Signs along New Hampshire 153

National Geographic Guide To

Scenic
Highways and
Byways

Prepared by
The Book Division
National Geographic Society
Washington, D.C.

Contents

New England   *page 14*

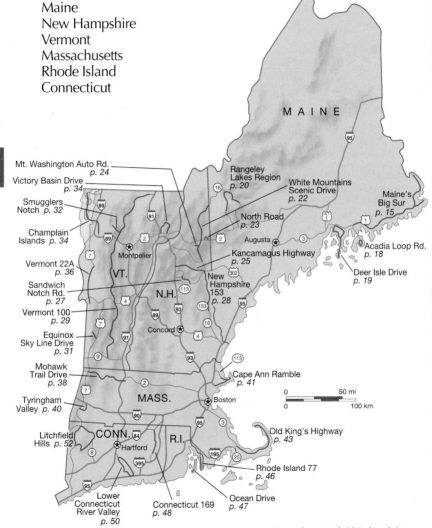

Maine
New Hampshire
Vermont
Massachusetts
Rhode Island
Connecticut

4

MAINE

Mt. Washington Auto Rd.
            p. 24
Victory Basin Drive
        p. 34

Rangeley
Lakes Region
p. 20

White Mountains
Scenic Drive
     p. 22

Maine's
Big Sur
p. 15

Smugglers
Notch p. 32

North Road
    p. 23

Champlain
Islands p. 34

Augusta

Acadia Loop Rd.
        p. 18

Vermont 22A
        p. 36

Montpelier

Kancamagus Highway
          p. 25

Deer Isle Drive
        p. 19

Sandwich
Notch Rd.
    p. 27

VT.

New
Hampshire
153
p. 28

Vermont 100
    p. 29

N.H.

Equinox
Sky Line Drive
      p. 31

Concord

Mohawk
Trail Drive
    p. 38

Cape Ann Ramble
        p. 41

Tyringham
Valley p. 40

MASS.

Boston

0   50 mi

0   100 km

Litchfield
Hills p. 52

CONN.

R.I.

Old King's Highway
        p. 43

Hartford

Lower
Connecticut
River Valley
    p. 50

Connecticut 169
        p. 48

Rhode Island 77
        p. 46

Ocean Drive
    p. 47

Cover photo: Humboldt Redwoods State
Park, California
Previous pages: Teton Range at sunset
from the Big Hole Mountains, Idaho

New York
New Jersey
Delaware
Pennsylvania
Maryland
West Virginia
Virginia

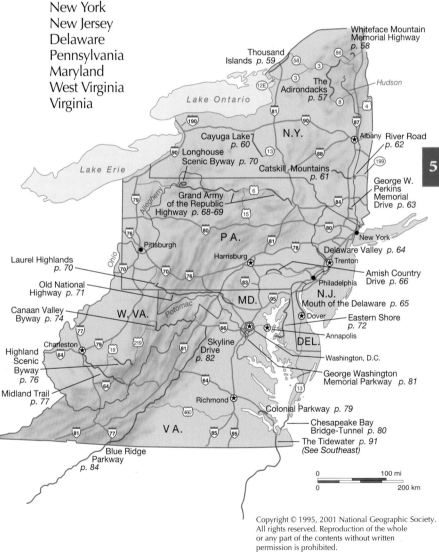

Whiteface Mountain
Memorial Highway
p. 58

Thousand
Islands p. 59

Lake Ontario

The
Adirondacks
p. 57

Hudson

Cayuga Lake
p. 60

N.Y.

Albany River Road
p. 62

Longhouse
Scenic Byway p. 70

Lake Erie

Catskill Mountains
p. 61

George W.
Perkins
Memorial
Drive p. 63

Grand Army
of the Republic
Highway p. 68-69

Allegheny

Pittsburgh

P.A.

Harrisburg

New York

Delaware Valley p. 64

Laurel Highlands
p. 70

Ohio

Trenton

Amish Country
Drive p. 66

Old National
Highway p. 71

Philadelphia

N.J.

Mouth of the Delaware p. 65

Canaan Valley
Byway p. 74

W. VA.

Potomac

MD.

Dover

Eastern Shore
p. 72

Charleston

Annapolis

Highland
Scenic
Byway
p. 76

DEL.

Washington, D.C.

Skyline
Drive
p. 82

George Washington
Memorial Parkway p. 81

Midland Trail
p. 77

Richmond

Colonial Parkway p. 79

Chesapeake Bay
Bridge-Tunnel p. 80

VA.

The Tidewater p. 91
(See Southeast)

Blue Ridge
Parkway
p. 84

| 0 | | 100 mi |
| 0 | | 200 km |

5

Contents

Southeast

North Carolina
Tennessee
Kentucky
Mississippi
Alabama
South Carolina
Georgia

Great Lakes

Michigan
Ohio
Indiana
Illinois
Wisconsin
Minnesota

Central Plains

page 146

Oxbow Overlook
Scenic Drive *p. 151*

North Dakota 22
p. 150

Sakakawea Trail
p. 148

Black Hills
p. 152

Peter Norbeck
Scenic Byway *p. 155*

Custer Scenic
Byway *p. 157*

South Dakota 44
p. 158

Nebraska 29
p. 162

North Dakota
South Dakota
Nebraska
Kansas
Missouri
Iowa

Grand Forks

N. DAK.

Fargo
Bismarck
Kathryn
Road *p. 147*

Badlands
p. 159

Rapid
City
Pierre
Missouri River

S. DAK.

Loess Hills
Scenic Byway
p. 169

Great River
Road *p. 170*

Mississippi River

Sioux
City

Pine Ridge
Country *p. 161*

NEBRASKA

Des
Moines

IOWA

Woodlands Scenic
Byway *p. 168*

Omaha

Lincoln

Missouri Valley
Wine Country
p. 166

KANSAS

Topeka

MO.

Kansas City

St. Louis

Flint Hills
p. 163

Jefferson
City

Wichita

Springfield

Missouri Ozarks
p. 164

0   100 mi
0   200 km

Glade Top
Trail *p. 165*

7

South Central

page 172

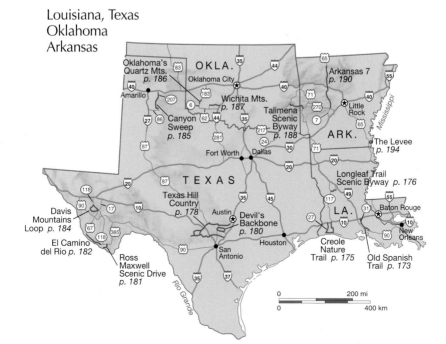

Louisiana, Texas
Oklahoma
Arkansas

Oklahoma's
Quartz Mts.
p. 186

OKLA.

Oklahoma City

Arkansas 7
p. 190

Amarillo

Wichita Mts.
p. 187

Little
Rock

Canyon
Sweep
p. 185

Talimena
Scenic
Byway
p. 188

ARK.

The Levee
p. 194

Fort Worth   Dallas

Longleaf Trail
Scenic Byway *p. 176*

TEXAS

Texas Hill
Country
p. 178

Austin

Devil's
Backbone
p. 180

LA.

Baton Rouge

Davis
Mountains
Loop *p. 184*

New
Orleans

El Camino
del Rio *p. 182*

Ross
Maxwell
Scenic Drive
p. 181

San
Antonio

Houston

Creole
Nature
Trail *p. 175*

Old Spanish
Trail *p. 173*

Rio Grande

0   200 mi
0   400 km

Contents

Southwest

Utah, Arizona, New Mexico, Colorado

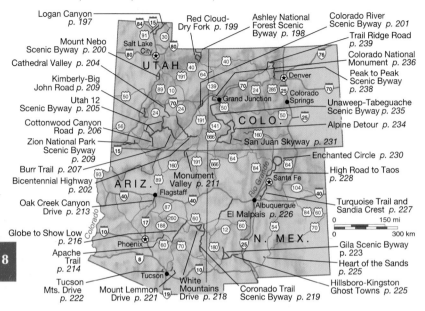

Rocky Mountains

Montana, Wyoming, Idaho

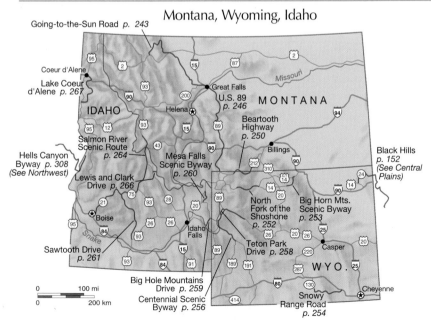

Northwest

page 268

Alaska, Washington, Oregon

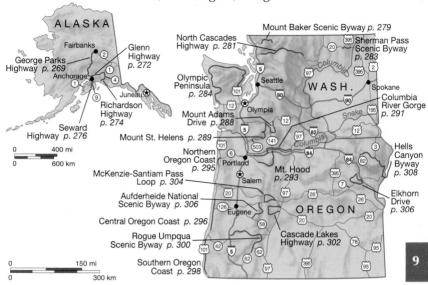

ALASKA

Fairbanks

Glenn Highway p. 272

George Parks Highway p. 269

Anchorage

Juneau

Richardson Highway p. 274

Seward Highway p. 276

North Cascades Highway p. 281

Mount Baker Scenic Byway p. 279

Sherman Pass Scenic Byway p. 283

Olympic Peninsula p. 284

Seattle

WASH.

Columbia

Spokane

Columbia River Gorge p. 291

Olympia

Mount Adams Drive p. 288

Snake

Mount St. Helens p. 289

Columbia

Northern Oregon Coast p. 295

Portland

Hells Canyon Byway p. 308

McKenzie-Santiam Loop p. 304

Salem

Mt. Hood p. 293

Aufderheide National Scenic Byway p. 306

Elkhorn Drive p. 306

Central Oregon Coast p. 296

Eugene

OREGON

Rogue Umpqua Scenic Byway p. 300

Cascade Lakes Highway p. 302

Southern Oregon Coast p. 298

0   400 mi
0   600 km

0   150 mi
0   300 km

9

Far West

page 310

Nevada
California
Hawaii

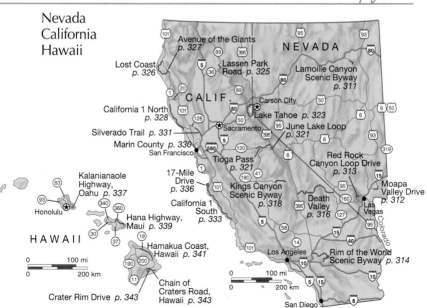

Avenue of the Giants p. 327

NEVADA

Lost Coast p. 326

Lassen Park Road p. 325

Lamoille Canyon Scenic Byway p. 311

CALIF.

Carson City

California 1 North p. 328

Lake Tahoe p. 323

June Lake Loop p. 321

Silverado Trail p. 331

Sacramento

Marin County p. 330

San Francisco

Tioga Pass p. 321

Red Rock Canyon Loop Drive p. 313

Kalanianaole Highway, Oahu p. 337

17-Mile Drive p. 336

Kings Canyon Scenic Byway p. 318

Moapa Valley Drive p. 312

Honolulu

California 1 South p. 333

Death Valley p. 316

Las Vegas

Hana Highway, Maui p. 339

HAWAII

Hamakua Coast, Hawaii p. 341

Los Angeles

Rim of the World Scenic Byway p. 314

0   100 mi
0   200 km

Crater Rim Drive p. 343

Chain of Craters Road, Hawaii p. 343

0   100 mi
0   200 km

San Diego

*F*or the past dozen years, I have been a travel writer, moving across continents, oceans, and sometimes hemispheres. Yet my best moments—the kind that distill all the pleasure of being alive—have occurred on the back roads of America: Booming past Wyoming buttes, with the west wind shoving at the car and a huge blue sky overhead; tunneling beneath a chromatic woodland of fall oaks and maples somewhere in the Virginia mountains; or winding along the California coast, with the sea stacks shimmering in the Pacific mist.

Roads web this country in a labyrinth of possibilities. As a nation of road builders, we have been hacking and cajoling trails, traces, country lanes, and superhighways out of the wilderness for almost 400 years now. Happily, most of the old, slow-moving thoroughfares are still out there, weaving in and around the brash new ones. Ambling across the most scenic corners of the country, they are the thin meandering lines on the map that make you want to wander for the sheer sake of wandering. Just the names of some of these byways—the Blue Ridge Parkway, California 1, the Great River Road, the Going-to-the-Sun-Road, the Natchez Trace—are part of our national psyche.

"Great beautiful clouds floated overhead, valley clouds that made you feel the vastness of . . . America from mouth to mouth and from tip to tip."

Jack Kerouac
On The Road

Twenty years ago, one social commentator remarked that we Americans had "become space-eaters, mile-consumers: Unless we can gulp distances down, we feel laggard as lizards." But in the current age of global living and virtual reality, many of us are ready to slow down and step backward a little in time. And nothing seems to bring the world back to a personal dimension better than a drive down these scenic highways and byways. Far from cyberspace, they still travel the true spaces of America, celebrating the regional diversity and hard-won histories that give this land its character.

In a place like Louisiana, for example, you can travel in a matter of miles from the robust high-spiritedness of Cajun swamp country to the manicured grace of an antebellum town. In the Northwest you can climb into mountains dense with fog-fed evergreens, then cascade down into the arid grandeur of the high desert. In New England you can wind through white-washed villages as solid as Plymouth Rock or along coastlines whose ruggedness has inspired generations of painters. In the Southwest you can explore adobe pueblos that haven't changed much in 200 years or deserted mining towns that lasted less than a decade. And in the Central Plains you can follow the bends of the Missouri River as it weaves through an exuberant wine country.

Each byway has its own character, its own promise. But all of them will give you back that sense of adventure that Walt Whitman proclaimed a century ago in his "Song of the Open Road": "Afoot, light-hearted, I take to the open road. Healthy, free, the world before me."

K. M. Kostyal

South Dakota 240 through Badlands National Park

About the Guide

Sacred datura

merica's landscape has long been celebrated for its beauty and magic, and studies show that driving for pleasure is the nation's most popular outdoor pastime. This book combines the scenery with the activity to bring you a guide you'll use both in planning unforgettable trips and as an indispensable mile-by-mile companion.

To come up with 200 drives that reveal the scenic wonder and diversity of the 50 states, the staff considered many hundreds of possibilities—federal and state highways and parkways, county and local routes, National Park, National Forest Service, and Bureau of Land Management roads. We painfully winnowed the list to the selection before you, then sent writers out to drive every mile and report on what they saw. All states have scenic highway programs, and their travel offices can tell you about other excellent drives.

Some of the longest roads have been written in segments. For example, we treat Mississippi's Great River Road in six drives covering four states. The Mississippi River Parkway Commission (P.O. Box 59159, Minneapolis, Minnesota 55459) offers a free map of the entire route.

"I might have seen more of America when I was a child if I hadn't had to spend so much of my time protecting my half of the back seat from incursions by my sister."

Calvin Trillin
Travels With Alice

To the best of our knowledge, information about the sites is accurate as of press time, but call ahead when possible. In addition to the stated days of operation, many sites close on national holidays. Seasons in the headings are writers' recommendations of when best to go; unless otherwise stated, though, the roads are open year-round. All mileages are approximate, and drive times allow for little or no stopping. To savor the drives fully—to stop at sites and overlooks and to take side trips and hikes—leave considerably more time.

With this book and a good road map you're sure to enjoy your rambles across America's enthralling landscape.

Appalachian Trail, Great Smoky Mountains N.P.

MAP KEY and ABBREVIATIONS

National Conservation Area — N.C.A.
National Historical Park — N.H.P.
National Historic Site — N.H.S.
National Lakeshore — N.L.
National Memorial — NAT. MEM.
National Monument — NAT. MON.
National Park — N.P.
National Preserve
National Recreation Area — N.R.A.
National River
National Scenic Riverways
National Scientific Reserve
National Seashore
National Volcanic Monument

Forest Reserve
National Grassland
National Forest — N.F.
State Forest — S.F.
Wilderness

National Wildlife Refuge — N.W.R.
National Wildlife and Fish Refuge
Wildlife Refuge

State Historic Site
State Historical Park — S.H.P.
State Natural Area
State Park — S.P.
State Recreation Area — S.R.A.
State Reserve — S.R.

Indian Reservation — I.R.

■ Point of Interest

Featured Scenic Drive

Interstate Highway — (40)

U.S. Federal Highway — (17)

State Road — (29)

County, Local, or Provincial Road — 9

Trail

Ferry

State or National Border

Forest / Wilderness Boundary

POPULATION
●San Antonio — 500,000 and over
●Lancaster — 50,000 to under 500,000
●Williamsburg — under 50,000

⊛ State Capital   ) (Pass
❘ Dam   ＝ Falls

13

Point Piños, Monterey Peninsula, California

New England

Maine, New Hampshire, Vermont, Massachusetts, Rhode Island, Connecticut

Maine

Maine's Big Sur

Ellsworth to Calais on U.S. 1 and Maine 186, 187, 189, 190

● 197 miles ● 1 day ● April through October. Road to Schoodic Point is one way.

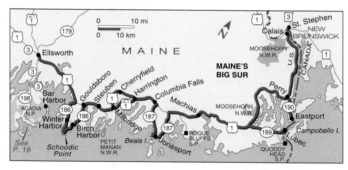

U.S. 1 from Ellsworth to Calais is truly a road less traveled. Most tourists never get past Bar Harbor and miss the crashing surf at Acadia National Park's Schoodic Point, the tiny fishing villages that dot the coast, and the small cities a stone's throw from the Canadian border. This is the route that links them all.

Start at **Ellsworth** and head north on U.S. 1 for 9 miles to the Hancock-Sullivan Bridge across **Taunton Bay.** Pull over after 1 mile at the **Sullivan Harbor Scenic Turnout** for views of Cadillac Mountain and Mount Desert Island. Sixteen miles east of Ellsworth, turn right on Rte. 186 for Acadia National Park's Schoodic Point. For the next 6 miles the road winds along the eastern shore of **Frenchman Bay** to Winter Harbor Village. Less than a mile from town, turn right for a side trip to **Schoodic Point,** a 2,016-acre preserve with a 6-mile scenic drive along the windswept granite shores of **Schoodic Peninsula,** views of Mount Desert and Cadillac Mountain, hiking trails, and tidal pools full of life. The park road ends at the tiny fishing village of Wonsqueak Harbor.

Pick up Rte. 186 a few miles north at Birch Harbor. At the end of Rte. 186, continue north again on U.S. 1 and continue for 2 miles, turning right to visit **Bartlett Maine Estate Winery** (*207-546-2408. Tastings May-Oct.*),

Former U.S. Coast Guard Station along Old King's Highway, Eastham, Mass.

Corea, coastal fishing village

where the Bartlett family has been making fruit wines since 1983.

Follow U.S. 1 for 3 miles to reach Washington County, the Sunrise County. Once the territory of the Passamaquoddy Indians, it is larger than Delaware and earned its sobriquet by being the first place in the U.S. to greet the rising sun each morning. It could as easily have been called the Blueberry County—about 30 million pounds are harvested each year.

Turn right onto Pigeon Hill Road in **Steuben** (Stoo-BEN) to visit the 6,950-acre **Petit Manan National Wildlife Refuge** *(207-546-2124)*, where more than 300 bird species—including bald eagle, peregrine falcon, and roseate tern—have been sighted. A few miles farther, at the head of **Narraguagus Bay,** is

Intertidal starfish

Milbridge, home to one of the world's largest blueberry processing plants. Stay on U.S. 1 at the junction of U.S. 1A to visit Cherryfield, the "blueberry capital of the world." To skip **Cherryfield** and cut out several miles of driving, take 1A north for 8 miles to Harrington.

Continue for 3.5 miles past Harrington to **Columbia Falls** and stop by the elegant **Thomas Ruggles House** *(207-483-4637. June–mid-Oct.; donation)*, built for a rich lumber dealer in 1818. Just past Columbia Falls is a right turn onto Rte. 187 for a 10-mile side trip to the boatbuilding and fishing communities of **Jonesport** and **Beals.** In Jonesport, look for the puffin mailbox of **Capt. Barna Norton** *(207-497-5933. June-Aug.; fares)* to sign on for a cruise to **Machias Seal Island** or **Petit Manan Island.** Take Rte. 187 back along the shore of **Chandler Bay** to U.S. 1.

Once back on U.S. 1, it's less than 2 miles to the turnoff for **Roque Bluffs State Park** *(207-255-3475. www.state.me.us/doc/prkslnds/roque.htm. May–late-Oct.; adm. fee)*, with its sandy beach and freshwater swimming pond. The shire town of Machias is just 5 miles beyond the turnoff. Turn right on Rte. 92 just south of town to visit the **Fort O'Brien State Historic Site** *(207-726-4412. www.state.me.us/doc/prkslnds/obrien.htm. Mem. Day-Labor Day)*, near where the first naval battle of the Revolution was fought in 1775, and **Jasper Beach,** with its wave-polished pebbles of jasper and rhyolite.

About 16 miles past Machias, turn right onto Rte. 189 for Quoddy Head State Park, Lubec, and Campobello Island. Turn off Rte. 189 after 9.5 miles to go to **Quoddy Head State Park** *(207-733-0911. May–mid-Oct.; adm. fee),* with adjacent **West Quoddy Head Light.** The park's steep ledges offer a terrific vantage point for the famous **Bay of Fundy** tides, which rise 20 to 30 feet. The candy-striped lighthouse, perched atop a 90-foot cliff on the easternmost point of land in the U.S., is visible from 20 miles at sea.

Once back on Rte. 189, continue toward **Lubec.** This easternmost town in the U.S. was once home to 19 sardine factories. It's also the access point for the **International Bridge** to New Brunswick, Canada's **Campobello Island,** and the 2,800-acre **Roosevelt Campobello International Park** *(506-752-2233. www.nps.gov/roca. Late May–mid-Oct.),* summer home of Franklin D. Roosevelt. As you climb the hill after clearing customs, turn around and look across the **Narrows,** where the strongest tidal currents on the East Coast flow at 15 mph. **Friar's Head Picnic Area,** on the left just before the entrance to the international park, offers views of Lubec, Eastport, Cobscook Bay, and the mouth of **Passamaquoddy Bay.** If you're headed for Eastport and want to save about 40 miles of driving, consider taking the ferry. The Deer Isle ferry leaves just a few miles past the park entrance; from Deer Isle you can take another ferry to Eastport.

Retrace Rte. 189 to the junction of U.S. 1 and head north toward Calais. After 3 miles the road enters the southern boundary of the Edmunds Unit of the **Moosehorn National Wildlife Refuge** *(207-454-7161. www.mainebirding .net/moosehorn),* a breeding ground for migratory birds and other wildlife, including the reclusive American woodcock. Many of its 6,700 acres border **Cobscook Bay,** and when you watch the tide come in from the shores of **Cobscook Bay State Park** *(207-726-4412. www.state.me.us/doc/prkslnds/ cobscook.htm. Mid-May–mid-Oct.; adm. fee),* it's easy to understand why the Indians named the bay "boiling tides"— they average 24 feet in height.

Seven miles past the state park entrance, watch for the turnoff to **Pembroke Falls,** one of the nation's largest reversing falls, a tidal phenomenon. The road to the falls is poorly marked: Turn right off U.S. 1 onto Leighton Point Road; after 3.2 miles, turn right and continue for 1.2 miles past the Clarkside Cemetery. When the road forks, go left and continue 1.7 miles into the park. The tip of **Mahar Point** provides a fine view of the fierce white water created when **Dennys Bay** and **Whiting Bay** flow into Cobscook Bay. Watch for bald eagles, ospreys, and seals.

Halfway between the Equator and the North Pole lies the town of **Perry,** named for Commodore Oliver H. Perry, a hero of the War of 1812. Two miles from the Perry town line, at the junction of U.S. 1 and Rte. 190, turn right onto 190 for Eastport. For the first few miles the road passes by the **Pleasant Point Indian Reservation,** home to over 850 Passamaquoddy Indians. It's another 5 miles to downtown **Eastport.** To see **Old Sow Whirlpool,** one of the world's largest, turn left onto Water Street at the end of Rte. 190, pass the entrance to the Deer Isle ferry, and continue to **Dog Island** at the end of the road. The whirlpool is best seen about two hours before high tide.

A pet plan of FDR, the Passamaquoddy Tidal Project, begun in 1934, would have used the rise and fall of the bay tides for electricity— but it never got off the ground.

17

Back at the junction of U.S. 1 and Rte. 190, continue north on U.S. 1 for 2 miles to the **45th Parallel Picnic Area.** The red granite stone marking the halfway point was erected in 1896 by the National Geographic Society. About 5 miles from here, pull over at the next rest area to view the red granite cliffs of the **St. Croix River.**

Between Robbinston and Calais look for 12 small, sequentially numbered granite markers on the river side of the road. Lumberman and journalist James S. Pike put them there in 1870 to time his racehorses. **St. Croix Island International Historic Site** *(207-726-4412. www.nps.gov/sacr)*, at the Calais town line, is named for two long coves that meet to form a cross. Samuel de Champlain landed here in 1604, making this island in the middle of the St. Croix River the site of the country's first white settlement north of St. Augustine, Florida.

The city of **Calais** (CAL-lus), along the bank of the St. Croix River across from St. Stephen, New Brunswick, is one of the busiest ports of entry along the 3,000-mile U.S.-Canada border. Continue north on U.S. 1 through town for 5 miles to the 16,080-acre Baring Unit of the **Moosehorn Wildlife Refuge** *(207-454-7161).* With the Edmunds Unit to the south, it's the northernmost in a chain of migratory bird refuges that extends from Maine to Florida. A fitting sentinel at the end of this road to the border, the American bald eagle has taken up residence here. Nesting areas line the entrance to the refuge at Charlotte Road.

18

Acadia Loop Road

Acadia National Park on Mount Desert Island

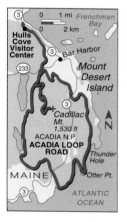

● 27 miles (20-mile loop, plus 7-mile round-trip up Cadillac Mountain) ● 2 hours ● Spring through fall. Expect traffic in July, August, and late September (for foliage). Not maintained in winter. Adm. fee to park May-October

The Park Loop Road of **Acadia National Park** *(www.nps.gov/acad)* is a gently graded, two-lane blacktop winding through dense woodland and along rocky shoreline to the top of 1,530-foot Cadillac Mountain, with 360-degree views of the Atlantic Ocean and Maine coast. (If you're an early riser, drive to the summit before dawn for a spectacular sunrise.)

Begin at the **Hulls Cove Visitor Center** *(207-288-4932. Mid-April–Oct.)* near Frenchman Bay, first explored by Samuel de Champlain in 1604. After 5 miles, turn off for **Sieur De Monts** to visit the **Nature Center** *(207-288-3338. Phone for hours)* and the **Robert Abbe Museum of Stone Age Antiquities** *(207-288-3519. Mid-May–mid-Oct.; adm. fee).*

Continue for 1 mile to the **Champlain Mountain Overlook,** offering a magnificent panorama of the Gouldsboro Hills, Frenchman Bay, and the tip of Schoodic Peninsula. As you leave, look back to the left toward **Thrumcap Island,** a rookery for gulls and cormorants. Four miles farther is **Sand Beach,** consisting mostly of crushed marine shells.

Stop a half mile past the beach at **Thunder Hole.** When seas run high, huge

Acadia National Park, Mount Desert Island

waves rush into a narrow slot in the rocks, forcing air trapped at the back of the chasm to compress and make a thundering sound. A mile past Thunder Hole, near the pink granite **Otter Cliffs,** explore the tidal pools an hour or two before low tide at **Otter Point.** Just beyond, the road enters a spruce-fir forest. **Wildwood Stables** *(207-276-3622. Mid-June–early Oct.; fee),* 4.5 miles past Otter Point, offers wagon rides on some of the 57 miles of wide, gravel **Carriage Roads** begun by John D. Rockefeller, Jr., in 1917; they're also open to horseback riders, hikers, bikers, and cross-country skiers.

A mile past the stables, stop at **Jordan Pond House** *(207-276-3316. Mid-May–mid-Oct.)* for a meal or the century-old tradition of tea on the lawn. Four miles beyond, turn right off the main road to ascend the 3.5 miles to the top of **Cadillac Mountain,** the highest point on the eastern seaboard north of Brazil. To return to the Visitor Center, follow the signs.

19

Deer Isle Drive

Orland to Deer Isle on Maine 175, 166A, 166, 199, 15

● **82 miles round-trip** ● **½ day** ● **May through October.** The roads here intersect constantly, looping back on one another and often sharing multiple designations. Pay close attention to directions.

This drive is a Down East sampler, circuiting a peninsula that juts into Penobscot Bay. You'll visit historic Castine and the fishing villages of Deer Isle and Stonington, then head back through the interior to Blue Hill.

Begin in **Orland** at the junction of U.S. 1 and Rte. 175, near where the **Penobscot River** meets **Penobscot Bay.** Follow Rte. 175 south a short way to the junction of Rte. 166A, then continue south on 166A for a few miles to **Castine,** home of the **Maine Maritime Academy** *(www.mainemaritime.edu).* Markers around town chronicle the 200-year-old history of this strategically located settlement. At the waterfront, you can tour the academy's training vessel, the *State of Maine (207-326-2420. July–Labor Day).* From here go north for a few miles on Rte. 166 toward **Penobscot,** and then north on Rte. 199 for 3 miles to Rte. 175 south toward Brooksville. After about 6 miles, you'll come to the **Bagaduce River** bridge. Stop here to see the **Reversing Falls,** a phenomenon caused by the fast-flowing tides.

Six miles beyond the falls is the **Caterpillar Hill Rest Area,** where you can view Deer Isle, Penobscot Bay, Camden Hills, and the Bay Islands. About a half mile past the rest area, go south on Rte. 15 and over the suspension bridge to the island communities of **Deer Isle** and **Stonington.** On Deer Isle turn right and follow signs to Sunset, overlooking **Southwest Harbor.** Continue south 4 miles to **Stonington Harbor,** a charter boat port, and the ferry for **Isle au Haut** *(Isle-au-Haut Co.*

Clambake fixings

207-367-5193. No service Sun. in winter. Fares), about half of which is parkland.

To return to U.S. 1, head north on Rte. 15 for 20 miles to **Blue Hill,** which prospered during the late 1700s as a shipbuilding and trading center and is now known for its pottery. From there continue north on Rte. 15 for another 12 miles to rejoin U.S. 1 at Orland.

Rangeley Lakes Region

Madrid to Houghton on Maine 4 and 17

● **44.5 miles** ● **2 hours** ● **April through October. Watch out for fast-moving lumber trucks and slow-moving moose.**

Waterfalls, lakes, mountains, gold mines, great sunsets—this wishbone-shaped route offers the best of western Maine's Rangeley Lakes region.

Start by heading west on Rte. 4 at the **Madrid** town line. Following the west branch of the **Sandy River,** the route climbs for 3 miles to the beginning of a 20-mile state-designated scenic highway at the entrance to **Smalls Falls Picnic Area.** A good path leads across the cataracts, at the confluence of **Chandler Mill Stream** and Sandy River. The nearby Appalachian Trail ascends to the top of 4,116-foot **Saddleback Mountain.**

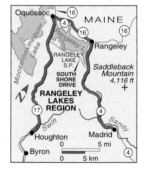

Eight miles past the picnic area, turn left for a 5-mile side trip on South Shore Drive to **Rangeley Lake State Park** *(207-864-3858. www.state.me.us/doc/prkslnds/rangeley.htm. Adm. fee).* This beautiful 691-acre park on **Rangeley Lake** is a popular place to fish for trout, salmon, black bass, togue, and pickerel.

Continue on Rte. 4 for 1.5 miles past the state park turnoff to the official beginning of the Rangeley Lakes region. The region is actually made up of numerous lakes, including Rangeley, Mooselookmeguntic, Richardson, Umbagog, Parmachenee, and Kennebago.

To visit **Saddleback Ski Area** *(207-864-5671),* one of the state's largest, turn right on Dallas Hill Road, which climbs 7 miles to the base of Saddleback Mountain. **Rangeley Center** on Rangeley Lake is on Rte. 4 just a mile past this turnoff. The tiny town retains its frontierlike feeling, even though it has been the area's major service center since tourists started arriving more than a hundred years ago. Before that, the area was a logging center.

Dawn over Rangeley Lake

Timber was hauled across the lake and through the dam near Oquossoc into Mooselookmeguntic Lake, through the Richardson Lakes and Lake Umbagog to the Androscoggin River to Berlin, New Hampshire.

Continue on Rte. 4 for 3.5 miles to **Orgonon** and the **Wilhelm Reich Museum** *(207-864-3443. July-Aug. Wed.-Sun., Sun. only in Sept.; adm. fee)* to learn about the controversial physician-scientist who once lived and worked here. A nature study center and hiking trails are open all year. Continue 3 miles past Orgonon to the junction of Rtes. 4 and 17 and turn left onto 17 to begin a 32-mile state-designated scenic highway.

Just past the junction, a scenic overlook offers a panorama of Rangeley Lake, Saddleback Mountain, and ranges to the east. **Bald Mountain** is between Rangeley and **Mooselookmeguntic Lakes;** to the north are the **Kennebago Mountains,** and to the south of Mooselookmeguntic are **Bemis Mountain** and **Elephant Mountain,** with the **White Mountains** in the distance. Five miles past this overlook, pull off at the rest area on the right for a view of Mooselookmeguntic Lake. The view from the **Height of Land Overlook,** just half a mile past the lake turnoff, is spectacular at sunset.

Keep an eye out for moose and an ear cocked for loons at **Beaver Pond,** 1 mile farther up on the right. The turnoff for 90-foot **Angel Falls** is 4.5 miles from Beaver Pond. Turn right immediately before the brown trailer, cross the bridge, and head down Bemis Road, an old railroad bed. From the road's end, it's an easy 45-minute hike to the falls.

Continue down Rte. 17, through hardwood forest, watching for the bridge just 3.7 miles past the Angel Falls turnoff. Park by the green gate and wade up the **Swift River** a little bit to explore an old gold-panning area. Nearby **Byron** is purported to be the site of America's first gold strike, in 1848.

If you want to try your luck at gold panning, continue 1 mile to **Coos Canyon Wilderness Campground** *(207-364-3880. Mid-April–mid-Nov. Fee for supplies),* which offers demonstrations. At the **Coos Canyon Rest Area,** right across the way, the Swift River has carved a gorge into the bedrock. Staurolite crystals, jasper, garnets, and gold have been found here.

Continue on a few miles to Houghton and the end of the drive.

New Hampshire
White Mountains Scenic Drive

Wentworth Location to Glen on N.H. 16

● **74 miles** ● **2 hours** ● **Especially beautiful in fall. Driving north to south offers the most dramatic views of the mountains and valleys. This is moose country; collisions can be disastrous, so watch out for the huge beasts on the road.**

This drive follows the wild Androscoggin River, the water highway of the old-time log drivers who shuttled timber to the mills at Berlin. South of Berlin, the route winds along the floor of Pinkham Notch, in the shadow of mighty Mount Washington.

Begin on Rte. 16 in **Wentworth Location,** a speck on the map along the Maine border. For information on **Umbagog Lake,** partly in Maine and partly in New Hampshire, stop a short distance south at the **Lake Umbagog National Wildlife Refuge** *(603-482-3415. Mon.-Fri.).* Umbagog, which means "clear water" in the local Abenaki dialect, teems with pickerel and salmon. The lake's outlet on its western shore is the headwaters of the **Androscoggin River.** Follow the Androscoggin to **Errol,** settled when lumbering began here in the late 1800s. Rte. 26 west out of Errol goes to **Dixville Notch,** famous as the first place to report results in national elections.

Continue south on Rte. 16 for about 16 miles to **Pontook Reservoir Recreation Area and Hydro Station** *(603-449-2903),* where a diagram explains the workings of the hydroelectric dam. Shortly after the dam look to the south for a view of the **Presidential Range.**

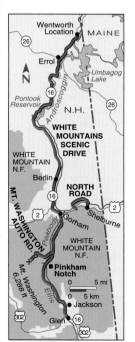

On days when the wind is "right," you can smell the distinctive aroma of **Berlin**'s pulp and paper mills long before the huge smokestacks come into view. To the east is the **Mahoosuc Range.** Berlin (BER-lin) sits on a flank of granite that is part of **Jefferson Dome.** Inside the city limits is **Nansen Wayside State Park** *(603-752-6060),* a popular fishing and hiking spot, known for its ski jump.

Continue south to **Gorham,** nestled in a sheltered valley at the junction of the Androscoggin and **Peabody Rivers.** When the Atlantic & St. Lawrence Railroad completed laying its track in the mid-1800s, Gorham became a gateway for tourists visiting the northern mountain resorts. (Go east on U.S. 2 for 3 miles to take the North Road scenic drive; see page 23.)

Proceeding south on Rte. 16, you follow the Peabody River through **Pinkham Notch.** Carved by stream and glacial action, it was named for Daniel Pinkham, who arrived from the coast in the late 1700s—on a sled pulled by a pig. At

Peabody River, White Mountain Natl. Forest

North Road

Off U.S. 2 near Gorham

- 8.5 miles • ½ hour or less
- Best as a fall foliage trip; the views along much of the route are obscured by trees.
See map page 22.

This forgotten byway of New Hampshire's North Country meanders along the Androscoggin River, passing family farms, old cemeteries, and a venerable country inn.

Turn left from U.S. 2 onto North Road 3.5 miles east of Gorham at the 1884 stone house. Stop at the hydroelectric dam a short distance ahead for a view of the **Presidential Range** to the west.

the entrance to the 740,841-acre **White Mountain National Forest** *(www.fs.fed.us/r9/white)* is a **Ranger Station** *(603-466-2713. Closed weekends)* offering information. Continue into the forest, stopping a few miles from the entrance at the viewing area for the **Great Gulf**—a huge glacial cirque encompassed by the Great Gulf Wilderness. Go another mile for the entrance to the Mount Washington Auto Road (see p. 24). The parking area of the **Glen House** *(603-466-3988),* a former grand hotel at the base of the auto road, offers a magnificent view of **Tuckerman Ravine,** a glacial cirque formed by small glaciers that followed stream valleys during the last ice age.

Look to the right as you pass by thick stands of white birch for views of **Middle Moriah Mountain** and the **White Mountain National Forest.** The **Mahoosuc Range** to the left is mostly obscured. The surrounding forest has been heavily logged and is mostly new growth.

To visit the grave of Peter Poor, a white man killed in 1781 by Indians working for the British, park at the Appalachian Trail's **Austin Brook Trailhead** about 3 miles past the dam and walk down the hill to the right. Just ahead, visit **Cobblestone Farm** *(603-466-2621),* where the Danforth family raises sheep, spins yarn, and makes apple cider.

Continue a short distance to **Philbrook Farm Inn** *(603-466-3831. Closed April and Nov.-Dec.).* Here the Philbrook family has put up travelers since 1861; non-lodgers can stop in for breakfast or dinner, if there's room. Follow North Road 4 miles farther as it narrows before intersecting with Meadow Road back over the Androscoggin River to U.S. 2 at Shelburne. Unpaved North Road continues into Bethel, Maine.

23

Birch trees along Androscoggin River

Wentworth Resort Hotel, Jackson

The **Wildcat Mountain Ski Area** *(603-466-3326)*, 2 miles past the Glen House, offers challenging downhill skiing and a breathtaking gondola ride *(Fee for nonskiers)*. From the ski area, continue for 0.75 mile to the Appalachian Mountain Club's **Pinkham Notch Visitor Center** *(603-466-2727)* and the trailhead for the short walk to the waterfall at **Crystal Cascade** and a longer climb into Tuckerman Ravine. A half mile farther south is the trailhead for the short walk to **Glen Ellis Falls.** As you proceed down Rte. 16, great views of the **Ellis River Valley** await you.

When you leave White Mountain National Forest, you enter the town of **Jackson** at the northernmost end of the **Mount Washington Valley.** The drive ends in Glen at the junction of U.S. 302.

Mount Washington Auto Road

Mount Washington Auto Road

N.H. 16 at Glen House

● 16 miles round-trip ● 2 hours
● Spring through fall. Closed in winter. Toll road (603-466-3988). Trailers and RVs not permitted. No services. Temperatures from the bottom to the summit can vary as much as 30°F. *See map p. 22.*

P.T. Barnum is supposed to have called the view from the top of 6,288-foot Mount Washington—extending into four states and Canada—the "second greatest show on Earth." The weather is equally impressive: Earth's highest wind speed of 231 mph was recorded at the summit in 1934, and the climate above timberline is ecologically similar to that of northern Labrador.

Opened in 1861, the road climbs about 4,700 vertical feet at an average grade of 12 percent. The first 4 miles cut through dense forest, revealing the succession from hardwoods to evergreens. As you approach timberline at 4,500 feet, the trees become stunted and twisted. Above 4,000 feet there are views to the north of the **Great Gulf**—the White Mountains' largest glacial cirque—as well as **Mounts Adams, Jefferson,** and **Madison.** Beyond lie the **Androscoggin River Valley** and the peaks of the **Mahoosuc Range.**

Just past the 6-mile marker is the **Alpine Garden Trail;** look for diapensia, Lapland rosebay, alpine azalea, and mountain avens. Just past Milepost 7, where the road parallels the **Mount Washington Cog Railway** *(Bretton Woods. 603-846-5404. May-Oct.; reserations required. Fare),* look down into two other glacial cirques. At the summit, visit the **Mount Washington Observatory Museum** *(603-356-8345. Mid-May–mid-Oct. weather permitting; adm. fee).*

Kancamagus Highway

Lincoln to Conway on N.H. 112

● 34 miles ● 1 hour ● May through Oct. Spectacular fall foliage

Famous for its magnif-
icent autumn color,
the Kanc stretches
from the Pemigewasset
River at Lincoln to the
junction of Rte. 16 in
Conway and crosses
several mountains,
climbing nearly 3,000 feet as it traverses the flank of **Mount Kancamagus.**
The views are breathtaking, the two-lane blacktop road is excellent, and
there are numerous places along the way to camp, hike, swim, fish, or just
enjoy the scenery.

There is a **New Hampshire Visitor Center** *(White Mountain Attractions
603-745-8720)* at the junction of I-93 and Rte. 112 in Lincoln. There are also
two centers specifically for the Kancamagus Highway: **Lincoln Woods Visitor Center** *(No phone. Mid-June–Labor Day and various times throughout
the year, depending on staff availability)* at the west end of the scenic highway
and the White Mountain National Forest's **Saco Ranger District Office and
Information Center** *(603-447-5448)* at the highway's east end.

The Kancamagus (pronounced Kan-kuh-MOG-us) Highway took

25

20 years to build starting in
the late 1930s, partly on the
bed of a narrow-gauge railroad
that originally carried timber
into Lincoln. The mountains
along the Kanc are named after
New Hampshire Indians. Kancamagus ("fearless one"),
grandson of the great chief
Passaconaway, served as the
third and final ruler of the Penacook Confederacy and led a
confederation of tribes in New
Hampshire in the late 1600s.

The Kanc's most scenic
section begins 3 miles from
Lincoln at the entrance sign to
the **White Mountain National
Forest.** The first parcels of this
770,000-acre woodland were
set aside in 1911; today,
114,932 acres are officially
designated as wilderness. Approximately 184 species of

Kancamagus Highway, White Mountain National Forest

birds have been sighted in the forest, including the green heron and the
peregrine falcon. Moose, deer, foxes, and black bears are permanent

residents here. Trees that thrive along the Kanc include the alder, spruce, pine, maple, white birch, black cherry, larch, and poplar.

For the first few miles, the road follows the east branch of the **Pemigewasset River,** popular with trout fishermen. The Lincoln Woods Visitor Center is a mile up on the left. The 8.9-mile **Wilderness Trail** begins at the parking lot just east of the highway bridge.

As the road begins to wind for 8 miles to the top of the 2,855-foot **Kancamagus Pass, Mounts Hancock, Hitchcock,** and **Huntington** rise up to the left; **Loon Mountain** and **Mount Osceola** are off to the right. The streams to the east empty into the **Saco River,** and those to the west feed the Pemigewasset. Pull in at the **C.L. Graham Wangan Ground** at the pass. You are now in the Saco River Valley section of the national forest.

Continue for 7 miles alongside the **Swift River** to **Sabbaday Falls Picnic Area,** trailhead for one of the most popular family hikes along the Kanc. It's an easy 0.4-mile walk on a graded path to the narrow flume and picturesque waterfalls. The falls owe their existence to the presence of a black basalt dike, which is beautifully exposed. Sand and gravel carved the potholes below the falls. Tradition says they were named by early explorers who discovered them on the Sabbath while searching for a mountain pass. There's excellent fishing along **Sabbaday Brook** *(License required).*

A few miles up at **Passaconaway Historic Site** *(Info at Saco Ranger District),* you'll find a little bit of everything: romance, history, legend, and nature. The only historic house on the highway, the **Russell-Colbath Historic Homestead** *(Mem. Day-Columbus Day; donation)* was built here about 1832. One day in 1891 Mr. Colbath left the house, telling his wife he'd be back soon. Every night for the next 39 years, Mrs. Colbath lit a lantern

Swift River's
rocky shore

and placed it in a window to help him find his way. He finally did, but by then Mrs. Colbath had been dead for three years. The house faces south, overlooking the **Albany Intervale** and **Mount Passaconaway,** the "monarch of the Sandwich Range" at 4,060 feet. Passaconaway, considered one of the greatest Indian leaders, was head of the Penacook Confederacy when the first Europeans arrived.

In the small cemetery next to the Russell-Colbath house, look for the grave of Orren A. Chase, who died July 25, 1864. On leave from the Civil War, he was riding home by train for his wedding when he was robbed and killed. The half-mile **Rail 'n' River Trail,** which leaves from the parking lot at the house, is accessible to strollers and wheelchairs.

Just a half mile past the Passaconaway Historic Site is the turnoff for Bear Notch Road. This 9-mile route to Bartlett passes by the 2,600-acre **Bartlett Experimental Forest,** where research on the growth, composition, and culture of a northern hardwood forest goes on. In winter the road is plowed for only a mile, up to the **Upper Nanamocomuck Ski Trail,** which runs alongside the Swift River.

To build the Kanc, Civilian Conservation Corps workers began hacking their way through the wilderness in the 1930s. Not until 1959 did the road open to through traffic.

Sandwich Notch Road in fall

Three miles past the Bear Notch Road turnoff, watch for the entrance to **Rocky Gorge Scenic Area,** between **Moat Mountain** and **Mount Chocorua,** designated a National Scenic Area in 1937. The gorge was once filled with basalt; however, over the years the fierce waters of the Swift River have eroded the basalt, leaving the harder granite, waterfall, and narrow gorge. The rocks alongside are composed primarily of quartz and feldspar. The swimming is great along the river (although not permitted right in the gorge), and the short **Lovequist Loop** circles trout-filled **Falls Pond,** formed during the Ice Age when a retreating glacier left a narrow ridge of gravel and sand. Beavers have raised the level of the water in the pond.

Save energy for the popular **Boulder Loop Trail,** which begins near the covered bridge just a few miles from Rocky Gorge. You need only hike a short way up the 2.8-mile loop to see the effects of the glaciers that moved south from Canada and covered New Hampshire during successive Pleistocene Ice Ages.

The scenic section of the Kancamagus ends a few miles past the covered bridge, at the sign "Leaving White Mountain National Forest." Continue toward **Conway** for 2.5 miles to visit the Saco Ranger District Information Center.

Sandwich Notch Rd.

Center Sandwich to N.H. 49

- ● 9.5 miles ● 30 to 45 minutes
- ● May through October. Closed in winter. Narrow, hilly dirt road. Not for RVs. No services

In the early 1800s the town of **Sandwich** spent $300 to build a road one rod (16.5 feet) wide over **Sandwich Notch** to the town of Thornton, so that upcountry farmers could reach market towns to the south. In its heyday the Notch Road had a couple of dozen families, two mills, three schools, and a tavern. Today, few traces of civilization remain along this bumpy dirt road that runs partly through the **White Mountain National Forest** *(603-528-8721).*

Before taking the drive, stop at **A.G. Burrows General Store** in the picturesque village of **Center Sandwich** to make sure the road is open. (For hikers, the **Town Hall,** open weekdays, offers a free brochure, "Bearcamp River Trail Guide.") Begin at Main and Grove Streets, following a sign for Sandwich Notch Mead Base, a Boy Scout camp. Grove Street soon becomes Diamond Ledge Road, a country lane flanked by stone walls marking the boundaries of bygone farms.

At the fork about 2 miles ahead, bear left onto Sandwich Notch Road, which now narrows to one lane and begins its climb up **Sandwich Notch.** Plants along the way range from balsam fir to wood sorrel to buttonbush. The 4.5-mile **Algonquin Trail,** about 4 miles ahead, ascends to the top of **Sandwich Mountain.** The road ends at Rte. 49.

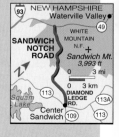

Conway to Sanbornville

● 35 miles ● 1 hour ● April through October. Spectacular fall foliage and less crowded than better known routes

Poor People's Pub, Sanbornville

The two-lane country road that winds southeast from busy Conway through dense woods and past small, tree-lined lakes along central New Hampshire's border with Maine is quiet, yet filled with surprises—a vest-pocket ski area, two wildlife sanctuaries, and a historic village noted for its 18th- and 19th-century buildings.

Head south on Rte. 153 from its junction with Rte. 16 in **Conway.** Once a mountain retreat for writers and artists, Conway today is a mecca for factory outlet shoppers. Slow down after about 5 miles, when you first see **Crystal Lake** ahead. It's worth turning left here for a short side trip to **Snowville,** a tiny village settled in the early 1800s. For a magnificent view of the **Presidential Range,** head a short distance up Stuart Road/Firelane 37 to **Snowvillage Inn** *(603-447-2818 or 800-447-4345)* or go 2.5 miles farther, up **Foss Mountain** to the blueberry barrens on top.

Returning to Rte. 153, turn left and follow Crystal Lake about 0.5 mile to **Eaton Center** and **The Inn at Crystal Lake** *(603-447-2120 or 800-343-7336),* where Irish bread is featured on the breakfast menu. The **Little White Church** up the road was built in 1879. Continue 2.5 miles to Purity Lake in East Madison, site of the **Purity Spring Resort** and **King Pine Ski Area** *(603-367-8896 or 800-367-8897),* Mount Washington Valley's smallest ski area, named for its towering pine trees. A short distance past the resort, turn left onto Horseleg Road to visit the New Hampshire Audubon Society's 135-acre **Hoyt Wildlife Sanctuary** *(603-224-9909. www.nhaudubon.org/sanctuaries/hoyt.htm).* This wetland is a haven for birds such as the great blue heron and the black-throated blue warbler; flora includes the insect-eating pitcher plant. Watch for beaver and deer.

Should you miss Hoyt, there's another sanctuary just 7 miles farther south—New Hampshire Audubon's **Charles Henry & Mabel Lamborn Watts Wildlife Sanctuary** *(603-224-9909. www.nhaudubon.org/sanctuaries/watts.htm).* This 380-acre preserve on the **Ossipee River** is composed of mixed forest and wooded swamp, and provides a diversity of habitats for creatures such as river otter and waterfowl. There are trail maps in the parking lot mailbox.

A stone marker in **Effingham,** 2 miles past the sanctuary, marks the site of the first normal school in New

See P. 25

Hampshire. Continue for about 6 miles to **Province Lake,** where ancient Indian hearths have been found on the western shore. It's only 10 miles from the lake to **Wakefield,** the self-described "center of New England." Turn right off Rte. 153 to visit the **Wakefield Corner National Historic Area** *(Town Hall 603-522-6205).* The town was developed 200 years ago at the intersection of two stagecoach routes. Twenty-six of its 18th- and 19th-century buildings are on the National Register of Historic Places. Though most are private residences, some are open to the public on special days throughout the year.

Finish the drive by continuing roughly 1 mile past the Wakefield Corner turn to reach the junction of Rtes. 153 and 109 in **Sanbornville.**

Foliage time along Vermont 100

Vermont 100

Wilmington to Newport

● **188 miles** ● **5 hours** ● Late spring through mid-fall. In the north, fall foliage peaks earlier; the display is usually over by mid-October. Traffic can be heavy in high summer and foliage season. Road is well maintained in winter.

Rte. 100 is the Main Street of Vermont's Green Mountains, running alongside the state's rugged spine from Massachusetts almost to Quebec. The road passes through many villages typical of this Yankee heartland.

Begin at **Wilmington,** where Rte. 100 crosses Rte. 9. Wilmington is a lodging and service center for several nearby ski areas and amply supplied with comfortable inns.

Follow Rte. 100 north out of Wilmington; soon the north branch of the **Deerfield River** will be on your right. Rising on your left is 3,400-foot **Haystack Mountain,** one of the southernmost peaks of the **Green Mountains.** A northern extension of the Appalachians, the Green Mountains were formed some 450 million years ago by the folding and faulting of sedimentary rock. Erosion and the action of ice age glaciers have since rounded them.

Covered bridge near Warren

Rte. 100 climbs toward **West Dover,** at 1,720 feet one of the loftiest villages in Vermont. Roughly 8 miles north of Wilmington, near the access road for the **Mount Snow Ski Area** *(802-464-3333),* you can see the slopes to the left. Rte. 100 soon cuts through a southern portion of the **Green Mountain National Forest** *(802-747-6700).* Land acquisition for the forest began during the 1930s; today it encompasses well over 350,000 acres greened by hardwoods.

Continue north on Rte. 100 as it descends through densely forested country to **West Wardsboro,** where a left turn would take you to 3,936-foot **Stratton Mountain** and its giant ski resort. **North Wardsboro** itself, 4.5 miles past the Stratton turnoff, is a quarter-mile-long string of small restaurants, general stores, and craft shops. From here, follow Rte. 100 for 4.5 miles to East Jamaica, then bear left for the 3-mile drive up the **West River Valley** to Jamaica.

To stay on Rte. 100, bear right at Rawsonville, 5 miles northwest of Jamaica, then left at South Londonderry toward Londonderry, where you take another left to reach **Weston.** Weston sums up so much of what outsiders find captivating about Vermont villages—the fenced green with its bandstand, the white steeples and cradling hills. It is home to two durable attractions: the **Weston Playhouse** *(802-824-5288. Summer)* and the **Vermont Country Store** *(802-362-4667),* a tribute to Yankee shopkeeping around the potbellied stove.

Bear right 3.5 miles north of Weston and follow Rte. 100 for 7 hilly miles into **Ludlow,** a former factory town that wears a cheerful new look now that the factory has been turned into a lively agglomeration of shops and restaurants.

Continue on Rte. 100 back into rural Vermont. On your right, **Lake Rescue** soon comes into view, followed by **Echo** and **Amherst Lakes**—all strung together by the **Black River,** a tributary of the Connecticut. Continue for 3 miles past the northern end of Amherst Lake to a right turn onto Rte. 100A and a 2-mile side trip into history. It was in tiny **Plymouth Notch** that Calvin Coolidge became President of the U.S. on August 3, 1923. Vice President Coolidge was visiting his boyhood home when word of President Harding's death arrived, and he was sworn in by his father, a notary public. The hamlet's houses, barns, and old Coolidge store are now part of the **President Calvin Coolidge State Historic Site** *(802-672-3773. www.state.vt.us/ dca/historic/Coolidg.htm. Late May–mid-Oct.; adm. fee).*

Return to Rte. 100 and continue north along the floor of the **Black River Valley,** reaching U.S. 4, central Vermont's principal east-west highway, at **West Bridgewater.** The **Ottauquechee River** here once turned the wheels of Bridgewater's woolen mills. As Rte. 100 and U.S. 4 follow the river, they are the same highway, climbing in elevation as they pass the **Killington Ski Area** *(802-422-3333),* Vermont's largest. The summit of **Killington Peak,** part of the 4,235-foot massif on your left, is visible ahead nearly 6 miles beyond the junction of Rte. 100 and U.S. 4.

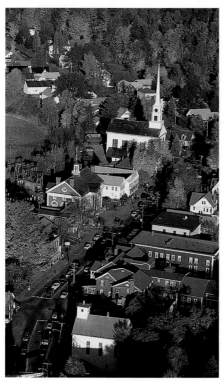

Above Stowe

Equinox Sky Line Dr.

Off Vt. 7A, south of Manchester Center

- 12 miles round-trip ● 45 minutes
- Toll road. Generally open May 1 to November ● Autumn foliage peaks around the first week of October, earlier at high elevations. *See map p. 30.*

The Taconic Range dominates the southwestern portion of Vermont, and highest among the slate-and marble-bearing hills is 3,852-foot **Mount Equinox.** The Equinox Sky Line Drive *(802-362-1115. www.equinox mountain.com),* which takes you to the summit, offers spectacular views of—and from—a mountain remarkably free of development. Three decades ago, businessman J.G. Davidson donated 8,000 Mount Equinox acres to the Carthusians, a Catholic monastic order committed to silence and self-sufficiency. The Carthusians currently make their home in a secluded granite monastery *(Not open to visitors)* on the southwest slope. The only other human presence on Equinox is the 20-room **Inn at Equinox Mountain.** *(Currently closed; scheduled to reopen summer 2001. Call 802-362-1115 for information.)*

Along the route, you can look out across the countryside from three parking areas, but the stellar vistas are from the summit. Immediately below are **Manchester** and the southern reaches of the **Valley of Vermont,** separating the Taconics from the Green Mountains. The **Berkshire Hills** in Massachusetts and New York's **Adirondacks** range to the south and west, and summit markers boast of clear-weather views of New Hampshire peaks and even Montreal's **Mount Royal.** Plan to sample the summit hiking trails, ranging from a half mile to 2 miles in length.

31

Smugglers Notch

Stowe to Jeffersonville on Vt. 108 and Mount Mansfield Toll Road

- 17.5 miles (plus 9-mile round-trip on the toll road) • 1 hour
- Summer and early fall. Road is plowed only to ski areas on either side of Smugglers Notch. Summit is usually snowed in between Nov. and early May. *See map p. 30.*

At 4,393 feet, **Mount Mansfield** is Vermont's highest mountain. It's accessible via a summit road and a highway that skirts its eastern flanks and traverses the rocky fastness called **Smugglers Notch.**

Start at the beginning of Rte. 108 in the ski capital of **Stowe.** The first few miles are thick with businesses serving the ski and summer trades; at mile 2 is the left turn for the famous **Trapp Family Lodge** *(802-253-8511).* Just beyond is a dramatic view of the profile of Mount Mansfield—the forehead, nose, and chin of what is said to resemble a reclining man's face. Follow Rte. 108 for 5 miles to reach the 4.5-mile **Mount Mansfield Toll Road** *(802-253-3000. Toll),* which leads to the 4,062 foot "nose." Views take in the northern **Lake Champlain Valley,** New York's **Adirondacks,** New Hampshire's **White Mountains,** and, on a clear day, the **Montreal** skyline.

Return to Rte. 108 and follow it as it climbs into the **Mount Mansfield State Forest.** The road twists through a series of steep switchbacks. The height of land at **Smugglers Notch,** a natural pass allegedly used for contraband during the War of 1812, is 2.5 miles past the entrance to **Smugglers Notch State Park** *(802-253-4014. www.vtstateparks.com/smuggler. Mem. Day-Columbus Day; adm. fee).* Enjoy sweeping vistas of the **Lamoille River Valley** as you descend 8 miles to the village of **Jeffersonville.**

Hiker on Mount Mansfield

In about 1.5 miles the routes diverge. Bear right to stay on Rte. 100, which enters a heavily wooded stretch of rolling, mountainous terrain, with the northern section of the Green Mountain National Forest on the left.

The village of **Pittsfield,** 7.5 miles from U.S. 4, is marked by a bandstand on the common. The road here follows the deep valley of the **Tweed River,** which empties into the White River, a tributary of the Connecticut, just ahead at Stockbridge. The waters on this side of the Green Mountains divide ultimately empty into Long Island Sound; west of the divide, the rivers drain into Lake Champlain.

Bear left to stay on Rte. 100 at the intersection with Rte. 107 at Stockbridge, then left again just after crossing the White River bridge. Ahead is **Talcville,** named after the former talc mines here. **Rochester,** less than a mile ahead, is the prettiest of the towns along this stretch of Rte. 100. The bandstand on its village green looks ready for a summer concert.

Head north beyond Rochester, skirting pastures and cornfields crowded along the floor of the steep-sided **White River Valley.** Once you pass Granville, the valley narrows beyond the possibilities of agriculture as Rte. 100 enters the **Granville Gulf Reservation,** where jutting escarpments and a heavy canopy of foliage in season cast the road in shade. Look to your left for lovely **Moss Glen Falls,** cascading down a sheer rock wall 1.4 miles into the reservation. The roadside vistas won't broaden for 3 miles, by which point Rte. 100 enters the **Mad River Valley.**

Now you're once again in ski country, as you can tell from the inns and restaurants as you drive through **Warren** and approach the regional commercial center of **Waitsfield.** A left turn on Rte. 17 at Irasville, about a mile south of Waitsfield, offers access to the **Sugarbush** and **Mad River Glen Ski Areas.**

The 12-mile stretch of Rte. 100 between Waitsfield and Waterbury is largely farmland, with fine mountain views. The highest peak you see here is 4,083-foot **Camels Hump,** fourth highest in Vermont.

Four and a half miles north of Waitsfield, bear left to stay on Rte. 100 and continue for another 7 miles to **Waterbury,** where the highway crosses the **Winooski River** and I-89. Just a mile past the interstate is one of Vermont's most popular attractions, **Ben & Jerry's** *(802-244-TOUR. Adm. fee for tours)* ice-cream factory. At the **Cold Hollow Cider Mill** *(802-244-8771),* 2.5 miles past Ben & Jerry's, you can watch cider being made.

Ten miles north of Waterbury is **Stowe,** a town long synonymous with skiing and, for many, with Vermont itself. If you've never been to Stowe, the tininess of the village may surprise you—it's barely more than a couple of blocks clustered around the needlelike spire of its **Community Church** and the 1833 **Green Mountain Inn** *(802-253-7301).* Most of Stowe's businesses, and its ski area, are spread along the Mountain Road (Rte. 108), which leads out of town toward Mount Mansfield (see Smugglers Notch drive p. 32).

Follow Rte. 100 north out of Stowe, but to avoid the traffic around the market town of Morrisville, bear left 1.8 miles past Stowe and take an 8.5-mile shortcut to Hyde Park on the Stagecoach Road (Rte. 108). On the left will be excellent views of **Mount Mansfield;** on the right, **Mount Elmore** rises beyond the Stowe Valley. At Hyde Park you can pick up Rte. 100 at Rte. 15.

Now Rte. 100's character changes—the terrain is wilder, more like the forested fastnesses of the nearby Northeast Kingdom. Up here, logging looms larger than agriculture, and moose and bear abound.

Go north through Eden and Lowell, beyond which the mountains give way to broader vistas. The last great sentinel of the Green Mountains,

Vermont 100 near Stockbridge

3,861-foot **Jay Peak,** stands just south of the Canadian border. You can see the summit poking above the mountains to the left at the junction of Rtes. 100 and 105, just outside little **Newport.** And that is where Rte. 100 ends, some 200 miles from the Massachusetts border.

> In 1934 a group of skiing enthusiasts pooled $500 to build Vermont's first ski tow. It was put together out of 1,800 feet of rope and an old Model T, but it was the start of a revolution in the Green Mountains.

33

Victory Basin Drive

U.S. 5 and Vt. 114 to U.S. 2 from St. Johnsbury

- 46 miles round-trip on paved and gravel roads
- 1¼ hours • Late spring through early fall. Black-flies are a problem in May and June. Foliage season arrives early in northern Vermont, usually by mid-September.

In this far northeastern corner of Vermont, a gravel road leads through remote and unspoiled **Victory Basin,** a hauntingly beautiful wetlands area surrounded by 13,000-acre Victory State Forest.

Begin in **St. Johnsbury,** which boasts an excellent art gallery at its 1871 **Athenaeum** *(30 Main St. 802-748-8291. Mon.-Sat.),* with paintings by artists of the Hudson River school, and the eclectic **Fairbanks Museum and Planetarium** *(Main and Prospect Sts. 802-748-2372. www.fairbanksmuseum.com. Adm. fees).* Follow U.S. 5 north to Lyndonville, and bear right onto Rte. 114 for East Burke. North of town is **Burke Mountain Ski Resort** *(802-626-3305),* where many U.S. Olympians train.

About 2.5 miles north of East Burke, turn right onto an unnumbered road, following signs for **Gallup Mills,** 7.5 miles away; along the way the road becomes gravel. This is the center of **Victory,** one of the last Vermont towns to receive electricity (1961). Turn right and follow the **Moose River** into the 5,000-acre **Victory Basin Wildlife Management Area.**

The wetlands, prized by naturalists for their vegetation and wildlife, are made up of swamps, marshes, and hard-to-reach bogs. Highly acidic and low in nutrients, bogs are characterized by a floating mat of vegetation over still water. Trees along the wetlands route include red and black spruce, speckled alder, willow, black cherry, and aspen. Mink, otter, moose, and bear are among the animal residents. The area is an important breeding ground for the unusual black-backed woodpecker.

Moose

As you continue south, the terrain's flat, subtly colored expanse makes a fine visual foil for ranks of spruce and fir in the middle distance and for the lonely peaks of **Umpire** and **Burke Mountains** off to the right. Eleven miles south of Gallup Mills, the Victory road meets U.S. 2 at North Concord. Turn right and drive another 11 miles back to St. Johnsbury.

Champlain Islands

Colchester to Alburg on U.S. 2

- 33 miles • 1 hour • Late spring to mid-fall. Lake Champlain is ice covered into April. Fall lingers here due to moderating lake influence; foliage peaks in early October

When Vermonters talk about "the islands," chances are they're referring to the archipelago in northern Lake Champlain. This drive follows the main route through the chain, with lake and mountain views on either side. Start where U.S. 2 leads west from I-89 at **Colchester,** 9 miles north of Burlington. After 2 miles you will cross the **Lamoille River** near its mouth at **Lake Champlain.** Beyond the broad, meandering river, the mainland is low and marshy, prime waterfowl habitat.

On your right at 4.7 miles is the entrance to **Sand Bar State Park** *(802-893-2825. www.vtstateparks.com/sandbar. Mem. Day–Labor Day; adm. fee),* with a fine bathing beach on a shallow lake cove. Just past the park, U.S. 2 crosses a causeway to **South Hero Island.** Look to the left for magnificent views of the broadest portion of the lake and of New York's **Adirondack Mountains.**

The islands and towns of North and South Hero were named after Vermont's two Revolutionary leaders, Ethan and Ira Allen; legend has it that the proud brothers themselves did the naming. South Hero is becoming a bedroom community for Burlington, but if you turn left onto South Street, 2.5 miles after reaching the island, you'll soon see acres of apple trees. Several orchards here run pick-your-own operations in early autumn, and during the first weekend in October, South Street is the setting for an annual **Applefest.**

Continue north on U.S. 2 for 2 miles past the South Street crossroads, with Lake Champlain's **Keeler Bay** on your right, to reach the intersection with Rte. 314. Turn left here and drive 3 miles if you have time for a scenic, 12-minute ferry ride to **Plattsburgh, New York** *(Ferry info 802-372-5550).* Opposite the ferry dock on the Vermont side is the **Ed Weed Fish Culture Station** *(802-372-3171),* which offers free self-guided tours.

Back on U.S. 2, you soon enter the town of **Grand Isle.** Here is the **Hyde Log Cabin** *(802-828-3051. July–Labor Day Wed.-Sun.; adm. fee),* built in 1783 and believed to be one of the oldest U.S. log cabins in its original state.

Hay and corn fields line the road north of the cabin, while off to the southeast are clear views of the northern **Green Mountains,** including the handsome profile of **Mount Mansfield.** Soon a drawbridge carries U.S. 2 across a Lake Champlain passage called **The Gut** to **North Hero Island.** The lake and Adirondack views to the left are especially fine. In summer Austria's famous Royal Lipizzan Stallions perform here *(802-372-5683).*

Drawbridge connecting Grand Isle and North Hero Island, Lake Champlain

As you drive along U.S. 2 just north of the drawbridge, look ahead and to the right to see the northernmost outrider of the Green Mountain chain, **Jay Peak.** The town center of **North Hero** rambles along **City Bay,** with none of its buildings more than a few yards from the water. Structures include the 1824 Greek Revival **Grand Isle County Courthouse,** in locally quarried stone.

Cabins along U.S. 2 in the Champlain Islands

Your next 2 miles on U.S. 2 take you along the narrow neck of land called the **Carrying Place,** a portage point used by Indians and early settlers crossing Lake Champlain. Beyond, North Hero Island widens into a landscape of cornfields and pastures, with the lake always on your right. Soon a road branches off to the right for **North Hero State Park** *(802-372-8727. www.vtstateparks.com/nhero. Mem. Day–Labor Day; adm. fee),* where lean-to campsites offer splendid lake and mountain views.

Continue 2 miles past the park road to the bridge across **Alburg Passage.** You are now in **Alburg,** which occupies a peninsula reaching down from Canada and separated from the rest of the U.S. by Lake Champlain. At the intersection with Rte. 129, turn left for a side trip onto **Isle La Motte,** smallest and least developed of the three main lake islands. In 1666 the French established Vermont's first white settlement here; the spot is marked by the outdoor **St. Anne Shrine** *(802-928-3362. Mid-May–mid-Oct.).*

Continue north on Rte. 2 for 6 miles past the Alburg Passage bridge to the intersection with Rte. 78. Unless you are heading north to Canada, turn right here to reach I-89 (11 miles east) by way of the **Missisquoi National Wildlife Refuge** *(802-868-4781. www.fws.gov/r5lcfwro/Miss.html),* a birder's paradise centered upon the delta of the **Missisquoi River** at Lake Champlain.

Vermont 22A

Vergennes to Fair Haven

● **41 miles** ● **1 hour** ● **Late spring to mid-fall. Autumn foliage is spectacular, and the warming influence of Lake Champlain often extends peak season well into October.**

Travel south along the rich bottomlands of the Lake Champlain Valley, where views of New York's majestic Adirondack Mountains rise above some of Vermont's choicest dairy lands.

Start at the northern end of Rte. 22A in **Vergennes.** At 1 square mile, it claims to be the smallest chartered city in the country—and you'll notice that the tidy 19th-century downtown quickly gives way to pastures.

Continue south on Rte. 22A into the predominantly agricultural community of **Addison.** The marshy lowlands that lie off to your right, starting about 5 miles south of Vergennes, are part of the **Dead Creek Wildlife Management Area,** a stopover for waterfowl using the Lake Champlain migration corridor. In the background in New York stand the high peaks of the **Adirondacks,** dominated by 5,344-foot **Mount Marcy.** Less imposing, though far more accessible, is 1,287-foot **Snake Mountain,** which rises in a long ridge to the left of Rte. 22A, just beyond the intersection with Rte. 17. (Turn right

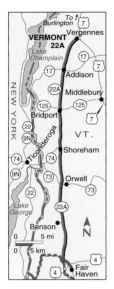

here if you want to take the **Lake Champlain Bridge** to New York State.) To reach the trail to the top of Snake Mountain, turn left onto Rte. 17, then right after a mile, and left after another 3.3 miles.

Mountains, high or low, do not figure in the immediate landscape as you drive south along Rte. 22A. Traditionally a dairy state, Vermont has been steadily losing individual farms over the past few decades. But in the gently rolling lowlands of the southern **Champlain Valley,** dairying is still king. Unlike the rocky Green Mountain foothills, this fertile terrain encourages the consolidation of smaller farms into large operations and the maintenance of economically viable herds of cows numbering in the hundreds. Head down Rte. 22A through Addison and Bridport, and you'll see pasture after pasture dotted with black-and-white holstein-friesians, Vermont's most popular dairy cow, as well as the occasional herd of fawn-colored jerseys or fawn-and-white guernseys.

As you enter the village of Bridport, 10 miles south of Vergennes, you will pass the right turn onto Rte. 125 west, an alternative way to the Lake Champlain Bridge. Just ahead on the left is Rte. 125 east to the college town of **Middlebury,** 8 miles away. Drive another 10 miles through the dairy country south of Bridport to reach **Shoreham,** whose antique shops, inn, and country store

lie just to the right of Rte. 22A on Rte. 74. Shoreham looms large in Vermont agriculture: Here, as in the Champlain island communities to the north, the temperature-moderating influence of the lake encourages apple growing. Late summer marks the opening of numerous roadside stands and pick-your-own orchards.

A right turn onto Rte. 74 at Shoreham leads you, in 5 miles, to the little ferry *(802-897-7999. Mid-April–mid-Oct.; fare)* for **Ticonderoga** in New York State. **Fort Ticonderoga** *(518-585-2821. www.fort-ticonderoga .org. Early May–mid-Oct.; adm.*

fee), now restored to its Revolutionary-era appearance, was the British stronghold captured on May 10, 1775, by Benedict Arnold and Ethan Allen, legendary leader of Vermont's Green Mountain Boys. If you take the ferry from Larrabees Point near Shoreham to the New York side, you will be following in the wake of Allen's wooden boats.

Back on Rte. 22A, continue 6 miles south past Shoreham to reach Rte. 73 at **Orwell.**

Vermont 22A sights: barn and barn tools (top)

A left turn here leads directly into the village, with its handsome green and 1810 Town Hall; a right will bring you, in 6 miles, to another Revolutionary War site, **Mount Independence** *(802-759-2412).* Interpretive trails here connect remnants of a 1776 fort built to block a southward British drive. The lake and mountain views alone are worth a ramble along the trails.

Just 1.5 miles south of Orwell on Rte. 22A, look to your left for **Historic Brookside Farms** *(802-948-2727)*, a 1789 farmhouse with a stately 1843 Greek Revival front and a beautiful free-standing curved staircase. Still a working farm, Brookside also serves as an inn and offers miles of trails for nature hikes and cross-country skiing.

As you drive south of Orwell, notice how the terrain becomes increasingly hilly, and the ubiquitous Champlain Valley dairy farms begin to give way to woodland. Roughly 5.5 miles past the Rte. 73 intersection, you can stop at a pleasant picnic area on the left. A mile and a half farther is a right turn for **Benson,** a tiny village from which a network of gravel roads spreads out toward the narrow southern tip of Lake Champlain. Continue south for little more than 6 miles to where Rte. 22A meets U.S. 4. Head east from here to Rutland on U.S. 4 or west into New York State; just ahead is the town of **Fair Haven,** where brick storefronts face the green in a scene little changed over the past century.

Massachusetts

Mohawk Trail Drive

Greenfield to Williamstown on Mass. 2

● 41 miles ● 1 hour ● Late spring to mid-fall. Rte. 2 can be very busy in summer and at peak foliage season (early to mid-October), but fall colors are magnificent and worth braving the traffic.

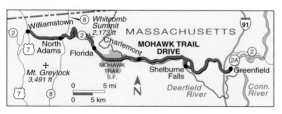

Named after a route followed by Mohawk Indians traveling between what are now Massachusetts and New York State, the Mohawk Trail has been a favorite scenic byway since it was first opened to automobile traffic in 1914. To follow this route across the **Hoosac Range** of wooded hills, head west from **Greenfield** on Rte. 2. (The actual Mohawk Trail begins at Orange, about 20 miles east.)

The road soon begins to climb out of the Connecticut River Valley. After 1 mile, stop at an observation tower to enjoy a view reaching northwards into New Hampshire and Vermont.

Continue west past the sort of roadside attractions that vanished from much of America with the coming of the interstate highways. Just 4.5 miles west of I-91 is the eye-catching **Mohawk Trading Post** *(413-625-2412)*, complete with tepee and totem pole. This is the first of several establishments along the drive that specialize in Native American crafts in a region that

Autumn in Massachusetts' Berkshires

has not had an appreciable Indian population for centuries. Within the first 7 or 8 miles west of Greenfield, two maple sugar houses offer demonstrations in early spring of how maple sap is boiled down into syrup. They sell the finished product all year.

Three miles past the Mohawk Trading Post, turn left off Rte. 2 for a half-mile side trip to **Shelburne Falls.** This snug mini-city, its tidy downtown mostly unchanged since early in the century, is graced by the **Bridge of Flowers** *(April-Oct.),* a 400-foot span across the **Deerfield River** built for a trolley line that stopped running in 1928. Ever since, the women's club has cultivated a garden along the bridge's pedestrian walkway.

Continue along Rte. 2 past the Shelburne Falls turnoff, crossing the Deerfield River and following its path through the town of Charlemont. One-half mile beyond Charlemont, you can rent a canoe at **Zoar Outdoor** *(413-339-4010. Daily May–mid-Oct.; March-April and mid-Oct.–mid-Nov. Wed.-Sun.; mid-Nov.–Feb. Tues.-Fri.)* and enjoy a water-level view of the Deerfield Valley.

Roughly 4 miles past Charlemont, Rte. 2 enters the **Mohawk Trail State Forest** *(413-339-5504. www.state.ma.us/ dem/parks/mhwk.htm).* The Mohawk Trail's commercial aspect abruptly ends here. The road follows a deep ravine, appearing almost to tunnel through trees whose crowns tower above: In autumn the effect is kaleidoscopic. You will find summer attractions as well—on your right, just over a half mile into the state forest, there's a picnic area with swimming in the river *(Parking fee Memorial Day-Columbus Day).*

Coming out of the state forest, Rte. 2 winds to the highest point along the Mohawk Trail at **Whitcomb Summit** (2,173 feet), reached just after you pass, on the right, the bronze "Elk on the Trail," dedicated by Massachusetts Elks to honor their World War I dead. The view from Whitcomb Summit takes in Vermont's **Green Mountains** to the north, New Hampshire's **Monadnock Mountain** to the northeast, the **Berkshire Hills** to the south, and, directly west, **Mount Greylock** (3,491 feet), the highest point in Massachusetts.

Mount Greylock dominates the western horizon as you descend through the Mohawk Trail's famous **Hairpin Turn,** 3.5 miles beyond Whitcomb Summit. The turn is situated on the shoulder of a ledge, with open views

The Hoosac Tunnel, near the town of Florida, was one of the greatest engineering accomplishments of the railway age. Completed in 1875, the 25,000-foot tunnel cost 20 million dollars and 195 lives.

of the valley below. If you'd rather enjoy the scenery while sitting still, there's the roadside **Golden Eagle Restaurant** *(413-663-9834. Daily in summer, Fri.-Sun. rest of year)* at the head of the turn.

Head downhill for 3 miles past the hairpin turn to enter **North Adams,** a

classic small New England factory city that, like so many similar places, has had to struggle through the loss of textile manufacturing jobs over the past half century. Follow Rte. 2 as it passes between somber brick mills built a century or more ago. For a glimpse of North Adams's industrial and railroad history, visit the **Western Gateway Heritage State Park** *(413-663-8059. www.state.ma.us/dem/parks/wghp.htm. Donation),* downtown on Rte. 8, just south of Rte. 2.

Drive west on Rte. 2 for 4 miles past North Adams to reach **Williamstown.** If North Adams is the factory city from central casting, Williamstown is the archetypal New England college town.

Deerfield River at Charlemont

Williams College *(413-597-3131)* has dominated the local landscape since its founding in 1793; its main buildings, many in Georgian and federal styles, surround the lovely village green that marks the end of this drive. Just off Rte. 2 and U.S. 7, a mile south of the town center, is one of the area's principal cultural attractions, the **Sterling and Francine Clark Art Institute** *(413-458-9545. Closed Mon. Sept.-June),* with magnificent collections of Old Master, French Impressionist, and 19th-century American paintings.

Tyringham Valley

Great Barrington to Lee on Mass. 23 and Tyringham and Main Roads

● 17 miles ● ½ hour ● Late spring to mid-fall. Foliage is spectacular from late September to early October.

No matter how well beaten the Berkshire paths have become, it's easy to wander onto roads less traveled. This route through Tyringham Valley combines forests and farms with a sculptor's storybook retreat.

Begin in **Great Barrington** at U.S. 7 and Rte. 23, heading east on Rte. 23. The road soon enters a hardwood forest filled with maples and a few elms that survived the Dutch elm disease.

Continue along Rte. 23 for 8 miles to the village of **Monterey,** named for an American victory in the Mexican War. Monterey today is an arts and crafts center; in the village and along local byways are a number of galleries and potters' studios.

At Monterey turn left onto the unmarked Tyringham Road at the big white church on the left. The road climbs through shady woods, with **Lake**

Garfield on the right within the first mile. About 2.5 miles out of town, expansive views of the northern Berkshires open up ahead.

Turn left at a T-intersection onto Main Road, 4 miles north of Monterey, to continue toward **Tyringham.** The town lies in the deep **Tyringham Valley** along Hop Brook, so named because of the wild hops early settlers found growing. The valley today is almost entirely agricultural—all pastures, barns, and fences, culminating in a town "center" with no more than a toylike stone post office, a tidy flower bed, and **Tyringham Cobble** *(Off Jerusalem Rd. Donation),* a little hill with a spectacular view of the valley.

Continue north 1 mile past the Tyringham post office to **Tyringham Galleries** *(413-243-3260. Mem. Day-Columbus Day; adm. fee),* a building straight out of J.R.R. Tolkien. The British sculptor Sir Henry Kitson, creator of "The Minute Man" stat-

Along Massachusetts 23

ue in Lexington, Massachusetts, built this medieval hideaway as a studio in the 1920s. The structure has chestnut beams, a layered shingle roof that suggests thatching, and great stone buttresses that seem to rise naturally out of the ground. Inside, contemporary paintings and sculptures are for sale; outside are a sculpture garden and a trail leading to a secluded lily pond alive with frogs and turtles.

Leaving the gallery, drive north along the remaining 4 miles of Tyringham Road. The road ends at U.S. 20 on the outskirts of Lee, with a Massachusetts Turnpike entrance nearby.

41

Cape Ann Ramble

Essex to Salem on Mass. 133, 127, 127A, and 1A

● **30 miles** ● **1½ hours** ● **Spring to late fall. Ocean views are usually fine. Roads can be crowded in high summer.**

Cape Ann is Massachusetts' "other cape"—not as well known as Cape Cod, but suffused with the traditions of New England seafaring and the tang of Atlantic breezes.

Start a Cape Ann circuit at Rtes. 22 and 133 in **Essex,** a village built along broad salt marshes. Essex was a shipbuilding center as early as the 17th century, and today is the home of the **Essex Shipbuilding Museum** *(978-768-7541. May-Oct. Wed.-Mon., Nov.–mid-May weekends; adm. fee).*

Just south of Essex center, at an intersection surrounded by antiques shops, bear left to follow Rte. 133 onto Cape Ann proper. The landscape for the next few miles is mostly suburban. Seven miles beyond the intersection is **Gloucester Harbor,** home of a commercial fishing fleet. Turn left onto Rte. 127 at its intersection with Rte. 133 and look to the right for the famous Fishermen's Memorial Statue, a bronze helmsman hunched over his wheel. "They that go down to the sea in ships 1623-1923," the

Geese in a pond off Mass. 127

inscription reads, and Gloucestermen still, in the rest of the words of that biblical passage, do business in great waters.

Follow Rte. 127 along Gloucester's waterfront; a mile past the statue, bear left (127A goes to the right) and follow signs for **Rockport.** In 3 miles

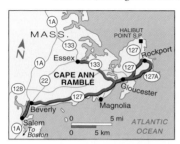

you will come to the second intersection with Rte. 127A. Turn left here for a side trip to **Halibut Point State Park** *(978-546-2997. www.state.ma.us/dem/parks/halb.htm. Parking fee Mem. Day-Columbus Day)*, where foot trails follow the cape's granite-bound northern tip. To stay on the scenic drive, veer right at the intersection onto Rte. 127A (Broadway), which leads to Rockport's quaint downtown.

Parking in central Rockport is often difficult (peripheral parking is offered in summer, with shuttle buses to downtown), but it's worth the extra effort to get out of the car and stroll along **Bearskin Neck,** a narrow strip of land projecting into the harbor and lined with craft shops and art galleries. Nearby, **Motif #1** is a little red fishing shack jutting into the harbor that earned its name because of its countless depictions by painters. Destroyed in the blizzard of February 1978, the beloved structure was immediately rebuilt.

Continue south on Rte. 127A as it reenters Gloucester, along that city's oceanside residential district, past **Long Beach** and **Good Harbor Beach** *(Adm. fee for both)*. If you stop for a swim, you'll find the Atlantic bracingly cold even in late summer. Follow Rte. 127A through the **Bass Rocks** area, where dramatic views of the rockbound coast are interspersed with textbook examples of the turn-of-the-century shingle style of New England seaside architecture—all turrets, wraparound porches, and weathered cedar siding.

Gloucester's rocky Atlantic coast

Head back along the coast toward the Gloucester business district, watching for two roads on the left. The first leads to **Eastern Point,** where Henry Davis Sleeper's mansion **Beauport** *(75 Eastern Point Blvd. 978-283-0800. Mid-May–mid-Oct.; adm. fee),* built between 1907 and 1934, is a mélange of styles. The second road, one-half mile past the Eastern Point road, leads to **Rocky Neck,** filled with artists' studios and galleries.

Head back into downtown Gloucester and pick up Rte. 127 again, heading west out of town. Rte. 127 next takes you through the region that late 19th-century Boston Brahmins called the North Shore. Nowadays, the term is applied loosely to the Massachusetts coast from Boston to New Hampshire, but it was the towns along the south coast of Cape Ann—**Magnolia, Manchester, Beverly Farms, Prides Crossing**—to which the upper crust of a century ago repaired in summer. Most of the surviving mansions are set back from the road with commanding ocean views. Just off Rte. 127 on Hesperus Avenue in Magnolia, the medieval stone pile of **Hammond Castle** *(978-283-7673. Adm. fee)* belongs to the post-World War I era. Its flamboyant builder, electronics innovator John Hays Hammond, installed a massive organ still used for concerts.

> The first fried clam is said to have been served about 75 years ago at Woodman's on Main Street, Essex, where they're still frying up the tender bivalves.

Rte. 127 ends at Rte. 1A in **Beverly,** where the first American privateer was commissioned; hence the city's claim as the "birthplace of the American Navy." Continue through downtown and cross the bridge over the harbor to reach the port city of **Salem,** with its many reminders of the 17th-century witch trials and its days as a late 18th- to early 19th-century maritime trading center. The **Salem Witch Museum** *(Wash. Sq. N. 978-744-1692. Adm. fee)* evokes the witch hysteria. Native son Nathaniel Hawthorne often visited a 1668 house, now the **House of the Seven Gables** *(54 Turner St. 978-744-0991. Adm. fee).* The federal **Custom House** is part of the **Salem Maritime National Historic Site** *(Derby St. 978-740-1650. www.nps.gov/sama).*

43

Old King's Highway

Sagamore to Provincetown on Mass. 6A and U.S. 6

● 59 miles ● 1½ hours
● All year. Cape Cod is best known as a summer resort, but spring and fall are lovely and uncrowded. Winter seas and skies are cast in somber grays and blues.

Of the three routes along the shoulder-to-elbow portion of Cape Cod's crooked arm, the most picturesque is along Rte. 6A and U.S. 6, the King's Road of colonial times. Beyond, U.S. 6 follows the majestic, lonely dunelands of Cape Cod National Seashore.

After crossing **Sagamore Bridge** over the Cape Cod Canal, follow the signs for Rte. 6A. Roughly 3 miles ahead is the right turn for **Sandwich,** the oldest town on the cape (settled 1637). The town is famous for its beautiful colored 19th-century glass, a craft celebrated at the **Sandwich Glass Museum** *(Main St. 508-888-0251. www.sandwichglassmuseum.org. Closed Mon.-Tues. Feb.-March plus all Jan.; adm. fee).*

At Cape Cod National Seashore you can see the site of the station from which in 1903 Guglielmo Marconi sent and received the first transoceanic radio messages between world leaders— Theodore Roosevelt and Britain's King Edward VII.

Driving in and around Sandwich offers a quick introduction to the cape's potpourri of architecture—somber 17th-century saltboxes, classically proportioned Georgians, and federal-style houses, and of course the region's signature Cape Cod cottages. As you head back to Rte. 6A and continue east toward Barnstable, note the attention Cape Codders pay to their gardens. Everywhere you look, you'll see the white snowball bushes and bright blue hydrangeas that thrive here.

Continue on Rte. 6A for 12 miles past the Sandwich turnoff to the center of **Barnstable,** the seat of Barnstable County, which encompasses all of Cape Cod. The grand Greek Revival **Court House,** a relic of New England's early 19th-century "granite age," dominates this tree-shaded town. Three miles down the road in **Yarmouth Port,** a domestic version of the Greek Revival style executed in wood can be seen at the **Capt. Bangs Hallet House** *(508-362-3021. June–mid-Oct. Thurs.–Sun.; adm. fee),* filled with treasures garnered during the captain's career in the Asia trade.

Follow Rte. 6A east out of Yarmouth Port into **Dennis.** Turn right onto Old Bass River Road at the Dennis village green, then left on Scargo Hill Road for a half-mile side trip to **Scargo Hill,** at 160 feet one of Cape Cod's highest points. Despite this modest elevation, the hill—topped by an observation tower—affords fine views of the cape terrain along the bay side as far north as Provincetown.

On the beach at Provincetown

Brewster, about 6 miles east of Dennis via Rte. 6A, is a town of 19th-century sea captains' houses, many serving today as inns and restaurants. The main street is also lined with an eclectic assortment of antique shops.

Continue on Rte. 6A for 3 miles past Brewster to reach the entrance to **Nickerson State Park** *(508-896-3491. www.state.ma.us/dem/parks/nick.htm. Camping fee),* nearly 2,000 acres of pond-studded scrub-conifer forest. The park is an access point for the **Cape Cod Rail Trail,** open to cyclists and walkers, which extends north to Wellfleet along a paved former rail bed.

44

Cape Cod National Seashore

Route 6A meets U.S. 6, the Mid-Cape Highway, near Orleans, 2 miles past the state park. You can continue directly north on U.S. 6 to Provincetown or stay on Rte. 6A for the 1-mile drive into the town center of **Orleans,** commercial hub of the Outer (or Lower) Cape. Beyond Orleans, U.S. 6 heads along the middle of the narrow forearm of Cape Cod, flanked on the right by the 43,500-acre **Cape Cod National Seashore** *(508-349-3785. www.nps.gov/caco),* which encompasses much of the Outer Cape. Stop at the **Salt Pond Visitor Center** *(508-255-3421),* 4 miles past the junction with U.S. 6, for information on the historic attractions, lighthouses, and ocean beaches that lie within this federal property.

For a marked contrast with the Outer Cape's oceanside environment of high dunes and white-capped breakers, head north for 3.5 miles past the Visitor Center to the Massachusetts Audubon Society's **Wellfleet Bay Wildlife Sanctuary** *(508-349-2615. www.wellfleetbay.org. Adm. fee),* a secluded tract of woods and salt marshes along the bay side. The town of **Wellfleet** itself, just off U.S. 6 to the left 5 miles past the sanctuary, is the last village south of Provincetown. Stay on U.S. 6 beyond Wellfleet to enter **Truro,** which offers what many visitors consider the purest distillation of the Cape Cod landscape: heather-blanketed moors, high dunes, and the sense that you are never far from the sea—as indeed you are not.

At North Truro, 7.5 miles north of Wellfleet, the road forks and Rte. 6A reappears. Bear right and continue on U.S. 6 past brackish **Pilgrim Lake** for access to the **Province Lands** *(Visitor Center 508-487-1256. End of April to Thanksgiving)* section of the national seashore. Its paths wind through dunelands fragrant with beach plum and bayberry, and its excellent beach overlooks Herring Cove. Or bear left to hug the bay shore for the final few miles to **Provincetown,** that peerless amalgam of beach resort, colonial village, Portuguese fishing port, and flamboyant art colony—all at the very tip of Cape Cod.

Rhode Island

Rhode Island 77

Tiverton to Sakonnet Point

● 14 miles ● ½ hour ● Late spring to mid-fall. Harvest season from late summer to early autumn is especially recommended, when roadside stands sell local produce.

Rhode Island's easternmost corner is separated from the rest of the state by Narragansett Bay and the Sakonnet River and by the Fall River area of Massachusetts. Worlds away from busy Newport and Providence, this often-overlooked part of "little Rhody" offers tranquil vistas of farmlands, vineyards, and the sea.

Start this short tour in the town of **Tiverton,** at the intersection of Rtes. 138 and 77, and head south on Rte. 77. Immediately to your right, as you drive out of Tiverton, is the narrow head of the **Sakonnet River;** opposite is the northeasternmost tip of **Rhode Island,** largest of the Narragansett Bay islands. Known by the Wampanoag Indians as Aquidneck, it was named by settlers who mistook it for a nearby island that the Florentine explorer Giovanni da Verrazano had named for the Mediterranean island of Rhodes. Rhode Island later gave its name to the colony and state that surround the bay.

Within the first mile south of Tiverton, the Sakonnet River—not a true river but a tidal channel—widens to reveal broad views of **Portsmouth** on the opposite shore and of tiny, rocky **Gould Island.** The protected waters of the Sakonnet are popular with boaters, and in summer this stretch of the "river" is flecked with white sails.

Continue on Rte. 77 as it veers eastward and farther inland along the shores of **Nannaquaket Pond** and across **Sin and Flesh Brook.** We can only guess whether this little stream was named by the Puritans as a general warning against the ways of the world, or because of some local reputation for misbehavior. Rte. 77 next passes through a patchwork of small farms, their fields marked off by old stone walls. Blueberries and corn are among the local crops available at roadside stands from midsummer. Also along here is the **Emilie Ruecker Wildlife Refuge** *(Right on Seapowet Ave., follow signs. 401-949-5454.*

Tiverton salt marsh in fall

46

www.asri.org/rueckr.htm) with three salt marsh trails.

Turn left at a point slightly more than 7 miles south of Tiverton to enjoy another local crop. **Sakonnet Vineyards** *(401-635-8486)* has been a leader among New England wineries since 1975; the vines here benefit from the moderating climatic influence of the ocean, and cultivation of Chardonnay grapes has been particularly successful. Tours highlight various aspects of wine making, and a tasting and sales room is open daily.

Along with Sakonnet's grapes, crops such as peaches and strawberries also benefit from the mild local climate, as evidenced by the farm stands that dot the roadsides around here. Proximity to the ocean, of course, also means fog.

Head south for another 1.8 miles beyond the Sakonnet Vineyard turnoff and turn left for the mile drive to **Little Compton Commons,** a secluded gem of a New England village. Little more than a crossroads with a restaurant (specializing in johnnycakes, a cornmeal-based Rhode

Sailboats at a Newport dock

Island tradition) and a century-old general store, Little Compton is clustered about the magnificently steepled 1832 **United Congregational Church.** Take a few moments to walk through the churchyard; the church was founded in 1704, and there are many 18th-century gravestones. Little Compton, which comprises not only the village of Little Compton Commons and its environs but the entire southern tip of this corner of the state, was where the famous Rhode Is-

Ocean Drive

Newport Loop

● 10 miles ● ½ hour ● All year, though crowded in summer.
See map p. 46.

The colonial seaport of Newport, at the entrance to Narragansett Bay, is perhaps best known for its extravagant turn-of-the-century "cottages." This circuit takes them in as well as the city's rugged shoreline. *(Mansions open to the public are under the direction of the Preservation Society of Newport County. 401-847-1000. www.newportmansions.org. Phone for schedule. Adm. fee.)*

From downtown Newport, follow Memorial Boulevard to the corner of Bellevue Avenue and turn right into the heart of mansion territory. Directly on your right is the 1839 Gothic Revival **Kingscote,** followed by **The Elms,** a 1901 château.

Turn left from Bellevue onto Narragansett Avenue, then right onto Ochre Point Avenue to reach **The Breakers,** the 1895 extravaganza designed for Cornelius Vanderbilt II. Head back up to Bellevue Avenue by turning right onto Ruggles Avenue, then left onto Bellevue. Over the next mile you will pass **Rosecliff** (1902), where *The Great Gatsby* was filmed in 1974; **Marble House** (1892), incorporating 500,000 cubic feet of marble; and the 1894 **Belcourt Castle** *(401-846-0669. Adm. fee).*

At the end of Bellevue Avenue follow signs for **Ocean Drive.** The route affords vistas of Rhode Island Sound and the rocky coast, passing **Brenton Point State Park** and **Hammersmith Farm** *(Private),* site of John and Jacqueline Kennedy's 1953 wedding reception. Continue past **Fort Adams State Park** *(www.riparks.com/fortadams.htm),* where there is a **Museum of Yachting** *(401-847-1018. May-Oct.; adm. fee),* and finish at the downtown waterfront.

47

land Red breed of chicken was developed in the 1850s. There is a monument to the bird in the community of Adamsville, near the Massachusetts border.

This part of the coast has long had the name Fogland, and the mist can badly hamper visibility any time of year, especially in the morning.

Return to Rte. 77 and turn left for **Sakonnet Point.** On the left, a mile past the Little Compton Commons turnoff, stands a 1690 structure housing the small museum of the **Little Compton Historical Society** *(401-635-4035. Late June-Labor Day and weekends in Sept. Call for other dates; adm. fee).* From here, the 2.5-mile drive that remains before land's end at Sakonnet Point takes you through rolling meadows and small farms, with occasional views of the 4-mile-wide Sakonnet River near its mouth at Rhode Island Sound. If wine, peaches, and berries haven't filled your picnic basket, you can still stock up at a roadside stand along the way back north. The end of the line, Sakonnet Point, comes at a little anchorage for fishing boats and pleasure craft, where a stone jetty is usually lined with anglers. There is a place to buy lobsters—and not much else, unless you count spectacular sunsets over Newport, just 6 miles across the sound.

Connecticut

Connecticut 169

Canterbury to North Woodstock

● 22 miles ● ½ hour ● Spring to mid-autumn. Foliage peaks in early to mid-October.

Although the roads of Connecticut's northeastern Quiet Corner were traveled by colonial settlers as far back as the 1680s, this unsung nook of the Nutmeg State still affords the pleasures of discovery. The secret is to stay off I-395, the area's main north-south artery, and follow the byways through a skein of unspoiled villages.

Begin by picking up Rte. 169 at Canterbury, just 4 miles west of I-395. Here, at the intersection with Rte. 14, is the 1805 **Prudence Crandall Museum** *(860-546-9916. Adm. fee),* the house where Prudence Crandall set out to educate young black girls in the early 1830s, and was hounded out of town for it. Fifty years later a penitent Connecticut voted the aged Crandall a pension.

Continue north on Rte. 169, past late 18th-century farmhouses and fields that have been tilled since before the Revolution. Along the way, you'll see many examples of classic New England stone walls. The low, even walls are remarkably durable monuments to early farmers' determination to find a practical use for the curse of Yankee agriculture—the glacially deposited rocks and boulders strewn throughout farm fields. In some places, the walls have outlasted the

Trinity Church, Brooklyn, Connecticut

fields: Areas once completely cleared for agriculture have long since reverted to forest, with the enduring stone fences surviving amid the trees. A little over 5 miles north of Canterbury, you'll pass through a thick stand of maple and pine, along a shady allée canopied by foliage in summer.

49

Follow Rte. 169 to **Brooklyn,** 6 miles north of Canterbury. Since 1852, the **Brooklyn Fair** has been held here the week before Labor Day. The fairgrounds are on your left, along Rte. 169 just south of town.

One-half mile past the fairgrounds, also on the left, stands the handsome **Israel Putnam Monument** to Brooklyn's most famous resident, a Revolutionary War major general. Born in Salem Village, now Danvers, Massachusetts, Putnam spent much of his life here and is buried beneath this monument. The command "Don't fire until you see the white of their eyes" was allegedly given by Putnam at the Battle of Bunker Hill.

Just past the Putnam monument is the Brooklyn town center, dominated by the lovely white spire of the 1771 Congregational **Meeting House,** which, in 1816, became Connecticut's first Unitarian church.

Stay on Rte. 169 past its intersection with U.S. 6 at Brooklyn and continue 7 miles into the town of **Pomfret,** clustered, like Brooklyn, around the simple antique spire of a Congregational church. This one was built in 1832 in the Greek Revival style. (The Congregationalists, so called because of the autonomy of their individual congregations, stem from England's original Puritan churches.)

In 1674 the Reverend John Eliot, "apostle to the Indians," preached to the local tribes near Woodstock, and 12 years later the first white settlers arrived.

As you drive through Pomfret, you'll notice that along with stone walls and churches, this corner of Connecticut is steeped in another New England tradition—private boarding schools. The campuses of the **Pomfret School** (1894) and the **Rectory School** (original building dates from 1792) both line Rte. 169 within a short distance of each other.

Woodstock, 4 miles ahead, lies along the route of the Connecticut Path,

Forest stream,
Woodstock

the wilderness link between the Massachusetts and Connecticut colonies, and it is possible that Thomas Hooker and his party passed near the present-day site of Woodstock en route to Hartford in 1636.

You won't be able to drive past the Woodstock town green without taking notice of the vividly painted house across the street. This is **Roseland Cottage** *(860-928-4074. Early June–mid-Oct. Wed.-Sun.; adm. fee)*, the summer home of abolitionist publisher Henry Bowen. Done in bright pink with green shutters, as if part of its lush gardens, the 1846 cottage is a masterpiece of the Gothic Revival style. Bowen hosted several U.S. Presidents here during his lavish July 4th celebrations; his barn houses perhaps the oldest indoor bowling alley in the U.S.

Head on to **North Woodstock,** a village that does as much as any place to help the Quiet Corner earn its sobriquet. Here, you can choose to continue north toward Southbridge and Sturbridge (home of Old Sturbridge Village) just over the Massachusetts line, or follow the tranquil east-west byways of northeastern Connecticut.

50

Lower Connecticut River Valley

Loop from Middletown on Conn. 66, 151, 149, 82, 156, I-95, Conn. 9 and 154

● 56 miles ● 2 hours ● May through October

The towns and harbors along the lower reaches of the Connecticut River have hummed with activity for over 300 years. This route explores the natural and man-made environments that inspired the Nature Conservancy to designate this area one of forty "Last Great Places" in the hemisphere. Start in **Middletown,** home of **Wesleyan University** *(860-685-2000)*, at the junction of Rtes. 9 and 66. Main Street parallels the **Connecticut River,** which stretches some 400 miles from near the Canadian border to Long Island Sound.

Head east on Rte. 66 across the river into **Portland,** settled in 1690 and once a brownstone quarrying center. Five miles farther, at the junction of 66 and 151 in the village of **Cobalt**—named for an early mining venture—turn right and head south for 8 miles on Rte. 151 and then south on Rte. 149 and continue 3 miles into **East Haddam,** home of the restored **Victorian Goodspeed Opera House** *(860-873-8668. April-Dec. Wed.-Sun.; adm. fee)*, where live musicals are performed.

From the junction of Rtes. 149 and 82 in East Haddam, go west on Rte. 82 and follow signs for **Gillette**

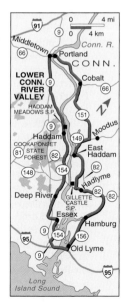

Castle State Park *(Via River Rd. 860-526-2336. http://dep.state.ct.us/rec/ parks.htm#Parks. Grounds open year-round. House under renovation and on restricted schedule).* The fieldstone castle, on a hill overlooking the Connecti-

cut River, was built in 1919 by actor William Gillette, famed for his portrayal of Sherlock Holmes.

Leaving the park turn left on Rte. 148 through the town of Hadlyme, then pick up Rte. 82 and continue east for 4 miles to the intersection with Rte. 156. Turn right and head south. The road crosses **Eightmile River,** site of **Joshua's Rock,** where the first Englishmen to sail up the Connecticut River

Haddam Meadows State Park on the Connecticut River

were killed by Indians, through Hamburg, and into the township of **Old Lyme.** To visit the town, which is filled with the mansions of 18th- and early 19th-century sea captains, take a left on Halls Road, then a right on Lyme Street. Otherwise, continue the drive south on I-95, cross over the Connecticut River, and take the first exit to Rte. 9. Take the second exit off Rte. 9 to Rte. 154.

One mile north on Rte. 154 is **Essex,** settled in 1690. The first Connecticut warship, the *Oliver Cromwell,* was built here in 1775. **Ivoryton,** a part of Essex, once manufactured ivory piano keys. Turn off onto Rte. 9 and follow signs for the historic waterfront to visit the **Connecticut River Museum** *(Foot of Main St. 860-767-8269. Closed Mon.; adm. fee).* Stop for lunch or dinner at the **Griswold Inn** *(860-767-1776),* open since 1776.

Middletown bridge

North on Rte. 154, past the junction with Rte. 9, is the **Essex Steam Train & Riverboat Ride** *(860-767-0103. Early May–late Oct.; call ahead for schedule; fare).* The **E.E. Dickinson Company,** famous as a distiller of witch hazel, is also here. The formula, based on a woodland shrub, was learned from the Indians. Continue north for 3 miles to **Deep River,** settled in 1635. Every third Saturday in July the town hosts the country's largest **Ancient Fife and Drum Muster.** Five miles north, you can turn west on Rte. 148 for about 5 miles, then right on Cedar Lake Road, and follow signs to Pattaconk Reservoir for a side trip to 16,000-acre **Cockaponset State Forest** *(860-345-8521. http://dep.state.ct.us/rec/parks.htm#Forests),* with some of New England's few tulip trees.

Drive north along the river 4 miles past Rte. 82 to **Haddam,** once an important salmon and shad fisheries center. According to the indigenous

Wangunk Indians, each year the Shad Spirit would lead the fish from the ocean to spawn in the Connecticut River. Turn left onto Walkley Hill Road to visit the 1794 **Thankful Arnold House** *(860-345-2400. Mon.-Wed. and second Sun. in month June-Oct.; donation).* Return to Rte. 154; on the right is the entrance to **Haddam Meadows State Park** *(http://dep.state.ct.us/rec/parks.htm#Parks),* a meadowland in the river's floodplain.

The scenic portion of Rte. 154 ends some 4 miles ahead, at a pretty waterfall in **Seven Falls State Highway Park.** Just past the falls on the left, the stone slabs of **Bible Rock** stand on edge like an open book. Directly across from Bible Rock is **Shopboard Rock,** a freestanding boulder with a flat top; it was brought here by a glacier some 25,000 years ago. About 1 mile from the park is an entrance to Rte. 9 back toward Middletown.

Litchfield Hills

Torrington loop on U.S. 202, 7, 44, Conn. 63, 109, 47, 45, 341, 8

● 87 miles ● ½ day ● May through October

Connecticut's gently rolling Litchfield Hills are often called the "foothills of the Berkshires," but they have a character all their own—country squire manners with just the right amount of rustic Yankee charm.

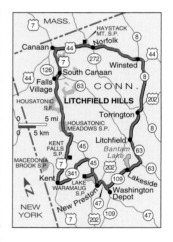

Begin this drive in **Torrington** by the Civil War statue at the junction of South Main Street and U.S. 202. Once one of the "brass towns" of the **Naugatuck River Valley,** Torrington has a rich industrial history. The source of waterpower for these early industries was the scenic **Naugatuck River,** which flows through town. Follow U.S. 202 for about 5 miles southwest as it climbs a plateau to the quintessential New England town of **Litchfield,** whose lovely town green is edged with stately colonial houses and elm trees. The **West Street Grill** *(43 West St. 860-567-3885)* on the green serves an excellent lunch and dinner. The **Tapping Reeve House and Law School** *(South St. 860-567-4501. Mid-April–late Nov.; adm. fee)* was America's first law school. Among the school's graduates were Vice President Aaron Burr—Reeve's first student—and Vice President John C. Calhoun.

For a side trip to the state's largest nature center, wildlife sanctuary, and natural lake, bear right and head west on U.S. 202 for a few miles to **White Memorial Foundation** *(860-567-0857).* This 4,000-acre sanctuary on **Bantam Lake** has a museum, hiking and cross-country ski trails, and bird observation platforms. The **Bantam River,** flowing through the grounds, is a spawning ground for the state's largest freshwater game fish, the northern pike, and offers some of the best flat-water canoeing in Connecticut. The scenic drive continues its climb south on Rte. 63. A few miles past the

Before sunrise on Lake Waramaug

junction is **White Flower Farm** *(860-567-8789. Mid-Feb.–Dec.)*, with 10 acres of perennial display gardens and 30 acres of growing fields. Less than a mile past the farm, at the junction of Rtes. 63 and 109, turn right and go west on Rte. 109 toward Washington Depot.

About 3.5 miles west on Rte. 109, in **Lakeside,** glass sculptor Larry LiVolsi welcomes visitors to his **Lorenz Studio and Gallery** *(226 Old Litchfield Rd. 860-567-4280)*. The farmland and rolling hills that Rte. 109 traverses farther west typify the New England uplands. At the junction of Rtes. 109 and 47 in tiny **Washington Depot,** turn right and head north on 47 toward Lake Waramaug State Park. If you're hungry, detour a few miles south on Rte. 47 to the elegant 1890 **Mayflower Inn** *(860-868-9466)*.

Continue on Rte. 47 for 3 miles, then turn left onto U.S. 202. Much of this area is marshy—in the summer, look for ferns and cattails. Turn right at the light onto Rte. 45 toward the **Connecticut Wine Trail,** which winds past local wineries between Brookfield and Clinton on the coast. In **New Preston,** the **Aspetuck River** once powered mills that manufactured wagons and sleighs. Today the tiny town is a mecca for antiques collectors. **Lake Waramaug,** a short distance from New Preston, lies in heavily forested country and is one of the state's largest natural lakes. Its Indian name, "good fishing place," is still apt: Large and smallmouth bass, chain pickerel, and yellow perch swim its waters. A few miles up Rte. 45, turn off onto Lake Road to visit **Lake Waramaug State Park** *(860-868-2592 or 860-868-0220. http://dep.state.ct.us/rec/parks.htm#Parks. Adm. fee)*. The park offers a bathing beach, hiking trails, and paddleboat rentals. On the way to the park, stop at the tasting room of **Hopkins Vineyard** *(860-868-7954. Daily May-Dec., Fri.-Sun. only Jan.-April)*. The soil is favorable for growing vinifera and French-American hybrid grapes; the Seyval Blanc is excellent. In season, the 19th-century **Hopkins Inn** *(860-868-7295. Restaurant open April-New Year's)* serves lunch and dinner on a terrace overlooking the lake.

Continue north on Rte. 45 for 3 miles past the turnoff for the state park to Rte. 341. Turn left and continue for approximately 10 miles to Kent. At the junction of Rte. 341 and U.S. 7, you can continue west on 341, then turn right on Macedonia Brook Road for a 4-mile detour to **Macedonia Brook State Park** *(860-927-3238. http://dep.state.ct.us/rec/parks.htm#Parks)*, whose hiking trails offer excellent views reaching far into New York State to the west.

Main Street, Winsted

Or you can turn right from Rte. 341 onto U.S. 7 and head into **Kent,** on the banks of the **Housatonic River.** The Housatonic, whose Indian name means "place beyond the mountains," has its source in the Berkshire Hills of Massachusetts and makes its way for 148 miles through Connecticut to Long Island Sound. Kent's Main Street is lined with beautifully detailed and well-preserved old houses, art galleries, and antiques shops. But in the mid-1800s this was a workaday town, with three stone blast furnaces busy turning ore into iron. The discovery of iron ore in marble bedrock led to a massive deforestation of western Connecticut, as vast amounts of charcoal were needed to keep the furnaces in blast. The last blast furnace—Beckley Furnace in East Canaan—quit in 1923, and the woods are beginning to recover as second growth replaces the vanished climax forest.

54

Stop about 1.5 miles north of Kent at the **Sloane-Stanley Museum & Kent Iron Furnace** *(860-927-3849. Mid-May–Oct.; adm. fee)* to visit the ruins of a blast furnace and to see works by Eric Sloane, author, artist, and celebrator of American folk technology. Just past the museum is **Flanders Historic District,** a group of buildings that were part of early Kent.

Continue north on U.S. 7 for 4 miles to **Kent Falls State Park** *(860-927-3238. http://dep.state.ct.us/rec/parks.htm#Parks. Parking fee May-end of foliage season).* For most of its way through Connecticut the Housatonic River flows through marble lowlands called the **Marble Valley.** In the park, a tributary of the river has eroded the marble bedrock, creating a spectacular waterfall that drops 200 feet in a quarter of a mile. You can see the waterfall from the road.

In colonial times 95 percent of the citizens of Connecticut, then known as the Provisions State, worked on farms; today less than one percent do.

North of Kent Falls, U.S. 7 follows the Housatonic through a mixed deciduous forest to **Housatonic Meadows State Park** *(860-927-3238. http://dep.state.ct.us/rec/parks .htm#Parks).* The river here is shallow, and only fly-fishing is permitted in the park. The **Pine Knob Loop Trail,** which joins the Appalachian Trail, begins on the left less than 1 mile north of the junction with Rte. 4. Watch for the right turn onto Rte. 128 for the covered bridge built about 1864 that links West Cornwall with Sharon. There are several buildings on the other side of the bridge, including a Shaker woodworking showroom, a bookstore, and a restaurant.

Continue north on U.S. 7 for 5 miles to reach the turnoff for **Music Mountain** *(860-824-7126. June-Sept.; adm. fee for concerts),* site of the oldest chamber music series of its kind in the country. Along the way, you'll pass through **Housatonic State Forest.**

One and a half miles past the Music Mountain turnoff, turn left on Rte. 126 and drive a half mile to **Falls Village,** a historic district dating from around 1739. A part of the town of Canaan, the town was named by settlers who saw the potential of the falls of the Housatonic. Sawmills and gristmills began tapping its power in 1741, and today hydroelectric power is generated here.

Beyond the Falls Village turnoff, U.S. 7 passes through South Canaan, then sidles along **Canaan Mountain.** The views here of **Mount Riga** and **Bear Mountain** are fine, particularly at foliage time. Up the road lies **Canaan Village,** another historic district that once served as the hub for the Connecticut Western Railroad.

At the junction of U.S. 7 and 44, turn right and head east on U.S. 44. The road parallels the **Blackberry River,** which furnished power for the area's early furnaces. At Norfolk, turn left onto Rte. 272 for a quarter-mile side trip to **Haystack Mountain State Park** *(Burr Pond: 860-482-1817. http://dep.state.ct.us/rec/parks.htm#Parks).* A 36-foot stone tower at the top of the 1,680-foot peak provides a wonderful view of the Berkshires to the north. In the late 1800s many rich families built summer homes in **Norfolk.** Today, music lovers are attracted to the town by the world-class artists performing each summer at the **Norfolk Chamber Music Festival** *(860-542-3000 in summer, 860-432-1966. www.yale.edu/norfolk. Sept.-May. Open late June–mid-Aug.; adm. fee).* The fountain on the green was designed by architect Stanford White, and the fountain at the southern corner of the green was designed by sculptor Augustus Saint-Gaudens and executed by White.

The next 10 miles of U.S. 44, leading to the intersection with Rte. 8, are heavily commercialized. The **Mad River Dam,** 7 miles east of Norfolk, is part of a project built by the U.S. Army Corps of Engineers after floods in 1955 inflicted heavy damage on this part of the state. In **Winsted** turn right and head south for 9 miles on Rte. 8 to return to Torrington.

Litchfield Hills

Middle Atlantic

New York, New Jersey, Delaware, Pennsylvania, Maryland, West Virginia, Virginia

New York

The Adirondacks

Speculator to Saranac Lake through Adirondack Park on N.Y. 30 and 3

● 92 miles ● 2½ hours ● Late spring to early fall. Fall colors occur early, about mid-September. Roads are well plowed, but snow is frequent and heavy in winter.

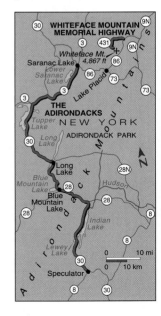

Lofty heart of a 6-million-acre state parkland, the Adirondack Mountains constitute one of the Northeast's last great wildernesses, with 42 peaks rising higher than 4,000 feet. Scoured by Ice Age glaciers, the area is now densely forested and pocked with countless lakes and ponds.

A choice Adirondack drive begins at the intersection of Rtes. 8 and 30 in the village of **Speculator,** a hunting, fishing, and skiing center. The mountains rise gradually as you follow Rte. 30 north through hardwood forests of maple, beech, and birch that explode with color in the fall.

After 12 miles, you come to **Lewey Lake** and the entrance to Lewey Lake Campground. *(For information on campgrounds, contact Forest Recreation 518-457-2500.)* Just beyond, the road crosses a stream linking Lewey Lake with larger **Indian Lake,** which forms part of the Hudson River's headwaters. Following Indian Lake for the next 8 miles, you'll crest a hill where views of the distant peaks of the northern Adirondacks open up. After several miles, a scenic turnoff takes in 3,353-foot Bullhead Mountain and surrounding peaks in the area.

One mile past the turnout, take a left at the T-junction in the hamlet of Indian Lake and continue on Rte. 30 across the **Cedar River,** another Hudson River tributary. After 10 miles, you'll cross the divide between the Hudson and St. Lawrence drainage systems. Beyond that point Adirondack lakes and streams do not drain into the Hudson but rather into the distant St. Lawrence River.

Amish country, Lancaster County, Pennsylvania

Franklin Lake and Whiteface Mountain

Whiteface Mt. Memorial Hwy.

N.Y. 86 to the summit of Whiteface Mountain on N.Y. 431

- 12 miles round-trip • ¼ hour
- Late spring to late fall only. Toll booth halfway up mountain; elevator to summit from end of roadway.

See map p. 57.

Whiteface Mountain isn't the loftiest of the Adirondacks—that distinction belongs to 5,344-foot Mount Marcy. But this 4,867-foot peak stands well enough apart from the rest of the range to offer the region's finest views. It's also the only Adirondack mountain whose summit can be reached by road.

The Whiteface Mountain Memorial Highway (Rte. 431) begins off Rte. 86, 9 miles east of Lake Placid, where the 1932 and 1980 Winter Olympics were held. Climbing along the sides of **Esther Mountain**, it offers broad views of the **Saranac River Valley**. After 1.5 miles, you pass the community of **North Pole**, where **Santa's Workshop** *(518-946-2211. Mid-June–Columbus Day and five weekends before Christmas; adm. fee)* caters to young-hearted visitors. The toll booth for the summit drive is 1.5 miles beyond.

For the next 3 miles, the road hugs the mountain's north and west faces and makes the final ascent via a pair of sharp switchbacks. From road's end, you can hike to the summit or go up via an elevator whose shaft was cut into the mountain rock when the road was built in 1932.

The summit offers striking views: east to Vermont's **Mount Mansfield** and adjacent peaks and north to the skyscrapers of **Montreal;** to the west and south, the **Adirondack Mountains** and much of northern New York State is visible, with **Lake Placid** shimmering in the foreground.

Thirteen miles past Indian Lake, the small resort town of **Blue Mountain Lake** offers outfitting services and a shop that sells the Adirondack's famous wooden slat chairs. Turn right to stay on Rte. 30. Ahead is the lake from which the town takes its name and on the right rises **Blue Mountain.** Its 3,759-foot summit is crowned by a fire tower and accessible by a 2.2-mile trail that begins about a mile north of town. Just before you reach the trailhead, you'll see the excellent **Adirondack Museum** *(518-352-7311. www.adkmuseum.org. June-Oct.; adm. fee).* Its collection includes such regional classics as antique guideboats, furniture, mementos of early resort life, and an opulent private railroad car.

From the museum, the road descends through forests to **Long Lake.** These larger Adirondack lakes continue to harbor trout and other fish, but the smaller ponds, particularly on the west side of the park, were the first bellwethers of acid rain and some no longer support fish.

Split Rock Falls in the Adirondacks

58

Turn left at the town of Long Lake, 11 miles from Blue Mountain Lake, to stay on Rte. 30. After a 20-mile forest drive, cross an arm of **Tupper Lake** and follow Rte. 3/30 signs through the town of the same name, notable for its early 20th-century facades. As the road crests a hill on the east side of town, look ahead for a view of 4,867-foot **Whiteface Mountain,** one of the highest peaks in the Adirondacks.

Bear right onto Rte. 3 about 5 miles past Tupper Lake. This forested, mountainous road leads 15 miles to the town of **Saranac Lake.** As you approach town, spectacular views of glistening **Lower Saranac Lake** open up. Famous a century ago for its tuberculosis sanatorium, the town itself is now the largest community in Adirondack Park and a hub for outdoor recreation. The drive ends at the intersection of Rtes. 3 and 86.

Thousand Islands

Cape Vincent to N.Y. 37 on N.Y. 12E and 12

● 53 miles ● 1½ hours ● Late spring to mid-fall; colorful fall foliage. Winters are usually long and snowy. Ship traffic on St. Lawrence Seaway best seen in ice-free months

The mighty St. Lawrence River flows out of Lake Ontario along the northwestern edge of New York State. Its broad channel, dotted with the Thousand Islands archipelago, is furrowed by big oceangoing ships headed through the St. Lawrence Seaway.

This route begins at **Cape Vincent,** a small residential community and sportfishing center whose **Tibbetts Point Lighthouse and Visitor Center** (*End of Tibbetts Point Rd. 315-654-2700. Daily in summer; weekends in spring and fall; closed winter*) offers fine views of the river and lake. From Cape Vincent, follow Rte. 12E for 4.5 miles through a predominantly agricultural area to **Burnham Point State Park** (*315-654-2324. Mid-May–early Sept. Vehicle fee*). Here, you can get a look at shipping on the **St. Lawrence Seaway.**

In the Thousand Islands

Continue on Rte. 12E 10 miles to **Clayton,** where pleasure boats and scenic cruises put out for various harbors along the waterfront. Clayton's **Antique Boat Museum** (*315-686-4104. Mid-May– mid-Oct.; adm. fee*) displays sailing and motor vessels. Rte. 12E ends in Clayton, and you pick up Rte. 12 heading east here.

Seven miles farther on, the **Thousand Islands International Bridge** (*Toll*) carries traffic from I-81 into Ontario, Canada. For a view of the river, islands, and seaway traffic, take the bridge partway across to **Wellesley Island.**

Four miles northeast of the bridge in the tourist town of **Alexandria Bay,** boat tours leave for **Boldt Castle** (*315-482-2520. www.boldtcastle.com. Mid-May–mid-Oct.; adm. fee*), a turn-of-the-century millionaire's extravaganza built on Heart Island. Beyond town, Rte. 12 has intermittent views of the river, particularly at a scenic turnoff 14.5 miles east. Here, you can see **Chippewa Bay,** the Canadian shoreline, and the easternmost Thousand Islands, which are composed of the same rock as the Adirondacks.

Paralleling the shoreline as it continues downriver from Chippewa Bay, the road offers good views of the narrowing St. Lawrence. The drive ends at the intersection with Rte. 37, near the riverside village of **Morristown.**

Cayuga Lake

Ithaca to Seneca Falls on N.Y. 89

● 39 miles ● 1 hour ● Summer and early fall are best for visits to wineries; winter, with its lack of foliage, allows good views of the lake.

Few geographical features are more aptly named than New York State's Finger Lakes, which fan across the Allegheny Plateau like outstretched digits of a hand. This drive winds along the shoreline of the longest of them, 40-mile-long Cayuga Lake, where the countryside is flavored by pleasant towns and fine wineries.

The drive begins in **Ithaca** at the southern end of **Cayuga Lake.** A Visitor Center *(904 East Shore Dr. 607-272-1313)* has information on sites in the area.

As Rte. 89 heads north, it first winds past Ithaca's outlying suburbs before cutting through **Taughannock Falls State Park** *(607-387-6739. Vehicle fee mid-May–mid-Oct.)*, 10 miles outside town. Here, you'll find boat launches and rentals, a beach, and the falls themselves. At 215 feet high, Taughannock is higher than Niagara—but don't expect a roaring cascade. Changing seasonally, the narrow white ribbon of water needles down into a cold green pool at the center of a vast natural amphitheater of shale.

North past the falls, Rte. 89 passes through tranquil lakeside farmland, with occasional views of Cayuga Lake and its eastern shore. This is

New York's Finger Lakes region ranks as the largest wine-producing area in the East.

wine country; you'll find almost a dozen wineries located just off the road. Most offer tours and on-site purchasing. Several roadside apiaries also sell honey along the way.

For a pleasant side trip with outstanding lake views, turn right 8 or 9 miles north of Taughannock Falls on Deerlick Springs Road, then left on Rte. 153, which winds through the little towns of Kidders and Sheldrake. Restaurants in **Kidders** serve local wines, and there are two B&Bs in **Sheldrake.** Otherwise, this route is uncommercialized, passing gracious Victorian homes framed by big weeping willows that drape their branches out across the water. The shore road, called Weyers Point Road, loops up and rejoins Rte. 89 after 4.5 miles, but the panoramas of the lake continue to the east. To the west, farmlands, orchards, and the occasional small town

Cayuga Lake countryside

occupy the gently rising pillow of land that reaches across to the shores of **Seneca Lake.** Two of the communities here, Ovid and Romulus, typify the penchant in the early 1800s for naming towns after people and places of classical antiquity.

You'll follow Cayuga Lake quite closely along much of the northern half of the route, with little to interrupt views of the water and of the patchwork of meadows and woods on the opposite shore. As recently as the 1920s steam ferries plied the lake, some running its entire length.

The drive ends in **Seneca Falls,** just west of Cayuga Lake on U.S. 20. Here, in the mid-19th century, Elizabeth Cady Stanton and Susan B. Anthony laid the groundwork for the modern women's movement. The small city is now home to the **National Women's Hall of Fame** *(76 Fall St. 315-568-8060. www.greatwomen.org. Closed Mon.-Tues. Nov.-April; adm. fee),* whose portraits and photographs tell the stories of distinguished American women.

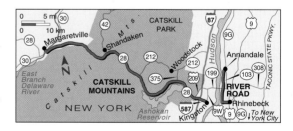

Catskill Mountains

Kingston to Margaretville on N.Y. 28

● 43 miles ● 1½ hours ● Fall foliage peaks in mid-October. In winter, ski resorts dot the snow-covered mountains, and small towns take on a festive Alpine air.

Hudson River school painters, beginning in the 1820s with Thomas Cole, celebrated the scenery of the Catskill Mountains, whose gentle slopes are laced with trout streams.

Start just west of **Kingston,** where Rte. 28 begins. After 6 miles— some of them heavily commercialized—turn right onto Rte. 375, and you'll soon reach the artist colony of **Woodstock,** made famous by the 1969 music festival that actually was held 50 miles southwest of here.

Returning to Rte. 28, you pass **Kenozia Lake** after several miles. To the left, though not visible from the road, is the **Ashokan Reservoir,** built in 1915 as part of New York City's water supply system. The reservoir was formed by damming **Esopus Creek,** the Hudson River tributary that Rte. 28 follows

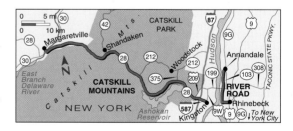

Eagle Lake, the Catskills

for a portion of its length.

The creek valley deepens as you drive along, with rising hills crowding in on both sides. The early Dutch settlers here called such deep ravines "cloves." The word survives in many local designations, describing the shady, sometimes almost somber defiles that give the region so much of its scenic flavor. A good example can be found along Rte. 42, a right turn off Rte. 28 near the village of Shandaken.

Roughly half a mile past the town of Pine Hill, take a left turn for **Belleayre Mountain Ski Center** (914-254-5600), a state-run facility that is open to hikers in the off-season (lifts operate only in winter). Mountain views are spectacular from the base lodge at 2,541 feet, and even better if you hike to the 3,375-foot summit of **Belleayre Mountain.**

End the drive with a right turn onto Rte. 30 at **Margaretville.** The bridge here crosses the **East Branch of the Delaware River,** a parent stream of the great river that flows into Delaware Bay some 200 miles to the south.

> **Perhaps the first mountains to strike Americans as anything other than a nuisance, the Catskills have attracted artists since the early 19th century.**

River Road

Rhinebeck to N.Y. 9G on W. Market St. and N.Y. 103

● 9 miles ● 20 minutes ● Spring to mid-fall; fine fall foliage.
See map page 61.

One of the earliest settled regions in the country, the Hudson Valley was home to Dutch colonists long before the Pilgrims landed at Plymouth. Sought out later by 19th-century barons of the Gilded Age, the valley wears the look of a well-used landscape that still possesses much of its natural charm.

Begin this drive in **Rhinebeck,** settled in 1686. The **Old Rhinebeck Aerodrome** (42 Stone Church Rd. 914-758-8610. Mid-May–Oct.; adm. fee) displays a collection of antique planes. The **Beekman Arms** (4 Mill St. 914-876-7077), an inn built in the 18th century, was the spot where Franklin Roosevelt held his election-night rallies.

Follow West Market Street, which becomes Rhinecliff Road. As you crest a hill, you'll see the distant Catskill Mountains across the **Hudson River.** About a mile from town, turn right onto Rte. 103, the River Road. (Despite the name, the road offers no direct views of the Hudson.) Along this winding, tree-canopied road, low stone walls and handsome gatehouses mark estates that date from the past century.

Turn left 6 miles down to enter **Montgomery Place** (914-758-5461. April-Oct. Wed.-Mon., Nov.-Dec. weekends only. Closed Jan.-March; adm. fee), a 434-acre estate and 1805 mansion with splendid views of the Hudson and Catskills. In early autumn you can pick and purchase the estate's apples.

The River Road soon takes you through the campus of **Bard College** in the village of **Annandale.** End the drive at the intersection with Rte. 9G.

Bear Mountain Bridge across the Hudson

George W. Perkins Memorial Drive

Seven Lakes Drive to the summit of Bear Mountain

● 5 miles ● 20 minutes ● Open daily 8 a.m. to dusk. Spring through fall; fine autumn foliage. Weekends crowded mid-spring through late fall. Winter weather often causes closings.

This drive climbs 1,305-foot Bear Mountain, second highest of the granite Hudson Highlands peaks (1,355-foot Storm King is first). The summit has commanding views of the lower Hudson Valley.

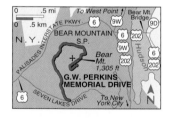

The drive begins off Seven Lakes Drive, the main route through **Bear Mountain State Park** *(914-786-2701. Parking fee except winter weekends).* The lower portion of the drive winds through deep woods and past exposed rock ledges characteristic of the region's upthrust Precambrian granite. Broad vistas of the **Hudson Valley** open up as you ascend.

The summit offers spectacular views. To the east is **Bear Mountain Bridge;** on the Hudson's opposite shore is a rocky promontory called **Anthony's Nose.** The northern view takes in the river valley toward **West Point** and **Storm King.** To the west the **Hudson Highlands** recede toward the lake-studded landscape of Harriman State Park. And to the south the broad swath of the Hudson River called the **Tappan Zee** is spanned by the **Tappan Zee Bridge.** On the clearest days, you can see the gleaming steel towers of the **George Washington Bridge** at the threshold of Manhattan Island.

New Jersey

Delaware Valley

Trenton to Frenchtown on N.J. 29

● 30 miles ● 1 hour ● Fine fall foliage

Prallsville Mills Historic District, Stockton

The small towns and green parklands that characterize New Jersey's Delaware River shoreline belie the state's popular image as a place of densely packed cities. Just over an hour from both New York and Philadelphia, this part of New Jersey is a world apart from urban bustle.

The excursion begins in **Trenton,** in the shadow of the golden-domed **State House** *(W. State St. 609-292-4661).* Drive a block north on State Street, turn left, and follow signs for Rte. 29 north. At 8 miles, turn right on Rte. 546 to visit 841-acre **Washington Crossing State Park** *(609-737-0623. Adm. fee weekends Mem. Day-Labor Day),* site of George Washington's tactically brilliant crossing of the Delaware River on Christmas night 1776.

The waterway visible on the left as you drive through the park—and along much of this route—is a 22-mile feeder channel of the 1834 canal, now preserved in the **Delaware and Raritan Canal State Park** *(732-873-3050. www.state.nj.us/dep/forestry/parks).* The canal was built to route barges around difficult stretches of the river.

After 14 miles on Rte. 29, bear left to see the neatly painted brick facades of **Lambertville.** George Washington visited here in 1777, at the Holcombe House *(Private)* at 260 N. Main St.

Go north for 3.5 miles to Stockton, where the **Stockton Inn** *(1 Main St. 609-397-1250)* has been in business since 1796 (the building dates from 1710). The inn is believed to have inspired the Rodgers and Hart song, "There's a Small Hotel." At nearby **Prallsville Mills Historic District,** canal-side mill buildings stand amid oaks and willows.

Delaware and Raritan Canal State Park

64

From here, the road heads through an oak and maple forest for 3 miles to the **Bull's Island Recreation Area** *(609-397-2949).* Part of the Delaware and Raritan Canal State Park, it welcomes canoeists, cyclists, and hikers. Past this northern end of the canal, Rte. 29 follows the Delaware to **Frenchtown,** whose streets are lined with 19th-century homes, antique shops, trim B&Bs, and the restored 1851 **National Hotel** *(31 Race St. 908-996-4871).*

Dairy farm outside Dover, Delaware

Delaware
Mouth of the Delaware

New Castle to Dover on Del. 9 and 8

● 45 miles ● 1½ hours ● Spring and fall; summer is hot, humid, and bug-ridden along the marshes.

The Delaware River, navigable from Delaware Bay to Trenton, New Jersey, has long been an important highway of commerce for tankers and freighters, but this drive explores a different aspect of the river. Ambling through the northern end of the Delmarva (Delaware, Maryland, Virginia) Peninsula, it passes through small towns and salt marshes where herons and egrets wade.

Begin at **New Castle**. Founded in 1651 as a Dutch outpost, the town went on to become the capital of the colony. New Castle's **Old Court House** *(211 Delaware St. 302-323-4453. Closed Mon. Donation)* is one of the nation's oldest public buildings, dating from 1732. Heading west, Rte. 9 twists through several miles of industrial and residential neighborhoods. In vacant lots you'll see *Phragmites communis,* the tall feathery-topped marsh reed characteristic of wetland environments. Phragmites quickly takes over when pollution has extirpated more delicate marsh plants.

Ten miles down the road, a high bridge carries Rte. 9 across the **Chesapeake and Delaware Canal,** which links the upper reaches of Chesapeake Bay with the lower Delaware River. The bridge affords a commanding view of the surrounding territory: On the left is the **Delaware River;** ahead lies the New Jersey shore and the massive cooling tower of the Salem nuclear power plant; to the west, the canal and marshes spread toward Maryland.

Three miles past the bridge, the road enters the small town of **Port Penn,** whose name harks back to William Penn, founder of the Pennsylvania

colony. In 1682 a British land grant also awarded him what is now Delaware. The **Port Penn Interpretive Center** *(302-836-2533. Mem. Day-Labor Day Wed.-Sun.; adm. fee)* focuses on the interplay between the region's natural environment and the human uses of it.

Beyond Port Penn, the countryside is dominated by fields of corn and soybeans. Horses graze in pastures, and in summer the buzzing of cicadas accentuates the bucolic atmosphere. The fields alternate with stretches of salt marsh, such as those at the Augustine, Cedar Swamp, and Woodland Beach Wildlife Areas, all three of which lie along Rte. 9.

The **Woodland Beach Wildlife Area** is worth a detour. At an intersection roughly 20.5 miles south of Port Penn, turn left and drive 3 miles through the wildlife area's pristine tidal marshes—prime feeding grounds for great blue herons and snowy egrets. Cross Duck Creek to enter the tiny Delaware River hamlet of Woodland Beach.

Continue roughly 3 miles past the Woodland Beach turnoff to the **Bombay Hook National Wildlife Refuge** *(302-653-9345. http://northeast.fws.gov/de/bmh .htm. Adm. fee)*. This is one in a string of preserves along **Delaware Bay,** a major stopover for birds migrating along the Atlantic flyway.

After the village of Leipsic, the road continues 6 miles south through more farmland to the intersection with Rte. 8. This leads 4 miles west to **Dover,** Delaware's small but pleasant capital.

Workboats near New Castle, Delaware

Pennsylvania

Amish Country Drive

Gap to Marietta on Pa. 772

● 35 miles ● 1 hour ● All year. Summers crowded; all shops and facilities closed Sunday. Horse-drawn buggies have the right-of-way.

This drive traverses Lancaster County, center of Amish life in the East and one of the nation's most productive agricultural communities. As you drive past the farm fields, small towns, and developing suburbs

Amish house

of southeastern Pennsylvania, you'll be sharing the road with the horse-drawn buggies of the Amish.

Begin your tour at **Gap** and head northwest on Rte. 772. In about 5 miles the road hits the center of **Intercourse,** located at the intersection of two roads. The complex of buildings, shops, and galleries at the **People's Place** is a must-see *(3513 Old Philadelphia Pike. 717-768-7171. Closed Sun.).* Here, the documentary "Who Are the Amish?" *(Adm. fee)* explains that the bearded, black-coated Amish men and plainly dressed Amish women of today are members of a Protestant sect that developed in Switzerland in the 16th century.

> **Despite the devotion of the Amish, you won't see their churches along the drive. These "plain people" worship in private homes, rotating from house to house.**

About 19,000 Amish now live in Lancaster County, working their family farms with draft horses instead of tractors, which gives the landscape a distinctive look. Thanks to the presence of the Amish, the county now draws about five million visitors a year.

Outside Intercourse, stop at one of the many farm stands for fresh fruits, vegetables, cider, and wonderful butter and cheese. After about 12 miles, you'll come to **Lititz.** The handsome square in the middle of town is dominated by the **Moravian Church** *(717-626-8515),* built in 1787, and by **Linden Hall.** Begun in 1746, it's the oldest girls' boarding school in the country. Across the street, the **Lititz Historical Society** *(717-627-4636. Mem. Day-Oct. Mon.-Sat. Adm. fee)* features exhibits and old photographs of the Moravian community in this area. The nearby **Sturgis Pretzel House** *(219 E. Main St. 717-626-4354. Closed Sun.; adm. fee)* claims to be the oldest commercial pretzel bakery in the nation. If you have a longing for chocolate, stop at the **Candy Americana Museum and Wilbur's Chocolate Factory** *(46 N. Broad St. 717-626-3249. Closed Sun.).*

For 12 miles past Lititz, Rte. 772 dips through farm country. When it crosses Rte. 283, the scenery becomes more developed and suburban.

Rte. 772 ends in the town of **Marietta,** on the **Susquehanna River,** where the streets are lined with restored 19th-century homes.

Amish buggy and farm fields of Lancaster County

Grand Army
of the Republic Highway

Clarks Summit to Towanda on U.S. 6

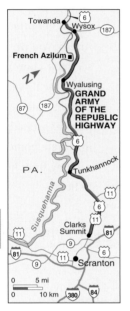

● **68 miles** ● **2 hours** ● **Spring through fall; fine fall foliage**

As U.S. 6 crosses northern Pennsylvania, it follows the Susquehanna River past rolling hills, forested mountains, and historic small towns. One of the nation's first transcontinental highways, U.S. 6 has linked the East and West Coasts since 1927. In 1948 Pennsylvania's portion was dubbed the **Grand Army of the Republic Highway,** in honor of Union Civil War veterans. These days, it is traveled mostly by local people and those who come to sightsee, hike, fish, and hunt.

From I-81 or I-84 near Scranton, pick up U.S. 6/11 to **Clarks Summit.** This small town is in Pennsylvania coal country, and not long ago the hills you're traveling past were barren, the streams polluted from a mining industry that dated back to the 1840s. In the past 30 years, reforestation and housing projects have replaced mounds of coal refuse.

Near **Tunkhannock,** about 17 miles from Clarks Summit, you start seeing the **North Branch Susquehanna River.** For the rest of the drive, you have occasional grand vistas of the rock-strewn river, as it makes a series of turns in a narrow valley. This natural pathway cut by the river through the mountains has been used by Indians, by wagoners, by the railroad, and now by U.S. 6 on its way across the country.

Beyond Wyalusing, stop at the **Marie Antoinette Lookout** and gaze down on the site of the **French Azilum** *(570-265-3376. Mid-May–Aug. Wed.-Sun., Sept.–mid-Oct. weekends only; adm. fee).* In 1793 a band of aristocrats fleeing the French Revolution began building a mini-Paris

Susquehanna River near Tunkhannock

out of log cabins arranged on broad avenues here. To visit the Azilum, turn left in Wysox onto Rte. 187, then follow the signs for 7 miles.

Back on U.S. 6, the drive ends 2 miles farther on in **Towanda,** where local artifacts and memorabilia are displayed at the **Bradford County Historical Society Museum** (*21 Main St. 570-265-2240. Thurs.-Sat.; donation*).

Wellsboro to Warren on U.S. 6

● **129 miles** ● **5 hours** ● **Spring through fall**

This portion of the Grand Army of the Republic Highway takes you through hills and mountains that look pristine—but that's an illusion. This land gave up its wealth of coal, oil, and timber to make Pennsylvania and

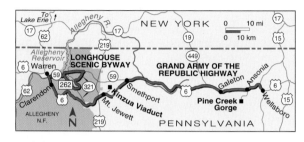

much of the nation into an industrial powerhouse. Fortunes were made here, and the face of the land changed forever.

The drive begins in **Wellsboro.** Head 12 miles west to the town of Ansonia and turn left on Colton Road to visit **Pine Creek Gorge,** locally known as the Grand Canyon of Pennsylvania. The road leads 6 miles through a mixed hardwood forest to **Colton Point State Park** (*570-724-3061*), where overlooks and walkways offer views of the 830-foot-deep gorge.

Return to U.S. 6, which follows **Pine Creek** to the town of **Galeton,** formerly home to one of the world's largest sawmills. The **Allegheny Mountains** surrounding the town were stripped in the 19th century by timbermen greedy for their hemlock and white pine. Cherry, maple, and beech have since taken the conifers' place. For 13 miles beyond Galeton trundle through these forests before reaching the **Pennsylvania Lumber Museum** (*814-435-2652. www.lumbermuseum.org. Closed weekends Dec.-March; adm. fee*), featuring exhibits on the life of 19th-century lumberjacks.

From here, follow the **Allegheny River** as forests give way to farmlands interspersed with towns. After 35 miles you reach Smethport; for the next 15 miles the road curves through forests along trout-laden **Marvin Creek.** Just before you enter Mount Jewett, a turnoff on the right leads 2.5 miles to the 301-foot-high **Kinzua Viaduct,** highest railroad viaduct in the world when it was built in 1882. Views from the bridge are still breathtaking.

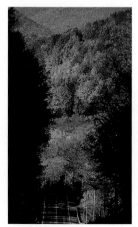

In the Alleghenies

Back on U.S. 6, you enter the 250,000-acre **Allegheny National Forest** (*814-723-5150. www.fs.fed.us/r9/ allegheny*). Between Wetmore and Ludlow, look for a sign for the **North Country National Scenic Trail,** a segment of the 3,200-mile trail being built between New York and North Dakota. Around **Clarendon** you'll begin to see scattered oil wells—reminders that the modern oil industry started southwest of here in Titusville.

Stay on U.S. 6 to the drive's end in **Warren,** where well-appointed mansions built from timber, oil, and coal money line the boulevards.

Longhouse Scenic Byway

Loop around Allegheny Reservoir on Pa. 59 and 321 and Forest Road 262

● 29 miles ● 1 hour ● All year; fine fall foliage. *See map p. 69.*

Looping through the Allegheny National Forest, the byway encircles the Allegheny Reservoir, offering lovely vistas of the Allegheny Mountains.

Start the tour 3 miles southeast of Warren, where Rte. 59 branches east off U.S. 6. Along the way here, you can view the **Kinzua Dam,** which formed the reservoir, and hike the half-mile **Little Boulder Nature Trail** that begins at the Big Bend Access Area.

For thousands of years, this area was inhabited by Indians. The large, communal longhouses of the Seneca Indians gave the drive its name. Back on Rte. 59, you cross the reservoir on **Casey Bridge** and climb a forested plateau. At its top, stop at the **Rimrock Overlook** for a spectacular view of the reservoir.

Make a hard right at Rte. 321 and follow **North Fork Creek,** then **Chappel Creek** to dramatic views of

Longhouse Scenic Byway in fall

Chappel Bay. Complete the loop by making another hard right onto FR 262, which follows a twisting course along the reservoir.

Laurel Highlands

Farmington to Normalville on Pa. 381

● 17 miles ● ½ hour ● All year; fine fall foliage. *See map page 71.*

Frank Lloyd Wright's Fallingwater

Tucked between ridges of the Alleghenies, this road through the picturesque Laurel Highlands is a short drive, but you could spend days exploring its attractions.

From **Farmington** follow Rte. 381 north for about 8 miles to **Ohiopyle State Park** *(724-329-8591)*. At the **Ohiopyle Falls** day-use area, stop for a look at these 20-foot falls tumbling down sandstone ledges. They are part of the **Youghiogheny River Gorge**, about 14 miles of which cut through the park. The "Yock" offers some of the best white-water rafting in the East. For an easy hike, sample the 4 miles of trails across the river on the **Ferncliff Peninsula,** famous for its wildflowers and other flora and for its excellent overlooks of the gorge.

Continue up Rte. 381 a couple of miles, where a left turn leads to **Fallingwater** *(724-329-8501. Tues.-Sun. mid-March–Nov., Sat.-Sun. mid-Nov.–March; adm. fee)*. Designed by Frank Lloyd Wright in the 1930s, this dramatic house is cantilevered over a waterfall on Bear Run. It was rated the "best all-time work of American architecture" in a poll taken of the American Institute of Architects.

Back on Rte. 381, you come almost immediately to the turnoff for **Bear Run Nature Reserve,** where there are more than 20 miles of marked trails through forests rich in rhododendron and mountain laurel.

The drive ends about 6 miles beyond in the small town of **Normalville.**

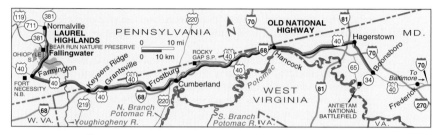

Maryland

Old National Highway

Boonsboro, Maryland, to Fort Necessity National Battlefield, Pennsylvania, on U.S. 40A and 40

● **131 miles** ● **4 hours** ● **Spring and fall. Drive overlaps I-68 in several places.** *See map above.*

U.S. 40 and 40A follow Indian paths through the mountains, overlapping the country's first federally funded highway— the National Road. Begun in 1806 and linking Cumberland, Maryland, with Vandalia, Illinois, the route became a vital thoroughfare on the great trek west.

Begin your tour in the small town of **Boonsboro.** First detour to **Antietam National Battlefield** *(301-432-5124. www.nps*

Pastureland near Grantsville, Md.

.gov/anti. Adm. fee) by turning left onto Rte. 34 for 5 miles. On September 17, 1862, Antietam saw the single bloodiest day of battle in the Civil War.

After Boonsboro, U.S. 40A continues about 5 miles west to the outskirts of **Hagerstown,** where you'll see a sign reading "Dual Highway"; turn left onto U.S. 40. For a look at life here in the early 18th century, when this area was still mostly wilderness, head to the beautifully restored **Hager House** *(110 Key St. 301-739-8393. April-Dec. Tues.-Sun).*

After Hagerstown, U.S. 40 weaves 18 miles west through rolling countryside, until you join I-70 briefly before exiting west onto Scenic 40. Follow signs, as U.S. 40 frequently overlaps with I-68. Twenty-eight miles past Hancock, stop at **Rocky Gap State Park** *(301-777-2139)*, where **Lake Habeb** sits amid the rugged **Allegheny Mountains.**

Back on the road, you soon enter **Cumberland,** site of the famous Cumberland Narrows, a well-trod pass through the Allegheny Mountains. To visit the town's historic area, turn off U.S. 40/I-68 and follow the tourist information signs to the **Western Maryland Station Center** *(13 Canal St.).* This restored 1913 railroad station houses a Visitor Center, art gallery, transportation museum, and rail station where you can take an excursion on Maryland's only coal-fired train *(800-TRAIN-50. May-Oct. Tues.-Sun., Nov.-Dec. Sat.-Sun; adm. fee).*

As you leave Cumberland on U.S. 40A and plod briefly past strip malls, watch to your left for a little octagonal brick building: one of the few remaining tollhouses standing along the old National Road. In 1806, the U.S. Congress approved the road's construction as a means to unite the new nation. It was the federal government's first foray into the road-building business.

Emerging into open countryside, U.S. 40A continues to **Frostburg.** Founded because of the National Road, this town once revolved around coal but now revolves around Frostburg State University. As you head to **Grantsville,** the horse-drawn buggies of the Mennonites, a religious group that practices a simple lifestyle, begin to appear.

At **Keysers Ridge,** U.S. 40A merges into U.S. 40 and you soon cross into the rolling Pennsylvania countryside. Just past Farmington, the **Fort Necessity National Battlefield** *(724-329-5512. www.nps.gov/fone. Adm. fee)* commemorates the 1754 battle in which 22-year-old George Washington led British troops against French forces, sparking the French and Indian War. Don't miss the **Mount Washington Tavern** here. Among the numerous taverns that once lined the National Road, this was considered one of the most elegant.

Eastern Shore

Chesapeake City to Tilghman Island on Md. 213, 662, 322, 33, and U.S. 50

● 80 miles ● 2 hours ● Spring and fall; winter brings a certain brooding charm to Tilghman Island.

Swans on the Chesapeake Bay

Although close to the fast-paced world of the Eastern megalopolis, this peninsular portion of Maryland still remains a place apart. Here, broad tidal rivers drain tranquil farmlands, and watermen in wooden skipjacks sail out to harvest the Chesapeake Bay's legendary abundance.

Begin in **Chesapeake City,** a handsomely restored 19th-century town. Sitting near the western end of the Chesapeake and Delaware Canal, it's dotted with pleasant inns, cafés, and marinas.

Driving south along Rte. 213, you'll pass fields green in summer with corn and soybeans, two Delmarva (Delaware, Maryland, Virginia) Penin-

sula staples. Within the first 15 miles, the highway crosses the **Bohemia** and **Sassafras Rivers,** the latter thought to have been explored by Capt. John Smith during his 1608 reconnoiter of the Chesapeake Bay. In the following century of colonization, rivers like these were indispensable highways for the great tobacco plantations of the area.

Continue on to **Chestertown,** which has stood on the banks of the Chester River since 1706. The **Historical Society** *(410-778-3499. Mon., Wed., Thurs. year-round; also weekends May-Oct.)* functions as a colonial house museum, and you can take afternoon tea at the 18th-century **White Swan Tavern B&B** *(410-778-2300)* on High Street. Or you can just ramble the town's shaded streets, past stately Georgian and gaily painted Victorian homes.

The wooden Chesapeake Bay skipjacks are the nation's last commercial fishing fleet working under sail.

A mile past its intersection with U.S. 50, Rte. 213 ends at **Wye Mills** *(410-827-6909. Donation),* the last in a line of grist mills built on this site. This mill is preserved in its 19th-century state, its massive granite millstones still using waterpower to grind grain into flour. Just south of the mill on Rte. 662, another landmark has stood for over 400 years: the enormous, gnarled **Wye Oak,** said to be the country's largest white oak.

The Wye Oak marks the end of the first part of this drive. To continue, head south on U.S. 50 toward Easton. Nearby, at the mouth of the Wye, stands **Wye House** *(Private),* once the seat of a vast plantation where the great abolitionist leader Frederick Douglass spent his boyhood as a slave.

Near Easton, turn right onto Rte. 322, then right again onto Rte. 33 east. Eleven miles down the road is **St. Michaels,** an old harbor town graced by tidy inns and good restaurants—of both the candlelit and boisterous crab-cracking varieties. The excellent **Chesapeake Bay Maritime Museum** *(410-745-2916. www.cbmm.org. Adm. fee)* is dedicated to the history and workaday lore of the bay.

If you don't notice the little bridge over **Knapps Narrows,** 13 miles beyond St. Michaels, you won't realize that you have left the mainland and are on **Tilghman Island.** The island has been home for centuries to the hardy individuals who harvest the bay's bounty. Less than half a mile from the bridge, turn left on Dogwood Harbor Road to see one of their most durable legacies—the famed Chesapeake Bay skipjacks,

Skipjack at Hooper Strait Light

73

wooden sailing vessels ranging from 25 to 60 feet in length. Several are usually docked here.

At the fork 2.5 miles farther on, bear right for a fine view of the bay along Black Walnut Point Road. The road ends in half a mile at the gate for the **Black Walnut Point Inn** *(410-886-2452)*, perhaps the most secluded B&B on the Eastern Shore.

Historic Beiswanger Henn House, Chesapeake City, Maryland

West Virginia

Canaan Valley Byway

Blackwater Falls State Park to the Virginia border on W.Va. 32 and 55

● 99 miles ● 3 hours ● Spring through fall; fall foliage peaks in mid-October. Watch for fast-moving trucks.

This lovely rural route will lead you through some of the best sights that West Virginia has to offer, from Blackwater Falls to Seneca Rocks, through parts of both the Monongahela and George Washington National Forests, and past roadsides sprinkled with wildflowers.

Begin at **Blackwater Falls State Park** *(304-259-5216. www.blackwaterfalls.com)*, a mile off Rte. 32 near Davis. From the parking lot, stairs and a gently sloping trail lead down to a view of the 60-foot-falls plunging into an 8-mile-long gorge. Leached tannic acid from fallen hemlock and red spruce needles give the water its black appearance.

Follow Rte. 32 south about 10 miles from the park to the **Canaan Valley Resort State Park** *(304-866-4121 or 800-622-4121. www.canaan resort.com)*. Popular with hikers and skiers, the park also operates a chairlift during the summer that offers a panoramic view of the

Mountain hollow near Harman

mountains and valleys of the Potomac Highland.

Continue along this winding, wooded road to the intersection of Rte. 32 and Rte. 55, in the town of **Harman.** From here, head east on Rte. 55. After 3 miles you'll begin to climb **Allegheny Mountain,** cresting it at 3,293 feet. The road curves down the far side of the mountain, and you pass through the small town of Onego.

White churches steeple the landscape as you follow **Seneca Creek** to the **Spruce Knob–Seneca Rocks National Recreation Area** *(304-567-2827. Visitor Center mid-April–Nov., weekends only Dec.–mid-April),* 3 miles beyond Onego. Seneca Rocks is a spectacular 900-foot sandstone formation created over millions of years by erosion. A trail leads to an observation deck with a stunning view of the valley and the river; the Visitor Center has exhibits on the geology and history of the area. The **Sites Homestead** has a reconstruction of the single-room log cabin built in 1839 by Jacob Sites, who was one of the early settlers in the Potomac Highland.

Rocky meadows, almost alpine in appearance, open up on either side of the road, and flocks of sheep graze on distant hillsides.

75

For the next 6 miles the road follows the **South Branch of the Potomac River** past fields and farms to **Champe Rocks.** Similar to Seneca Rocks, the formation was named for John Champe, who lived nearby. A sergeant in the Revolutionary War, he was sent by Gen. George Washington on an unsuccessful mission to kidnap the traitor Benedict Arnold from behind British lines.

Continuing beyond the town of Hopeville, you'll find **Smoke Hole Caverns** *(304-257-4442 or 800-828-8478. Adm. fee),* a commercialized but nonetheless unique natural formation. Nearly 225 million years old, the caverns feature the world's longest ribbon stalactite, as well as an underground lake filled with golden and rainbow trout.

At **Petersburg Gap,** 1.5 miles farther on, the north fork of the **South Branch of the Potomac River** breaks through **North Fork Mountain,** forming a cleft 800 feet deep as it does. Another 2.5 miles will bring you to a picturesque little park overlooking the Potomac.

Continue through the city of Petersburg, and 7 miles on the other side you'll find the **West-Whitehill Winery** *(304-538-2605. Sat.-Sun.*

Moonrise above Seneca Rocks

or by appt.). This region is ideal for growing wine grapes, and you can stop here for tastings and for information on the local wine industry. About 5 miles farther on in **Moorefield,** charming antebellum houses and public buildings line the main street. Beyond town, Rte. 55 climbs into the mountains through a series of hairpin turns; watch for lovely mountain views along this stretch.

As you continue toward the Virginia border, you'll be in poultry country; the road cruises through farmland then winds up a steep grade to a mountain crest. For its final 9 miles the byway weaves amid the mixed hardwoods of the **George Washington National Forest** *(540-265-5100. www.southernregion.fs.fed.us/gwj)* before ending at the Virginia border.

Highland Scenic Byway

Richwood to U.S. 219 on W.Va. 55 and 150

● **45 miles** ● **1 hour** ● **Spring through fall; fine spring wildflower bloom and fall foliage**

Winding through the Monongahela National Forest, this National Forest Scenic Byway traverses a narrow valley and passes a unique bog wilderness where cranberries grow before climbing into the forests of the Appalachian Plateau.

Take Rte. 55 north out of **Richwood,** the gateway to the **Monongahela National Forest.** At the head of the Cranberry, Williams, Gauley, and Cherry Rivers, Richwood supports a thriving timber industry.

The **Gauley District Ranger Station** *(304-846-2695)* is 2 miles northeast of Richwood. From here, the road meanders through a dense forest of oak, poplar, maple, beech, hemlock, and red spruce. Be on the lookout for wildlife. While the area's black bear and wild turkey will not generally appear on the side of the road, you may well spot white-tailed deer, fox, or see a hawk soaring overhead.

About 4 miles past the ranger station, you arrive at the North Bend Picnic Area, and just beyond a 2-mile access road leads to **Summit Lake.** This man-made lake, rimmed by forests, is stocked with trout from April to early June.

One of the highlights of this drive is the **Falls of Hills Creek,** about 15 miles southeast of Richwood. A steep trail leads past two of the waterfalls; the lower of these, at 65 feet, ranks as one of the highest waterfalls in West Virginia.

Back on the road, turn left 5.5 miles beyond the falls onto Public Road 102 and drive 2 miles to the **Cranberry Glades Botanical Area.** Similar to the Arctic tundra, this unique glade features plants that are not generally found this far south. A half-mile boardwalk crosses the bogs. For more information, stop at the **Cranberry Mountain Visitor Center** *(304-653-4826. April-Nov.)* at the junction of Rte. 39 and Rte. 150.

From the Visitor Center, take Rte. 150 north as it skirts the edge of the **Cranberry Wilderness.** Moving into the mountains and valleys of the **Appalachian Plateau,** the highway tops off at elevations over 4,000 feet. Here,

Monongahela National Forest in the Allegheny Mountains

the road runs through hardwood forests, broken by open areas speckled with mountain ash. Views of the surrounding valleys are spectacular. After a few miles you'll come to the **Cranberry Glades Overlook,** where a short path leads to a beautiful view of the Cranberry Glades.

As this hilly, curving road winds toward its end at the junction with U.S. 219, be sure to enjoy the vistas from several scenic overlooks, including **Little Laurel,** about 17 miles from Cranberry Mountain, and **Red Lick,** 3 miles farther on.

Midland Trail

Charleston to White Sulfur Springs on U.S. 60

● 115 miles   ● 4 hours   ● Spring through fall. Fine foliage

This state scenic route follows the Kanawha River out of Charleston, then snakes along the New River Gorge before veering through rolling farmlands. Along the way, you'll find a hidden waterfall, historic towns, and a resort hotel that has catered to Presidents.

Begin in **Charleston** at the **State Capitol** (*Kanawha Blvd. E. 304-558-4839. Tours Mon.-Sat.*), a majestic golden-domed Greek Revival structure completed in 1932. Continue east on U.S. 60 half a mile to **Daniel Boone Park.**

It was across the Kanawha River at this location that frontiersman Daniel Boone lived in the late 1700s.

Four miles ahead, U.S. 60 enters the small town of **Malden,** which developed as a center of salt production in the early 19th century. The African American educator, Booker T. Washington, worked at the salt licks here when he was young, and a park in his honor stands on the site of his sister's home.

Landing a trout

Drive east through the **Kanawha River Valley,** barges and pleasure boats ply the river. In the town of **Belle,** you'll find **Shrewsbury House** *(Belle town offices for info. 304-949-3841. Tues. only; adm. fee).* Built about 1800, this small homestead is one of the few older structures that has survived the industrialization of the region.

Tunneling through woods, the road passes Cedar Grove and the small redbrick **Virginia's Chapel,** built in 1853 as a graduation present for Virginia Tompkins, the daughter of a prominent pioneer citizen.

For the next 17 miles, the Midland Trail follows the Kanawha through small towns, with wildflowers growing in abundance along the roadsides. At **Kanawha Falls** you can picnic or fish while enjoying the 10-foot-high falls. Two miles farther on, the **New** and **Gauley Rivers** join to form the Kanawha. Soon thereafter, take a sharp left turn into the pullover for **Cathedral Falls;** a short but steep trail leads to the top of the falls.

From here, the drive climbs high above the New River, with overlooks of the mountains and the river. At **Hawks Nest State Park** *(304-658-5212. www.hawksnestsp.com. Adm. fee),* you can walk a couple of hundred feet from the parking area for a particularly dramatic view of the New River and the sheer sandstone cliffs of its gorge. The park's small **Museum** *(April-early Nov.)* features pioneer exhibits, Indian artifacts, and a natural resources exhibit. A half mile farther, a park tram will take you down into the gorge itself, where there is a marina with paddleboats for rent.

After leaving the park, U.S. 60 continues to weave through more rural countryside, past small farms, rolling green hills, and forests that flame with color in October. You may want to take a detour about 5 miles south on U.S. 19 to the **New River Gorge National River.** The **Canyon Rim Visitor Center** *(304-574-*

New River Gorge

2115) here features a local history and natural resource museum, as well as a stunning view of white water riffling through the gorge. To get a closer look, take the boardwalk and staircase that wind down into the gorge.

Back on U.S. 60, you meander for the next 50 miles through country dotted with cattle, sheep, and horses. As you climb **Sewell Mountain,** you may pass logging trucks, a reminder that the nearby town of Rainelle was once home to the world's largest hardwood mill.

Beyond the crossroads called Sam Black Church, lovely old farmhouses punctuate the landscape on the way to **Lewisburg,** a Southern outpost during the Civil War and the site of an 1862 engagement between Union and Confederate forces. Graced with many beautiful 18th- and 19th-century houses and a number of cemeteries, the old part of town is now a national historic district. Stop at the **Visitor Center** *(105 Church St. 304-645-1000 or 800-833-2068. Daily Mem. Day-Oct., closed Sun. rest of year)* for information on the self-guided walking tour of this lovely town.

Ten miles past Lewisburg, the Midland Trail ends in the town of **White Sulfur Springs,** whose mineral springs have lured visitors since the 1700s. The town's elegant old hotel, the **Greenbrier** *(304-536-1110 or 800-624-6070),* has played host to Presidents and other luminaries.

Historic Lewisburg, West Virginia

Virginia

Colonial Parkway

Jamestown to Yorktown through the Colonial National Historical Park

● 23 miles ● 40 minutes ● All year; fine spring bloom and fall foliage

Crossing the Virginia Peninsula from the James to the York Rivers, this parkway leads through pristine tidewater countryside and 175 years of colonial history.

For a chronological orientation, begin at **Jamestown Island** *(757-229-1733. Adm. fee),* where excavated foundations of the 17th-century settlement overlooking the **James River** are preserved. Take the Island Loop Drive to see the wilderness as the colonists found it, then leave via the causeway across Sandy Bay.

On the mainland, the **Glasshouse** features costumed craftspeople demonstrating 17th-century glassblowing—one of America's earliest industries. The nearby **Jamestown Settlement** *(757-229-1607. www .historyisfun.org. Adm. fee),* a living history museum, holds reproductions

Colonial Parkway

Chesapeake Bay Bridge-Tunnel

Virginia Beach to the Eastern Shore

● **17.6 miles** ● **½ hour**
● **All year. Toll**

The longest bridge-tunnel complex ever built, this spectacular stretch of U.S. 13 links Virginia Beach and Norfolk with Virginia's Eastern Shore. Completed in 1964, the structure is a unique combination of trestles, tunnels, bridges, man-made islands, and a causeway. In 1987 the complex was officially renamed the Lucius J. Kellam, Jr. Bridge-Tunnel to honor the project's visionary chairman.

From the south, you pass through the toll plaza onto the first section of trestled roadway and are suddenly flanked by open sea: the **Atlantic Ocean** on the right and on the left the **Chesapeake Bay,** the largest estuary in the country.

After 3.5 miles you come to **Sea Gull Island,** the first of four man-made islands and the only stopping point. From the 625-foot bayside fishing pier here, you can watch ships plying busy **Hampton Roads** harbor. Leaving the island, the road enters 5,734-foot-long **Thimble Shoal**

of a fort, an Indian village, and the three tiny ships that brought the colonists from England in 1607.

For the next 5 miles or so, the parkway wends along the James River, passing marshes frequented by egrets, herons, and other birds. Approaching Williamsburg, woodlands of oak, white-barked American sycamore, and poplar predominate.

Colonial Williamsburg *(800-447-8679. www.history.org. Adm. fee)* is the country's largest living history museum, with more than 500 original and reconstructed buildings and 90 acres of gardens and greens. Costumed interpreters throughout the village re-create life here in the 18th century, when this was the capital of Virginia.

As you exit the tunnel at Colonial Williamsburg, bear right toward Yorktown. The parkway winds 5 or 6 miles through the woods until it picks up the **York River**. Soon you'll see the **Yorktown Victory Center** *(Old Rte. 238. 757-887-1776. www.historyis fun.org. Adm. fee)* off to the left. This museum of the American Revolution features a re-created farmstead, a Continental Army camp, and military demonstrations.

The parkway ends in the small colonial seaport of **Yorktown,** where American Revolutionaries scored their decisive victory against the British in 1781. Exhibits at the park **Visitor Center** *(757-898-3400)* detail the siege and a driving tour of the battlefield leads past redoubts to **Surrender Field.**

Tunnel, one of two tunnels underlying shipping channels. More trestled roadways lead to the 5,423-foot-long **Chesapeake Channel Tunnel,** then across **Fisherman Island** *(757-331-2760),* a natural island preserved as a national wildlife refuge.

A bridge across the Inland Waterway brings you to the drive's end at the southern tip of Virginia's bucolic **Eastern Shore.**

George Washington Memorial Parkway

Mount Vernon to I-495

● 25 miles ● 45 minutes ● All year. Rush hour traffic can be heavy.

George Washington's Mount Vernon

This sinuous park-scape traces the Virginia shoreline of the Potomac River, linking historic sites and showcasing the capital's skyline.

The route begins at **Mount Vernon** *(703-780-2000. www.mountvernon .org. Adm. fee),* the Potomac River plantation that was George Washington's home from 1754 to 1799. Now a national icon and the site of the first President's grave, Mount Vernon enshrines Washington's private life as a Virginia planter.

From here, the parkway winds past stands of maple, oak, beech, and tulip poplar. Modeled after New York's Bronx River Parkway, the first 15.5 miles of this road were completed in the 1930s and carefully landscaped to capture the look of the Virginia countryside.

About a mile past Mount Vernon, a lovely bridge, first in a series of low-slung concrete spans, arches across the roadway. Soon the woods clear and the wide **Potomac River** comes into view at **Riverside Park.**

A mile farther on, 156-acre **Fort Hunt Park** preserves the batteries that from 1898 to 1918 guarded the river approach to Washington. Across the Potomac stands the masonry ramparts of **Fort Washington** (1824), an example of a 19th-century coastal fortification.

As the road veers briefly away from the river, a turnoff to the right leads to **River Farm** *(703-768-5700. Mon.-Fri.; donation).* Once part of George Washington's estate and now headquarters of the American Horticultural Society, it features gardens and the original 18th-century house.

As the parkway passes Belle Haven Marina, you have a great view downriver. Birdwatchers will want to check adjacent **Dyke Marsh Wildlife Preserve,** a 240-acre wetland that attracts over 250 different bird species. The parkway becomes Washington Street as it enters **Old Town Alexandria.** Founded in 1749 as a colonial port, Old Town holds many historical highpoints. For information on the town, visit **Ramsay House Visitor Center** *(221 King St. 703-838-4200).*

Beyond Old Town, the parkway passes 106-acre

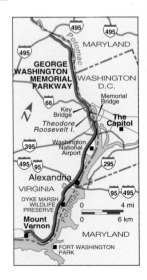

Daingerfield Island, a great spot to stroll or birdwatch. After you curve past **Reagan National Airport,** the Washington skyline looms into view. Continue under **Memorial Bridge,** built as a visual link between hilltop **Arlington House** *(703-557-0613)*, Robert E. Lee's home as an adult, and the **Lincoln Memorial.**

Beyond Roosevelt Bridge, there's a turnout for 88-acre **Theodore Roosevelt Island** *(703-289-2550. www.nps.gov/gwmp/ tri.htm)*, a nature preserve threaded by wooded trails. Past the island, as you dip below **Key Bridge,** the spires of **Georgetown University** come into view.

As the drive climbs above the Potomac, overlooks afford views of the increasingly wild and rocky river. The parkway ends at its junction with I-495.

George Washington Memorial Parkway

Skyline Drive

Front Royal to Rockfish Gap through Shenandoah National Park

● 105 miles ● 4 hours ● Spectacular spring bloom and fall foliage. Fall weekends are crowded; in winter road occasionally closes due to weather. Distances designated by mileposts. Adm. fee to park

Teetering atop the narrow spine of the Blue Ridge, the Skyline Drive gazes down on the fertile Shenandoah Valley to the west and rolling foothills to the east. Once inhabited by Indians, then mountaineers, this wild backcountry was reclaimed in the 1930s, when Shenandoah National Park was created.

From Front Royal, follow U.S. 340 south 1 mile to the entrance to **Shenandoah National Park** *(540-999-3500. www.nps.gov/shen. Adm. fee)*. As the road climbs forested **Dickey Ridge,** patterned lowlands appear to the east through the hickories and oaks. Below the **Shenandoah Valley Overlook** *(Mile 2.8)* stretches the fabled valley that the Indians purportedly called "Daughter of the Stars"—Shenandoah. Through it the **Shenandoah River** wanders amid barns and farm fields. Bisecting the

See P. 84

valley is the long rampart of **Massanutten Mountain.** The nearby **Dickey Ridge Visitor Center** *(Mile 4.6. April–mid-Nov.)* offers park information.

Six miles beyond, the road runs into the **Blue Ridge** at **Compton Gap,** and from here follows the mountain crest. In spring the Blue Ridge is vibrant with blossoming redbud, dogwood, azalea, and mountain laurel, and in fall its forested ridges are painted in rich autumnal hues.

At **Hogback Overlook** *(Mile 21)* stop to look down on the looping course of the Shenandoah River. From here, the road snakes down to **Thornton Gap** then enters **Marys Rock Tunnel** *(Mile 32.4)*. At its southern portal, the **Tunnel Parking Overlook** peers into a hollow where more than 20 families lived when the park was established.

Blue periwinkle

The park's third highest peak is **Hazel Mountain,** whose 3,815-foot summit may be seen at **Hazel Mountain Overlook** *(Mile 33)*. Hikes into the area called Hazel Country, along rocky streams and through forests of hemlock and mountain laurel, begin a half mile ahead. Relics of former inhabitants are visible everywhere: rock walls, split-rail fences, abandoned orchards.

Moseying south, the road winds around **The Pinnacle,** then **Stony Man Peak.** Keep a lookout for white-tailed deer, prominent throughout the park, as well as less visible denizens—skunks, barred owls, and the occasional black bear. At mile 41.7, the parkway reaches its highest point—3,680 feet at **Skyland** *(540-999-2211. Late April-Nov.)*. Now a hub of park facilities, this historic mountain resort was founded in the 1890s.

At the **Old Rag View Overlook** *(Mile 46.5)*, note the ancient Old Rag granite visible on this venerable mountain's upper peaks. Two fine hikes can be accessed along the next several miles. From **Upper Hawksbill Parking** *(Mile 46.7)* a mile-long trail leads to the top of 4,050-foot **Hawksbill Mountain,** the park's highest peak. Farther on, a steep trail descends less than a mile past ferns and liverworts to **Dark Hollow Falls.** Thomas Jefferson once stood below this 70-foot cascade, admiring its beauty.

Beyond, the road enters an open area called **Big Meadows** *(Mile 51)*, remnant of an ancient plain that once extended over the entire region. Blueberries and strawberries grow here, and deer like to browse along the edges. At the **Byrd Visitor Center** *(540-999-3283. April-Nov.)*, a movie depicts the history of the park.

A wonderful view of the Blue Ridge's classic smoky peaks ap-

Autumn along the Skyline Drive

pears at **Hazeltop Ridge Overlook** *(Mile 54.4)*. As you continue along the ridgetop, watch for **Bearfence Mountain Parking** *(Mile 56.4)*, where you can scramble up a short, boulder-strewn trail leading to one of the few 360-degree vistas in the park.

Stony Man Peak, Skyline Drive

After that the road curves in long, lazy turns to **Swift Run Gap** *(Mile 65.7)*, an important Blue Ridge crossing for decades. Beyond here, the views overlook a sea of undulating blue ridges, especially striking at the **Big Run Overlook** *(Mile 81.2)*.

After passing through the park's southern boundary, the parkway ends at **Rockfish Gap,** where a buffalo path, then a colonial road, once ran.

Blue Ridge Parkway

Rockfish Gap, Virginia, to Great Smoky Mountains National Park, North Carolina

● 469 miles ● 2 days ● Spring through fall. Fine fall foliage and spring bloom. Higher elevations occasionally close in winter. Distances designated by mileposts.

84

Showcasing the age-old beauty of the southern Appalachians, the Blue Ridge Parkway is one of America's most popular scenic drives. Connecting Shenandoah and Great Smoky Mountains National Parks, the two-lane drive rides the crest of the Blue Ridge and other ranges, occasionally dipping into hollows or climbing above timberline to heights over 6,000 feet.

The road begins where Skyline Drive leaves off (see p. 82), at **Rockfish Gap** near Waynesboro. After a brief heavenward climb—perhaps the most dramatic stretch in Virginia—the road gracefully rises and falls along the narrow, forested spine of the **Blue Ridge.** The mountain drops off sharply on both sides, leaving the parkway to soar above foothills to the east and the Great Valley of Virginia, the Shenandoah, to the west.

Until the road was built in the 1930s, mountaineers, mostly of Scotch-Irish and German descent, led hardscrabble lives in these timbered hollows. Some of their restored rock-and-timber farm buildings can be visited at **Humpback Rocks Pioneer Exhibit** *(Mile 5.8. 540-943-4716. May-Oct.).*

Beyond, the forested parkway winds alongside spritely Dancing Creek, then Otter Creek. **Otter Lake** is one of the parkway's man-made embellishments.

Midway to Roanoke, the road dips to its lowest elevation, 649 feet, at the **James River** *(Mile 65)*. The **James**

River Visitor Center *(Mile 63.6. 804-299-5496. May-Oct.)* tells the story of this river, its 7-mile gorge through the Blue Ridge, and the adjacent Kanawha Canal, a Civil War supply route.

Winding sharply up to the crest line again—about 3,300 feet in 13 miles—the Blue Ridge Parkway reaches **Apple Orchard Mountain,** its highest point in Virginia (3,950 feet). Whipping winter winds twist the northern red oaks that predominate between here and the Arnold Valley Overlook into spindly shapes resembling apple trees.

At mile 85.6, the parkway reaches historic **Peaks of Otter Lodge** *(540-586-1081),* surrounded by Sharp Top, Flat Top, and Harkening Hill—the three Peaks of Otter. A **Visitor Center** *(Mile 86. 540-586-4357. Mid-April–Oct., weekends only in Nov.)* has information on the area.

Entering the **Roanoke River Basin,** the parkway cruises for about 30 miles in the shadow of a discontinuous series of free-standing peaks. Then, south of Roanoke, the scenery turns exceedingly pastoral as the road climbs onto the **Blue Ridge Plateau.** Distant views alternate with closeups of small highland farms, where tobacco, hay, and vegetables grow in neat fields and Herefords graze behind split-rail fences.

At mile 176.2, **Mabry Mill** *(540-745-9662. May-Oct.)* demonstrates the importance of self-sufficiency in this remote corner. Far from any towns, local farmers relied on the ingenuity of Ed Mabry, who built this gristmill, along with a sawmill and blacksmith shop, in the early 1900s.

To learn to identify the kinds of split-rail fences that divide the farmlands and edge the roadsides, stop at **Groundhog Mountain** *(Mile 188.8),* where an exhibit identifies snake rail, buck rail, and post-and-rail; a fire tower here yields sweeping views of the high country.

The road continues south, with the distinct outline of **Pilot Mountain** on the eastern horizon. At mile 216.9, it crosses the state line into North Carolina and the rolling plateau begins to build into the soaring mountains and deep valleys of **Pisgah National Forest** *(828-257-4200).*

With its array of regional crafts, antiques, and homemade pastries, the **Northwest Trading Post** at mile 258.6 adds local color. Beyond, the solitary bulk of **Mount Jefferson** looms over the town of Jefferson as the road drops down into **Deep Gap.** This wild, rugged area was known only to the Cherokee and buffalo in the late 1700s when Daniel Boone, a nearby resident, forged a path through here to Kentucky. Look for **Boone's Trace** at mile 285.1.

The road continues past **Blowing Rock,** a pleasant mountain resort, and **Moses H. Cone Memorial Park** *(Mile 294. 828-295-7938. March-Nov.).* Built as

View from Craggy Gardens Overlook, North Carolina

a mountain retreat by Cone, a textile magnate, the manor houses a Visitor Center and the **Parkway Craft Center.**

Just down the road hulks 5,964-foot **Grandfather Mountain,** the highest mountain in the Blue Ridge and one of the oldest in the world.

(Geologists say its quartzite is over a billion years old.) Head west 1 mile on U.S. 221, then take the 2-mile entrance road that twists up to a **Visitor Center** *(800-468-7325)*. Here, you'll find spectacular views and a pedestrian swing bridge crossing to **Linville Peak.**

Spring rhododendron bloom,
Blue Ridge Parkway

Back on the parkway, the drive now encounters the "missing link," the last 7.5-mile section of the road, completed in 1987. To preserve Grandfather Mountain's fragile environment, 153 precast segments specifically fitting the mountain's contours were used to build the S-shaped **Linn Cove Viaduct,** which snakes along its rocky slopes. At the **Linn Cove Parking Area** *(Mile 304.4. 828-733-1354)*, a trail leads to a view of the elevated roadway.

The terrain's ruggedness persists at **Linville Falls Recreation Area** *(Mile 316.5. Follow spur road 1.4 miles along Linville River. 828-765-1045. May-Oct.)*. Here, the river drops over rock ledges then flows between 2,000-foot-high walls—the deepest cleft this side of the Grand Canyon. The mile-long trail to the falls passes through one of the few remaining virgin stands of eastern hemlocks.

As you continue, the parkway enters the mining district of **Spruce Pine,** where 57 different types of minerals are found, including emeralds and rubies. To learn more, stop at the **Museum of North Carolina Minerals** *(Mile 331. 828-765-2761. Closed Mon.-Tues. Nov.-April; adm. fee)*.

Farther south, the parkway explores beautiful forests. The big bold **Black Mountains,** named for the black-green Fraser fir and red spruce that carpet their slopes, rise darkly in the distance.

Beyond **Crabtree Meadows Recreation Area** *(Mile 339.5. 828-675-4236. May-Oct.)*, the road begins its last climb on the Blue Ridge. Views widen of surrounding blue peaks and the vegetation changes from that of southern forests to northern spruces and firs.

After about 15 miles, the highway leaves the Blue Ridge at **Ridge Junction** and begins its traverse across a jumble of colliding ranges. It briefly skirts the southern edge of the Black Mountains, then at Balsam Gap begins a tipsy ride across the **Great Craggy Mountains.** At **Black Mountain Gap,** a 5-mile detour on Rte. 128 climbs **Mount Mitchell** *(Visitor Center 828-675-4611)*, at 6,684 feet the highest peak in the East. A short walk leads to the summit, where a sweater is needed for the Canadian-like climate (snow in July is not impossible).

Back on the parkway just past mile 361, look for views of **Glassmine Falls** tumbling down Horse Range Ridge, and of **Graybeard Mountain,** a prominent Blue Ridge peak that, if surrounded by clouds, indicates rain.

In mid-June, the slopes of **Craggy Dome** are carpeted with the red-purple blossoms of catawba rhododendron. The **Craggy Gardens Visitor Center** *(Mile 364.6. May-Oct.)* has exhibits on heath gardens.

Leaving the Great Craggies, the road begins its gradual descent into the **French Broad River Valley** and Asheville. The **Folk Art Center** *(Mile 382. 828-298-7929)* displays traditional Appalachian crafts—quilts, woven baskets,

Black bear cubs

furniture—and sells them in the outlet run by the Southern Highlands Handicraft Guild. Here you can detour to the highlands city of **Asheville** and palatial **Biltmore Estate** *(3.5 miles north of parkway on U.S. 25. 828-255-1700 or 800-543-2961. Adm. fee)*, a château built by George Vanderbilt at the turn of the century.

Crossing the **French Broad River** beyond Asheville, the tree-framed road plays hide-and-seek with a series of tunnels, climbing onto the rocky, rugged back of **Pisgah Ledge.** Soon you see **Mount Pisgah** looming to the right. When Vanderbilt came to the area in 1884, he became so enraptured with Mount Pisgah that he bought it. His lands became the nucleus of Pisgah National Forest and site of the first U.S. Forestry School. The **Pisgah Inn** *(Mile 408.6. 828-235-8228. April-Nov.)* has a panoramic mile-high view of this rugged land.

At Tanassee Bald the parkway swings northwest along the Great Balsams, sharply climbing and dropping on a winding road. Intermingled with dense forests are increasingly breathtaking panoramas of bold mountain peaks: **Cold Mountain, Looking Glass Rock,** and **Devil's Courthouse,** which the Cherokees believed to be the dancing chamber of their devil. The parkway reaches its highest point (6,047 feet) at **Richland Balsam** *(Mile 431).* Below, the ranges of the southern Appalachians ripple to the horizon. For its last 10 miles, the parkway passes through these beautiful ranges, once home to the Cherokee Nation and now part of the Cherokee Indian Reservation.

87

The parkway ends in a pastoral valley on the **Oconaluftee River.** To the right, on U.S. 441, lies **Great Smoky Mountains National Park** (see Newfound Gap Road, page 95). To the left is **Cherokee** and the **Museum of the Cherokee Indian** *(U.S. 441N and Drama Rd. 828-497-3481. www.cherokeemuseum .org. Adm. fee).*

Sunset over the Great Smokies

Southeast

North Carolina, Tennessee, Kentucky, Mississippi, Alabama, South Carolina, Georgia, Florida

North Carolina

Cape Hatteras National Seashore

Kill Devil Hills to Ocracoke on U.S. 158, N.C. 12, and the Hatteras Inlet Ferry

● 80 miles ● 3 hours ● Spring through fall

North Carolina's Outer Banks—a 200-mile-long chain of low, slim barrier islands—arc out from the mainland, protecting the coast and shallow sounds from the battering Atlantic. This drive takes in the Cape Hatteras National Seashore, established in 1953.

From the mainland, U.S. 158 crosses **Albemarle Sound** to the Outer Banks. Several miles down, the road passes through **Kill Devil Hills,** where you'll find the **Wright Brothers National Memorial** *(252-441-7430. Adm. fee),* site of the first mechanically driven flight in 1903. A few miles beyond, the **Jockey's Ridge State Park** *(252-441-7132)* boasts the East Coast's highest dune (130 feet); prevailing winds across the dune attract hang gliders. From Jockey's Ridge, turn east on one of the numerous side roads that connect U.S. 158 with Rte. 12, which hugs the coastline.

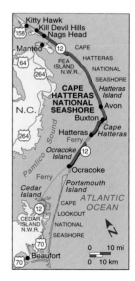

Rte. 12 plows south past the beach houses of Nags Head to Whalebone Junction, where an Information Center has maps and brochures on **Cape Hatteras National Seashore** *(252-987-2401. www.nps.gov/caha).* After crossing the grassy marshlands of **Bodie** (pronounced Body) **Island** for about 6 miles, you reach the dunes near **Coquina Beach,** and, just beyond, the 1872 **Bodie Island Lighthouse** *(Visitor Center 252-441-5711. Mem. Day-Columbus Day).*

Beyond Bodie, you cross **Oregon Inlet** and have a sweeping vista of the **Atlantic Ocean** and **Pamlico Sound.** On the far side of the bridge lies the 5,915-acre **Pea Island National Wildlife Refuge.** Located on the Atlantic flyway, it attracts more than a million migratory birds in spring and fall. It's also one of the northernmost nesting grounds for threatened loggerhead sea turtles.

Cape Hatteras Light Station

Here, the route is flanked by salt flats stretching into Pamlico Sound and man-made barrier dunes edging the Atlantic, stabilized by beach grasses and sea oats. Continuing south, you pass **North Pond,** site of a 5-mile interpretive trail and the **Pea Island National Wildlife Visitor Center** (*252-987-2394. Daily April-Nov., some weekends rest of year*). For the next 2 miles or so, a wall of sandbags replaces seaside dunes flattened by a storm in 1991. Coastal processes—waves, winds, tides, currents, storms—are pushing the islands ever westward, constantly challenging attempts to maintain permanent structures.

On **Hatteras Island,** you'll pass historic **Chicamacomico Coast Guard Station** (*252-987-2401. Tues., Thurs., Sat. May-Oct. and by appointment*). Built in 1874 as a U.S. Life Saving Service Station, it's now a museum displaying maritime rescue equipment and early Coast Guard memorabilia.

Called the "graveyard of the Atlantic," the shoals off the Outer Banks have taken down hundreds of ships since the 16th century.

For the next 20 miles the road passes through the beach communities of Rodanthe, Waves, Salvo, and Avon. Pockets of coastal forest once dotted this area, but in the 1800s the trees were felled to build clipper ships. Along this stretch are fine views of Pamlico Sound. Covering more than 1,800 square miles, Pamlico is the largest sound on the East Coast, and the steady winds here draw hundreds of windsurfers.

The next town, **Buxton,** features the **Cape Hatteras Light Station and Hatteras Island Visitor Center** (*252-995-5209. Visitor Center year-round; lighthouse closed Columbus Day-Good Friday*). The 210-foot lighthouse, built in 1870, is the nation's tallest brick lighthouse. You'll also find the north end of **Buxton Woods** here, as well as a wonderful beach where you can see the tip of **Cape Hatteras** jutting into the Atlantic. The notorious **Diamond Shoals** offshore have caused hundreds of ships to run aground.

From Buxton the road burrows through the woods about 5 miles to **Frisco,** where you hit a touristy strip for the final 5 miles to the resort town of **Hatteras.** Once there, follow the sign for the **Hatteras Inlet Ferry** *(800-BY-FERRY or 800-368-8949)*, a delightful 40-minute, free ferry trip across **Hatteras Inlet** to **Ocracoke Island.** Once on the island, Rte. 12 leads 14 miles to the village of Ocracoke, the island's only settlement. Along the way, you'll pass pristine seacoast and marshland, where you may spot some of the island's legendary Banker horses, popularly believed to be descended from purebred Spanish mustangs.

Hugging the tidal harbor of **Silver Lake, Ocracoke** was settled by ship pilots—and haunted by Blackbeard. The notorious pirate was captured and beheaded here in 1718. The historic town features the state's oldest operating lighthouse (1823) and a national seashore **Visitor Center** *(End of Rte. 12. 252-928-4531. Daily Easter weekend-Columbus Day)*.

Ferries crossing Pamlico Sound from Ocracoke connect to **Cedar Island National Wildlife Refuge** *(252-225-2511)*.

The Tidewater

Portsmouth, Va., to New Bern, N.C., on U.S. 17

- **173 miles** ● **4 hours**
- **Fall through spring**

Newbold-White House, near Hertford

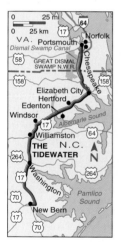

Part of the old Ocean Highway linking New York and Florida, this section of U.S. 17 meanders through the lush lowlands and historic tidewater towns of Virginia and North Carolina.

From **Portsmouth,** head south past several miles of strip centers and suburbs. In the adjacent city of **Chesapeake,** signs lead to **Deep Creek Lock,** one of the two remaining locks of the **Dismal Swamp Canal.** Cross the bridge over the canal—now part of the **Atlantic Intracoastal Waterway** that runs between Boston and Key West—and turn right onto an open stretch of road.

Once in the countryside, the drive begins running parallel to the 200-year-old canal, which links Virginia's Chesapeake Bay and North Carolina's Albemarle Sound. Built by slaves, it ranks as the country's oldest continually operating artificial waterway and is now used by recreational boaters. Off to the right sprawls the dense vegetation of the 107,000-acre **Great Dismal Swamp National Wildlife Refuge** *(757-986-3705)*, a fine example of freshwater swampland. Forested mostly by red maple and juniper, the refuge centers around 3,100-acre **Lake Drummond.**

After about 4 miles the road enters a wooded stretch then emerges into fields cultivated in corn, wheat, and potatoes. Continue across the North Carolina border, and in about 3 miles you'll see the **Dismal Swamp Canal Visitor–Welcome Center** *(252-771-8333. Closed Sun.-Mon. Nov.-Mem. Day)*. Here, you can get a closeup look at the canal's black waters, the result of juniper and cypress tannins.

The roadside becomes cluttered for several miles as you approach **Elizabeth City.** A commercial center at the narrows of the **Pasquotank River,** it was incorporated in 1793. Stop at the **Museum of the Albemarle** *(1116 U.S. 17 S. 252-335-1453. Closed Mon.)* for regional history and culture, then take a turn through the historic district and waterfront.

Leaving town, you have to bear with several more miles of strip centers before crossing the wide and lovely **Perquimans River,** where knobby cypress knees poke from the water. Continue through the town of **Hertford,** and 3 miles south of it, you'll see signs for the 1730 **Newbold-White House** *(1.5 miles south on Rte. 1336. 252-426-7567. March-Thanksgiving Tues.-Sun.; adm. fee),* the state's oldest house.

The landscape now becomes rural again, edged by fields of corn, soybeans, peanuts, and cotton. The elegant colonial town of **Edenton** *(Historic Edenton Visitors Center, 108 N. Broad St. 252-482-2637),* beautifully set at the junction of the **Chowan River** and **Albemarle Sound,** is worth a short detour

Great Dismal Swamp

on Rte. 32. Leaving Edenton, you soon rejoin U.S. 17 south, which crosses over the Chowan River. For the next 30 miles the landscape is coastal plain, consisting of sandy soil.

Coming into **Windsor,** you'll see signs for historic **Hope Plantation** *(4 miles west of U.S. 13 Bypass on Rte. 308. 252-794-3140. Adm. fee).* This 19th-century federal-style home of Governor David Stone is furnished with 18- and 19th-century Carolina antiques.

At Windsor, U.S. 17 takes a turn south and for the next 6 miles passes more farmland before the landscape turns lush and dense as you drive through the 18,060-acre **Roanoke River National Wildlife Refuge** *(252-794-5326. http://roanokeriver.fws.gov)*—a wetlands preserve on the river's floodplain.

After crossing the Roanoke River, the road enters Williamston before returning to farmland, some 10 miles south in Beaufort County. These once boggy lands now support fields of soybean, tobacco, and corn cultivated by families whose ancestors have farmed here for generations.

The town of **Washington** *(Chamber of Commerce, 102 Stewart Pkwy. 252-946-9168),* the "original Washington," was incorporated in 1782 and is the country's first community named for George Washington. Set at the confluence of the **Tar** and **Pamlico Rivers,** the town was destroyed by fire during the Civil War and rebuilt. Then in 1900 its downtown burned once again. A walking tour here takes you along the river-front and through the town's historic district.

George Washington, the great canal developer, had an early hand in planning the Dismal Swamp Canal.

From Washington, the road weaves through suburbs for 7 miles then reenters endless fields. If you're here during harvest time, you may share the road with carts packed with big-leaf tobacco.

Dense brush and forest flank the roadside as you near the bridge over the **Neuse River** to the drive's terminus in **New Bern** *(Convention and Visitors Bureau, 219 Pollock St. 252-637-9400).* Set at the confluence of the Neuse and the **Trent River,** the former colonial and state capital—and the state's second oldest town—was founded in 1710 by German and Swiss settlers, who named it after Bern, Switzerland. Along with its federal-style buildings, New Bern's main attraction is **Tryon Palace Historic Sites and Gardens** *(George and Pollock Sts. 252-514-4900. www.ah.dcr.state.nc.us/ sections/tryon/default.htm. Adm. fee),* the restored estate of colonial governor William Tryon.

Forest Heritage Scenic Byway

Loop from Brevard on U.S. 64 and 276 and North Carolina 215

● 80 miles ● 2 hours ● All year. Blue Ridge Parkway occasionally closed due to weather. Fine fall color

Passing the waterfalls, streams, and pastures that sprinkle the forested foothills and upper slopes of North Carolina's Blue Ridge Mountains, the byway loops through the sylvan lands that gave birth to America's forestry program.

Charming **Brevard,** dating from the 1860s, is known for the summer concert season at its **Music Center.** From Brevard, the drive heads northeast on U.S. 64, then northwest on U.S. 276, soon passing

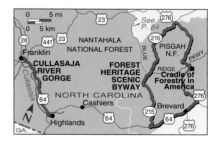

through the venerable stone entrance gate of **Pisgah National Forest.** The serene road twists beneath oaks, poplars, balsam firs, and birches along the **Davidson River.** Stock up on information at the **Pisgah Visitor Center** *(828-877-3265),* 1.5 miles inside the entrance.

Forest Heritage Scenic Byway in autumn

Nearby **Looking Glass Falls** thunders 60 feet into a dark pool by the roadside, and 2 miles farther on, **Sliding Rock** creates a natural, 60-foot water slide. After this, the road begins its heavenward ascent up **Pisgah Ledge,** a long, wooded ridge topped by Mount Pisgah. In the woodlands ahead is the **Cradle of Forestry in America** *(828-877-3130. www.cradleof forestry.com. Mid-April–early Nov.; adm. fee),* where a modern Visitor Center and restored dwellings celebrate the birthplace of American forestry in 1889. The idea is attributed to wealthy conservationist George Vanderbilt, who once owned the lands now composing the nucleus of Pisgah National Forest.

Past **Pink Beds,** where massive beds of rhododendron, azalea, and mountain laurel bloom in early summer, U.S. 276 curves up the mountainside toward **Wagon Road Gap** (elevation 4,533 feet). Here, you'll find a junction with the Blue Ridge Parkway (see page 84). For soaring views, head to **Mount Pisgah,** about 3 miles north on the parkway.

Back on U.S. 276, you drop precipitously off the northern side of Pisgah Ledge and twist between the steep slopes of **Mount Pisgah** and **Cold Mountain.** At the parking lot by the **East Fork of the Pigeon River,** trails lead into 18,500-acre **Shining Rock Wilderness.**

The road continues through mountain-ringed **Cruso Valley,** dotted with grazing cows, green pastures, and leaning barns. Development marks the approach to Cruso, but when you reach Rte. 215 and turn south, you're back in more pastoral countryside.

About 8 miles farther on, the byway climbs back up Pisgah Ledge again, with long views of roadside waterfalls and the glorious backcountry of Shining Rock and **Middle Prong Wildernesses.** Cresting at **Beech Gap,** the drive passes back under the Blue Ridge Parkway and plummets off Pisgah Ledge's southern slope, offering views of tree-carpeted foothills.

Continuing to descend, you thread through mountain pastures and pass under the open jaws of **Alligator Rock.** Rte. 215 ends at its junction with busy U.S. 64, which leads 6 miles back to Brevard.

Cullasaja River Gorge

Franklin to Highlands on U.S. 64

● 18 miles ● ½ hour ● Spring through fall. *See map p. 93.*

Clinging to a mountainside high above the Cullasaja River, this steep mountain road showcases a number of breathtaking waterfalls.

Start in the town of **Franklin,** which calls itself the "gem capital of the world," due to a score of nearby ruby, garnet, and sapphire mines. Head south on U.S. 64 through genteel countryside that gives no sense of the road ahead.

After 7 miles the pastures disappear, and the road swings onto **Higdon Mountain,** a towering hulk of granite gneiss flanked by **Cullasaja Gorge.** The narrow, curving ribbon of pavement passes **Lower Cullasaja Falls,** an unmarked but obvious cascade plummeting 150 feet beside the road. Winding between towering cliffs, the road follows the **Cullasaja River** through forests of pine, hemlock, and maple.

Dry Falls, about 6 miles ahead, is found at the end of a short trail; a path tunnels under the 75-foot falls. A mile farther on, the drive reaches **Bridal Veil Falls.** While the current road skirts around the falls, a portion of the old road passes under it, and you can still drive on it, conditions permitting.

The route ends in **Highlands,** at 4,118 feet North Carolina's highest and wettest town. Some 80 inches of rain a year explain the lush flora in this popular summer and fall resort.

Dry Falls, Cullasaja Gorge

Tennessee

Newfound Gap Road

Sugarlands Visitor Center, Tenn., to Oconaluftee Visitor Center, N.C., through Great Smoky Mountains National Park

● **40 miles** ● **2 hours** ● **Bloom for dogwood and wildflowers best mid-March into July. Fall foliage peaks mid-October. Traffic heaviest in summer and fall.**

Traversing the East's most massive mountain uplift, Newfound Gap Road in Great Smoky Mountains National Park *(www.nps.gov/grsm)* climbs through a unique botanical paradise, where the vegetation ranges from southern hardwood forests to alpine spruce and fir forests. Constructed in the 1930s, the scenic road through this gap in the Appalachian Mountains features such artful touches as stone bridges, sweeping curves, and stone guardrails.

Begin at the park's **Sugarlands Visitor Center** *(865-436-1200),* located in a valley rich in sugar maples and pioneer history. As you head east, the road wanders through a gorge carved by the **West Prong Little Pigeon River,** through a cove hardwood forest of red maples, white oaks, tulip trees, basswoods, and magnolias. Several trails, designated **Quiet Walkways,** amble through the woodlands, offering a chance to escape the often crowded road in this, the nation's most visited national park.

About 2 miles from the Visitor Center, the first sweeping views appear, showcasing **Mount LeConte**—at 6,593 feet the highest peak, from base to summit, east of the Mississippi. For a closer look, stop at **Campbell Overlook.** From here, the road begins its ascent, gentle at first, winding along the West Prong. After about 2 miles, the jagged **Chimney Tops** appear. Three pullouts give slightly different perspectives of these 4,700-foot twin peaks of quartzite and slate.

Early snow on Chimney Tops

Cades Cove

Blue-eyed grass

Just beyond, the road curves more dramatically and soon enters the forest transition zone, where northern hardwood forests begin to dominate the slopes. Lush rainfall (averaging more than 85 inches annually) and mild temperatures contribute to the park's diverse flora, which includes more than 1,500 species of flowering plants. You get an idea of the terrain's increasing complexity less than a mile ahead. To negotiate the steep, crowding mountains, the road passes through a tunnel, then loops up, around, and over itself.

Beyond this, several pullouts along the river allow contemplation of the Smokies' lifeblood. The 900 billion gallons of water pulsing through the park each year nourish abundant plant life and feed rivers that eventually drain into the Gulf of Mexico.

Farther on, the road passes the parking area for the 2.5-mile-long **Alum Bluffs Trail** to the summit of Mount LeConte. Still climbing, you pass **Anakeesta** (Cherokee for "place of balsam") **Ridge,** covered with spruce and fir, then sidle alongside its base. You are now in a harsh vegetation zone, characterized by steep slopes and rocky outcrops and dominated by Fraser fir and red spruce.

The Cherokees gave the Smokies their name, calling them Shaconage, "the place of blue smoke."

At sky-high **Morton Overlook** you can look down on the **Sugarlands Valley** or up to the notch in State Line Range, where **Newfound Gap** joins Tennessee to North Carolina.

The views are even better just around the corner at the **Newfound Gap Overlook** (elevation 5,048 feet), the road's highest point. From here, you can peer into Tennessee or into North Carolina's **Oconaluftee Valley.**

It's downhill from here, unless you opt to visit 6,643-foot **Clingmans Dome,** the park's highest peak. A 7-mile spur road (Closed in winter) climbs along the ridge of the dome. From the parking area at the road's end, a steep but short half-mile hike leads to a lookout tower with 360-degree panoramas of the hazy, undulating peaks and rounded summits that are this park's signature. Whether mist veils the mountains or clear skies illuminate the endless ridges, the view is beautiful.

Back on Newfound Gap Road, the drive soon passes **Ocolonee Valley Overlook,** perched atop the long ridge of **Thomas Divide.** A Tennessee mountainman who made one of the first trips on the road reacted this way to the view: "If the world's as big back thataways as it is out yonder, then she's a whopper."

As the road switchbacks down the divide, the views of the Smoky Mountains backcountry are breathtaking. At **Webb Overlook,** you can gaze up at Clingmans Dome. Beyond here, you enter a deciduous forest. Soon, the road picks up the **Oconaluftee River** and follows its curves and bends to **Mingus Mill** (May-Oct.). Built in 1886, it is now one of two working mills in the national park.

At the end of the road the **Oconaluftee Visitor Center** features a mountain farmstead of historic log buildings transplanted here to demonstrate pioneer life.

Cades Cove Loop Drive

Loop road off Laurel Creek Road in Great Smoky Mountains National Park

● 11 miles ● 1 hour ● One way. Spring through fall. Allow ample time to reach loop road. Speed limit is 20 mph. *See map page 95.*

Hidden from the world by big, rumpled mountains, Cades Cove retains the pastoral beauty of the early 19th century, when settlers first cleared the land. At its peak in the 1850s, the picturesque valley was the remote home of 680 mountaineers. Today, a loop road through the cove passes the restored remains of their farms and villages.

From the **Sugarlands Visitor Center** *(865-436-1200)* in Great Smoky Mountains National Park, follow Little River and Laurel Creek Roads 25 miles to the Cades Cove Loop.

The drive leads through a nostalgic landscape, where weathered fence posts, bounding deer, majestic oak trees, and bales of hay recall a different era. Along the way, you can visit 18 marked sights, including the **John Oliver Place,** a small cabin with split-wood shingles and hand-hewn logs; the plain white-frame **Primitive Baptist Church,** organized in 1827; the **Elijah Oliver Place,** a rustic farmstead with a smokehouse, springhouse, and corn crib; and the **John Cable Mill,** where corn was ground into meal.

Midway is the **Cades Cove Visitor Center,** with exhibits illustrating turn-of-the-century rural life.

Kentucky

Kentucky Heartland Drive

Lexington to Harrodsburg on U.S. 68

● **30 miles** ● **1 hour** ● **All year**

Following a former buffalo trace and an early 19th-century Shaker toll road, this rolling rural drive takes you into central Kentucky's famed Bluegrass region and through the rugged Kentucky River Gorge.

The drive begins in **Lexington,** center of the state's lucrative tobacco and horse industries. Head south from downtown on busy South Broadway (U.S. 68). Soon after passing **South Elkhorn Creek,** the road—now narrower and less trafficked—begins sweeping around precipitous bends and curves as urban development gives way to modest plots of burley tobacco and lush pastures dotted with dairy cows and bales of hay.

The most prominent feature of this region is its miles and miles of black and white plank fences, behind which statuesque Thoroughbreds graze in manicured meadows. Here in the heart of Kentucky's Bluegrass country, the world's finest racing stock is born, raised, and bred.

Perhaps the most famous horse farm along the route is the old **Almahurst Farm,** 10 miles outside Lexington. Dating from the land grant days, it boasts cream-colored barns trimmed in forest green and burgundy.

Beyond Almahurst, U.S. 68 winds past more posh horse farms,

Mares and foals of Bluegrass country

roadside stands selling fresh corn and watermelon in summer, and weather-beaten tobacco barns where the state's largest cash crop is hung to cure.

Several miles after entering Jessamine County, the drive begins its descent into a narrow side valley of the **Kentucky River Gorge.** After 1.5 miles of tricky driving, you cross the deep, olive green **Kentucky River** on the Brooklyn Bridge, with a fabulous view of the river's 300-foot-high limestone palisades. The road crawls along the valley for a bit, following the river. Then, suddenly it begins climbing up the sloped southern wall. After 2 miles the land opens up into rough, rolling farmland.

Shaker Meeting House, Pleasant Hill

Note the native limestone fences bordering much of this section of road. These mortarless fences were built by Irish stonemasons, who came to the region to build roads in the mid-1800s.

Soon the substantial buildings of the **Shaker Village of Pleasant Hill** *(606-734-5411. Adm. fee)* appear on the right, behind a maze of limestone fences. A religious sect that spread down from New England, Shakers first came to this high plateau above the Kentucky River in 1805 and established a self-sufficient colony known for its industriousness and celibacy. Though the colony effectively disbanded in 1910, many of their buildings have been restored and can be toured.

The drive continues another 7 miles, past more rolling pastureland, antebellum mansions, and groves of walnut and oak trees, before ending in **Harrodsburg.** Kentucky's oldest permanent settlement, the town began as a palisaded village in 1775, built to protect settlers from hostile Indians. A reproduction of the fort can be seen at **Old Fort Harrod State Park** *(606-734-3314. www.state.ky.us/agencies/parks/ftharrd2.htm. Adm. fee),* situated near the original site. The **Lincoln Marriage Cabin,** where the parents of Abraham Lincoln were married in 1806, was moved to the park from its original location a few miles west.

Land Between the Lakes

Barkley Canal, Kentucky, to the South Welcome Station, Tennessee, on the Trace

● **40 miles** ● **1 hour** ● **All year**

Called the Trace, the drive meanders the length of a long, narrow wooded peninsula jutting between Kentucky Lake and Lake Barkley and straddling the Kentucky-Tennessee border. Ravaged by floods, wars, and poverty, the region—originally known as the "Land Twixt the Rivers"—was converted to a recreation area by the Tennessee Valley Authority in the 1960s. This natural wonderland is rich in wildlife, including a variety of fish that delights anglers.

The drive begins in Kentucky just south of the bridge over **Barkley Canal,** which connects the two lakes. For vistas of the canal and **Kentucky Lake,** detour onto Kentucky Lake Drive, a pretty, 3.2-mile loop tour. Back on the Trace, you can pick up maps and brochures at the **North Welcome Station.**

From here, the Trace proceeds 17 miles through a genteel corridor of white oaks, sugar maples, black walnuts, and dogwoods. The **Golden Pond Visitor Center and Planetarium** *(270-924-2233)* has information and regional exhibits explaining, among other things, the area's moonshining past. Dur-

The Homeplace–1850

ing Prohibition this isolated pocket was home to one of the nation's most notorious moonshining operations, which capitalized on the limestone-rich mineral water and the abundant corn of this area.

About 8 miles farther, just across the Tennessee border, lies **Cedar Pond,** a pleasant picnic spot and prime wildlife-viewing area.

Continue 1.5 miles to the **Homeplace–1850** *(931-232-6457. Closed Dec.-Feb.; adm. fee),* a farm worked by costumed interpreters. Across the road a herd of American bison roams a 200-acre pasture.

The remains of a flourishing iron industry can be found at the nearby **Great Western Iron Furnace.** Deterred from farming by constant flooding and poor soil, many early settlers turned to iron, and by the 1830s Kentucky ranked third in the nation in iron-ore production.

The drive ends at the **South Welcome Station** 9 miles ahead, but don't leave the area before exploring its many recreational opportunities.

Mississippi
Natchez Trace Parkway

Nashville, Tennessee, to Natchez, Mississippi, on Tennessee 96 and the Trace Parkway

● 443 miles ● 2½ days ● Spring and fall. Only one service station on parkway at mile 193; otherwise you must exit for gas, food, and lodging. Wildlife sightings more likely in early morning and late afternoon. Speed limit of 50 mph strictly enforced. Mileposts record mileages in reverse, from Natchez to Nashville.

Stretching from the Tennessee Valley to the Mississippi River, the richly scenic Natchez Trace Parkway is one of America's most famous frontier trails. From buffalo paths used by prehistoric hunters, the Trace became a series of Indian trails later trod by French and Spanish trappers, traders, missionaries, and soldiers. The current two-lane parkway, administered by the National Park Service, meanders through forest, farmland, marshland, and

Mississippi River at Natchez

prairie, more or less paralleling the original Trace.

The parkway begins at Hwy. 100 in the outskirts of Nashville. Continue on to **Franklin** *(Chamber of Commerce, City Hall, 109 Second Ave. 615-794-1225 or 800-356-3445)*, site of a bloody Civil War battle in 1864. The town now boasts a handsomely restored, 19th-century downtown and significant antebellum landmarks including graceful **Carnton Plantation** *(1345 Carnton Ln. 615-794-0903. Adm. fee)*. From here, drive west 8 miles on Rte. 96 to enter the parkway.

The Trace gets off to a slow (40 mph) start, sweeping in great, elegant curves through the woods. Emerging into open fields, it rolls along for the next 20-some miles through idyllic Tennessee horse and farm country. At mile 407.7 **Gordon House** survives as one of the few structures from the old Trace.

Three miles beyond, a paved path leads to a pool at the base of **Jacksons Falls,** and a little farther on lies a **Tobacco Farm** featuring farm buildings with exhibits on tobacco-growing. A 2-mile drive along the original **Old Trace** begins here.

At the park dedicated to explorer **Meriwether Lewis** *(Mile 385.9)*, you'll find a reconstruction of the old log inn, or "stand," where he died in 1809 of gunshot wounds The building now holds a ranger station and history exhibit. Lewis's grave and a symbolic broken obelisk are also here.

Continue through the woods and across the **Buffalo River.** About 10 miles down, turn left on Old Trace Drive, which loops along a scenic ridge (one-way northbound) on a section of the old road.

South of here, you leave the woods behind for a breather of open farmland. Then the trees return, and you soon see **Sweetwater Branch** *(Mile 363);* in spring, wildflowers garnish the nature trail here. After about 20 miles of moving in and out of forests of oak and hickory, the Trace then crosses into Alabama and the land becomes noticeably flatter, marked by red-clay plains and cotton fields.

At mile 327.3 you cross the wide **Tennessee River** at **Colbert Ferry,** where in the mid-19th century itinerant preacher George Colbert ran a stand and a ferry "over the worst natural obstacle on the trace." Cultivated fields and low hills dominate for the next 10 miles. At **Freedom Hills Overlook** *(Mile 317)* a quarter-mile trail leads to the 800-foot hilltop, the highest point on the Alabama portion of the Natchez Trace.

In the early 18th century this 500-mile path through the wilderness was so hazardous that travelers called it the "devil's backbone."

Continuing south into Mississippi, you start to see more wetlands. About 9 miles across the state line, you reach the **Jamie L. Whitten Bridge** over the **Tennessee-Tombigbee Waterway.** Finally completed in 1985 (the idea was first proposed in the mid-1700s), the Tenn-Tom, as it's called, provides a 459-mile-long navigable link between the Tennessee River and the Gulf of Mexico.

After a few miles, watch for **Pharr Mounds**—the largest, most important archaeological site in northern Mississippi. The ancient Mound Builder culture constructed eight great, dome-shaped burial mounds here about 2,000 years ago, scattering their handiwork across 90 acres.

Crossing a boggy area that is habitat for great blue herons, egrets, and other birds, the road winds past **Donivan Slough,** where an interpretive trail leads through a fascinating hardwood swamp.

Continue on past fields of cotton, soybean, and milo (used for making sorghum and cattle fodder) to **Dogwood Valley** *(Mile 275.2).* The stand of large old dogwoods blooms profusely in the early spring.

If you pull off at the next **Old Trace** marker about 5 miles beyond, you can follow a short trail to a clearing in the woods that is believed to hold the graves of 13 unknown Confederate soldiers.

Along the original Trace

The **Natchez Trace Parkway Visitor Center** *(Mile 266. 800-305-7417. www.nps.gov/natr)* serves as park headquarters and offers exhibits and an audiovisual presentation about the Trace. From here, a 5-mile detour off the Trace on U.S. 45 will bring you to **Tupelo.** Legendary birthplace of Elvis

Presley, the small town celebrates its favorite son in several museums.

Back on the Trace, the **Chickasaw Village** at mile 261.8 marks the site of a former Native American settlement and interprets Chickasaw life. The glorious, open country you're now in—called the **Black Belt** for its black soil, in which cedar and oak thrive—is the remnant of a vast prairie.

You reenter an oak, hickory, and pine forest that is part of the **Tombigbee National Forest.** Before you leave the forest, take a stretch under the fragrant pines at magical **Witch Dance** before heading south, past the twin **Bynum Mounds**—more Mound Builder remains.

The next 40 miles offer a constantly changing picture of pretty farmscapes, pasturelands, and forests. **Jeff Busby Site** *(Mile 193.1)* has the only services along the Trace and offers a view from 603-foot **Little Mountain.** From here, the Trace soon crosses a bottomland, where shrubs replace trees. Down the road is the site of a former inn that became **French Camp Academy** *(662-547-6482).* The name refers to the inn's original French-Canadian proprietor. Now a Christian school-home, the grounds contain a visitor center, bed and breakfast, and historic buildings.

The landscape turns swampy over the next few miles, and the trail at **Cole Creek** leads through this fecund, fragrant bottomland hardwood forest. At mile 160 **Kosciusko,** pronounced koz-ee-ES-ko *(Chamber of Commerce, 124 N. Jackson St. 662-289-2981),* was named for the Polish soldier who became a hero during the American Revolution. The town is also the birthplace of talk-show star Oprah Winfrey. Aside from the new **Kosciusko Visitor Center,** this Victorian village boasts a charming town square and some fine historic homes.

103

Continuing through more swamp and bottomland for 30-some miles, the Trace passes **River Bend** *(Mile 122.6),* where you have a splendid view up the **Pearl River.** Just beyond, a boardwalk trail penetrates the eerie forest of bald cypress and tupelo at **Cypress Swamp.**

Picking up the shoreline of the scenic **Ross Barnett Reservoir,** the parkway follows it for 8 miles before reaching the **Mississippi Crafts Center at Ridgeland** *(601-856-7546),* which sells traditional Choctaw baskets, pottery, quilts, and other crafts. South of this, the parkway is interrupted; detour on I-55 and I-220 south and I-20 west toward Vicksburg, then follow signs to rejoin the Trace.

Mississippi's gracious capital, **Jackson** *(Jackson Visitor Information Center, 1150½ Lakeland Dr. 601-960-1891),* offers such attractions as museums, gardens, and a walking tour of the historic downtown.

From here you soon enter some of the most productive farmland in the state.

Cypress Swamp along the Natchez Trace

Rolling through this pastoral countryside for about 25 miles, the Trace passes the silent site of a 19th-century cotton town, where an old church and cemetery survive and the trees are draped in Spanish moss.

Crossing **Big Bayou Pierre** four times, you get a view of its cultivated floodplain before reaching peaceful Mangum Site and Grindstone Ford. Now the parkway sweeps south past farms and wetlands, passing at mile 41.5 the **Sunken Trace,** a short trail along a deeply eroded portion of the old Trace. Leaving the gently rolling countryside, the road begins to climb an upland ridge forested with hardwoods and pines. At **Mount Locust** *(Mile 15.5)* you can visit the only inn still remaining on the Trace and one of the oldest structures in the state. And at **Emerald Mound** *(Mile 10.3)* you can see the second largest Indian mound in the country: an 8-acre, earthen temple built about 600 years ago by ancestors of the present-day Natchez Indians.

The parkway winds to its current southern terminus 2 miles farther on when it intersects U.S. 61. Seven miles southwest lies **Natchez** *(Convention & Visitor Bureau, 422 Main St. 601-446-6345 or 800-647-6724),* an elegant vestige of the Old South containing a wealth of historic homes.

Hospitality Highway

Clermont Harbor to Ocean Springs on South Beach Boulevard and U.S. 90

● 32 miles ● 1 hour ● Fall through spring

This drive along Mississippi's Gulf Coast traces a section of the Old Spanish Trail. Along the way it passes scenic shorelines, a profusion of subtropical flora, some charming towns—and some casino stretches.

From **Clermont Harbor,** follow South Beach Boulevard east along **Mississippi Sound,** where the birdwatching is superb. The drive passes **Buccaneer State Park,** a 400-acre shoreline park *(228-467-3822),* then continues through the small town of Waveland, into the heart of historic **Bay St. Louis.** Long a favorite getaway for New Orleanians, this colorful little resort community holds galleries, antique shops, and impressive vintage architecture, including Spanish and old classical revival buildings.

Beach Boulevard brings you to U.S. 90 at the bridge over **St. Louis Bay.** Less than half a mile east of the bridge, you come upon a magnificent view of **Mississippi Beach**—the longest man-made strand in the world—at a bend in the road leading toward **Pass Christian** (pronounced Chris-CHAN). Known as The Pass, this was once the playground of wealthy southern planters and New Orleanian aristocrats. Take the designated scenic drive for a look at the antebellum mansions they once occupied.

The drive feeds back into Beach Boulevard after several miles, and you continue east through **Long Beach.** Here you see the **Port of Gulfport** ahead, and some 4 miles farther you enter the city of **Gulfport.**

The 12 miles from Gulfport to Biloxi are dotted by casinos and commercial strips, relieved intermittently by stretches of open beach. In **Biloxi** *(Visitor Center, 710 Beach Blvd. 228-374-3105)* the Old South returns,

Treasure Bay Casino, Biloxi, Mississippi

particularly in the town's historic district and at gracious veranda-fronted **Beauvoir** *(2244 Beach Blvd. 228-388-1313. Adm. fee)*, the last home of Confederate president Jefferson Davis.

The bridge over **Biloxi Bay** puts you in the lovely artist community of **Ocean Springs,** known for the **Walter Anderson Museum of Art** *(510 Washington Ave. 228-872-3164. Adm. fee)*, and **Shearwater Pottery** *(102 Shearwater Dr. 228-875-7320)*, featuring works by Anderson family members.

Alabama

Talladega Scenic Byway

U.S. 78 to Pinhoti Trailhead at Adams Gap on Ala. 281

● 27 miles ● ½ hour ● Spring and fall

Winding atop the long, narrow spine of Horseblock Mountain then scaling Alabama's highest peak— Cheaha Mountain—this drive offers dreamy views of the southern Appalachian's wooded valleys and ridges.

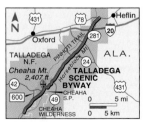

The byway begins 3 miles west of Heflin, where you head south on Rte. 281 through a wooded corridor in **Talladega National Forest** *(256-463-2272)*. Almost immediately, overlooks on the road's eastern side introduce shady ridges and valleys rolling far off in the distance.

About a mile ahead a sign emblazoned with a hiker marks the **Pinhoti Trail** *(accessible from several points along the byway)*. The 80-mile-long path winds through forested coves and past rocky streams. Wander a bit down

Along the Talladega Scenic Byway, Alabama

the trail—you might spot a wild turkey or a white-tailed deer.

Beyond I-20 and U.S. 431, the byway climbs the long slender ridge of **Horseblock Mountain.** Through pine forests, you have views of the rugged **Coosa River Valley,** whose gentle ridges mark the southern reaches of the Appalachians. Continuing south, the undulating byway passes Rte. 24, which leads west to **Morgan Lake** and east to sinewy **Ivory Mountain.** Past the Rte. 24 turnoff, the drive tackles the steep slopes of **Cheaha Mountain,** Alabama's highest peak (2,407 feet). On the mountain's wooded crest you'll find **Cheaha State Park** *(256-488-5115. Adm. fee),* a rustic haven with a restaurant, lodge, and rental cottages. From **Bunker Tower,** a 1930s stone observation tower at the summit, you can see peaks and valleys 60-some miles away on clear days.

Beyond the park, the road plummets 1,200 feet through the mountainous backcountry of the 7,490-acre **Cheaha Wilderness.** Continue on Rte. 281 for 7 miles, past signs for the turnoff for **Lake Chinnabee Recreation Area** *(256-362-2909),* where the 2-mile **Lakeshore Trail** circles the picturesque lake toward Turnipseed Camp. The drive ends at the parking area for the Pinhoti Trailhead at Adams Gap. A dirt road continues from here, but it is best driven with a four-wheel-drive vehicle.

Produce of the Cherokee foothills

South Carolina

Cherokee Foothills Scenic Highway

Gaffney to Lake Hartwell State Park on S.C. 11

● **130 miles** ● **2½ hours** ● **Peach bloom peaks in May; fall foliage peaks in mid-Oct.**

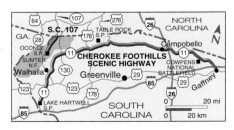

Following a path trodden by Cherokee Indians, frontier traders, and bootleggers, the drive ambles through Blue Ridge foothills, past peach orchards, soaring mountain peaks, lakes, and fish-filled streams.

Begin in **Gaffney,** one of the world's largest peach-shipping centers. Towering above the town is a pink-and-orange "peachoid." The million-gallon water tank is a reminder that this region produces nearly a quarter of South Carolina's peaches. As you head northwest from town, the flat, rural landscape is sprinkled with small homes, churches, and barns. Roadside stands sell peaches in summer and apples in fall. In the distance, smoky, forested hills darken the horizon.

At **Cowpens National Battlefield** *(864-461-2828. www.nps.gov/cowp)*, about 9.5 miles from Gaffney, a quiet green meadow commemorates one of the most strategic battles of the Revolution, where in 1781 American colonists scored a triumph in their fight for independence.

From Cowpens, Rte. 11 begins to roll gently, undulating more and more as the rumpled mountains ahead grow closer. Along the roadsides, ruler-straight rows of peach trees edge back into the hills.

About 9 miles beyond Campobello, the road passes just south of **Hogback Mountain,** then along the base of **Glassy Mountain.** You are now in the Blue Ridge foothills. A roadside mixture of rhododendron, mountain laurel, hemlock, dogwood, hickory, oak, and wild cherry guarantees an explosion of color in spring and fall.

A collection of gentle mountains older than the Alps, the Blue Ridge once towered as high as the Himalayas.

Crossing the **North** and **Middle Saluda Rivers,** the byway enters Cleveland, where a 6-mile detour on River Falls Road leads to **Jones Gap State Park** *(864-836-3647. www.southcarolinaparks.com)*. Here, in a pleasant wooded glen, picnic tables sit beside the clear, murmuring Middle Saluda River.

107

As the byway continues beside the **South Saluda River,** you'll pass the cars of anglers who congregate here to try their luck on the river, stocked with rainbow and brown trout. The 1,200-foot rock precipice protruding from a forested mountainside is **Caesars Head.** If you take a 7.5-mile detour up precipitous U.S. 276, you can walk out to its edge at **Caesars Head State Park** *(864-836-6115. www.southcarolinaparks.com)*. The sudden drop in elevation here provides a soaring view of the Blue Ridge and three states—South Carolina, North Carolina, and Georgia.

Back on Rte. 11, roadside stands sell hot boiled peanuts and quilts. **Table Rock,** revered by the Cherokee as the dining spot of the Great Spirit, hulks over the rolling landscape.

In the shadow of Table Rock lies **Aunt Sue's Country Corner** *(864-878-4366. April-Nov. Tues.-Sun.), a* quirky, old-time village of craft and food shops, where the

Caesars Head State Park

employees call each other "Cousin."

Table Rock State Park *(864-878-9813. www.southcarolinaparks.com. Vehicle fee),* 2 miles down the road, is the halfway point of the drive. The east gate leads to historic **Table Rock Lodge** *(864-878-9065. Closed Mon.),* famous for its spectacular views and country-style Sunday buffets. The west gate accesses **Pinnacle Lake,** with trails up the slopes of **Pinnacle** and **Table Rock Mountains.**

Forested ridges soon envelop the road, and the state's highest peak, **Sassafras Mountain,** towers 3,554 feet above the hills. Shortly after the junction with U.S. 178, **Keowee-Toxaway State Park** *(864-868-2605. www.southcarolinaparks.com)* straddles the road. To the left, a museum and interpretive trail with exhibits explore the history and culture of the Upper Cherokee, who lived on these lands until they were forced to move in the late 18th century.

Soaring across the **Keowee River,** whose forested banks were once edged by Indian settlements, the byway is soon intersected by Rte. 25, which leads 5 miles to **Devils Fork State Park** *(864-944-2639. www.south carolinaparks.com).* Nestled on the shores

Roadside offerings, South Carolina 107

of lovely **Lake Jocassee** against a backdrop of rippling mountain slopes, the park is especially popular with anglers and boaters.

The road dips and rises beyond Devils Fork through a secluded region, setting the scene for historic **Oconee Station** *(Right 2 miles on Oconee Station Rd. 864-638-0079. Thurs.-Sun. Closed Jan.-Feb.),* one of several outposts erected in the early 1790s to protect frontier families from Indians. The oldest building in Oconee County, it is also a state park. Not far ahead is the small town of **Walhalla,** its Main Street lined with

South Carolina 107

Oconee State Park to the North Carolina border on S.C. 107

● 12 miles ● ½ hour ● Spring through fall; fine spring bloom and fall foliage. *See map p. 106.*

Rustic and remote, Rte. 107 heads into the Blue Ridge foothills, climbing 1,122 feet in 12 miles. Along the way, side roads lead to various recreational opportunities.

Begin at **Oconee State Park** *(864-638-5353. www.southcarolinaparks .com. Adm. fee weekends Mem. Day-Labor Day)* on the wooded shores of a 20-acre lake. A mantle of loblolly and white pine, hickory, and oak drapes the road as it winds northward through **Sumter National Forest** *(864-638-9568. www.fs.fed.us/r8/fms).* In spring, mountain laurel, dogwood, and rhododendron color the understory.

Lake Cherokee, a mile-long lake surrounded by hills, lies 4.5 miles east on Tamassee Road (FR 710), an old Cherokee trail. The 43-mile-long **Foothills Trail** passes by the lake on its way through some of the most rugged terrain in the Carolinas.

Back on Rte. 107, you'll soon pass a pleasant picnicking and camping spot at **Moody Springs Recreation Area.** A mile beyond, a 3-mile side trip on Burrells Ford Rd. (FR 708) leads to the **Chattooga River.** The rapids-filled river, a national wild and scenic river, drops almost 2,500 feet in 50 miles. It's popular with anglers fishing for trout.

Ahead on Rte. 103, the road to the **Walhalla National Fish Hatchery** *(864-638-2866)* twists 2 miles down the mountain, following the **East Fork of the Chattooga River.** You can also take a walk here in the **Ellicott Rock Wilderness,** rich in old-growth white pines and eastern hemlocks. The drive ends at the North Carolina border, but the road continues into that state's rugged mountains.

majestic antebellum homes. Settled by Germans in the mid-19th century, the town was named after the mythical Norse paradise, Valhalla.

As the road veers south, watch as the Blue Ridge becomes more hazy and distant in your rearview mirror, then fades altogether. Soon you're back in the "down country," the same flat, rural landscape in which the drive began. The final stop on the drive is **Lake Hartwell State Park** *(864-972-3352. www.southcarolinaparks.com)*. Huddled on the shady banks of **Lake Hartwell,** the park features shoreline picnic tables, boating, and a nature trail.

Georgia

Russell-Brasstown Scenic Byway

Loop drive from Helen on Georgia 17/75, 180, 348, and 75A

● 38 miles ● 1 hour ● Spring through fall; fine fall foliage

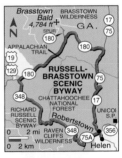

This drive travels through the forested foothills, mountains, and valleys of Chattahoochee National Forest, climbing to the top of Georgia's highest peak.

Begin in charming **Helen,** a former sawmill town that has redecorated its facades with a Bavarian motif and now bustles with German-style biergartens, inns, and shops. From Helen head north on Rte. 17/75 as it follows the headwaters of the **Chattahoochee River** through the southern end of the **Chattahoochee National Forest**

Autumn view from Brasstown Bald

(770-297-3000. www.fs.fed.us/conf), one of the most extensive and productive hardwood forests in the world.

Russell-Brasstown Scenic Byway

A mile ahead in Robertstown, you can detour 3 miles on Rte. 356 to the wilderness haven of **Unicoi State Park** *(706-878-2201. www.dnr.state.ga.us/dnr/ parks. Vehicle fee)*. The park's 7 miles of hiking trails wind into the surrounding hills. If you continue 1.5 miles farther on Smith Creek Road, you'll come to **Anna Ruby Falls** *(706-878-3574. Vehicle fee)*, where a half-mile paved trail through the forest leads to a twin waterfall.

Back on Rte. 17/75, the road now moves alongside crystal-clear **Andrews Creek,** wending through pines, poplars, hemlocks, and oaks. After 3 miles it ascends the rumpled slopes of the Blue Ridge. Along this stretch, you'll find a shady picnic spot by **Andrews Creek.**

The precipitous road crests at 2,949-foot **Unicoi Gap,** where the **Appalachian Trail** crosses on its 2,100-mile journey from Georgia to Maine. Just beyond, **High Shoals Scenic Area** has a 1.2-mile trail past Blue Hole and **High Shoals Falls.** Back on the road, turn left onto Rte. 180. This quiet country road climbs the lower slopes of **Brasstown Bald,** Georgia's highest mountain. You'll get a closer look at the actual bald—the treeless area on the mountain's summit—by following the Rte. 180 spur. From the parking area, you can either be shuttled or you can hike the last half-mile to the 4,784-foot summit, with a modern, exhibit-filled **Visitor Center** *(706-896-2556)* and a 360-degree view of misty mountain peaks reaching into Tennessee and the Carolinas.

Back on Rte. 180, the drive continues through some of Georgia's most spectacular Blue Ridge country, then enters a rolling, mountain-fringed valley. At Rte. 348 turn left on the Richard Russell Scenic Byway, which follows the headwaters of the **Nottely River.**

The countryside gives way to hills, then steep mountains, as the road climbs to 3,137-foot **Tesnatee Gap,** then to 3,480-foot **Hogpen Gap.** The steep, rugged drainage on the left is, appropriately, **Lordamercy Cove.** You are now on top of the Blue Ridge Divide; water flowing west from here drains into the Tennessee River and east into the Chattahoochee.

As you descend, stop at the overlook perched on the divide for a view of the wild backcountry of the **Raven Cliffs Wilderness.** Descending along **Piney Ridge,** with splendid views of the wilds to the right, the road comes to **Dukes Creek Falls** about 4.5 miles ahead, where a short trail wanders to an observation platform. Soon after, you turn left onto busy Rte. 75A, which leads back to Helen.

Ferns, Chattahoochee NF

Sea Islands

Jekyll Island to Savannah on Ga. 520, 99, and U.S. 17

● 81 miles ● 2 hours ● All year

So interlaced with sea marshes, swamps, mudflats, and sloughs is Georgia's shoreline that no coastal road exists to showcase its quiet beauty. The closest thing is U.S. 17, which, though it lies a few miles from the sea, swings to and fro through grassy tidal estuaries, pine thickets, and quaint shrimping villages. Along the way, causeways and bridges meander off to explore a few of Georgia's splendid "golden isles," a string of subtropical barrier islands that hold everything from posh resorts to the tangled wilds of coastal salt marshes.

The drive takes off from **Jekyll Island,** purchased in 1886 as the exclusive winter playground of 50 business magnates, including William Rockefeller, William Vanderbilt, and J.P. Morgan. Their luxurious "cottages" may now be seen in the **Jekyll Island Historic District** (*912-635-2236. Vehicle and tour fee*).

From the island, follow the Jekyll Island Causeway (Rte. 520) to U.S. 17 and head north across the **Brunswick River** to **Brunswick,** founded in 1771 and one of Georgia's largest shrimping and oystering ports. Brunswick's **Old Town** is lined with restored turn-of-the-century homes.

111

To the north and east of Brunswick lie the **Marshes of Glynn.** Beneath the marshes' soft facade of cordgrass hides one of the most biologically productive environments on earth, teeming with microscopic creatures, as well as crabs, shrimp, oysters, fish, alligators, and even bobcats. A short boardwalk at the marshes' **Overlook Park** *(Junction of U.S. 17 and Rte. 25)* provides a good vantage on marsh life.

Three of Georgia's barrier islands cluster together just east of Brunswick. **Little St. Simons** is accessible only by boat, but St. Simons and Sea Island are a quick jaunt across the marshes via the F.J. Torras Causeway. Before cross-

Springtime in Savannah

ing, load up on information at the **Brunswick-Golden Isles Welcome Center** (*912-264-5337 or 800-933-2627*).

At oak-shaded **St. Simons Island,** you can explore **Fort Frederica National Monument** (*912-638-3639. www.nps.gov/fofr. Vehicle fee*), a fortified town built in the mid-1700s to protect against Spanish invasion; **St. Simons Lighthouse and Museum of Coastal History** (*101 12th St. 912-638-4466. Tues.-Sun.; adm. fee*); and miles and miles of shell-strewn beaches.

Exclusive, manicured **Sea Island,** the next island over, boasts the **Cloister**

Georgia's Sea Islands

(912-638-3611), a Mediterranean-style resort dating from the 1920s, as well as Sea Island Drive, called Millionaires' Row.

Back on U.S. 17 you drive through a mixed stretch of urban development, backwater towns, marshlands, and woodlands full of loblolly pines and moss-draped oaks. Ten miles ahead, at **Hofwyl-Broadfield Plantation State Historic Site** *(912-264-7333. www.dnr.state.ga.us/dnr/parks. Tues.-Sun.; adm. fee),* rice fields crossed with dikes and floodgates testify to the area's rich rice culture, which flourished along the coastline throughout the 1800s.

The drive continues across the mazelike flood delta of the **Altamaha River.** Part of the 27,078-acre **Altamaha State Waterfowl Management Area,** the delta attracts herons, egrets, ducks, and other wading birds.

The Marshes of Glynn stretch in a serene landscape of swaying cord-grass and mirror-smooth ponds.

As you cross **Butler Island,** look on the left for the white house and crumbling brick rice-mill chimneys of **Butler Island Plantation,** a former rice plantation that is now a private home. On the river's north bank is **Darien.** A quiet town founded as a military outpost in 1736, it has gained renown for its annual April blessing of the shrimp fleet. If you follow the road immediately to the right, past the **Darien Welcome Center** *(912-437-6684. Closed Sun.),* you'll come to **Fort King George State Historic Site** *(912-437-4770. www.dnr.state.ga.us/dnr/parks. Tues.-Sun.; adm. fee).* This is a reconstruction of the British Empire's southernmost outpost, occupied by its troops from 1721 to 1736.

From Darien, U.S. 17 continues through the same coastal-plain scenery. Or you can take Rte. 99 (Just north of the McIntosh County Courthouse), a country road leading off to places like the **Thicket** *(5 miles north of Darien),* with its ruins of a sugar mill and rum distillery, and the shrimping community of **Valona.**

Rte. 99 rejoins U.S. 17 at Eulonia. Eight miles farther, another detour will take you to **Harris Neck National Wildlife Refuge** *(7 miles east on Rte. 131.*

912-652-4415. *http://harrisneck.fws.gov).* As many as 30,000 wading birds congregate here in late summer and fall.

Back on U.S. 17, the drive passes under I-95, and the scenery begins to fluctuate between interstate commercialism and timeworn towns like **Midway.** At the **Midway Museum** *(On U.S. 17. 912-884-5837. Tues.-Sun.; adm. fee),* you'll find colonial furnishings and documents. Next door, the white clapboard **Midway Congressional Church** *(Key available at the museum)* has stood since Massachusetts Puritans built it in 1792.

The drive ends 30 miles farther in **Savannah.** With its open squares, live oaks, historic inns, and flowering gardens, this city embodies classic southern charm. Along the restored **Savannah Riverfront,** visit the **Savannah History Museum** *(303 Martin Luther King Blvd. 912-238-1779. Adm. fee)* or tour the city's historic districts, dating from the 18th-century era of the cotton barons.

Seaside, Florida

Florida

Panhandle Scenic Drive

Pensacola to Panama City on U.S. 98 and Fla. 30A

● 103 miles ● 3½ hours ● All year

Never straying far from the Gulf of Mexico, the Panhandle Scenic Drive wanders by lucid blue-green waters and sugar white beaches, through live oak thickets and ubiquitous tourist strips.

The drive begins in **Pensacola,** best known for its nearby naval air station. The **Pensacola Historical Museum** *(405 S. Adams St. 850-433-1559. Adm. fee)* has exhibits that explain why this town has flown five different flags. A bit of the rural charm of the Old South can be found at bougainvillea-draped **Seville Square** *(Between E. Government and S. Alcaniz),* one of three historic districts.

Head east on Main Street (Bayfront Pkwy./U.S. 98) past Pensacola Harbor. **Pensacola Bay** shimmers on the right, and the road soon crosses 3-mile-long **Pensacola Bay Bridge** to Gulf Breeze. Here the road forks and you can continue east on U.S. 98, through the **Naval Live Oaks Area,** a trail-laced thicket of live oak trees that is part of the 150-mile-long **Gulf Islands National Seashore** *(Visitor Center, 1801 Gulf Breeze Pkwy./U.S. 98. 850-934-2600. www.nps.gov/guis).* Or you can pick up Rte. 399 to **Santa Rosa Island,** whose eastern end is known as Okaloosa Island. A barrier island that is also

Sunset over the Gulf lowlands

14

part of the national seashore, it offers unspoiled miles of live oaks, sea oats, and billowing sand dunes topped by miniature magnolias.

The two roads reconvene in the town of **Navarre.** From here, neon-lit hotels, roller coasters, beach boardwalks, and condominiums line much of the rest of the way to Panama City, relieved only by a few undeveloped beaches.

Beyond the town of Fort Walton Beach, U.S. 98 returns to Santa Rosa Island, where a recreation area on **Choctawhatchee Bay** offers swimming and boating. The road cuts through a pretty stretch of pine-dotted dunes with Gulf vistas before crossing the mouth of the Choctawhatchee Bay and entering **Destin,** a town popular with charter-fishing enthusiasts.

Beach at Seaside

As you continue to head east through pine thickets and urban development, small side streets wander down to lovely sand beaches.

Three miles west of Sandestin, you can detour onto Rte. 30A, a secondary road that angles 20 miles past lily-dotted lakes, pine thickets, and backwater towns. Highlights include **Grayton Beach State Recreation Area** *(850-231-4210. Vehicle fee)* and **Seaside,** a resort village with small pastel villas bordered by white picket fences.

About 9 miles beyond Seaside, Rte. 30A joins U.S. 98 for the last brassy stretch to **Panama City,** known for its 27 miles of beaches.

Southern Everglades

Main Visitor Center to Flamingo on the main park road

● 38 miles ● 1 hour ● Dry winter months preferable for sighting animals and for the relative lack of mosquitoes, but insect repellent and long clothing advised year-round. Birdwatching best at dawn and dusk. Adm. fee to park

A slow-moving, freshwater river measuring 50 miles wide and 6 inches to 2 feet deep, the Everglades crawls seaward through a horizon-wide landscape of pale green saw grass. The only place on earth where such a vast wetland exists, this is one of the best wildlife viewing areas in the country.

The drive begins at the entrance gate to 1.5-million-acre **Everglades National Park,** *(305-242-7700. www.nps.gov/ever. Adm. fee).* Established in 1947, it now ranks as the third largest park in the continental U.S. Just inside the entrance, the **Ernest F. Coe Visitor Center** offers park information, exhibits, and films on the natural history of the area. Heading southwest, the flat road arrows through the endless river of grass, where regal egrets poise stone-still to catch fish, and black-and-white anhingas perch in trees with their great wings spread out to dry.

After crossing over marshy **Taylor Slough,** one of many drainages in the Everglades, detour 2 miles to **Royal Palm Visitor Center** *(305-242-7700),* which is named for the palms that dominate the area. Here you'll find two trails that, despite their proximity, couldn't be more different. The half-mile-long **Anhinga Trail** wanders on boardwalks over Taylor Slough, promising glimpses of turtles, garfish, and an American alligator or two. Nearby is the **Gumbo Limbo Trail.** Also a half mile long, it leads through one of the Everglades' many hardwood hammocks. Raised just a few feet in elevation, the hammock provides a dry environment for a luxuriant forest of gumbo-limbo, strangler fig, poisonwood, and other tropical trees.

Back on the road, you'll soon notice slash pines dotting the saw grass prairie. Once covering much of southern Florida's higher, drier ground, the vast pine forests have

Nine Mile Pond

been lost to loggers. But you can detour 1.7 miles to **Long Pine Key,** an island of pines, saw palmettos, and hardwood hammocks, where a 7-mile network of trails weave beneath the tall, skinny trees. Or take the half-mile loop in **Pinelands,** farther up the road, where interpretive signs explain

Slash pines and palmettos

the pines' dependence on fire. Without fire, hardwoods would shade out the more fire-resistant pines and predominate.

Soon you reach **Rock Reef Pass,** a 3-foot-high limestone ridge that is one of the highest spots in the southern Everglades. Beyond it you'll soon spot a forest of dwarf cypress, a variety of bald cypress stunted by the area's poor, shallow soil. A half mile farther on at **Pa-hay-okee Overlook** (pa-hay-okee is an Indian term meaning "grassy waters"), a boardwalk provides a popular perch from which to study wildlife; an observation tower offers a perspective on the vastness of the swaying saw grass, which covers nearly 8 million acres.

From here, the road turns due south to **Mahogany Hammock,** where a boardwalk penetrates a cluster of mahogany trees that includes the largest living mahogany in the country. As you near the coast, the mixing of saltwater with the Glades' freshwater becomes evident as salt-tolerant mangroves replace the saw grass, palms, and mahoganies. The mangrove-filled estuaries produce a nutrient-rich soup, the food base for a vast variety of marine life.

Roseate spoonbills find dinner by swinging their spoon-shaped bills back and forth in shallow water to capture small fish.

The best way to travel the tangled, mangrove wilderness is by canoe, and several access points are found along the roadside between here and Flamingo. Along the way, too, are ponds that attract majestic wading birds in winter. Good places to watch for egrets, roseate spoonbills, ibis, and herons are brackish **Nine Mile Pond, West Lake** (which has a boardwalk trail leading through mangroves), **Mrazek Pond,** and **Coot Bay Pond.**

The road dead-ends in **Flamingo** on **Florida Bay.** Settled in the late 1800s by fishermen, plume hunters, and moonshiners, the small community is now the southern hub of the national park. It has a **Visitor Center** *(941-695-2945),* ranger station, motel, restaurant, and marina, where cruise boats depart for Florida Bay and the mangrove-tangled backcountry. If you haven't spotted a roseate spoonbill on your way through the park, stop at lovely **Eco Pond,** just past the motel on the main park road.

Roseate spoonbill

Bahia Honda State Park, Florida Keys

Florida Keys

Florida City to Key West on U.S. 1

● 126 miles ● ½ day ● Fall to spring; summers can be hot, bug-ridden, and subject to thunderstorms. The crowded tourist season runs from October through March.

Mangrove-fringed and water-bound, the Overseas Highway (U.S. 1) links a chain of subtropical isles that arc off the tip of Florida. Delving ever deeper into a tropical terrain, the route reveals a land of hammocks and reefs, miniature deer, and, at last, the fanciful, idiosyncratic town of Key West.

The drive begins a mile below Florida City on the mainland, where mile marker 126 starts counting down the miles to Key West. Following the former roadbeds and bridges of the Florida East Coast Railway, which was completed from the mainland to Key West in 1912, the highway shoots across the southern edge of the Everglades.

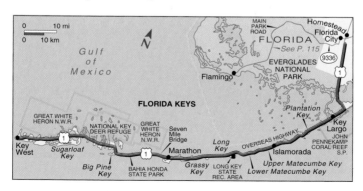

Southernmost house, Key West

A mile beyond **Lake Surprise,** named by early railroad explorers who weren't expecting to find it, the highway enters **Key Largo,** the largest and northernmost key along U.S. 1. Bustling with activity, Key Largo contains all aspects of the keys, from their rich tropical vegetation and opalescent waters to their billboards, dive shops, hamburger stands, and mom-and-pop motels.

At **John Pennekamp Coral Reef State Park** (*Mile 102.5. 305-451-1202. www.dep.state.fl.us/parks. Adm. fee*), the first underwater state park in the U.S., you can take snorkeling, diving, or glass-bottomed boats out to the lacy coral reef that parallels the keys' Atlantic shoreline from here all the way to the Dry Tortugas.

Continuing through **Plantation Key,** where pineapple and banana plantations flourished at the turn of the 20th century, U.S. 1 crosses **Snake Creek** on one of the 42 bridges that connect the keys. At Windley Key the **Theater of the Sea** (*Mile 84.5. 305-664-2431. www.theaterofthesea.com. Adm. fee*) features sea lions, sharks, and dolphins.

Islamorada (Spanish for "purple isle"), the only settlement on Upper Matecumbe Key, marks the beginning of the Middle Keys. The island's **Hurricane Memorial** (*Mile 82*) honors victims of the Labor Day hurricane in 1935, which washed out much of the railroad and was one of the most powerful ever recorded in the U.S.

Two sites can be visited off Lower Matecumbe Key. **Lignumvitae Key State Botanical Site** (*Accessible via boat*

Long a gathering place for writers, entertainers, and other members of the glitterati, Key West also boasts the country's largest historic district.

Little Palm Key

tours from Robbie's Marina. 305-664-2540. www.dep.state.fl.us/parks. Thurs.-Mon.; fare), an uninhabited 280-acre island, contains a rare virgin tropical hardwood forest that includes gumbo-limbo, pigeon plum, and poisonwood. At the **Indian Key State Historic Site** (*Also accessible via boat tours from Robbie's Marina. 305-664-4815. www.dep.state.fl.us/parks. Thurs.-Mon.; fare*), the foundations of buildings and cisterns from an 1830s wrecking village, established to salvage ships that had run aground on the reef, are still visible amid the tropical undergrowth.

At the **Long Key State Recreation Area** *(Mile 67.5. 305-664-4815. www.dep.state.fl.us/parks. Adm. fee)*, swimming is poor, but beachcombers may find the rubbery egg cases left by sea turtles. The **Golden Orb Trail** here leads through a delightful mangrove-edged lagoon.

The **Long Key Viaduct** sweeps toward tiny **Conch Key,** then Rte. 1 angles across **Grassy Key** and into **Marathon,** the heavily developed commercial center of the Middle Keys. Amid the sprawl is **Crane Point Hammock,** where you'll find a thatch-palm hammock with the combined **Museum of Natural History of the Florida Keys and Florida Keys Children's Museum** *(Mile 50. 305-743-9100. Adm. fee).*

South of Marathon, U.S. 1 crosses the spectacular **Seven Mile Bridge.** One of the world's longest bridges, it offers sweeping views of the open Atlantic on the left and the **Gulf of Mexico** to the right. On the other side of the bridge, **Bahia Honda State Park** *(Mile 37. 305-872-2353. www.dep.state.fl.us/parks. Adm. fee)* has white-sand beaches, rare in the keys. Satinwood, key spider lily, and other West Indian plants can be found along the **Silver Palm Trail.**

As the road pushes southwest, the keys seem more isolated and less populated. Bridges become shorter, and islands begin to merge. Eagles, falcons, and red-tailed hawks like this area, and it's not uncommon to see a large osprey nest perched atop a telephone pole.

Big Pine Key, unusual for its large slash pines, is the only place in the world where endangered Key deer live. Standing only 2½ feet tall, the dainty subspecies of the Virginia white-tailed deer might be spotted if you take a 2.5-mile detour onto Key Deer Boulevard through the **National Key Deer Refuge** *(305-872-2239. http://nationalkeydeer.fws.gov).*

For its final 30 miles, U.S. 1 crosses one small tropical key after another until it reaches **Key West,** an eccentric tropical town whose atmosphere is more Caribbean than American. Here, you can poke through the shops on **Duval Street;** see the southernmost point and the southernmost house at 1400 Duval St. *(Private)* in the continental U.S.; wander streets lined with fine Victorian homes and quaint white-frame "conch" cottages; visit the **Ernest Hemingway Home and Museum** *(907 Whitehead St. 305-294-1575. Adm. fee);* or simply soak up the town's distinctive ambience.

Sunset fishing in the Florida Keys

Great Lakes

Michigan, Ohio, Indiana, Illinois, Wisconsin, Minnesota

Michigan

Whitefish Bay Scenic Byway

Brimley to Whitefish Point on Lakeshore Drive, Curley Lewis Road, Mich. 123, and Whitefish Point Road

● 54 miles ● 2 hours ● Spring through fall

Tracing the shoreline of Lake Superior's Whitefish Bay, this lonely byway on Michigan's Upper Peninsula delves deep into the North Woods, where the air is fresh and wildflowers and white birch trees abound. Leaving **Brimley,** a commercial fishing and agricultural community, the drive enters pristine hardwood forest—mainly birch, maple, and oak, scattered with pine. Watch for black bears and, more likely, white-tailed deer. Periodically, St. Marys River appears to the right through the trees.

The drive passes through the community of **Bay Mills,** within the Bay Mills Indian Reservation, and arcs around placid South Pond. Just beyond town, look for Tower Road on the left. This 1-mile, partly paved detour leads to **Spectacle Lake Overlook.** And what a sight: glimmering Spectacle Lake, St. Marys River, and the distant Canadian shore.

Back on the road, the drive enters **Hiawatha National Forest** *(906-635-5311. www.fs.fed.us/rd/hiawatha),* an 860,000-acre preserve named after Longfellow's poem. A shady, mile-long side road about a mile ahead takes you to secluded **Monocle Lake.** The drive continues through the woods, framed by a constant profusion of wildflowers: white trilliums in spring, bunchberries and gaywings in summer, and blue asters and chickories in fall. A mile beyond the lake, **Point Iroquois Light Station** *(906-437-5272. Mid-May–mid-Oct.; donation)* comes into view. For 107 years, the light guided ships through the channel between shallow Point Iroquois and the rocky shore of Canada's Gros Cap. You can climb to the top of the 65-foot tower to view the headwaters of St. Marys River—the only passage between Lake Superior and the other Great Lakes. Down below, two rooms of a keeper's residence are preserved, and a small museum explains the light's history.

Palisade Head overlooking Lake Superior, North Shore Drive, Minnesota

Hiawatha National Forest

The road continues west through the town of **Dollar Settlement,** and a mile beyond, **Big Pines Picnic Area** offers a choice spot along a section of Whitefish Bay's 19 miles of accessible beach. The white sand is lovely, but Lake Superior—coldest of the Great Lakes—seldom warms to 60°F.

The road reenters the forest, now dominated by white birches. At **Pendills Creek National Fish Hatchery** *(906-437-5231. www.fws.gov/r3pao/pend_crk. Closed weekends)*, 3 miles beyond the picnic area, lake trout are raised to re-stock the Great Lakes. A half mile farther is **Salt Point** turnout, where the bay's turquoise waters lap against a gorgeous stretch of sandy beach. On calm days you can see the ribs of a sunken salt barge that washed ashore during a storm.

Farther west, occasional waysides permit closer inspection of the bay. The road then climbs away from the shoreline along the base of Naomikong Point, then returns to the bay. Near Naomikong Creek the **North Country National Scenic Trail** *(www.nps.gov/noco)* crosses the road, then follows it for about 4 miles. (When completed, the trail will extend from New York to North Dakota.) About 5.5 miles beyond, the drive leaves the water through a pretty stretch of trees to the junction with Rte. 123.

As you veer north on Rte. 123, the drive is straighter, faster, and edged with development. Bee-lining back to the bay's western shore, it crosses over the marshy, cattail-filled mouth of the **Tahquamenon River** beyond the fishing hamlet of **Emerson,** once a wild lumbering town. A picnic area here overlooks the river's confluence with Whitefish Bay.

Roadside shops sell fresh and smoked whitefish caught in local waters.

The drive continues through stands of pine, cedar, birch, and maple, crossing over Black Creek, passing through the village of Clarks, then on to the rustic resort town of **Paradise.** A beautiful 10-mile detour west on Rte. 123 leads to **Tahquamenon Falls State Park** *(906-492-3415. www.dnr.state.mi .us. Vehicle fee)*, which boasts one of the largest falls east of the Mississippi.

Continue the drive north on Whitefish Point Road, along the bay's northwestern shore. The road is narrower now and a bit cluttered with vacation cabins, but stretches of forest and water views remain pristine. About 10.5 miles north of **Paradise,** the road becomes twisty, and soon **Whitefish Point Lighthouse** peeks through the trees. Believed to be the oldest active lighthouse on Lake Superior, dating from 1849, the steel light replaced a brick tower in 1861. Fateful lake journeys are detailed at the **Great Lakes Shipwreck Museum** (*906-635-1742. www.shipwreckmuseum.com. Adm. fee*)*.* The nearby **Whitefish Point Bird Observatory** (*906-492-3596. www.wpbo.org. Mid-April–mid-Oct.*), only a few miles from the Canadian shore, is an excellent place to view hawks, owls, waterfowl, and songbirds on their spring and fall migrations.

Cherries

Cherry Orchards Drive

Cross Village to Traverse City on Mich. 119 and U.S. 31

● **96 miles** ● **3 hours (Add 36 miles and 1 hour for round-trip to Old Mission Peninsula)** ● **Spring through fall**

Prolific cherry trees, handsome summer resort towns, stunning fall foliage, and Lake Michigan vistas highlight this eastern lakeshore drive—a route once trod by Indians, French fur traders, and Jesuit missionaries.

From **Cross Village,** a historical center of Catholic missionary work, Rte. 119 begins a lovely 27-mile drive through oaks, maples, birches, and cedars, along an old Ottawa Indian trail sprinkled with secluded summer dwellings. It traces a hump of Michigan's rugged shoreline through an area known as *l'arbre croche*—the crooked tree, named by early voyageurs who used a lone gnarled fir on the lakeshore as a landmark. Only sometimes can you catch glimmers of Lake Michigan through the trees, but the dense foliage lends beauty to the winding road. Scattered pullouts permit longer looks at the lake.

You know you're nearing **Harbor Springs** when the road passes a golf course and opulent houses. The small downtown is a pleasant cluster of boutiques, ice-cream parlors, and fine restaurants. Nearby **Thorne Swift Nature Preserve** (*Lower Shore Dr. 231-526-6401. www.nature.org/thorne/ thorne.htm. Memorial Day-Labor Day and weekends in May and Sept. Vehicle fee*) offers a sampling of pre-resort Michigan, with dunes, wetlands, and woods of birch, cedar, balsam, willow, and quaking aspen. Rte. 119 wends southeast around Little Traverse Bay (you can't see it) and past **Petoskey State Park** (*231-347-2311. Vehicle fee*). About 1.5 miles farther south, the road ends, and the drive continues west on U.S. 31, past a fast-food stretch, to **Bay View.** Perched atop limestone bluffs overlooking Little Traverse Bay, the charming town was founded by Methodists in 1876 as a summer retreat. Leafy, winding streets harbor more than 500 Victorian "cottages" decorated with ornamental cornices and high gables.

Among early vacationers to **Petoskey,** west of Bay View, was Ernest Hemingway, who spent 20 summers in a nearby cottage and set many of his stories in the area. An exhibit at the **Little Traverse History Museum** *(1 Waterfront Park. 231-347-2620. Mon.-Sat. Memorial Day-Labor Day, Tues.-Sat. May, Sept., and Oct. Adm. fee)* honors him. Try to catch one of the

Little Traverse Bay

famous sunsets from **Sunset Park Scenic Overlook,** down by the waterfront. Beyond Petoskey, U.S. 31 follows the shoreline of **Little Traverse Bay,** then veers south where the coast dips into Grand Traverse Bay. A scattered forest of birch and pine fringes the highway, and in spring wildflowers carpet the roadside meadows. An **M-DOT Roadside Park,** 9.5 miles west of town, has a lovely picnic spot on a sandy cove, one of many along the lakeshore.

On Petoskey's beach, look for Petoskey stones—300-million-year-old coral fossils.

When you see the tip of **Lake Charlevoix** through the trees to the left, you'll know **Charlevoix** is only a mile or so ahead. Straddling a strip of land between Lake Michigan and Lake Charlevoix (the third largest inland lake in the state), the resort community—with its boutiques, restaurants, yacht-dotted harbor, and bluff-top cottages—has been luring wealthy families for six generations. You can catch a 2¼-hour ferry ride to **Beaver Island** *(Beaver Island Boat Co. 103 Bridge Park Dr. 231-547-2311. Fare),* the largest in a group of islands in the northern part of Lake Michigan, inhabited by Mormons in the mid-1800s. Today you'll find sandy beaches, hiking trails, and the **Marine Museum** *(Main St. 231-448-2254. Mem. Day-Labor Day; adm. fee).*

As U.S. 31 continues south, the woods give way to rolling farmland. Every now and then, the road crests a high hill, providing panoramas of shimmering Grand Traverse Bay to the west, with the forested hills of the Leelanau Peninsula beyond. Just before **Atwood,** you begin to see rows and rows of cherry trees. Temperate weather from the nearby lake and deep alluvial soil help this region produce more than 100 million pounds of cherries a year. The trees blossom beautifully but only briefly in spring; in summer you can sample the harvest from a roadside stand.

Just north of the town of **Torch Lake,** look for **Barnes County Park,** located west on Barnes Park Road. Here you'll find a secluded beach on **Grand Traverse Bay.**

You can get a close-up view of **Torch Lake**—a spring-fed lake once fished at night by Indians with torches—by detouring east from U.S. 31 onto Barnes Road, about 3 miles south of town. Ranging from pale aqua to deep violet, the lake is part of a chain of lakes created when glacial meltwater filled in the valleys. From here, veer right on West Torch Lake Drive, and follow it to Campbell Road, which takes you back to U.S. 31.

Back on U.S. 31, an **M-DOT Roadside Park** just 2.5 miles south offers a picnic spot next to serene **Birch Lake.** The road continues for 12 miles past more cherry orchards and farmland, through the former lumber towns of **Elk Rapids** and **Acme.** At this point, you hit the congested stretch, alongside beautiful Grand Traverse Bay, that leads into **Traverse City.**

From this lakeside resort town and host of the National Cherry Festival in July, you can drive out to **Old Mission Peninsula** on Rte. 37, a narrow ridge road overlooking the west and east arms of Grand Traverse Bay. The road meanders north through vineyards and the nation's greatest concentration of cherry trees, breathtaking in mid-May. At the end stands the 1870 **Old Mission Lighthouse,** located just south of the 45th parallel—halfway between the Equator and the North Pole.

Sleeping Bear Dunes National Lakeshore

Pierce Stocking Scenic Drive

Loop Road off Mich. 109

● 7 miles ● 1/2 hour ● Closed mid-Nov. through April. *See map p. 123.*

Winding atop sand dunes with gorgeous views of Lake Michigan, the Pierce Stocking Scenic Drive is an interpretive (and often crowded) drive across one of the nation's most fascinating landscapes. The centerpiece is **Sleeping Bear Dunes,** a 4-square-mile expanse of sand between Glen Lake and Lake Michigan. Created about 10,000 years ago, the dunes are the sand-covered remains of hills and ridges left behind when great sheets of glacial ice melted. Some are as high as 500 feet. Cottonwoods, junipers, sand cherries, and beach grass have since grown to stabilize them.

125

The drive's 12 overlooks and pullouts have plaques describing the region's diverse ecology. Highlights include views of **Glen Lake,** renown for its beauty, and the **Cottonwood Trail,** a 1.5-mile loop through the dunes with a first-hand look at "ghost" forests—clusters of trees buried by sand for a century or more, then uncovered by wind. At times, the road dips into lovely stretches of beech-maple forest.

The drive's history revolves around Pierce Stocking, a lumberman so awed by the beauty of the dunes that in the 1960s he built the road in order to share them with visitors. Today, the drive is part of **Sleeping Bear Dunes National Lakeshore** *(www.nps.gov/slbe),* which includes 31 miles of Lake Michigan shoreline.

Driving tour maps and other information are available in **Empire** at the **Visitor Center** *(9922 Front St./Mich. 72. 231-326-5134).*

Ohio

Covered Bridge Scenic Byway

Marietta to Woodsfield on Ohio 26

● 48 miles ● 2 hours ● Spring through fall. Heavy snows may close the road in winter.

The Covered Bridge Scenic Byway traverses a pastoral corner of southeastern Ohio through Wayne National Forest, either snaking along the muddy Little Muskingum River or climbing onto steep, forested bluffs. Along the way, tiny towns, century-old covered bridges, and weathered barns recall quieter days. But the starting point, **Marietta,** has bustled since its beginning in 1788 as the first permanent organized settlement in the Northwest Territory. After boning up on outpost history at the **Campus Martius Museum** *(601 Second St. 740-373-3750. www.ohio history.org/places/campus. Daily May-Sept., closed Mon.-Tues. Oct.-Nov. and March-April; adm. fee),* head north on Rte. 26 through Marietta's outskirts.

About 4 miles ahead, the road twists along a wooded ridgetop that overlooks hilly fields, deep hollows, and tree-covered ridges, then descends to the river valley floor. Along the river's floodplain you'll see small fields of corn and hay. Isolated oil wells, some of the nation's oldest, produce a few barrels each month.

Detour 0.5 mile east on Rte. 333 to **Hills Covered Bridge.** Built in 1878, it's one of the more than 2,000 bridges, covered to protect the main structural timbers from inclement weather, that once spanned Ohio's rivers.

Barns painted with catchy Mail Pouch Tobacco slogans dot the countryside, a post-World War II legacy.

Back on the byway, the **Little Muskingum River** soon appears on the right, in the shade of sycamores, box elders, and silver maples. The river's name is Indian for "muddy river." Popular in spring and fall with canoeists, the Little Muskingum also draws anglers with more than 40 species of fish, including spotted and rock bass and sunfish.

Continue along the river valley, meandering onto bluffs and through towns. Watch for **Hune Covered Bridge,** built in 1879. Cross it to hike part of the **North Country National Scenic Trail,** which one day will link New York and North Dakota. Though the byway leaves the river beyond Rinard Mills, you have two more chances to enjoy its serenity: at picturesque **Knowlton Covered Bridge,** built in 1887 and set in a tangle of wildflowers and native grasses, and at **Ring Mill** (follow gravel Rte. 68 east for 3 miles), a historical house and former mill in use between 1846 and 1921, with a lovely riverside park. Back on the byway, the road continues through hilly farm country. At the junction with Rte. 800, head north 3 miles to **Woodsfield,** a nice rural town at the end of the drive.

Farm country near Marietta, Ohio

127

Indiana

Amish Country

Elkhart to Lagrange on U.S. 20 and Rtes. 16, 250N, and 200N

● 28 miles ● 1 hour ● Spring through fall

This rambling drive across northern Indiana's Amish country features well-groomed farms and quaint villages, offering an intimate look at a religious community that thrives on centuries-old traditions.

From **Elkhart,** a manufacturing center with a Norman Rockwell collection at the **Midwest Museum of American Art** *(429 S.*

Main St. 219-293-6660. Closed Mon.; adm. fee), head east for 10 miles on busy U.S. 20. At Rte. 13, veer north into **Middlebury,** a town on the edge of Crystal Valley, the heart of Amish country. Amish families from Pennsylvania first arrived in this region in the 1840s, attracted by the rich glacial-till soil. Following the tenets of a 17th-century Mennonite elder, the Amish live, without modern conveniences, as productive farmers.

At East Warren Street (which begins as Rte. 16, then turns into 250N) turn right. Immediately you'll sense the change of scene. **Forks County Line Store,** on the left, has hitching posts for horses. Lining the roadside are barns with gambrel roofs and trim, white frame houses. Horses graze in lush

Amish washday

pastures, and corn, rye, oats, and hay grow in manicured fields. Be careful on this narrow road when passing horse-and-buggies. Three miles east of Middlebury at **Deutsch Käse Haus** *(219-825-9511. Closed weekends. Phone for cheese-making schedule)*, you can watch Colby and Colby Jack cheeses being made.

About 3 miles farther, you enter **Shipshewana,** the Amish market center with home-style restaurants and craft shops. At Van Buren Street (Rte. 5), turn right and head south. To learn more about the Amish and Mennonites, stop by the **Menno-Hof Mennonite-Amish Visitors Center** *(510 S. Van Buren St. 219-768-4117. Closed Sun.year-round and Sun.-Mon. Jan.-March; donation)*, just ahead on the right.

At the stoplight, turn left onto Farver Street (Rte. 200N) and head east, back into farm country. The road leads past **Wana Cabinets and Furniture** *(7245 W. 200N. Closed Sun.)*, custom builders of oak furniture. (More than half of the area's Amish heads of household work in factories.) **Babers Blacksmith Shop** and **M&M Harness Shop**, a mile on the right, are typical cottage industries. Three miles down the road you'll reach Rte. 9. Turn right into **Lagrange,** where the drive ends. Consider touring the **Lagrange County Courthouse** *(105 N. Detroit St. 219-463-3442. Tours by appt. Closed weekends)*, a marvelous redbrick structure built in 1878.

Ohio River Scenic Route

Aurora to Madison on Indiana 56 and 156

● 57 miles ● 1½ hours ● Spring through fall

Following the Ohio River for 57 miles of its 981-mile length, this well-marked route ambles across southern Indiana's bountiful tobacco region. From **Aurora,** whose steamboat legacy lives on at **Hillforest** *(213 Fifth St. 812-926-0087. www.aurora.in.us/hillfor .html. Adm. fee)*, a "steamboat Gothic" mansion, go south on Rte. 56. The road crosses Laughery Creek, then cuts through tobacco fields interspersed with corn and soybeans. Tobacco-curing barns, with slits in their sides for ventilation, dot the landscape.

About 8 miles ahead lies **Rising Sun,** platted in 1814 and allegedly

128

named for the spectacular sunrises over the hills in nearby Kentucky. Beyond town, the drive continues on Rte. 156, which follows the river's hills and curves. Though wide and serene, the Ohio works hard: Navigational dams enable it to haul more freight than the Panama Canal. Perhaps you'll see a barge pushing coal, oil, or sulfur from Pittsburgh—the river's birthplace—to Cairo, Illinois, where it meets the Mississippi.

Passing through the faded river towns of **Patriot**—beyond which the river swings westward—and **Florence,** the drive alternates between farmland and riverside bluffs and woods. Swiss wine makers settled **Vevay** (pronounced VEE'VEE), about 8 miles ahead, in 1801. The vineyards have vanished—the residents made a better living off tobacco and wheat—but more than 300 19th-century buildings still line the town's streets. Ask at the **Switzerland County Welcome Center** (*209 Ferry St. 812-427-3237 or 800-HELLO V.V.*).

Main Street, Rising Sun

Continue west on Rte. 56. About 5 miles beyond Lamb, the road climbs for a mile or so up the lower slopes of **Big Cedar Cliffs**—a twisty, narrow, stunning ride right beside the river.

Madison (*Visitor Center 301 E. Main. 812-265-2956 or 800-559-2956*), just ahead, was once Indiana's most prominent town—a prosperous 19th-century hub of riverboats, railroads, and wagons. Today the great antebellum mansions fill 133 city blocks. **Lanier Mansion State Historic Site** (*511 W. First Street. 812-265-3526. www.state.in.us/ism/sites/lanier. Closed Mon.; donation*), a Greek Revival edifice built in the 1840s, commands a panoramic view of the Ohio River and the Kentucky hills. One mile west of town on Rte. 56 is **Clifty Falls State Park** (*812-265-1331. www.state.in.us/dnr/parklake/parks/cliftyfalls.html. Adm. fee Mem. Day-Labor Day and spring and fall weekends*), a haven of deep-cut gorges, sheer rock walls, and waterfalls with hiking trails.

129

Lincoln Hills Scenic Drive

Corydon to Dale on Ind. 62

● **62 miles** ● **2 hours** ● **Spring through fall**

A scenic alternative to I-64, Rte. 62 bisects a portion of southern Indiana that Ice Age glaciers never reached. Instead, their torrential meltwaters carved out a hilly landscape of limestone caverns, deep woods, disappearing rivers, steep meadows, and broad lakes.

Snuggled in the Blue River Valley, **Corydon** is your starting point. The town's restored 19th-century buildings recall its place in history as the state's first capital. On High Street you can see the stunted trunk of the **Constitutional Elm,** beneath which the first state constitution was drafted in 1816. The drive leaves town through a mixed stretch of farmland, houses, and forested hills. Soon you cross the **Blue River** and enter Appalachian-like woodlands, thick with black walnut, oak, hickory, flowering dogwood, and sassafras. You might spot white-tailed deer and wild turkey. Walls of rugged limestone rise above the road as it winds among the hills. Near the

Crawford County line, detour to the **Wyandotte Caves State Recreation Area** *(812-738-2782)*, which showcases **Wyandotte Cave** *(Closed Mon. in winter. Fee for tours)*, Indiana's largest commercial cave with multiple levels and over 8 miles of explored passages.

About 4 miles ahead in the hilltop town of **Leavenworth,** the road curves, revealing a splendid horseshoe bend in the **Ohio River.** Leavenworth was down by the river until 1937, when a flood forced it to relocate. Beyond town, the drive enters 197,000-acre **Hoosier National Forest** *(812-275-5987. www.fs.fed.us/r9/hoosier)*, a favorite camping, boating, and hiking place known for undulating hills and sharp ridges. Once stripped of trees, the forest has been restored to its previous glory by the Forest Service. The road continues up, down, and around the hills, passing through the little towns of **Sulphur** (named for nearby sulfur springs), **West Fork, St. Croix,** and **Uniontown.** Far removed from large cities, locals live quiet, hard lives as cattle and pig farmers.

Just beyond the junction with Rte. 145, the road crosses the **Anderson River,** then continues through patches of corn and soybean fields squeezed into any available space between the hills. Upon rounding a curve into **St. Meinrad,** you sight the spires of the Benedictine **St. Meinrad Archabbey** *(812-357-6585 or 800-581-6905. Tours on Sat. except Dec.-Feb.)*, a Romanesque structure built in the mid-19th century. Its community became self-sufficient through farming and quarrying. The road continues through barndotted fields, and gradually the terrain flattens out. Coal and petroleum reserves are rich here—you can see oil pumps rising above the soybean fields.

The drive ends in the town of **Dale,** with several historical sites nearby, including a living history farm at the **Lincoln Boyhood National Memorial** *(2 miles E of Gentryville on Rte. 162. 812-937-4541. Adm. fee)*, which celebrates Lincoln's 14 years in Indiana, and the **Lincoln State Park** *(812-937-4710. www.state.in.us/dnr/parklake/parks/lincoln.html. Mem. Day-Labor Day and weekends in late spring and early fall. Adm. fee)*, where his sister, Sarah, is buried.

130

About 350 million years ago, a warm, shallow inland sea deposited layers of limestone, which eroded over time, creating southern Indiana's extensive cave systems.

Hemlock Cliffs, Hoosier National Forest

Illinois

Shawnee Hills on the Ohio

*Mitchellsville to Golconda on Illinois 34, Karbers Ridge
Road, and Illinois 1 and 146*

● 70 miles ● 1½ hours ● Spring through fall

Rising and dipping across southern Illinois's forested ridges and hollows,
this scenic byway reveals a rare midwestern pocket unscoured by Ice Age
glaciers, which stopped just 10 miles north of the Shawnee Hills.

From **Mitchellsville,** take Rte. 34 across rolling corn and soybean fields.
Within 5 miles, the road becomes steep and curvy, and the farmland gives
way to forest. These are the Shawnee Hills, also known as the Illinois Ozarks,
part of the nearly 300,000-acre **Shawnee National Forest** *(618-253-7114.
www.fs.fed.us/r9/shawnee).* Composed of sediments from an ancient inland
sea, the hills started forming some 70 million years ago when the continent's
crust uplifted. Since then, erosion has sculptured their valleys and ridges.

A few miles south of Herod, turn left onto Karbers Ridge Road, a quiet
country road (except during spring and foliage season) that roller coasters
through the forest. Watch for white-tailed deer,
foxes, and wild turkeys.

Three miles down the road, make a detour to
the **Garden of the Gods** *(2 miles N, follow signs.
618-287-2201).* A trail with boardwalks and rock
steps winds around sandstone towers, overhangs,
and balancing boulders that have eroded into
strange and beautiful shapes over the last 200
million years. Signs explain the geology. For
other intriguing rock formations and spectacular forest vistas, take the 2.5-mile gravel detour
to **High Knob,** about 2 miles farther east on
Karbers Ridge Road. Trails lead from the picnic
area to the bottom of the bluffs.

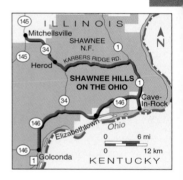

Back on the byway, you continue through the tiny town of Karbers
Ridge, with views of the Shawnee Hills. **Rim Rock National Recreation Trail**
(618-287-2201), just west of Pounds Hollow, wanders 3 miles through woodlands. The first mile has interpretive signs about the area's history and
geology. Down the road at **Pounds Hollow Recreation Area** *(618-287-2201),*
you can drive to 25-acre Pounds Hollow Lake.

The drive continues on Karbers Ridge Road to the junction with Rte. 1,
where you turn south into farmland. At the end of Rte. 1, about 13 miles
ahead, lies **Cave-in-Rock,** an Ohio River village with the river's only car and
passenger ferry. Follow the signs to **Cave-in-Rock State Park** *(618-289-4325.
http://dnr.state.il.us/lands/landmgt/parks/caverock.htm),* on the eastern edge
of town, where a short trail leads to a 200-foot-deep, cryptlike cavern overlooking the Ohio. A skylight carved in the cave's roof gives you a bird's-eye
view of the hideout used as early as 1797 by river pirates, who preyed upon

Illinois 34 near Herod

passing flatboats and keelboats.

Retrace your steps 2 miles north on Rte. 1 to the junction with Rte. 146 and continue west about 5 miles. Here, signs direct you (on a part-gravel road) to 160-foot **Tower Rock** *(618-287-2201)*, the highest point in Illinois along the river. A great view of the river and hills of Kentucky and Illinois awaits hikers at the top.

The road continues through rolling woods and farmland to **Elizabethtown,** poised on a rocky bank above the Ohio. The historical **Rose Hotel** *(Rte. 146 at the Ohio River)* is a gracious frame building that took in guests between 1812 and 1965.

Ahead you can take another side trip to the **Illinois Iron Furnace** *(3.3 miles N of jct. of Rtes. 34 and 146. 618-287-2201)*, built in 1837 and used for smelting iron ore during the Civil War. A trail along Big Creek points out natural and historical features.

Back on the byway, continue to **Golconda** *(Chamber of Commerce 618-683-9702)*, settled in 1798. At the foot of Columbus Avenue, a levee offers a superb view of the Ohio River and the Kentucky hills. Some 15,000 Cherokee crossed the river here in 1838 on their forced westward march, now known as the Trail of Tears.

The most scenic part of the drive ends here, though the official scenic byway continues south for 22 miles to the **Smithland Locks & Dam** *(618-564-2315)*. There you can watch barges pass through the lock—which lifts the river pool 22 feet, creating a 23,000-acre fishery for bluegill, crappie, and bass—and learn about river history at the Visitor Center.

Great River Road

Nauvoo to Hamilton on Illinois 96

● **10 miles** ● **¼ hour** ● **Spring through fall**

This shady, exceptionally scenic portion of the Great River Road in western Illinois closely traces the Mississippi River. The drive begins in **Nauvoo,** a clean, quaint town founded on swampy land by Mormons in 1839. Many 19th-century buildings still stand, including the 1840 **Hotel Nauvoo** *(1290 Mulholland St. 217-453-2211. Closed mid-Nov.–mid-March).*

As you head west on Mulholland Street, the **Mississippi River** shimmers at the foot of the road. You pass by the remains of the **Nauvoo Temple** *(217-453-2512)*, torched by hostile citizens who chased the Mormons west and murdered their leader, Joseph Smith. In a grassy park stand the 20 restored, redbrick structures in which Smith and his disciples lived and worked. Stop

by the **Joseph Smith Visitors Center** *(149 Water St. 217-453-2246)* for tour information and exhibits. Where the road veers south and leaves town, **Nauvoo State Park** *(217-453-2512. http://dnr.state.il.us/lands/landmgt/parks/nauvoo.htm)* perches on a grassy knoll. In addition to recreational facilities, the park has a vineyard and the **Icarian Museum** *(Mid-May–mid-Oct.)*, with early town artifacts.

The road immediately wraps around a wooded, undulating bluff. On the right is the boggy **Nauvoo Flat.** Soon, the rich bottomland joins the Mississippi River, here a wide stretch named Lake Cooper was formed by Keokuk Dam, the river's widest at nearly a mile. On the other side of the river, you see Iowa's forested bluffs and, for awhile, the Union Electric plant. The road follows a succession of bluffs, with the river to the right. Turnouts allow you to enjoy the view. In fall the hickory nut, maple, oak, and sumac trees turn scarlet, orange, and gold.

Mississippi River at Nauvoo

133

About 9 miles south of Nauvoo, the road turns sharply left, then right, veering into the town of **Hamilton.** Sometimes, especially on January mornings, you can see bald eagles around Keokuk Dam. For information, visit the **Alice Kibb Life Science Field Station of Western Illinois** *(Hamilton-Warsaw Road. 217-256-4519).*

Kampsville to Alton on Ill. 100

● 45 miles ● 1 hour ● Spring through fall

Following the course of the Illinois River to where it joins the Mississippi, this portion of the Great River Road (Rte. 100) ends with a wonderful drive along white limestone palisades. Begin in **Kampsville,** a tiny Illinois River town with intriguing exhibits on the region's prehistoric Indians at the **Kampsville Archeological Museum** *(618-653-4316. www.caa-archeology.org. Mid-April–mid-Nov.).*

Leaving town, Rte. 100 wends along steep limestone bluffs, draped with honeysuckle and wildflowers, on the western edge of the **Illinois River Valley.** After about 9 miles the road enters **Hardin,** the Calhoun County seat with two buildings to note: the nicely landscaped courthouse and the limestone jail out back.

Cross the river on Joe Page Bridge. The road jogs to the other side of the valley, edged with corn and soybean fields and roadside stands that offer peaches, tomatoes, and watermelons in season. A row of cottonwoods and birches down the middle of the valley is the only sign of the river now. Soon the road reaches the valley's eastern edge and veers south along its bluffs. About 10 miles ahead, you'll find **Pere Marquette State Park** *(618-786-3323. http://dnr.state.il.us/*

lands/landmgt/parks/peremarq.htm) and its scenic drive up the flank of **McAdams Peak,** with views of the valley. The rustic **Pere Marquette State Park Lodge** (*618-786-2331*), built in the 1930s, is listed on the National Register of Historic Places. Near the park's east entrance stands a stone cross marking the spot where, in 1673, French explorers Jacques Marquette and Louis Jolliet began their journey up the Illinois River to the Great Lakes.

Five miles south of the park at **Grafton,** the Illinois and Mississippi Rivers meet but don't mingle. One clear and the other muddy, they flow side by side for several miles. Here the road—now called the **Palisades Parkway**— squeezes between steep limestone bluffs and the Mississippi. Turnouts along the 14-mile stretch offer good views of the river. On sunny days, barges share the waterway with Jet Skis, motorboats, and sailboats.

Chautauqua, about 5.5 miles south of Grafton, is a national historic district dating from the 19th century, when it was a cultural center. Take time to meander through **Elsah,** just 2 miles farther. Tucked in a hollow between bluffs, the entire Victorian village, with its narrow, flower-lined streets and one-lane bridges, seems to have been forgotten by time.

A modern rendition of a fearsome Piasa bird decorates high rocks 2 miles before Alton, near Norman's Landing. A similar Indian painting impressed Marquette upon his 1673 visit to the region.

From here the road takes on a decidedly industrial character. In **Alton,** visit the **Alton Museum of History and Art** (*2809 College Ave. 618-462-2763. www.altonweb.com/museum. Tues.-Thurs. p.m. and Sun, or by appt. Closed Jan.*), with local artifacts and memorabilia of Mississippi River steamboat life.

134

Wisconsin
Kettle Moraine Scenic Drive

Greenbush to County Rte. H on County Routes

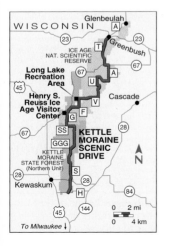

● 33 miles ● 1 hour ● Spring through fall. Open in winter, but icy conditions can make driving the many sharp turns tricky.

This northern portion of the Kettle Moraine Scenic Drive—part of a marked 120-mile route through southeastern Wisconsin—winds through wooded hills, ridges, and valleys that reveal a dramatic landscape sculptured by glaciers. More than 20,000 years ago, during the Wisconsin era of glaciation, two great wedges of ice—the Green Bay Lobe from the west and the Lake Michigan Lobe from the east— collided in this area. Eventually the mass melted, leaving jumbles of rock and debris as high as 300 feet. The drive traverses one of nine units of the **Ice Age National Scientific Reserve,** the northern portion of **Kettle Moraine State Forest** (*262-626-2116*). These units preserve glacial deposits and offer a roadside geology lesson.

From Glenbeulah, the drive wends south on Rte. A through farmland to **Greenbush,** a pleasant rural town. Here, the **Old Wade House State Park** *(Jct. of Kettle Moraine Scenic Dr. and Rte. T. 920-526-3271. Closed Nov.-April; adm. fee)* features an 1850s stagecoach inn. Take Kettle Moraine Scenic Drive out of town. The road suddenly climbs steeply onto the **Green Bay Terminal Moraine,** looping around the ridges that mark the farthest advance of the Green Bay Lobe. Covered with oaks, sumacs, and sugar maples, the enclave shelters deer, barred owls, weasels, red foxes, and more than 230 bird species.

Kames (conical hills), kettles (depressions), eskers (ridges or mounds), and other landforms along the drive demonstrate the awesome power of glaciers.

About 2 miles ahead, the **Ice Age National Scenic Trail** *(www.nps.gov/iatr)* crosses the road. When completed, this statewide hiking path will follow the end moraines of the most recent glaciation. The **Greenbush Kettle Geological Marker,** a mile farther on the right, showcases one of the area's deep ground depressions, formed when thick layers of glacier-deposited sediment settled over a melting ice block.

Beyond the marker, head east on Rte. 67, then south on Rte. A. The drive descends off the moraine into a glacial outwash area, a plain of sand and gravel (now covered with cornfields) deposited by glacial meltwater. These fine silts nourish some of Wisconsin's best farmland. The drive jogs across the flat plain then, after about a mile, enters the steep, wooded hills of the **Lake Michigan Terminal Moraine**—the farthest advance of the Lake Michigan Lobe.

135

At Rte. U, turn west. A quarter mile ahead, the **Parnell Observation Tower** yields an above-treeline view of the region. From here, the drive continues southwest on Woodside Road, Shamrock Road, and Scenic Drive, descending into another glacial outwash plain. On the left and right are examples of kames—steep-sided conical hills formed as debris flowed through holes in the ice, much like inverted funnels. Where Scenic Drive veers south, the road climbs through a stretch of maples and oaks, back into the hilly Lake Michigan Terminal Moraine, which it traverses for 2 miles or so.

At Butler Lake Road, head south, then west. The road climbs onto **Parnell Esker,** a serpentine, grass-covered ridge of gravel formed by a subglacial stream. The drive returns to the glacial outwash, passing Butler Lake and, where **Butler Lake** and Division Roads meet, **Long Lake Recreation Area.** The state forest service has worked to make this area a recreationist's paradise. Lakes, some glacial, offer swimming and canoeing; and woodsy trails through the moraines attract hikers, bikers, and cross-country skiers.

Follow Division Road south, then turn west on Rte. F. The

Above Kettle Moraine State Forest, Wisconsin

Fall foliage along Kettle Moraine Scenic Drive

massive hill to your right is **Dundee Mountain,** an example of a kame. Beyond the town of Dundee, pick up Rte. 67, which climbs onto the Green Bay Terminal Moraine. To gain a better understanding of the region's geology, go straight at the junction with Rte. G to the **Henry S. Reuss Ice Age Visitor Center** *(920-533-8322).*

As you head south on Rte. G, the drive descends into the **Jersey Flats,** extremely fertile farmland dotted with barns and cornfields. Turn east on Rte. SS to **New Prospect,** which lies on the edge of the Lake Michigan Terminal Moraine, then follow the moraine's spine south via Rte. GGG. Just before Tower Drive, the road crosses the Ice Age National Scenic Trail again, then touches an outwash plain. Beyond **New Fane,** continue south to Rte. H, the end of the drive.

Though the northern unit of the forest features the most dramatic glacial formations, the official Kettle Moraine Scenic Drive continues for some 90 miles south through populated towns, ending in the Kettle Moraine State Forest, Southern Unit.

Wisconsin River Scenic Drive

Sauk City to Prairie du Chien on Wis. 60

● 80 miles ● 1½ hours ● Spring through fall

This farm-to-market road in southwestern Wisconsin follows the Wisconsin River—the state's longest river, running 430 miles from Lac Vieux Desert in the north to its confluence with the Mississippi—through a region of rugged limestone bluffs and rich farmland. Beyond **Sauk City,** take Rte. 60 into **Fair Valley,** a narrow, steep-walled coulee carpeted with cornfields. The road descends past several sloughs, typical offshoots of the river's main channel formed by high water full of frogs, turtles, and snakes. Where the sloughs widen and join the **Wisconsin River,** you see the vast alluvial plain of the "river of a thousand isles."

In the valley's heart is **Spring Green,** a pleasant, elm-shaded town best known as the home of Frank Lloyd Wright, whose architectural philosophy—to meld the structure with its landscape—was partially inspired by the surrounding country-side. You can visit nearby **Taliesin East** (*3 miles S of Rte. 60 on Rte. 23. 608-588-7900. Adm. fee*), Wright's residence and studio.

Beyond town, the drive shoots 10 miles across fertile fields of corn and hay interspersed with copses of pine. Ridges stippled with oaks, maples, basswoods, and hickorys edge both sides of the wide riverbed, marking the level of the land before the river carved the valley. This

On the Wisconsin

region of limestone-capped bluffs, sand-stone outcroppings, and narrow wooded valleys—known as the Driftless Area—is the only part of Wisconsin left untouched by the last glaciers.

Just beyond **Gotham,** the road curves onto the lower slope of protruding **Bogus Bluff,** where local legend says counterfeit-ers operated in a cave before and during the Civil War. Soon, the Wisconsin River comes into view. With over 40,000 acres preserved for hunting and recreation, the river's lower reaches look much as they did when French explorers Jacques Marquette and Louis Jolliet paddled the route in 1673, searching for the Mississippi. Herons and kingfishers nest on wooded islands. Marsh-lands and timber stands shelter woodcock and grouse.

For 2 miles or so, the road twists along steep limestone bluffs with river views, then ducks into rich dairy land. The river appears again as the road enters **Port Andrew,** once the busiest port along the lower Wisconsin. You can picnic at a river wayside near the town's entrance.

From here, the road alternates between farmland and river-edged bluffs. West of **Wauzeka,** where the **Kickapoo River** spills into the Wisconsin, cornfields cover the flood-plain, now vast and fanlike. In the olden days, the smoke of stern-wheelers might be visible ahead, beyond the Mississippi River's hazy bluffs.

At Bridgeport, Rte. 60 joins U.S. 18, which leads to **Prairie du Chien,** a 19th-century river town 3 miles north of the confluence of the Wisconsin and Mississippi.

137

"The Wisconsin River is very broad, with a sandy bottom forming many shal-lows which render navigation difficult."

Father Jacques Marquette, 1673

Great River Road

Prairie du Chien to La Crosse on Wisconsin 35

● **53 miles** ● **1 hour** ● **Spring through fall. Excellent foliage**

Squeezing between steep, verdant bluffs and the wide Mississippi, this segment of the Great River Road (Rte. 35) passes through western Wisconsin river towns dating from before the days of steamers and Mark Twain.

Prairie du Chien, a former outpost for French voyageurs, takes pride in **Villa Louis** *(521 Villa Louis Rd. 608-326-2721. May-Oct.; adm. fee),* a fur trader's Victorian country house. The town sits 3 miles north of the confluence of the Wisconsin and Mississippi Rivers (see Wisconsin River Scenic Drive p. 136) on a heavily farmed terrace. Leaving town, the drive enters an area of cornfields, weathered barns, and dairy cows. About 5 miles ahead, it wraps around the base of high sandstone bluffs—forested with hardwoods—and continues on in their shadow. In about 3 miles the river appears, dotted with wooded islands that create a maze of sloughs, marshes, and ponds. The rich bottomland harbors 305 bird, 57 mammal, and 118 fish species. Protected by the **Upper Mississippi River Natl. Wildlife and Fish Refuge** *(507-452-4232),* it stretches 260 miles from Wabasha, Minn., to Rock Island, Ill.

Lock and Dam Number 9, about 6 miles north, creates a wide and beautiful pool that edges close to the bluffs, with the road snaking between. Similar pools to the north make this a virtually continuous lakeside drive. Over the next 40 miles, Rte. 35 passes through a string of fishing villages that are fun to wander through, including **Ferryville,** perhaps the nation's longest one-street village (more than a mile); **De Soto,** named for the Spanish explorer who crossed the Mississippi in the 1540s; and **Victory,** the site of the 1832 battle that ended the Black Hawk War.

Genoa, 7 miles north of Victory, was renamed in 1868 by Italian settlers, though the town little resembles its Mediterranean namesake. Just south, you see **Lock and Dam Number 8,** with an informative wayside park, and Dairyland Power Cooperative's former nuclear and coal-fire plant. About 2 miles north of Genoa, a climb up to **Old Settlers Overlook,** on a 500-foot bluff, yields a breathtaking view of the river.

The road continues through the town of **Stoddard,** with a river beach at **Stoddard Park** *(W on Center St., S on Pearl St.),* and by **Goose Island County Park** *(608-785-9770. Mid-April–mid-Oct.),* a recreational area on several islands. Five miles north is **La Crosse** at the confluence of the La Crosse, Black, and Mississippi Rivers. For a taste of olden days, catch a ride on a paddle-wheeler, or visit the **Hixon**

Lock and Dam Number 9, on the Mississippi

House *(429 N. 7th St. 608-782-1980. Mem. Day-Labor Day; adm. fee)*, exactly as it was in the 1880s. Or take in the valley view (with parts of three states) from atop 1,100-foot **Grandad Bluff** *(2 miles E on Main St.)*.

Apostle Islands Country

Ashland to Superior on Wisconsin 13

● 95 miles ● 2 hours
● Spring through fall.
In winter, when the average
temperature is 17°F, you can
walk to the islands on the
frozen lake.

Rte. 13 traces Lake Superior's southern shore, a remote North Woods landscape of windswept fishing villages and vistas of the low-lying Apostle Islands. Just west of **Ashland**— where the Soo Line Iron Ore Dock serves as a reminder of the area's mining and shipping legacy—the route follows Lake Superior's **Chequamegon Bay** north, its shimmering water visible through the trees.

Washburn, about 10 miles ahead, has an old bank building, courthouse, and other edifices made of brownstone originally quarried nearby and on Basswood Island, near Bayfield. In the 19th century Basswood stone was used in building construction all over the country.

The road moves on past farms cut out of the forest, their individualism expressed in the art painted on their barns—a rainbow stretches across one. Where the road returns to the bay shore, you can see forested **Van Tassells Point** ahead, a great hogback protruding lakeward onto which the road soon climbs. The drive continues through the hilly woods, with glimpses of the water and islands, then twists and turns back down the bluff to sheltered Pikes Bay. Across Pikes Creek, **Bayfield State Fish Hatchery** *(715-779-4021)* explains how lake trout, chinook salmon, and other fish are raised for lake stocking.

Victorian-style inns and shops signal the approach to **Bayfield,** a fishing and tourist village with fairy-tale mansions once owned by lumber magnates. Stroll along the deep-water harbor, where the **Apostle Islands** appear to float offshore. Most prominent are Madeline and Basswood, resembling green pancakes. For maps and information on boat tours, drop by the **Apostle Islands National Lakeshore Visitor Center** *(415 Wash. Ave. 715-779-3397. www.nps.gov/apis. Daily May-Oct., weekends Nov.-April).* **Red Cliff Indian Reservation** encircles the tip of Bayfield Peninsula, north of where Rte. 13 heads west. La Pointe Chippewa Indians have lived here since 1854, when a treaty giving them 14,142 acres was negotiated by Chief Buffalo. Beyond the town of **Red Cliff,** turn right on Cty. Rd. K and right on Little Sand Bay Rd. to reach the **Little Sand Bay Visitor Center** *(715-779-3459)*. Stroll along the sandy crescent overlooking the lake.

As they retreated nearly 12,000 years ago, Ice Age glaciers left behind the 22 Apostle Islands, where wind and water sculptured fantastic bays, red cliffs, and pink-sand beaches.

Back on Rte. 13, zigzag across the peninsula, then descend to Siskiwit Bay and tiny **Cornucopia.** Here, a 19th-century fishing village has been reborn with craft shops and a café. **St. Mary's Greek Orthodox Church** belies the town's Scandinavian roots.

Wetlands border the road west of Cornucopia, where **Lost Creek No. 1, Lost Creek No. 2,** and **Lost Creek No. 3** wander through a wide floodplain cut by a postglacial river and now drained by a river and a creek. Tiny **Herbster,** down the road, has a nice beach at the end of Lake Avenue.

Amnicon Falls State Park, Wisconsin

West of the small fishing village of **Port Wing,** Rte. 13 enters dense new-growth forest similar to what the first settlers encountered more than a century ago. The road crosses the **Iron River** and, soon after entering **Brule River State Forest** *(715-372-4866),* veers south. Watch for Brule River Road, which leads 4 miles to the mouth of the **Bois Brule River** at Lake Superior. Wisconsin's premier trout stream, the Bois Brule has been fished by five U.S. Presidents, starting with Ulysses S. Grant.

Beyond the river, the road dips into stream-filled valleys and climbs over high glacial hills covered with trees and wildflowers. After crossing the **Amnicon River,** look to the left for the green-roofed Davidson windmill, built in 1885 by a Finnish settler who hand-carved the gears. The last stop before Superior is **Amnicon Falls State Park** *(3 miles S on Rte. U. 715-398-3000. www.dnr.state.wi.us/org/land/parks/specific/index.html. May-Sept.; adm. fee),* where the Amnicon River tumbles through a red sandstone and basaltic lava escarpment. Ancient volcanic activity and thick Ice Age glaciers created this lovely landscape.

About 3 miles ahead, on the world's largest freshwater lake, **Superior** has the world's largest grain elevators, iron ore docks, and coal-shipping terminal. You can see them from **Barkers Island** or **Connors Point.**

Minnesota

North Shore Drive

Duluth to international border on Minn. 61

● **150 miles** ● **3 hours** ● **Spring through fall**

Skirting the jagged, glacier-worn Sawtooth Mountains, this winding road follows the rocky shoreline of Lake Superior, passing lighthouses and cascading streams and penetrating the only part of the continental U.S. where the northern boreal landscape thrives. The drive begins in **Duluth,** where you can obtain a free guide to the area from the **Duluth Convention and Visitors Bureau**

(Endion Station, 100 Lake Place Dr. 218-722-4011 or 800-4-DULUTH). After viewing the **Aerial Lift Bridge** and visiting the eclectic mix of museums known as **The Depot** *(506 W. Mich. St. 218-727-8025. Adm. fee),* pick up Rte. 61—the old meandering route, not the new four-lane expressway—and head northeast. Resort development sprinkles the first 30 miles or so, relieved by stands proffering wild rice and smoked fish. About 4 miles beyond downtown Duluth at **Lester River**—the traditional beginning of the North Shore—walks, overlooks, and stairways reveal the lake's immensity. In surface area, it is the world's largest freshwater lake.

> Lake Superior's volume of water—2,900 cubic miles—is greater than that of the rest of the Great Lakes combined.

Beyond Two Harbors the road climbs and twists among steep headlands, passing through tunnels bored through **Silver Cliff** and **Lafayette Bluff** to avoid the precipitous outer edge. Ancient volcanoes created the North Shore's bedrock, which was then sculptured by the same glaciers that carved out the Great Lakes. A remnant of virgin white pine forest is visible as you cross the **Encampment River.** From the Gooseberry River highway bridge, you can see the Gooseberry River drop 100 feet into the lake. This series of three cataracts, the centerpiece of **Gooseberry Falls State Park** *(218-834-3855. One permit fee good for all Minn. state parks),* is the first of eight extraordinary state parks along the drive. Though this sight is all most visitors see of the park, other highlights include the **Gitchi Gummi Trail,** with lake vistas and access to the **Superior Hiking Trail,** a 200-mile path along the North Shore's rocky spine.

The road continues east, crossing over Split Rock River to **Split Rock Lighthouse State Park** *(218-226-6377. Permit fee),* where a restored lighthouse sits atop a 130-foot cliff that juts into rocky shoals. First lit in 1910 after 215 men drowned during a disastrous shipping season, it now only serves visitors. The **Split Rock History Center** *(218-226-6372. Closed Mon.-Thurs. mid-Oct.–mid-May; adm. fee)* has exhibits on shipwrecks and commercial lake fishing.

Between Split Rock and **Beaver Bay**—one of the oldest continuous white settlements along the North Shore, platted in 1856—the terrain becomes more precipitous. But beyond the planned community of **Silver Bay,** the landscape softens, reflecting the widening of the Lake Superior watershed and the erosion of unforested lava flows. Just ahead is **Tettegouche State Park** *(218-226-6365. Permit fee),* with 22 miles of trails through mountainous hardwood forest dotted with lakes. One of the park's newest acquisitions, **Palisade Head,** rises 214 feet above the lake, with a spectacular view of the far-off Apostle Islands. Peregrine falcons nest nearby, and in summer look for blueberries in the scrub.

The drive continues across several rivers to **Taconite Harbor Observation Area,** where you can watch ore carriers load up. Just beyond Cross River, 3 miles or so farther, a road winds down a bluff to a windy peninsula, where you find a replica of **Father Baraga's Cross.** The missionary erected the cross in the mid-1840s in thanks for his safe passage across the lake in a severe storm.

Soon the drive enters **Superior National Forest** *(218-626-4300.*

Kayaker on Beaver Bay, Lake Superior

142

http://snf.toofarnorth .org), the heart of the boreal forest, characterized by mixed stands of balsam fir and spruce interspersed with red pine, white birch, and quaking aspen. Its inhabitants include moose, wolves, black bears, and loons. Nearby **Temperance River,** part of **Temperance River State Park** *(218-663-7476. Permit fee),* allegedly was named because no bar of sand blocks its mouth. Beneath the highway bridge, water crashes through a red rocky chasm filled with spillways and potholes, just before entering Lake Superior. Trails follow both riverbanks. Near **Tofte,** outcroppings such as 1,526-foot **Carlton Peak** break the gentle terrain. For a sweeping view of Lake Superior, hike to the peak top from a Superior Hiking Trail parking lot *(Look for the Sawbill Trail N of Tofte).* From up there you can also see how jagged the Sawtooth Mountains have become. Now paralleling the shore, their peaks have earned their name.

The drive continues through Lutsen to **Cascade River State Park** *(218-387-3053. Permit fee).* If you take a short walk upstream, you'll see the river dropping off a cliff. A bit farther and you'll find a rain forest setting, with water spilling over mossy ledges. A 2-mile stretch of beach east of the park is the best known place in the world to find thomsonite, a mineral that forms in volcanic rock. Beyond the beach, the road passes **Cutface Wayside,** featuring a massive lava wall with red sandstone deposits.

Grand Portage
Natl. Monument

About 5 miles ahead is **Grand Marais,** a resort town and artist colony at the base of a hill. With a picturesque natural harbor and lighthouse, fine restaurants and shops, it is the end of the road for most weekenders. But if you don't go on, you'll miss the most spectacular stretch of the drive.

A sense of remoteness envelops the road as it continues deeper into the realm of the early fur trappers and missionaries. Except for some ruggedness around Hovland, the road is relatively level as it crosses a series of rivers and creeks. Breaks in the trees frame Lake Superior to the right; calm and serene on one day, it may quickly release its legendary fury, thrashing icy waves against the shore. Just past the second intersection with Rte. 14, look for the "Moose Area" sign. It is one of the best spots along the drive to see a moose. Mile-long **Paradise Beach** *(No signs, but look for the pull-off near the small pond)* is a wonderful place to experience the area's solitude. Turn off the car motor and listen to the wind in the forest and to the lake's surf. Heavily forested **Judge C.R. Magney State Park** *(218-387-3039. Permit* *fee),* just 2 miles east, has the mighty Brule River as its centerpiece.

The road continues through Hovland and enters the **Grand Portage Indian Reservation,** an area where Ojibwa Indians have lived since before the fur traders. Beyond this point, geologic processes have created some of the shore's most spectacular mountains, ridges, and peninsulas. **Grand Portage Bay,** surrounded by jagged peaks, was the start of the historic Grand Portage between Lake Superior and Fort Charlotte, an 8.5-mile trail trudged by voyageurs and Indians to avoid the rapid-filled Pigeon River. Their story is preserved at **Grand Portage National Monument** *(218-387-2788. www.nps.gov/grpo. Mid-May–mid-Oct.; adm. fee),* a reproduction of the stockade of the North West Company, which operated here from 1784 to 1803.

Beyond Grand Portage, the road climbs several hundred feet to a crest near 1,348-foot **Mount Josephine,** which juts at a right angle into Lake Superior, forming a protective arm around Grand Portage Bay. From a scenic overlook you can see the rugged escarpment, Lake Superior, Wauswaugoning Bay, the Susie Islands, and, on a clear day, Michigan's Isle Royale. Farther north along the road, a state rest area *(May-Oct.)* overlooks the bay and offers regional information. Beyond, another scenic overlook shows you **Teal Lake,** lovely in autumn when birches turn gold.

If time permits, follow the North Shore Drive across the international border into Canada, where it officially ends at Thunder Bay.

Great River Road

Lake Itasca to Bemidji on County Routes

● 31.5 miles ● 1 hour ● Spring through fall. Roads part-gravel, part-paved. In winter, driving can be difficult.

Accompanying the fledgling Mississippi River on the first few miles of its 2,350-mile journey to the Gulf of Mexico, this portion of the Great River Road penetrates northern Minnesota's dense North Woods. Begin in **Itasca State Park** *(218-266-2114. www.dnr.state.mn.us/parks_and_recreation/ state_parks/itasca. Permit fee)* by wading across the Mississippi's headwaters—an ankle-deep brook gurgling over slick rocks from serene, pine-edged Lake Itasca. (Explorer Henry Schoolcraft is credited with discovering the headwaters in 1832.) Then hop in the car and follow Rte. 2 out the park's northern entrance into a rolling landscape of scattered birches and jack and red pines.

Mississippi River near Lake Itasca

For its first 80 miles, the Mississippi wanders northeast between two nearby watersheds, away from its final destination in far-off New Orleans. The Continental Divide, beyond which rivers flow north to Hudson Bay, rises a few miles away. Had the land been drawn just a bit differently, the river would never have become the Midwest's lifeblood.

Because of the river's finicky course, no road parallels its route across wetlands dotted with beaver dams. But 6 miles into the drive you'll cross the placid stream as it meanders through a meadow. At Rte. 40 turn right passing red barns, pine and birch copses, and dark, glassy lakes where you may hear a loon's call. About 2 miles ahead, the slightly fuller Mississippi appears beneath a bridge surrounded by cattails.

At the Hubbard County line, where the road becomes gravel (Rte. 9), is **Coffee Pot Canoe Landing,** one of five landings between Lake Itasca and Bemidji. To see the stream, follow a path to the banks fringed with alder, dogwoods, and reeds. Only about 10 feet wide, it resembles dozens of other streams that crisscross Minnesota.

For the next 15 miles, thick woods alternate with farmland. Erratics left by glaciers clutter the fields, showing the difficulties Scandanavian settlers had in tilling the soil. The road becomes paved again at the junction with Rte. 3, but returns to gravel along Rte. 10. You don't see the Mississippi again until right before **Iron Bridge.** Here, the floodplain widens, and the river flows more like a river.

The drive continues through farm country to **Bemidji,** the first northern town on the river, but among the last towns to be settled. Follow the pilot-wheel signs to the Mississippi River Bridge, where you find the Mississippi again at the point where it joins **Lake Bemidji** at the rate of 100 cubic feet a second. Assured that the river is on its way, take time to stroll along the lakefront, where 18-foot-high statues of **Paul Bunyan** and **Babe the Blue Ox,** the legendary lumberman and his pet, serve as reminders that this is a land that gives birth to giants.

La Crescent to Red Wing on U.S. 61

● 82 miles ● 1½ hours ● Spring through fall

Virtually every bend of this scenic stretch of the Great River Road (U.S. 61)—often compared to the Hudson River palisades and the Rhine River Valley—opens up a new panorama of the slow-moving Mississippi, buttressed between steep, verdant headlands. This portion of the drive begins in **La Crescent,** Minnesota's apple center, with the annual Applefest held in mid-September. Towering above the river on the Wisconsin side just beyond LaMoille is **Trempealeau Mountain,** the only rock island along the river's length as high as the surrounding bluffs. Pullouts provide stopping places.

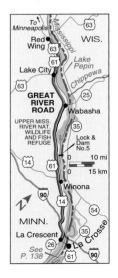

The 19th-century lumber town of **Winona** lies about 4 miles north on a giant sandbar, created centuries ago by the meandering Mississippi. During fall migration, about half of North America's canvasback ducks come to feast just south along the river. The road bypasses town, but make a point of stopping by the **Julius C. Wilkie Steamboat Center** (*1 Main St. 507-454-1254. May-Oct. Off season by appt. only; adm. fee*), whose reconstructed riverboat holds a museum full of memorabilia, and **Garvin**

Heights Park *(W of town, at end of Huff St.)*, with splendid river vistas.

About 7 miles ahead, the road hugs the bluffs and, beyond Minnesota City, rejoins the river. The drive continues past **Lock and Dam No. 5,** which has an observation deck, and the five prominent bluffs (including Faith, Hope, and Charity) of **John A. Latsch Wayside State Park.** Their bird's-eye views are accessible only by hiking trails.

A farm-covered floodplain announces the approach to **Wabasha,** sitting on a 12-square-mile area of bottomland forests, sloughs, islands, and marshlands that attracts eagles, tundra swans, canvasback ducks, and songbirds. In town, the gracious **Anderson House** *(333 W. Main St. 651-565-4524. Closed Mon.-Tues. Nov.-March)*, Minnesota's oldest hotel (1856), is known for its Pennsylvania Dutch food and bedtime cat companions.

Across the river valley from **Reads Landing,** Wisconsin's **Chippewa River** flows rapidly into the Mississippi, depositing sand to form a natural sandbar. The water has backed up, creating 22-mile-long **Lake Pepin,** which reaches as far north as Red Wing. A scenic overlook about a mile ahead provides a view of the bluff-bound pool, which the road follows for the next 8 miles. Jet Skis, sailboats, and motorboats coexist with traditional river barges. At **Lake City** the road wends by the river's largest marina and a sandy beach, then follows the river-lake for 3 more miles before veering away, through farmland. High atop the bluffs in **Frontenac State**

The Mississippi near La Crescent

Park *(651-345-3401. www.dnr.state.mn.us/parks_and_recreation/state_parks/ frontenac. Permit fee)*, about 8.5 miles ahead, trails offer sweeping vistas of sparkling Lake Pepin. Back on the road, the drive enters a hanging valley—a steep-walled hollow formed by the river's ancient meanderings. When you see **Barn Bluff,** rising 300 feet above its surroundings, you'll know that **Red Wing** is just around the corner. Famed for its pottery and Red Wing shoes, the river town has restored 19th-century buildings, including the elegant 1875 **St. James Hotel** *(406 Main St. 651-388-2846)*, where steamboat pilots once slept.

Central Plains

North Dakota, South Dakota Nebraska, Kansas, Missouri, Iowa

North Dakota

Kathryn Road

Valley City to Fort Ransom State Park on County Rtes. 21 and 58

● 33 miles ● 1 hour ● Spring through fall

Through the rolling farmland and forest of southeastern North Dakota, Kathryn Road (County Rtes. 21 and 58) follows the narrow Sheyenne River south from I-94 to Fort Ransom State Park. The road passes open prairies and Norwegian settlements dating from the 19th century.

Though you begin at the busy town of **Valley City** (pop. 7,200), the first several miles quickly immerse you in a landscape of huge dairy farms and grainfields. In spring and summer the roadsides bloom with wildflowers, and toward autumn vast fields are aflame with sunflowers, harvested for oil. Here and there, tumbledown farms dot the countryside, adding a melancholy note. While enjoying the pastoral scenery, be sure to watch for slow-moving farm machinery.

After 16 miles you can take a right to **Clausen Springs** (6 miles), a park offering picnicking, fishing, hiking trails, and a boat dock. Or turn left to **Kathryn.** Just off the main road, this tiny agricultural town has 40 households and a dirt-and-gravel main street with weather-beaten buildings that give the appearance of a Western ghost town. At the end of the road stand a fertilizer plant and a branch of Valley City State University.

Back on the road, follow signs to the **Fort Ransom Historic Site,** where a military post was established in 1867 to protect frontier settlements. The fort is gone, but worn earthworks are visible in a mowed field. Named for Civil War general T.E.G. Ransom, the fort was garrisoned for five years during the building of the Northern Pacific Railroad. With the railroad came more homesteaders and agricultural development.

Continue 1 mile to the town of **Fort Ransom,** which holds the **Ransom County Historical Museum** at the **T.J. Walker Historic Site** *(701-973-2651. May-Sept.; adm. fee)* and the attractive, white-washed **Standing Rock Lutheran Church** (1882). Outside town, the hilltop statue of a Viking pays tribute to Norwegian settlers who claimed that early Vikings landed here. Many area farmers still speak with Scandinavian accents.

Two miles farther on, 887-acre **Fort Ransom State Park** *(701-973-4331.*

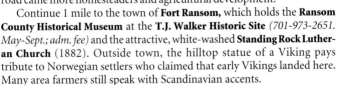

View from Chadron State Park in northwestern Nebraska's Pine Ridge country

Farm near Fort Ransom

148

www.state.nd.us/ndparks/Parks/FRSP.htm. Adm. fee) straddles the Sheyenne and features a dramatic overlook of the wooded hills, upland prairies, and farmlands stretching into the distance. Along the river valley grow bur oak, green ash, and elm, which blaze with colors come autumn. Among the park's many animal species are deer, fox, blue heron, and Hungarian partridge.

Sakakawea Trail

Washburn to Grassy Butte on N.D. 200A and 200

● 109 miles ● 2 hours ● Spring through fall

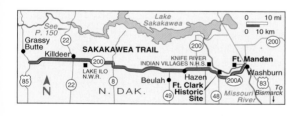

This east-west drive traverses the open ranges and rolling grainfields between U.S. 83 and U.S. 85, south of Lake Sakakawea. From the unspoiled banks of the Missouri River to the striking mesas and buttes of the badlands, the road runs traffic-free through scenic western North Dakota. En route, a handful of historic forts and Indian sites attract motorists hypnotized by the highway. Anchoring the drive's east end, the agricultural town of **Washburn** occupies a bluff on the Missouri, an ideal site for riverboat trade in the late 1800s. Two later arteries—the railroad and U.S. 83—have kept the town vigorous into the 21st century.

Head 3 miles west of town on Rte. 17 to **Fort Mandan** *(701-462-8535. www.fortmandan.org/fortmandan.html. Visitor Center mid-May–mid-Oct.),* which commemorates the 1804-05 winter quarters of Lewis and Clark. The site has a reproduction of the wooden fort the explorers stayed in on their way up the Missouri. Here, Sakakawea, the "bird woman" who helped guide the expedition to the Pacific coast, gave birth to a son.

Back in Washburn on Rte. 200A, take the bridge across the broad Missouri. The picture is not so different from what Lewis and Clark saw. Sandbars may have shifted over the years, but the tree-lined shores remain undeveloped in this area of long, severe winters. Summers carpet the lumpy hills in shades of brown and green.

Fishing Lake Sakakawea

Continue west on Rte. 200A for 10 miles, past rolling ranchland and fields of corn, wheat, and hay. Soon you begin to see the kinds of mesas and buttes that become more and more prominent as you travel west. Along here too you get glimpses of the scenic Missouri out your right window. About 3 miles after the Arroda Lakes, turn right to the **Fort Clark Historic Site** *(701-328-2666. www.state.nd.us/hist/sitelist.htm#clark. Mid-May–mid-Sept.).* Nothing remains of the fort on this deserted, windswept prairie. On-site brochures and plaques detail the history of the fur-trading post that operated on the river here from 1831 to 1860. Passengers on one steamboat brought smallpox, nearly wiping out the local Mandan Indians.

To learn more about the area's Native Americans, travel 8 miles west to the **Knife River Indian Villages National Historic Site** *(701-745-3309. www.nps.gov/knri).* An interpretive center traces the life of the Hidatsa through artifacts, exhibits, and a full-size reproduction of an earth lodge. Ground depressions offer evidence of the Mandan and Hidatsa villages that thrived here from the early 16th century to the late 19th century.

149

Over the next 40 miles the drive, now Rte. 200, opens up to huge, lump-in-the-throat panoramas of rolling farmlands. And along here small towns such as **Hazen** and **Beulah** stoke the fires of local industry. Miners extract lignite coal from the hills, which is then turned into gas or burned in one of six area electric power plants.

The western part of the drive takes you past beautiful gulches and buttes that become deeper and taller the farther west you go. Late afternoon light etches these landforms into striking relief, and breezes make the tall prairie grass shimmer like swells on an ocean.

Though the ocean is far away, drive 1.5 miles west of Dunn Center to see flocks of waterfowl on their semiannual layovers at the **Lake Ilo National Wildlife Refuge** *(701-548-8110. Headquarters closed weekends).* The 4,043-acre refuge provides feeding and nesting grounds for up to 20,000 birds each spring, including herons and Canada geese. A few miles beyond, in the mining town of Killdeer, is the start of another scenic drive, North Dakota 22 (see page 150). Or follow Rte. 200 20 miles to the intersection with U.S. 85, near Grassy Butte.

The Lake Ilo area has produced an astounding cache of prehistoric human artifacts, especially stone tools.

Lake Sakakawea

North Dakota 22

Killdeer to New Town

● **64 miles** ● **1½ hours** ● **Spring through fall**

A road noticed by few outsiders, Rte. 22 dips and curves over the rumpled hills of the western part of the state. Several highlights make the excursion well worth your while, and in between you'll feast on vistas that seem to go on forever.

Start out from **Killdeer,** home to cowboys and coal miners. Oil wells used to dot the nearby landscape, but many have recently been played out. Be sure to gas up in town since there's not another drop to be found until Mandaree, 37 miles north.

Two miles north you can take a 14-mile roundtrip to the **Killdeer Battlefield State Historic Site,** but you'll find only a marker. Better to drive on, observing the **Killdeer Mountains** to the west and noting that here, on July 28, 1864, Gen. Alfred Sully with 2,200 troops dispersed a Sioux encampment of some 6,000 warriors in retaliation for an uprising in Minnesota.

Drive northward 12 miles or so past dun hayfields, and suddenly you approach the badlands. For a closer look at the stunning scenery, turn right 15 miles after Killdeer Battlefield turnoff and drive 2 miles on a gravel road to **Little Missouri State Park** *(701-328-5357. www.ndparks.com/Parks/Little_Mo/ Home.htm. Vehicle fee).* The striated knobs and pinnacles and the beehive-shaped masses of stone resulted from the erosion of crumbly sedimentary rock deposited millions of years ago by streams flowing from the young Rocky Mountains. This 5,700-acre park offers horseback riding *(May-Oct.),* hiking trails, and camping.

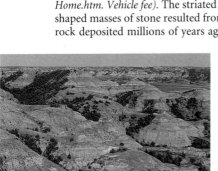

Little Missouri State Park

A bridge across the **Little Missouri River,** a few miles north, replaces the **Lost Bridge,** which provided passage to ranchers on their way from winter camps in the bottomlands to their ranches around the mountains.

After crossing the Little Missouri, you are on the **Fort Berthold Indian Reservation,** inhabited by the Hidatsa, Arikara, and Mandan. The 450,000-acre reservation was partially flooded by the creation of Lake Sakakawea in the early 1950s. Cattle and horses graze the wide pastures on this beautiful, rugged land.

Continue north through the reservation about 25 miles until the highway ends at Rte. 23. Head east on Rte. 23 about 7 miles to **Four Bears Memorial Park,** which was named for a Mandan chief and honors local Indians who died in conflicts from World War I to Vietnam. An A-frame houses the **Three Tribes Museum** *(701-627-4477. www.ndlewisandclark.com/sites/ 3tribes.html. Adm. fee),* a good introduction to tribal history and culture.

See P. 148

Next door, the **Four Bears Casino and Lodge** offers slot machines, video poker, and blackjack tables.

Cross **Four Bears Bridge** and turn left at the historical site marker for **Crow Flies High Butte.** This spectacular panorama of sparkling water and rolling hills came about in 1955 when the Garrison Dam backed up the Missouri and made 178-mile-long **Lake Sakakawea.** The dam protects downstream states from flooding and provides water for irrigation, navigation, and electricity. Buildings from the town of Old Sanish (now a bay) were moved east to what is now known as **New Town.** It has motels, restaurants, and gas stations.

Oxbow Overlook Scenic Drive

Theodore Roosevelt National Park (North Unit)

● 14 miles ● ¾ hour ● Spring through fall

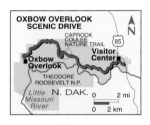

Meandering through the magnificent badlands of western North Dakota so beloved by Theodore Roosevelt, this park road traverses the length of the 24,000-acre North Unit of the **Theodore Roosevelt National Park** *(701-842-2333. www.nps.gov/ thro. Adm fee).* Traffic tends to be light for a national park, and you have ample opportunities for viewing wide prairies, wildlife, and the wonderful badlands rock formations. Pullouts en route have interpretive plaques and hiking trails.

The drive begins at the **Visitor Center,** a worthwhile stop with good displays and films and a friendly staff. The park was named for the man whose experiences in North Dakota helped mold him into a world leader. Roosevelt first visited the badlands in 1883 to hunt bison and other big game. A vigorous conservationist, he set aside a tremendous amount of land for parks, forests, and wildlife refuges during his terms as President (1901-09).

The **Longhorn Pullout** (Mile 2) is situated on the edge of a prairie where a small herd of longhorn steers graze. Longhorn in the area date from an 1884 Texas trail drive that pushed 4,000 head into an open range vacated by dwindling bison. Thousands of longhorn followed in subsequent drives, but in 20 years they too had gone, victims of overgrazing and hard winters.

The scenery that captured Roosevelt's imagination is evident at every

151

Little Missouri River from River Bend Overlook

When his mother and wife died within hours of each other in 1884, Theodore Roosevelt sought the solace of a strenuous life, returning to North Dakota to become a rancher.

bend in the road. Climbing through hills laced with juniper trees, the road soars above the canyons and draws characteristic of the badlands. Watch for wildlife, often not far from the road—mule deer, prairie dogs, bison, and more. The **Caprock Coulee Nature Trail** (Mile 6) takes about an hour (or longer if you make a loop) and offers an up-close examination of the local geology. Interpretive brochures are available at the trailhead.

River Bend Overlook (about Mile 8) affords splendid views of peaks and rounded buttes and the cottonwood-lined Little Missouri far below. The multicolored rock formations are layers of sandstone, clay, shale, and petrified wood deposited millions of years ago. Easily eroded by the elements, the rocks have become infinitely varied in shape—from drip castles to capped pillars and buttes. In 1864 Gen. Alfred Sully described the region as "hell with the fires out." The fires sometimes still burn when seams of lignite coal catch fire from lightning and bake the surrounding clay into a sienna red substance.

The road ends at **Oxbow Overlook,** another breathtaking vantage point. Here you can see where the Little Missouri once flowed north toward Hudson Bay. Forced by a glacier to find a new course, the river turned east and began running to the Mississippi during the last ice age.

152

South Dakota

Black Hills

Spiderwort

Devils Tower Junction, Wyoming, to Custer, South Dakota, on U.S. 385, 85, 14A; Wyo. 24; and S.D. 34

● 155 miles ● 4 hours ● All year

A crescent-shaped drive around the famous Black Hills of western South Dakota, this route connects five different highways in two states. Highlights include natural landmarks, historic mining towns, and views varying from immense rolling ranches to the pine-covered mountains and upthrust granite of the Black Hills.

From Devils Tower Junction, Wyoming, travel north on Rte. 24 through rugged rangeland toward **Devils Tower National Monument** (*307-467-5283. www.nps .gov/deto. Adm. fee).* Winding through this first section of the drive, you see big red capstones and beautifully exposed red clay hills. After about 3 miles you also glimpse

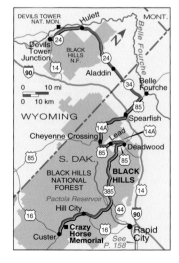

See P. 158

Black Hills National Forest, South Dakota

153

Devils Tower sprouting from the landscape. This stone monolith, a 60-million-year-old fountain of magma that cooled and fractured into long columns, rises 867 feet from its base. Indian legend maintains the tower was the stump of a great tree clawed by a bear.

The entrance to the monument lies 6 miles from U.S. 14. A road through the monument grounds passes a prairie dog community and ends at the **Visitor Center,** where a 1.3-mile trail circles the tower and provides great views of rock climbers scaling the heights. Bring binoculars.

Continue north on Rte. 24 past ranchlands that open out to a backdrop of rocky hills stippled with pines. Sheep and cattle graze the abundant grasslands. In 10 miles you go through the cowboy and logging town of **Hulett,** where the road begins to climb to an upland forest of tall pines and hardwoods. The signature dark green ponderosa pines cover the landscape so thickly that from a distance the hills look black—hence the area's name. The jagged schist and granite outcroppings that punctuate the hills were exposed millions of years ago when overlying sedimentary layers began eroding away.

The whole **Black Hills** area roughly describes an oval—120 miles north to south and 50 miles west to east—with the highest, and oldest, rocks in the center. To the Indians the Paha Sapa, or Black Hills, were a sacred place. By the 1840s trappers and traders had infiltrated the region, and the discovery of gold brought a wave of white settlers. Today, though altered, the Black Hills continue to give of their richness and beauty.

After Hulett, Rte. 24 veers east through forests and meadows. In about 20 miles watch for a sign that marks Lt. Col. George A. Custer's 1874 expedition into the Black Hills. With 1,000 men, 110 wagons, and 200 animals, Custer's survey team marched through here to verify rumors of gold. Ruts from the expedition remain just off the highway.

Not much remains of **Aladdin,** 4 miles farther on, other than a saloon and a century-old general store. Just east of town, the **Aladdin Tipple**

Historical Park *(Info at Aladdin Store 307-896-2226)* recounts the coal-mining heyday of the area, which at its peak supported 500 people. The site preserves a turn-of-the-century mine shaft and wooden coal chute.

Crossing the South Dakota state line, Rte. 24 becomes Rte. 34. In 10 miles you'll be near **Belle Fourche,** a sheep and cattle shipping center. The fertile valley of the **Belle Fourche** ("beautiful fork") **River,** named by French trappers, has long supported the area's large farms.

Head 10 miles south on U.S. 85 to **Spearfish**, home of the popular Black Hills Passion Play. While in town, visit the **High Plains Heritage**

Belle Fourche River and Devils Tower

Center Museum *(825 Heritage Dr. 605-642-WEST. www.members.mato.com/hpmuseum. Adm. fee),* with Western art and artifacts. The Spearfish Canyon Scenic Byway (U.S. 14A) leads you southward out of town, following lovely **Spearfish Creek,** which flows north. Modern fishermen, though not equipped with spears, find this stream burgeoning with trout. Waterfalls and high rock walls make this a picturesque drive.

At Cheyenne Crossing take U.S. 85 north up out of the canyon to the little mining town of **Lead** (Leed). Perched on a steep hill, Lead owes its existence to the 1876 gold rush. The **Homestake Gold Mine** *(605-584-3110. www.homestake.com. Adm. fee),* still in operation after some 120 years, yields more than 350,000 ounces of gold a year. Lead's steep slopes and 5,400-foot elevation also attract skiers and other winter sports enthusiasts.

> Visitors gravitate to Devils Tower much the way the aliens did in Steven Spielberg's *Close Encounters of the Third Kind.*

The road now descends precipitously 4 miles down into shadowy **Deadwood Gulch.** The town of **Deadwood** sprang to life soon after the discovery of gold nearby, when hundreds of people flooded into the area and began panning and sluicing the creek and then dynamiting the hills. By 1877 the government had imposed a treaty that forced the Sioux to sell the Black Hills.

Deadwood's downtown buildings of brick and stone maintain a solidly Western flavor with their flat facades and ornate rooflines. Wild Bill Hickok was shot dead in a saloon here in 1876. The **History and Information Center** *(3 Siever St. 605-578-2507),* in the old railroad depot, has exhibits and a brochure for a walking tour that takes you along three blocks of Main Street, where the clinks and beeps of more than 40 casinos keep Deadwood alive at all hours. Legalized in 1989, gambling has turned the town again into a frenzy of small-time speculation.

Backtrack on U.S. 85 up the forested hills from Deadwood and veer south on U.S. 385. After about 30 miles, just after the turnoff for Rte. 44, you'll see **Pactola Reservoir,** created by a dam on Rapid Creek. **The Black Hills National Forest** *(605-673-2251. www.fs.fed.us/outernet/bhnf)* maintains a Visitor Center here.

Back on the road, travel southward through a long stretch of dips and rises offering yet more beautiful views of the pine-covered hills and the exposed peaks looking like whitecaps on a dark sea. The highway passes towering stone cliffs near the small town of **Hill City** (4,980 feet), which has camping areas, motels, and a menu of trailheads.

About 8 miles later you pass **Crazy Horse Memorial** *(605-673-4681. www .crazyhorse.org. Adm. fee),* where the sculpture of the Sioux leader on horseback continues to emerge. For the best views of the Crazy Horse project, you must pay to enter the grounds. Ambitious work remains to be done. Begun in 1948 by the late Korczak Ziolkowski, the monumental tribute is being chiseled from the mountain under the direction of Ziolkowski's family.

Continue south about 6 miles to the town of **Custer,** where George Custer's 1874 expedition found gold nearby and precipitated a rush. The population quickly rose, then plunged as more gold was discovered in the northern Black Hills. But enough people stayed to establish a town. Today tourism, lumbering, ranching, and mining support the economy.

Peter Norbeck Scenic Byway

Loop from Custer past Mount Rushmore on U.S. 16A, Iron Mountain Road, and S.D. 244, 87, and 89

● 56 miles (add 18 miles for Custer State Park Wildlife Loop Road) ● 3 hours ● Iron Mountain Road is closed in winter.

This loop through the Black Hills offers an ever changing backdrop of close-up and distant views. It takes in the gentle prairie and diverse wildlife of Custer State Park, climbs Iron Mountain Road for spectacular views of Mount Rushmore, passes mountain lakes, and descends back to the historic town of Custer. Named after Peter Norbeck, a South Dakota governor and senator who guided the building of the road in the 1920s, the byway offers some of the best touring in the Black Hills.

Heading east from **Custer** on U.S. 16A, you'll pass forested hills and RV parks alternating with open meadows and ranchlands. In a few miles you enter **Custer State Park** *(605-255-4515. www.state.sd.us/sdparks/custer/custer.htm. Adm. fee).* Two jewel-like lakes near the entrance— **Bismark** and **Stockade**—offer swimming, fishing, boating, and camping; more camping is available a little farther down the road at **Legion Lake.** Beside Stockade Lake stands a reproduction of **Gordon Stockade,** where a

Granite Presidents' heads, Mount Rushmore

party of 27 gold prospectors spent the winter of 1874-75 in defiance of the U.S. Cavalry, which was trying to maintain the Fort Laramie Treaty by keeping the area free of white settlers. Though the Gordon party was removed, more whites soon slipped in, and the Sioux were forced to give up their sacred hills.

In Custer State Park glimpses of wildlife are almost guaranteed. Bison, elk, pronghorn, and burros are some of the animals that make their homes here, while fields of coneflowers, wild roses, bluebells, and other wildflowers brighten the grasslands and hills.

Continue east on U.S. 16A about 6 miles past the Needles Highway (Rte. 87) turnoff and stop in at the **Peter Norbeck Visitor Center** *(605-255-4464. May-Oct.),* which will help satisfy your curiosity about area history, geology, and flora and fauna. Just after the Visitor Center, you can turn right and take the 18-mile Wildlife Loop Road through the park's grassy prairies, then head up Rte. 87 to rejoin U.S. 16A. Or continue past the Wildlife Loop and follow U.S. 16A as it turns left onto the fabulous **Iron Mountain Road.**

For a special treat, drive up to Mount Rushmore on a summer night between 9:30 and 10:30, when spotlights draw the sculptures from the darkness.

A winding highway to the monumental sculptures on Mount Rushmore, this 17-mile stretch goes up and down, loops around hairpin curves, and

156

Stockade Lake, Custer State Park

threads through tunnels that frame the four Presidents' heads on the opposite mountain. Peter Norbeck tramped and rode horseback through these woods to help lay out the byway and also is largely responsible for founding Custer State Park. The **Norbeck Memorial Overlook**, at 5,445 feet the highest point on the drive, gives you one of the best views of Mount Rushmore (from 3 miles south). Seeing these American icons staring out from a range of ragged peaks, you get a sense of the boldness of a colossal project undertaken nearly 70 years ago.

The first tunnel occurs about 5 miles from Mount Rushmore. The second tunnel provides a good rearview shot of the monument. Just afterward, you cross the first of three rustic bridges supported by logs cut from the surrounding woods. Feats of engineering, these bridges are neither straight nor level. You now take a one-way right around a grove of shimmering aspen and birch, and head into the last and longest tunnel. The second rustic bridge follows shortly, curling gently down. After the third bridge you drop into a valley and cross **Grizzly Bear Creek.**

The road delivers you to the **Mount Rushmore National Memorial** (*605-574-2523. www.nps.gov/moru*), where the

Along Custer Scenic Byway

60-foot-high heads of (from left to right) Washington, Jefferson, Theodore Roosevelt, and Lincoln emerge from a wall of granite. Begun in 1927, the carving took 14 years. Though more was planned, chief sculptor Gutzon Borglum died in 1941. His son

Custer Scenic Byway

Jct. of U.S 385 and S.D. 87 in Wind Cave National Park to Sylvan Lake

● 33 miles ● 1½ hours ● Spring through fall. Needles Hwy. closed in winter. Adm. fee to state park. *See map p. 155.*

This spectacular Black Hills drive follows Rte. 87 north from Wind Cave, through Custer State Park, to the junction with Rte. 89 at Sylvan Lake. (The 14.5-mile section of Rte. 87 north of U.S. 16A is known as the **Needles Highway.**) Traveling south to north, you ascend the area's highest mountains and enjoy a marvelous finale.

At **Wind Cave National Park** (*605-745-4600. www.nps.gov/wica. Fee for tours*), you'll have a chance to see some of the extensive subterranean architecture sculptured over the eons in the porous limestone surrounding the Black Hills. Begin the drive at the junction of U.S. 385 and Rte. 87 and stop at the **Prairie Dog Pullout.** If you stay in the car, you'll have more to watch; cars don't spook the rodents but people do. Continue north on Rte. 87 into **Custer State Park** (*605-255-4515. Adm. fee*), contiguous with the national park, where you're likely to encounter more wildlife.

The road soon begins winding up through the dense pine forest. Near **Mount Coolidge** you'll notice vast tracts of charred forest from the 1988 and 1990 fires that devastated the park. For a 360-degree panorama of the Black Hills, take the 1.3-mile gravel road (on the left) to the **Mount Coolidge Fire Tower.**

The last few miles of the drive are thrilling. As you cruise the needles, or upthrust pylons of granite, in the heart of the Sioux holy land, amazing views seem magically to appear before your windshield. The drive ends at beautiful **Sylvan Lake.**

157

Asters

continued the project until funding dried up a few months later. An orientation center has information and a four-minute film.

Traveling down from Mount Rushmore on Rte. 244, you continue to have startling views of rock ledges sprouting from dense forest. Road cuts reveal granite, feldspar, and veins of sparkling quartz. And the light tones of aspen and paper birch accent a dark green sea of ponderosa pine and spruce.

Much of the area outside Custer State Park is part of the 35,000-acre **Norbeck Wildlife Preserve,** established by Congress in 1920. **Harney Peak** (7,242 feet), on your left as you descend Mount Rushmore, is the highest mountain east of the Rockies. Trails from Sylvan Lake and other points ascend the peak.

Take Rtes. 87 and 89 south to Custer, named for the flashy army officer who in 1874 opened the area to a flood of settlers by publicizing his expedition's discovery of gold. Though George A. Custer died two years later at age 37 in the infamous Battle of the Little Bighorn, his legend lives in the Black Hills, visited by more than 3.5 million people a year.

South Dakota 44

Rapid City to Badlands National Park

● **65 miles** ● **1½ hours** ● **All year**

A scenic alternative to I-90, Rte. 44 travels between the Black Hills and Badlands National Park, passing farms and ranches, Wild West towns, and open prairies. Going east from Rapid City, the highway follows the Rapid Creek Valley for about 30 miles, then enters the White River badlands area, crosses Buffalo Gap National Grass-

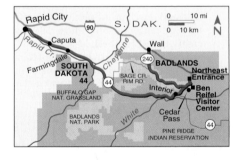

land, skirts the Pine Ridge Indian Reservation, and ends at the Cedar Pass entrance to Badlands National Park.

Situated on the eastern edge of the Black Hills, **Rapid City** dates back to 1876, two years after Custer's noisy expedition infected the region with gold fever. South Dakota's second largest city with 62,000 people, Rapid City functions as a tourism center, while mining, agriculture, and lumber also add to the economy. A powwow takes place here in July.

Driving east from Rapid City, you follow the hardwood-lined valley of **Rapid Creek** through the tiny agricultural communities of **Caputa** and tumbledown **Farmingdale.** The elms and cottonwoods along the creek make a river of green through an otherwise monochromatic prairie. After about 30 miles the creek joins the Cheyenne River and heads north, while the road continues southeast, gradually heading up to a vast plateau.

About halfway into the drive, you find yourself engulfed in a shallow bowl of long, rolling, brown-carpeted prairie creased with gullies. To a non-native, the immensity of space is almost overwhelming: You can see buttes and tablelands 30 miles away, with no sign of civilization anywhere.

Scattered throughout this area are the expanses of **Buffalo Gap National Grassland** *(www.fs.fed.us/r2/ nebraska/bgng.html),* one of 20 such areas in the Great Plains. In the 1930s the federal government started buying up land that had been overplanted or overgrazed, then drought stricken, to try to stabilize the soil and restore the grass. Some 4 million acres of this land became national grasslands in 1960 under the U.S. Forest Service. Ranchers graze cattle by

Sweet clover in bloom, Badlands National Park

permit, and anyone can hike or pitch a tent for free on Buffalo Gap's 591,000 acres. Contact the **National Grasslands Visitor Center** *(708 Main St. 605-279-2125)* in Wall for more information.

Nearing **Badlands National Park,** you see to your left the magnificent saw-toothed wall of stone pyramids and castles stretching 60 miles east to west. South of here is the **Pine Ridge Indian Reservation,** site of the 1890 massacre at Wounded Knee. The last major conflict between Indians and the U.S. Army, the battle ended the ghost dances that the Sioux thought would banish the whites and bring back the buffalo. Today 23,000 Oglala Sioux live on the reservation, and many old traditions survive. To hear the sound of Lakota (a Sioux dialect), tune your radio to 90.1 FM, "Voice of the Lakota Nation," which broadcasts music and cultural programs. **Interior** and **Cedar Pass** have lodging, food, and gas. **Cedar Pass Lodge** *(Inside the park. 605-433-5460. April-Oct.),* run by the Oglala Sioux tribe, sells Lakota arts and crafts.

Badlands

Northeast entrance of Badlands National Park to Wall on S.D. 240

● **30 miles** ● **2 hours** ● **All year but spring and fall best. Adm. fee to park mid-March through November. See map p. 158.**

This tour takes you through the starkly beautiful scenery of Badlands National Park, traversing the 300-foot-high escarpment that divides the upper from the lower prairie. Numerous overlooks and short trails provide visitors with a chance for further exploration.

Heading south from the northeast entrance to **Badlands National Park** *(605-433-5361. www.nps.gov/badl. Adm. fee)* on Rte. 240, pull over at the **Big Badlands Overlook** for an outstanding view. You stand atop the **Badlands Wall;** flat prairie stretches both behind you and in the far distance ahead.

In the middle lie the odd spires and knobs, steep gulches and ravines of the badlands. From here you can appreciate why French fur trappers in the early 1800s called the area *les mauvaises terres à traverser*—bad lands to cross.

Stop at the next pullout and take one of the short trails. The **Door** (0.75 mile), **Windows** (0.25 mile), and **Notch** (1.5 miles) **Trails** lead through a wonderland of high buttes and pinnacles, eroded from clay stone and volcanic ash deposits up to 38 million years old. The rugged **Castle Trail** (5 miles one-way) starts across the road and joins the **Saddle Pass Trail.** A little farther down the road, the **Cliff Shelf Nature Trail** makes a delightful half-mile loop through an island of juniper and features good views of the spreading prairie.

Stop at the **Ben Reifel Visitor Center** for a film, exhibits, and literature. Continuing west, you arrive in 4.5 miles at the **Fossil Exhibit Trail,** with its fossil reproductions displayed under clear plastic domes. Though the

160

Badlands under stormy skies, South Dakota

reproductions are hard to see, the trail offers proof that the badlands rank as one of the world's richest beds of prehistoric mammal fossils.

A little farther on, facing the less dramatic side of the road, **Prairie Winds Overlook** draws few motorists. But standing here at the edge of a prairie sea listening to the wind, you start to understand the homesteaders' attraction to the lonely prairie. Of the many overlooks, perhaps the most jaw-dropping is the **Pinnacles Overlook.** Here, almost surrounded by a badlands panorama, you can study the various landforms or just absorb the beauty. The rich interplay of light and shadow in the early morning or late afternoon adds another photogenic dimension.

You can continue on the gravel Sage Creek Rim Road, which overlooks the 64,250-acre **Sage Creek Wilderness Area** and offers likely sightings of bison, prairie dogs, and other animals. Or travel north 8.5 miles to the town of **Wall,** which has the **National Grasslands Visitor Center** *(708 Main St. 605-279-2125),* featuring excellent exhibits.

Nebraska

Pine Ridge Country

Gordon to Crawford on U.S. 20

- 67 miles • 1½ hours
- Spring through fall

Starting at the western edge of the Sand Hills, U.S. 20 travels west through hilly farm and ranch country into the rugged Pine Ridge area of northwestern Nebraska. Ranging through a diverse geographical region, the highway passes near picturesque state parks and connects several small agricultural towns noted

for their pioneer history. **Gordon** prides itself as the childhood home of writer Mari Sandoz (1896-1966), whose novels and nonfiction books about Indians, pioneers, and homesteaders gained her wide fame. The **Mari Sandoz Room,** a niche in the **Tourist Information Center** *(Ad Pad, 117 N. Main St. 308-282-9972),* contains first editions, letters, manuscripts, and memorabilia.

A block south of the tall, white grain elevator, Gordon's most prominent building, head west on U.S. 20. Ten miles to the south and east lie the western reaches of the **Sand Hills,** dunes stabilized by a layer of grass. In front of you, to the west, spread the flat plains, where cattle are common and trees scarce. With little annual rainfall, the main crops are wheat, alfalfa, and hay. Spring to fall wildflowers color the roadsides. Though the small towns of **Rushville** and **Hay Springs** each hold a historical museum, wayfarers will especially appreciate their oasislike parks.

On to the **Pine Ridge,** this is a country of high buttes and ridges, small streams and steep gullies. This narrow, 100-mile-long escarpment crosses the state's northwestern corner, defining the edge of the Nebraska High Plains. Prairie intermingles with pine-covered hills, and the landscape seems to change from mile to mile.

Three miles east of Chadron, the **Museum of the Fur Trade** *(308-432-3843. www.furtrade.org. June-Labor Day, winter by appt.;*

Near Fort Robinson State Park, Nebraska

adm. fee) tells the history of North American fur trading, with a collection of flintlock guns, a reconstructed trading post, and a garden of Indian crops.

Main Street in **Chadron** shows off a handsome row of Western-style, two-story buildings. About 10 miles south of town sits the lovely 974-acre **Chadron State Park** *(308-432-6167. www.ngpc.state.ne.us/parks/chadron.html. Adm. fee)*, which offers swimming, horseback riding, and hiking. Forest trails lead to good views at elevations of nearly 5,000 feet.

From Chadron, continue west along the **White River.** To the north lie rolling hills, the result of the erosion of ancient clay and clay-shale beds. To the south, you begin to see the buttes of the badlands. In 24 miles you reach the town of **Crawford,** known chiefly for **Fort Robinson State Park** *(308-665-2900. www.ngpc.state.ne.us/parks/frob.html. Parking fee)*, the largest state park in Nebraska. Centerpiece of the 22,000-acre park, Fort Robinson dates from the Indian battles of the 1870s. Chief Crazy Horse died here in 1877. During World War II German prisoners were held here. The complex includes a parade ground and twin rows of stately barracks and elegant officers' quarters (used as visitor accommodations in the summer). Trails explore the rocky bluffs and pine-clad slopes.

Agate Fossil Beds Natl. Monument, Nebraska

Within the park, the **Fort Robinson Museum** *(308-665-2919. April-Oct., weekends only Nov.-March; adm. fee)* showcases memorabilia in the old post headquarters. The **Trailside Museum** *(308-665-2929. May-Sept.)* interprets area geologic and natural history. North about 15 miles on Rte. 2 is the 95,000-acre **Oglala National Grassland** *(308-432-4475. www.fs.fed.us/r2/nebraska/oglala.html)*, popular for camping and hunting, and **Toadstool Park** *(308-432-4475)*, noted for its mushroom-shaped rock outcroppings.

Nebraska 29

Harrison to Agate Fossil Beds Natl. Monument

● 23 miles ● ½ hour ● Spring through fall *See map p. 161.*

A short ride south from Harrison takes you through high ridges and grassy ranchlands to an area rich in Miocene mammal fossils.

Offering motels and other visitor services, **Harrison** is the county seat—in fact the only town—of Sioux County. The village reached its peak population of 500 in 1940, but nothing could reverse the trend toward large, mechanized farms and ranches and a decentralized economy that spelled decline for Harrison. Now home to about 290 citizens, it struggles on.

Travel south on Rte. 29 along the swells of brown pastureland, relieved here and there by sharp-edged buttes and ridges and broken up by deep gullies. After 23 miles you arrive at **Agate Fossil Beds National Monument** *(308-668-2211. www.nps.gov/agfo)*. Situated along the meandering **Niobrara River,** this 2,770-acre park contains an astonishing wealth of fossilized mammals that roamed the plains from 13 to 25 million years ago. Named for nearby agate-rich rock formations, these beds of sedimentary rock preserve the bones of such odd creatures as the Moropus, an animal with the head of a horse, neck of a giraffe, and body of a tapir. The most common grazer was the Menoceras, a two-horned rhinoceros that ran in herds.

Along the river, cottonwoods and willows make a sinuous vein of green through the broad landscape of prairie sand reed, blue grama, and other grasses. A 2-mile interpretive walk explores the fossil sites on grassy hills 200 feet above the Niobrara River.

Kansas
Flint Hills

Manhattan to Cassoday on Kansas 177

● **84 miles** ● **2 hours** ● **Spring and fall**

This eastern Kansas byway arrows through the heart of the lovely Flint Hills, a region of rounded limestone hills covered by bluestem prairie. Along the way, it dips into the largest remaining tracts of tallgrass prairie in the U.S.

Start out in **Manhattan,** home of Kansas State University. The present town dates from 1855, when a steamboat full of settlers from Cincinnati ran aground nearby. With other area settlers they formed Manhattan. Its population drawn mostly from the North, the town remained abolitionist during the Bleeding Kansas and Civil War years.

Head south on Rte. 177 through rolling uplands pierced by limestone outcroppings. In about 8 miles, you pass the **Konza Prairie Research Natural Area** *(Right on Rte. 901 for 5 miles to entrance. 785-587-0441. www.tnc.org/infield/State/Kansas/kprairie.htm)*. Owned by the Nature Conservancy and run by Kansas State, this 8,616-acre parcel is one of the country's largest remaining pieces of virgin tallgrass prairie. Self-guided tour brochures are available.

After you cross I-70, the landscape unfurls in long pastures of green grass and delicate wildflowers. Tawny limestone peeks through the grass carpet. Much of the land in this 30- to 40-mile-wide band has remained unchanged for thousands of years. Indians used pieces of chert, or flint, found here for tools and weapons. Many pioneers, doubting such rocky ground would make for good farmsteads, moved on.

Continue south past tree-lined valleys and rocky ledges through shady **Council Grove.** For travelers on the Santa Fe Trail, the town was an important supply stop. In fact, Osage chiefs opened the Santa Fe Trail here in 1825, when they sold the right-of-way through their land for $800. The trunk of the **Council Oak,** where the agreement was penned, stands under a gazebo at 210 East Main Street. The popular **Hays House** restaurant *(Main St. between Neosho and Wood. 316-767-5911)*

163

Through the Flint Hills of Kansas

dates from 1857. For a good overview of area history, visit the **Kaw Mission State Historic Site** *(Mission St. N of U.S. 56. 316-767-5410. www.kshs.org)*, which houses Native American artifacts in an 1850s Indian school.

Continue south into Chase County, where waves of grass ripple off to the horizon, and low-lying hollows hold stands of cottonwood and scrub oak. Two miles north of Strong City looms the historic **Z-Bar/Spring Hill Ranch Headquarters Area** *(316-273-8494)*, just off the highway on your right. Built by cattle baron S.F. Jones in 1881, the three-story Second Empire-style ranch house was built of native limestone. In 1996, after years of intense debate by conservationists and landowners, the 10,894-acre ranch became the **Tallgrass Prairie National Preserve** *(www.nps.gov/tapr)*.

A few minutes south, **Cottonwood Falls** (pop. 890) claims the county seat and an architectural surprise. At the south end of the four-block main street, a French Renaissance-style building suddenly rears up from the prairie. Built with native limestone and walnut, the 1873 **Chase County Courthouse** *(316-273-6493. Open daily, tours weekends Feb.-Oct.; donation)* is the state's oldest courthouse still in use. The **Chase County Historical Society and Museum** *(301 Broadway. 316-273-8500. Afternoons only; donation)* displays the boots of author William Least Heat-Moon, who tramped nearly every inch of Chase County in the 1980s researching his best-seller *PrairyErth*.

Continue south through the **Flint Hills,** with views of native grasses and grazing cattle. In about 25 miles you reach the community of **Cassoday,** billing itself as the prairie chicken capital of the world. Hunted in fall, this short-tailed grouse is known for its noisy courtship dance. Other area wildlife includes the re-introduced pronghorn.

Ozarks blossoms

Missouri Ozarks

Salem to Eminence on Missouri 19

● **44 miles** ● **1 hour** ● **Spring through fall**

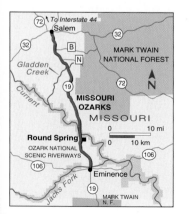

Coursing through the peaceful farm country and upland forests of southeastern Missouri, this winding road passes near a large section of the Mark Twain National Forest and crosses the Ozark National Scenic Riverways wilderness area. Most popular in spring and fall, the highway boasts redbud and dogwood in pink and white and a palette of brilliant autumn colors. Wildflowers from last frost to first frost enhance the beauty of the roadsides.

From **Salem,** seat of Dent County, head south past the courthouse (on your left) on Rte. 19. The first several miles envelop you in the big, undulant pastures typical of the region. Roads at 4 and 7 miles lead east to the Salem

Early morning fog along Missouri 19

and Potosi Districts of the 1.5-million-acre **Mark Twain National Forest** *(573-364-4621. www.fs.fed.us/r9/marktwain)*. After about 10 miles (from Salem), the wide green fields begin yielding to thick forests. Cross Gladden Creek and continue on the windy road through shadowed glens and grassy meadows. A brief stretch of mobile homes and shacks gives way to woods and long views of the misty blue-green Ozarks.

Traveling up now through the hardwood forest, Rte. 19 ascends the **Ozark Plateau,** an eroded tableland spreading from northern Arkansas to southern Missouri and west to northeastern Oklahoma. Continue south into the **Ozark National Scenic Riverways** *(573-323-4236. www.nps.gov/ozar)*, a National Park Service unit protecting more than 134 miles of the **Current** and **Jacks Fork Rivers.**

Cross the sparkling **Current River** and make a left into the **Round Spring** campground and picnic area. Here you can explore one of the area's many caves, tucked into the high limestone bluff. Continue south as the road begins climbing again to good views of the valley and hills. In about 3 miles you pass a tract of virgin pine. About 9 miles farther, a pull-off lets you savor the southern panorama of forested mountains before you begin a fairly steep descent to the Jacks Fork River. Just beyond, the town of **Eminence** has outfitters for river expeditions, trail rides, and other activities.

Glade Top Trail

Forest Road 147, Mark Twain National Forest

● 23 miles ● 1 hour ● Spring through fall. Gravel road

Built by the Civilian Conservation Corps in the 1930s, this two-lane gravel road traverses the gentle hills of Missouri's Ozark Plateau. Heading south from the northern boundary of the Mark Twain National Forest's **Ava Ranger District** *(417-683-4428)*, you come in about a mile to **Haden Bald,** an area managed by a controlled burn every four to six years. Just across the road lies the **Smoke Tree Scene** interpretive site. Locals call smoke trees "yellowwoods" for the color beneath the bark. Come autumn, the trees blaze with brilliant reds and golds.

The forest opens up to vistas 1.5 miles farther on, with **Arkansas View** offering on a clear day a look at the **St. François Mountains,** 40 miles to the southeast. This stop has a shady picnic area, strategically positioned for a panoramic view.

Continue south one mile to **Watershed Divide,** which splits the Little North Fork of the White River watershed on the east from the Beaver Creek watershed on the west. From here you can see an abundance of hardwoods and also observe your next stop, **Caney Lookout Tower,** 3 miles south.

A few miles beyond the tower, the forest road forks. FR 147 heads southeast toward Longrun, the trail's end, and FR 149 wanders southwest to Rte. 125. Take your pick: From both, peaceful hills and farms slip by your window like a dream.

Missouri Valley Wine Country

U.S. 61 to Hermann on Missouri 94

● **56 miles** ● **1½ hours** ● **Spring through fall**

Tracing the broad bends of the Missouri River, Rte. 94 ambles over sweeping green hills, past picturesque farmhouses, and into the heart of Missouri wine country just west of St. Louis. The drive ends at Hermann, a town of German architecture and heritage situated near several award-winning wineries.

Take Rte. 94 west from U.S. 61 and turn right in about 1 mile for the **August A. Busch Memorial Conservation Area** *(2 miles W on Rte. D. 636-441-4554)*, which, combined with two adjacent areas, offers 16,900 acres for fishing, hiking, hunting, biking, and picnicking. Back on Rte. 94, drive toward Defiance. The road soon becomes extremely twisty as it goes up and down the forested hills and past many small houses. After 6 miles, take Rte. F west for 5 miles to see the **Daniel Boone House** *(636-798-2005. Call for hours; adm. fee)* a four-story, Georgian-style house that the pioneer built with his son and lived in during his last years in the early 1800s.

Back on the highway, you'll see on the right the **KATY Trail** *(www.katy-trail.com)*, a 200-mile biking and hiking trail that follows abandoned railroad rights-of-way along the Missouri. A few miles west of Defiance, you encounter an attractive stretch of wineries around Augusta. As soon as you

Missouri River's 1869 Poeschel-Harrison House, built in typical German style

Missouri Valley Old World scene

pass one, you begin seeing signs for the next. **Montelle Winery** *(636-228-4464)*, perched 400 feet above the river valley, provides perhaps the most scenic views of the bluffs and verdant farmland below. All the wineries offer tours and tastings.

Proceed cautiously along the vertiginous highway. Detour, if you wish, 4 miles south of Dutzow to the riverfront town of **Washington,** a charming collection of restaurants, B&Bs, shops, and 19th-century houses built in the Missouri-German style. Washington also has the world's only corn-cob pipe factory.

Again on Rte. 94, drive a mile or so west of Dutzow to a side road leading to the **Daniel Boone Grave and Monument,** though no one knows for sure if Boone is buried there. Continue west through Marthasville and Treloar along the fertile **Missouri River Valley.** To your left lie flat fields of grain stretching to the Missouri, and beyond rises a ridge of bluffs several hundred feet high paralleling the river's course. On your right side loom the cliffs that define the north edge of the valley. Just over 3 miles after Treloar, you pass the lovely **St. Johns of Pinckney United Church of Christ** (1870) and its cemetery, sitting in a field at a curve in the road.

For the next 15 miles, a rich tableau unrolls—cornfields and cow pastures, one-lane bridges over small creeks, dips into shady vales, and rises to views of the river and the ranks of green hills.

At Rte. 19 take the truss bridge across the **Missouri River** into **Hermann.** From the bridge you can see the steeples and old brick buildings emerging from the limestone bluff on the south side of the river. German immigrants founded the town of Hermann in 1837 to preserve their language and customs. They also set about making Missouri the nation's second largest wine producer. Then Prohibition dried up the area. Missouri Valley wine making geared up again in the 1960s, and tourists now flock to Hermann to visit its German architecture, B&Bs, museums, and historic wineries.

Driving along the steep streets, you see charming houses with wide porches and hanging flowerpots, neatly groomed lots, clean sidewalks, and attractive shops. **Stone Hill Winery** *(573-486-2129. Fee for tours),* established in 1847, commands a fine view of the town and nearby countryside, and showcases an impressive array of vaulted cellars. Just east of the Missouri River bridge, the **Hermann-hof Winery** *(573-486-5959. Fee for tours)* dates from 1852 and features a smokehouse and brick wine cellars. The **Historic Hermann Museum** *(4th and Schiller Sts. 573-486-2017. Closed Thurs.; adm. fee),* housed in the 1871 German School Building, has displays on area shipbuilding, wine making, and early furniture, as well as a piece of the Berlin Wall.

The sweet wines of previous years are giving way to drier vintages made from more desirable French hybrids, resulting in a 15 million dollar industry for the state.

167

If you continue on Rte. 94 west of Hermann to Jefferson City (43 miles) you won't find any more wineries, but you'll travel through a similar stretch of gentle farmland with excellent views of valleys and bluffs interspersed with woodlands and a handful of tiny villages.

Iowa

Woodlands Scenic Byway

U.S. 34 near Ottumwa to Farmington on County Rtes. T61, T7J, J40, and W40; Iowa 273 and 2; and U.S. 63

- **74 miles** • **2 hours**
- **Spring through fall.** Some gravel roads

Along the back roads of south-eastern Iowa, this peaceful route takes travelers by cool forests and gentle glades, Amish farmsteads and historic riverfront hamlets. The tour connects several roads, varying from two-lane hard top to narrow gravel.

Start 12 miles west of Ottumwa and take Rte. T61 south from U.S. 34, following the "Scenic Byway" signs. Rolling farmlands and narrow valleys beckon. In about 4 miles you reach the small farming community of **Blakesburg.** Pass a row of clapboard houses along a shady main street, then turn right when the pavement ends, veer past the white-washed Christian Church, and continue south. After 5 more miles, turn left onto gravel Rte. T7J and travel along cornfields and feathery meadows. Along the way you'll see a private Christmas tree farm, an old cemetery, and, a few miles farther, broad views of the farmlands and glens off to your right.

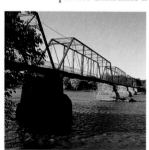

Keosauqua Bridge, Bentonsport

After about 9 miles the hard-top starts up again and takes you through **Drakesville.** Be on the look-out for slow-moving horse-drawn vehicles driven by black-clad Amish who adhere to a bygone way of life. Take Rte. 273 for 4 miles past Drakesville, turn right on U.S. 63, and go about 3 miles to **Bloomfield.** Stop in at the **Iowa Welcome Center** *(301 N. Wash. St. 515-664-1104)* for some friendly information, and then continue past the French Renaissance-style courthouse. Take a left at the square onto Rte. J40.

The next several miles feature fields of oats, corn, and beans. Stands of oak and hickory break the steady rhythm of the fields. In 11 miles, pass through the crossroads town of Troy and continue another 13 miles to the quaint village of **Keosauqua,** where the "steamboat Gothic" Manning Hotel sits by the wide **Des Moines River.**

Cross the river on the steel truss bridge and turn right for a detour through lovely **Lacey-Keosauqua State Park** *(319-293-3502. www.state.ia.us/parks/lacey keo.htm. Fee for camping),* which offers picnicking, hiking, and camping. Back on the road, travel about 6 miles to another historic port town, **Bentonsport.** You cross the river again to enter this tiny, tranquil mid-19th-century town. Cruise along the gravel riverside road by B&Bs, a blacksmith shop, general store, and arts and antiques shops. Then head back to Rte. J40 and up a steep, wooded bluff to an overlook of the river and hills.

In 4 more miles you arrive in the third erstwhile port town, **Bonaparte.** On the gentle Des Moines, this town preserves many buildings from the mid-1800s. Head south on Rte. W40 and then east on Rte. 2 through more pastoral landscapes to the pleasant town of **Farmington,** also on the river.

Loess Hills Scenic Byway

Iowa 127 to Smithland on Iowa 183, 37, 175, and Cty. Rtes.

● **45 miles** ● **1 hour** ● **Spring through fall**

Yucca blooms at sunset, Loess Hills

This section of the 220-mile designated byway courses through the heart of the Loess Hills region of western Iowa. Pieced together in the late 1980s and early 1990s, the byway comprises numerous rural roads that weave through picturesque farmlands and bluffs along the eastern side of the Missouri River Valley. Blue signs mark the main route and sometimes present an alternative route or loop for further exploration.

As you head north on Rte. 183, starting 3 miles east of Mondamin, cornfields stretch far to the west. Visible on both sides of the road are the bluffs that characterize the area. Loess (pronounced luss) is mainly a fine silt produced by glacial abrasion 12,500 to 150,000 years ago. Heavy winds blew this powdery soil and deposited much of it on the eastern edge of the Missouri River's floodplain, creating the hills. Over the years erosion sculptured the ravines and steps you see today. In 10 miles you come to the quaint town of **Pisgah,** dating from 1899 and typical of the region's small farming communities. (From here you can take the **Fountainbleu Loop,** 19 miles on dirt and gravel, for bluff-top scenic views.)

Continue northward on Rte. 183 for 5 or 6 miles to the sign for **Preparation Canyon State Park** *(712-423-2829. www.state.ia.us/parks/prepcan.htm. Closed in winter to vehicles),* a 3-mile detour. This peaceful, 344-acre preserve offers fine vistas of the verdant farmlands below and provides a home to wildlife, bur oaks, and prairie grasses.

Go north on Rte. 183 a couple of miles to another small town, **Moorhead,** where the **Loess Hills Hospitality Association** *(Main St. 712-886-5441. Closed Sun. in winter)* dispenses area maps. Stop in at the adjacent café or continue your tour on Rte. L16. Just out of town, you can take Rte. E54 west 3.5 miles to the simple **Ingemann Danish Lutheran Church** (1884). Very little interrupts the tranquillity of this spot. Here also is a chance to see some of the 350 species of glorious wildflowers found in these hills.

Back on Rte. L16, travel north into a flat-bottomed bowl with rounded hills. After about 10 miles, you veer onto Rte. 37 to tiny **Turin,** where a marker notes the 1955 discovery in the area of a 5,000-year-old human skeleton. From Turin to **Smithland** *(N on Rte. 175, W on Rte. E34, N on Rte. L20, W on E16, N on Rte. L12),* good views continue of the hills and farm country. The 623-acre **Southwood Conservation Area** *(712-258-0838. Utilities shut off Nov.-April),* 2 miles west of Smithland on Rte. 141, harbors such wildlife as white-tailed deer, wild turkey, and migrating waterfowl.

Great River Road

Marquette to Dubuque on Iowa 76, 340; U.S. 18, 52; and County Rtes. X56, C17, and C9Y

● 62 miles ● 1½ hours
● Spring through fall

Hilltop farms and expansive valley views distinguish this roller-coaster ride up, down, and around the bluffs surrounding Iowa's road along the Mississippi River. The drive begins at river level in **Marquette,** known as North McGregor in 1857, when it was founded as a railroad supply point. Before heading south, drive 3 miles north to **Effigy Mounds National Monument** *(319-873-3491. www.nps.gov/efmo. Adm. fee),* where a bluff-top trail weaves among 191 preserved Indian mounds dating from 500 B.C. Southbound, the road wriggles between tall, steep slopes and the wide Mississippi, with an eye-level view of barges, towboats, and pleasure craft. About a mile farther on the right is the **Upper Mississippi River National Wildlife and Fish Refuge Visitor Center** *(319-873-3423. www.umesc.usgs.gov/umr_refuge.html),* where you can learn about the 194,000-acre preserve, which stretches for 261 miles along the river's bottomlands from Wabasha, Minnesota, to Rock Island, Illinois.

The road veers west, away from the river into **McGregor,** a 19th-century ferry landing between the bluffs. Century-old buildings line the road—now called Main Street—many of which have been rejuvenated as shops and inns. Ringling Brothers Circus began in McGregor backyards in the 1870s. The **McGregor Historical Museum** *(Main St. June–mid-Oct. Tues., Thurs., Sat. p.m.)* has early circus posters and pictures.

Beyond town, the road snakes up into steep bluffs wooded with oaks,

Along Iowa's Great River Road

maples, and birches, climbing, climbing, until it emerges amid hilly corn-fields and weathered barns. **Pikes Peak State Park** *(319-873-2341. www.state.ia.us/parks/pike peak.htm)*, a half mile down the road (now Rte. 340), provides vistas of the river valley far below. The high bluff is named for Zebulon Pike, of Colorado fame, who led an expedition through here in 1805. Across the gorge you can see the **Wisconsin River** flowing into the Mississippi—the point at which French explorers Louis Jolliet and Jacques Marquette emerged in June 1673 on their canoe trip down the Wisconsin.

The river road climbs and swoops and winds its way among cornfields, descending to the hamlet of Clayton, then **Guttenberg,** both by the river's edge. In Guttenberg, settled in 1845 and named by German settlers for the inventor of the movable press (the extra "t" was a mistake), the road parallels lovely **River Front Park,** a mile-long, grassy stretch with picnic tables and views. The downtown is filled with limestone buildings from the 1840s and '50s. A walking tour map is available at the **Municipal Building** *(502 S. First St.)*. An observation platform offers a look at **Lock and Dam No. 10.**

Just beyond town, stop at the bluff-top scenic overlook for a good view of the river's deep-sided valley, etched with limestone strata and containing rich deposits of lead ore (mined in the region for 300 years). From here, the road continues through farmland, descending briefly into a valley created by the **Turkey River**, then climbing again onto the bluffs. An expansive view opens up of pastures dotted with dairy cows and trim barns. The road continues for about 9 miles before diving down to **North Buena Vista,** a river town with frame structures clinging to steep bluffs.

Returning to the bluff tops, the road veers from the river and becomes exceedingly precarious along a ridge. At points, you can see the river sparkling far below. The drive climbs higher, passing Balltown and Sherrill, towns seemingly on top of the world.

From Sherrill, the road descends into a valley, weaving around and down past barns, silos, and dairy cows. Little by little, more houses line the curvy road, and at the junction with U.S. 52, the route becomes a four-lane highway. **Dubuque** lies 5 miles away. In Iowa's oldest city you can brush up on 300 years of river lore at the **Mississippi River Museum** *(Third St. and Ice Harbor. 319-557-9545. www.mississippirivermuseum.com. Adm. fee)* complex.

The Mississippi River Valley was created over thousands of years—from the time it lay under Paleozoic seas to the most recent ice age, when glacial meltwaters scoured the river's course.

South Central

Louisiana, Texas, Oklahoma, Arkansas

Louisiana

Old Spanish Trail

*Houma to Breaux Bridge on U.S. 90 and
Louisiana 182 and 31*

● 108 miles ● 3 hours ● Spring and fall; summers are
hot and humid.

Originally a section of a 19th-century Spanish frontier trail and trading route, the drive wends through southern Louisiana's Cajun country. This low, flat land of bayous, moss-draped live oaks, sugarcane fields, and old plantation manors also sustains a burgeoning oil industry.

Begin in **Houma,** the seat of Terrebonne Parish and a center of Cajun culture. Before leaving town try a spicy étouffée dish or a rich gumbo. From town head west on Bayou Black Drive (U.S. 90), which hugs the bayou. Roadside signs advertise swamp tours, some run by the area's colorful Cajun entrepreneurs. The tours explore parts of the **Atchafalaya Basin,** which covers several hundred thousand acres and ranks as the continent's largest river-basin swamp.

A few miles outside Houma, the drive cuts through the first fields of sugarcane. After another 10 miles or so, it reaches the turnoff for **Wildlife Gardens** *(Right at Greenwood School, then left 2 miles to 5306 Black Bayou Dr. 504-575-3676. Closed Sun.-Mon.; adm. fee).* Featuring an alligator farm and trapper's cabin, the gardens also offer nature and swamp tours.

Back on U.S. 90, you see evidence of the region's rampant oil industry around **Gibson.** For the next 15 miles or so the drive passes oil-platform fabricators and other heavy equipment used by the inshore oil industry.

As you cross the bridge into St. Mary Parish along **Bayou Boeuf,** you can literally smell the industry generated by the enormous **McDermott Shipyard** on your left. Soon you enter **Morgan City,** a major port on the **Intracoastal Waterway.** The city's attractions include the 3.5-acre **Swamp Gardens** *(725 Myrtle St. 504-384-3343. Adm. fee),* where the 1917 Tarzan classic was filmed; and the **Turn-of-the-Century House** *(715 Second St. 504-380-4651. Closed Mon.; adm. fee).*

From Morgan City, follow signs for Berwick/Rte. 182, which will take you across **Berwick Bay** and the **Atchafalaya River** on the **Long-Allen Bridge,** then into the tiny towns of Berwick and Patterson. Paralleling the course of **Bayou Teche,** the drive now passes through one of the most fertile parts

Moss-draped live oaks along the Old Spanish Trail

of the state's "sugar bowl," where plantations—each with its own sugar mill—flourished prior to the Civil War.

On the outskirts of Patterson, Rte. 182 jogs left and feeds into U.S. 90 for about a mile before veering off again into flats and cane fields. After a couple of miles you enter **Centerville,** one of St. Mary Parish's oldest communities and a former sugar hub, with fine Victorian homes and antebellum planters' mansions.

Gulf oysters on the half shell

Passing through the small town of Garden City, the road soon arrives in **Franklin,** the seat of St. Mary Parish and an official Main Street, U.S.A., town. Rte. 182 now becomes a stately boulevard running through the restored downtown and the elegant historic district, where you'll find **Oaklawn Manor** *(Irish Bend Rd. 337-828-0434. Adm. fee)* and **Grevemberg House** *(Sterling Rd., Franklin City Park. 337-828-2092. Adm. fee).*

Continuing west on Rte. 182, you'll pass through more cane-field country. In **Jeanerette,** one of the state's 18 active sugar mills still processes cane into raw sugar. There's also the **Jeanerette Bicentennial Museum** *(500 E. Main St. 337-276-4408. Closed weekends; adm. fee),* with exhibits on the sugar industry and bayou life. As you pass **LeJeune's Bakery** *(1510 W. Main St. 337-276-5690. Closed weekends),* look for a blinking red light; this indicates the bakery has its famous French bread for sale, a town staple since 1884.

For the next 8 miles, the drive wanders through more flat cane country before entering **New Iberia** *(Tourist Commission, 2704 Hwy. 14. 337-365-1540),* another town that sugar built. Main Street leads through the handsome historic district. The crown jewel here is **Shadows-on-the-Teche** *(317 E. Main St. 337-369-6446. Adm. fee),* a restored 1834 plantation home with gardens. Other sights include the **Conrad Rice Mill** *(307 Ann St. 337-364-7242. Closed Sun.; adm. fee),* the oldest rice mill in the country; and the stunning

174

Antebellum mansion, New Iberia

Rip Van Winkle Gardens *(Rip Van Winkle Rd. 337-365-3332. Adm. fee).*

From here, you can detour 20 miles on Rte. 182 to **Lafayette,** a colorful hub of Cajun country and a fine place to enjoy zydeco music. Or you can continue on the drive by turning right on Rte. 31. After 10 more miles of cane fields, you enter **St. Martinville** *(La Remise Visitor Information Center, Evangeline Oak Park, Evangeline Blvd. 337-394-2233),* the seat of St. Martin Parish. Known as "Petit Paris," this elegant, French-style town was made famous by Henry Wadsworth Longfellow's poem *Evangeline;* it recounts the story of two Acadian exiles who fled from Nova Scotia in 1755 to escape British rule. You can see the famous **Evangeline Oak** in **Evangeline Town Park** *(E. Port St.).* On St. Martin Square you'll find the **Evangeline Monument** and the **Petit Paris Museum** *(337-394-7334. Adm. fee).*

A mile north on Rte. 31 is 135-acre **Longfellow-Evangeline State Commemorative Area** *(1200 N. Main St. 337-394-3754. Adm. fee),* with a plantation home, Visitor Center, and recreation area. Continuing on Rte. 31, you follow Bayou Teche to the town of Parks. Seven miles farther, the drive ends in the town of **Breaux Bridge.**

Creole Nature Trail

Sulphur to Lake Charles on La. 27, 384, and 385

● 105 miles ● 2½ hours ● Fall through spring. Summers hot and humid; bring insect repellent. Excellent birding area

Marshland, prairie, wildlife refuges, Gulf shoreline, and a variety of flora and fauna await you on this drive through southwestern Louisiana, an area favored by birding and shelling enthusiasts.

The drive begins in **Sulphur,** 5 miles west of Lake Charles on I-10. Its name derives from the huge mineral deposits found in a nearby salt dome. As the drive heads south on Rte. 27, you pass through a few miles of flat fields before crossing the **Intracoastal Waterway,** which runs from Florida to Texas. On the left **Calcasieu Lake,** 19 miles long and 8 miles wide, is linked by a separate shipping channel to the Gulf.

On the other side of the bridge, the landscape changes dramatically to brackish tidal marsh with few trees. Two miles beyond the bridge, you can see the shipping channel on your left and oil fields on the right. Continue to **Hackberry,** where you might spot shrimp boats with long, flat "butterfly nets" lowered into Calcasieu Lake to catch shrimp migrating to the Gulf.

Alligators in a Louisiana marsh

The drive soon enters 125,000-acre **Sabine National Wildlife Refuge** *(337-762-3816. http://sabine.fws.gov),* the Gulf Coast's largest waterfowl refuge with more than 250 species. Four miles beyond, the 1.5-mile **Marsh Trail** offers the chance to see alligators, egrets, roseate spoonbills, and a variety of other seasonal waterfowl.

Angling through a treeless landscape, the drive continues 7 miles to the town of **Holly Beach** on the **Gulf of Mexico.** The beach offers particularly good shelling from October through February.

Turn left on Rte. 27/82. As you head east, note the coastal oaks, cedars, and tallows bent from the winds off the Gulf. Nine miles farther on, take the free ferry across the shipping channel to the town of Cameron.

Coastal vegetation marks the 14 miles from Cameron to Creole, where you head north on Rte. 27. Again crossing the Intracoastal

Sunset at Sabine National Wildlife Refuge

Louisiana has 5,000 miles of ice-free navigable rivers, bayous, and canals—the most extensive water transportation network in the country.

Waterway, the drive enters the **Cameron Prairie National Wildlife Refuge** (*Visitor Center 2 miles beyond waterway. 337-598-2216. http://refuges.southeast.fws.gov/cameronprairie*). Distinctly different from Sabine's marshlands, its grasslands and farmlands attract ducks, doves, and rare black rails.

A few miles beyond, turn west on Rte. 384 and head through rice fields for 5 miles. Then turn north on Rte. 385 and continue to the drive's end in the port city of **Lake Charles** (*Southwest Louisiana Convention & Visitors Bureau, 1211 N. Lakeshore Dr. 337-436-9588 or 800-456-SWLA. www.visit lakecharles.org*). The town's historic **Charpentier District** preserves about 20 blocks of vintage Victorian architecture.

Longleaf Trail Scenic Byway

Louisiana 117 to Louisiana 119 on Forest Road 59 in Kisatchie National Forest

● 17 miles ● ½ hour ● Spring and fall; summers are hot and humid.

Winding through Louisiana's 600,000-acre Kisatchie National Forest, the drive traces a high ridge through beautiful pine forests.

Before starting at the western end of the marked byway, head south 3 miles on Rte. 117 to FR 350. Follow it east 1.9 miles to **Kisatchie Overlook** for views of **Kisatchie Bayou,** a state-designated natural and scenic stream. Return to Rte. 117 and head north to the beginning of the byway on FR 59.

After winding through a mixed pine forest for 3.5 miles, you cross Kisatchie Bayou. Unlike Louisiana's usually languid bayous, this one follows a steeper course, creating falls and rapids.

The drive ascends from here, past pastures and farms and through the community of Lotus Hill. Just beyond you enter the 38,450-acre **National Red Dirt Wildlife Management Preserve** *(Kisatchie National Forest 318-352-2568),* established in 1941 to protect game animals.

After passing the preserve's Cane Campground, you'll see a stand of longleaf pines, as well as taller, straighter "superior pines" that have been genetically engineered.

Farther on, the drive passes through a forest of longleaf, loblolly, and shortleaf pines. It's worth a detour to **Kisatchie Bayou Campground** *(4 miles south on FR 321, then west 2 miles on FR 366).* From the campground's bluffs, you have great views of the bayou's white-sand beaches, rapids, and forested bottomland flats.

Back on FR 59 east, you soon come to a stand of nursery pines on the right. Another half mile down on the left, look for white-banded "nest trees" set aside throughout the forest as habitat for the endangered red-cockaded woodpecker.

After about 3 miles the drive reaches the boundary of the **Kisatchie Hills Wilderness,** an 8,700-acre preserve featuring rugged sandstone bluffs, outcrops, and mesas. For the drive's remaining 7 miles, this wilderness monopolizes the view to the northeast.

At **Longleaf Vista** a short, paved interpretive walk offers superb views of the wilderness and the longleaf pine forest; the walk connects with a 1.5-mile nature trail that circles through these glorious pinelands.

Passing through the pines, Longleaf Trail Scenic Byway

177

The byway's final 2 miles follows a section of the old Opelousas–Fort Jesup Military Road, a major Civil War route. At **Bayou Cypre Overlook** stop for more views of the Kisatchie Hills Wilderness. The drive ends at the intersection with Rte. 119.

Texas

Texas Hill Country

Oak Hill to New Braunfels on U.S. 290, Texas 16, 27, 39, 46, and Farm-to-Market 187 and 337

● **280 miles** ● **2 days** ● **All year. Wildflower bloom peaks in April. The area is subject to flash floods.**

This lofty oasis is rife with rolling hills, plunging gorges, limestone bluffs, diverse wildlife, and charming villages that reflect the region's Old World heritage.

From **Oak Hill,** U.S. 290 west heads for the Texas Hills. You won't see much for the first 10 or 11 miles, aside from glimpses of the plains as you ascend the 100-million-year-old geologic region called the **Edwards Plateau.** After about 18 miles, you cross the margin of the plateau, a landscape strewn with limestone rubble and stands of gnarled oaks set off by shrubby hills and ridges. The deep limestone bedrock here was formed by the shells and skeletons of tiny creatures that lived in ancient, shallow seas covering much of present-day Texas. Later,

massive shifts inside the earth caused a giant surface bulge. When part of the bulge fell toward the Gulf of Mexico, it left the great ragged Balcones Fault and this uplifted plateau, since carved by erosion.

About 3 miles west of the hamlet of Henly is a right turnoff to 5,212-acre **Pedernales** (pronounced the LBJ way: perd'n-AL-es) **Falls State Park** *(6 miles north on Rte. 3232. 830-868-7304. www.tpwd.state.tx.us/park/pedernal/pedernal.htm. Adm. fee),* flanking the wooded **Pedernales River.** Pedernales Falls drops 50 feet over tilted limestone stair steps.

Continuing west on U.S. 290, you reach the junction with U.S. 281, leading 9 miles south to the Devil's Backbone drive (see page 180).

Six miles north, you enter **Johnson City** *(Visitor and Tourism Bureau, 406 W. Main. 830-868-7684. Closed weekends).* Lyndon Johnson was born nearby in 1908, and the town is named for his ancestors. The **Lyndon B. Johnson National Historical Park Visitor Center** *(100 10th St. 830-868-7128. www.nps.gov/lyjo)* contains the frame house that was **Johnson's Boyhood Home,** and the Johnson Settlement, the ranch complex where LBJ's forebears first settled.

Watch for deer as you drive west on U.S. 290; grazing buffalo on the right some 13 miles along mark a second unit in the national historical park. Here,

Chuckwagon at LBJ National Historical Park

bus tours depart for the **LBJ Ranch** *(830-868-7128. Adm. fee),* which preserves Johnson's birthplace and the one-room Junction School he attended. Nearby, the **Lyndon B. Johnson State Historical Park** *(830-644-2252. www.tpwd.state .tx.us/park/lbj/lbj.htm)* features a living-history farm, a nature trail, and wildlife.

The hills are barely visible as you enter the peach country of Gillespie County. The fruit of the vine also flourishes here, resulting in several wineries. The nearby town of **Fredericksburg** *(Chamber of Commerce, Main St. and N. Adams. 830-997-6523)* is 19th century in character and German in custom. The **Admiral Nimitz Museum and Historical Center** *(304 E. Main St. 830-997-4379. www.tpwd.state.tx.us/park/nimitz/nimitz.htm. Adm. fee)* includes the Museum of the Pacific War, housed in the 1850s Nimitz Hotel established by the admiral's grandfather.

From here, take an 18-mile detour north on Rte. 965 to **Enchanted Rock State Natural Area** *(915-247-3903. www.tpwd.state.tx.us/park/enchantd/enchantd .htm. Adm. fee).* Centerpiece of the 1,643-acre park is a massive 440-foot-high dome of pink granite—the second largest batholith on the continent.

Back in Fredericksburg, head south on Rte. 16, crossing through the rich, fertile country of the Pedernales River watershed. Gradually, the hills dissolve and the landscape flattens. After about 18 miles, the road begins twisting steeply down into the **Guadalupe River Valley.**

Another couple of miles puts you into the summer playground of **Kerrville,** home of the **Cowboy Artists of America Museum** *(1550 Bandera Hwy. 830-896-2553. Closed Mon. Sept.-May; adm. fee)* and the historical **Hill Country Museum** *(226 Earl Garrett St. 830-896-8633. Closed Sun.; adm. fee),* set in a stone Romanesque-Victorian mansion.

At this point, you can proceed south on Rte. 16 toward Medina through a breathtaking 35 miles, promising hairpin turns, lofty vistas, craggy canyons, and crystal streams. Or you can detour west to explore some of the Texas

Cattle roundup in Texas Hill Country

Texas bluebonnets and Indian paintbrush

Devil's Backbone

Loop from Blanco on U.S. 281 and Ranch-to-Market 32, 12, 2325, and 165

● 56 miles ● 2 hours ● Fall through spring. *See map p.178.*

This twisting, razor-backed ridge offers dramatic views of the Balcones Fault Zone, a 400-mile-long break in the Earth's crust. The road tops a broken, crumpled remnant of the Edwards Plateau.

From **Blanco,** named for the clear waters of the pretty **Blanco River** that runs through it, drive 3 miles south on U.S. 281 to Rte. 32. For the first 7 miles, the road rolls through limestone hills, past pasturelands scattered with oak and juniper. As you begin to climb, feast your eyes on the rugged stair-step hills on the northern skyline.

The next 10 miles or so offer ample opportunities to see how erosion has carved the layer cake of sedimentary deposits typical of Texas Hill Country.

After 18 miles on Rte. 32, stop at the picnic area on the left for a view of these colorful hills and incised valleys. The drive continues another 6 miles through karst terrain dotted with sinkholes before intersecting Rte. 12. Take Rte. 12 north for 5 miles through precipitous Hill Country to arty **Wimberley,** then follow Rtes. 2325 and 165 west 24 miles back to Blanco.

Hills' most remote and spectacular country. If you choose this second option, take Rte. 27 west to Ingram, where you pick up Rte. 39. At the junction of the two routes, historical murals on a lumber company building are evidence of the area's vigorous artist colony.

Roller coastering through dipping ranchlands, the road hugs the serpentine **South Fork Guadalupe River.** At Rte. 187 turn south toward Vanderpool and continue about 11 miles to a picnic area with a fabulous panorama of rugged hills and canyons. Descending steeply, the road pitches into **Sabinal River Canyon** and weaves past its towering limestone walls and buttes for 4 miles. At Rte. 337, a designated state scenic highway, turn west toward Leakey. For the next 17 miles, the drive skirts the sheer cliffs and deep gorges of the **Frio** and **Sabinal Rivers** before reaching **Leakey.** A pretty town on the Frio River, it's home to the **Wildlife Art Museum** *(Hwy. 337 E. 830-232-5607. Closed Sun. except by appt.; donation).*

From here, head east again on Rte. 337, which will return you to Vanderpool, and then back into rugged high country with more panoramic views.

Rolling through the pastoral valley of the **West Prong of the Medina River,** the road

Armadillo along Devil's Backbone

enters **Medina,** "apple capital of Texas." Turn southeast on Rte. 16, and continue 14 miles through the flat prosperous ranchland of Bandera County. The town of **Bandera** itself, a ranching center, has a real cowboy flavor with a frontier-style Main Street—and one of the oldest Polish communities in the country. Stop by the **Frontier Times Museum** *(13th St. 830-796-3864. Adm. fee)* to see exhibits on the Old West and the town's founding in 1852.

Continue east on Rte. 16 for about 12 miles across the southern end of the Edwards Plateau, with Hill Country now out of sight. At the intersection with Rte. 46, turn left and dip through low hills for about 12 miles to the restored Main Street, U.S.A., town of **Boerne** (pronounced BUR-nee). Settled by Germans in the 19th century, the town proudly preserves its Old World heritage and serves as an antiques hub. Its **Cibolo Wilderness Trail** *(830-249-4616)* is a 100-acre greenbelt with trails through four ecosystems.

About 13 miles east of Boerne, Rte. 46 passes Park Road 31, which leads 3 miles to the rugged and scenic **Guadalupe River State Park** *(830-438-2656. www.tpwd.state.tx.us/park/guadalup/guadalup.htm. Adm. fee).*

Back on Rte. 46, continue for 30 miles through rolling green hills edged in oak and cedar to **New Braunfels** *(Chamber of Commerce, 390 S. Seguin St. 830-625-2385 or 800-572-2626).* Texas' oldest community, it features the **Hummel Museum** *(199 Main Plaza. 830-625-5636. Adm. fee)* and the historic district of **Gruene** *(Gruene Rd.),* a restored, turn-of-the-century German-style town with half-timbered houses and shops.

Ross Maxwell Scenic Drive

Santa Elena Junction to Santa Elena Canyon Overlook in Big Bend National Park

● 32 miles ● 1 hour ● Unless you have a four-wheel-drive vehicle, route requires backtracking. Adm. fee to park

Within the big bend of the Rio Grande, which forms the U.S. border with Mexico, 801,163-acre Big Bend National Park contains deserts, canyons, mesas, and mountains. The drive—designed by Ross Maxwell, a geologist and the national park's first superintendent—gives you a look at the remarkably varied terrain.

From **Santa Elena Junction** in **Big Bend National Park** *(915-477-2251. www.nps.gov/bibe),* the drive heads south. Mountains command the left view, with **Burro Mesa** on the right. After about 2 miles, you can make out angular and domed formations in the mountain rock that indicate ancient volcanism. Fortress-like outcroppings called dikes are also common here.

For the next few miles you ascend steadily past boulder-strewn slopes. **Sotol Vista,** one of the best views in the park, offers a stunning perspective on **Santa Elena Canyon** and the floodplain of the **Rio Grande.** From here, the drive descends through a series of switchbacks, past views of the unmistakable **Mule Ears Peaks** formation; **Tuff Canyon,** named for its gray, volcanic ash rock; and **Cerro Castellan,** a pile of volcanic rock that towers 1,000 feet. As you continue down, the **Chihuahuan Desert** benchland suddenly opens before you.

Don't bypass the old Army compound of **Castolon,** a frontier trading

Santa Elena Canyon

post still open for business. Paralleling the Rio Grande, the road crosses a fertile floodplain. The scattered remains of old adobe buildings along this stretch mark former farms.

About 8 miles from Castolon, the **Santa Elena Canyon Overlook** offers a view down on the narrow Rio Grande flowing through a chasm with 1,500-foot limestone walls. The road ends half a mile farther, where a 1.5-mile trail leads into the mouth of the canyon.

El Camino del Rio

Lajitas to Presidio on Farm-to-Market 170

● 50 miles ● 1½ hours ● Fall through spring; summers are extremely hot. Be aware of steep grades, sharp curves, and poor shoulders along this route.

One of the most spectacular routes in Texas, El Camino del Rio—the River Road—plunges over mountains and into steep canyons, following the sinuous Rio Grande through the desolate but beautiful Chihuahuan Desert.

Begin by orienting yourself with a stop at the **Barton Warnock Environmental Education Center** *(1 mile east of Lajitas on Rte. 170. 915-424-3327. Adm. fee),* where you can pick up information on the **Big Bend Ranch State Park** *(915-229-3416. www.tpwd.state.tx.us/park/bigbend/big bend.htm),* a 438-square-mile preserve encompassing the River Road.

Continue on to the town of **Lajitas** (la-HEE-tahs), an Army post established in 1915 to protect settlers from Pancho Villa, the famed Mexican renegade.

Rte. 170 begins its roller-coaster course before you even leave town, following the **Rio Grande** west. A couple of miles out of town, the volcanism that shaped this region is obvious in dark lava flows topped by white tuff, or hardened volcanic ash.

After another couple of miles, the road swings away from the river, dips to cross spring-fed **Fresno Creek,** which is flanked by layered beds of buff-colored limestone, and returns to the river. After 2 to 3 miles you'll see a cluster of weathered volcanic ash formations called hoodoos along the river. Not far from here, colorful tepees mark a dramatic picnic spot overlooking the river at **Madera Canyon.**

Writer James Michener called the dusty little adobe town of Presidio his "favorite place in all Texas."

The drive now starts a steady, 5-mile climb up the "big hill" of **Santana Mesa.** A major engineering feat, this portion of the road ascends at a 15-percent grade. At the summit, an overlook affords superlative views of the canyon below and the rugged, rather forbidding volcanic landscape that sweeps to the horizon.

As you make your serpentine descent off the mesa, the Rio Grande winds below, a green path through the wild **Chihuahuan Desert.** The **Rio Grande Valley** continues to widen, filled with a sculptural array of eroded lava hills and mesas. You cross **Panther Creek** about 1.5 miles down, then pass a narrow fissure known as **Closed Canyon,** the first in a series of canyons along this undulating stretch.

Continuing on, you have expansive scenics of the arid valley below. After crossing **Tapado Canyon,** well watered for this dry region, watch for traces of a former smugglers path that is now a ranch trail in the bare

183

Main Street, Lajitas

mountain slopes to the north. About 10 miles farther on, the drive enters windblown **Redford,** an old farming community.

Pressing on through open range, the road finds the river again and passes through a couple of refreshingly green oases before entering **Presidio.** A former Spanish mission village, the small adobe border town now functions as a U.S. Port of Entry. Nearby **Fort Leaton State Historic Site** *(915-229-3613. www.tpwd.state.tx.us/park/fortleat/fortleat.htm. Adm. fee)*, built to protect settlers from hostile Indians and Mexican bandidos, serves as the western Information Center for visitors traveling the River Road.

Davis Mountains Loop

Loop from Fort Davis on Texas 118, 166, and 17

● 74 miles ● 2 hours ● All year

This drive weaves through the ragged Davis Mountains—the "Texas Alps"—and around 8,382-foot Mount Livermore, the state's second highest peak. But you'll also see desert, rolling hills, fantastic volcanic formations—and lots of stars.

Start in the frontier village of **Fort Davis** *(Chamber of Commerce, Union Trading Company at Town Square. 915-426-3015 or 800-524-3015. Closed Sat.-Mon.)*—at 4,900 feet the state's most elevated town. Its main attraction is the 1854 **Fort Davis National Historic Site** *(915-426-3224. www.nps.gov/foda. Adm. fee)*, the first military post on the San Antonio–El Paso Road and a home of the famed African-American buffalo soldiers.

Just past the fort, bear left on Rte. 118. Winding up **Limpia Canyon,** past walls of jointed lava columns, the drive parallels the cottonwood-lined banks of **Limpia** (Spanish for "clear" or "clean") **Creek.** For the next 8 miles through the canyon, you dip along foothills covered with oak woodlands, passing 2,800-acre **Davis Mountains State Park** *(915-426-3337. www.tpwd .state.tx.us/park/davis/davis.htm. Adm. fee)*. Vistas of hills and valleys, intruded by volcanic outcroppings and weathered, rounded slopes, predominate for a few more miles.

Beyond Prude Ranch, you drive out onto a beautiful expanse of Texas grassland. In this open country, you have views of **Mount Livermore** and the dome that tops 6,809-foot **Mount Locke.** This is the University of Texas' **McDonald Observatory** *(915-426-3640. www.as.utexas.edu/mcdonald. Visitor Center daily, scheduled observatory tours, and "Star Parties" on Tues., Fri., Sat. evenings)*. The observatory boasts a 432-inch telescope, the world's third largest.

Along the Davis Mountains Loop

Inspiring mountain views continue as the drive hugs the rim of **Elbow Canyon** for several miles before winding steadily down past sylvan **Madera Canyon,** greened by oak, juniper, and pinyon woodlands, toward the high desert.

At the Y-junction, turn left on Rte. 166 into an arid desertscape. Straight ahead looms landmark **Sawtooth Mountain,** a worn volcanic cone.

Officers Row, Fort Davis National Historic Site

Opposite its base stands the **Rock Pile,** a fine example of jointed lava blocks. A couple of miles beyond this, you enter a chaos of volcanism: precipitous slopes, jagged outcroppings, and towering rock peaks. The **Davis Mountains,** 35 to 39 million years old, represent one of the largest volcanic centers in the geologic belt stretching from Montana to Mexico.

The peaks subside during the next few miles, yielding to flat, big sky country for about 17 miles. Off to the southwest you can see miles into Mexico. The road swings eastward, and as you start to climb again through dun-colored hills, the trees gradually reappear.

Pass a dozen miles of green pastureland before reaching Rte. 17, which leads about 3 miles north to Fort Davis.

Canyon Sweep

Prairie dog

Silverton to Claude on Texas 86 and 207

● 53 miles ● 1 hour ● All year. Most scenic in the light of early morning and late afternoon

Traversing the vast, windswept High Plains that occupy the middle of the Texas Panhandle, this drive reaches its scenic height when it descends into splendid Palo Duro Canyon.

The drive begins in **Silverton,** commercial center for the area's farms and ranches and the Briscoe County seat. From here, you follow Rte. 86 west for 5 miles, then head north on Rte. 207 through several miles of unbroken flatness, where rows of milo and wheat alternate with pastureland. This region is part of the High Plains, the southernmost reach of the continent's Great Plains.

About 11 miles beyond Silverton, the road drops into **Tule Canyon,** a beautiful gorge worn by Tule Creek. Winding through a geologic jumble, the drive passes colorful rock strata and dramatic, sheer-faced buttes. After crossing **Tule Creek,** you begin to ascend, soon passing 896-acre **MacKenzie Reservoir,** which offers a variety of recreational opportunities, including boating, swimming, fishing, and picnicking.

For the next 15 miles the road stretches through tableland ranch country dotted with shrubby mesquite and juniper. Suddenly the plains part, revealing the spectacular, 9-mile-wide, 120-mile-long **Palo Duro Canyon.**

Palo Duro Canyon, Texas

In Spanish the name means "hard wood," a reference to the junipers growing from the canyon walls. As you approach the southern rim, a picnic area offers a sweeping view of the nearly 1,000-foot-deep canyon, whose colorful sedimentary layers span 250 million years. When you begin to descend, notice the distinctive color bands in the canyon rock; they represent five major geologic periods. Here and there in the lowest level, you'll see red formations veined by white gypsum. Sixteenth-century conquistador Francisco Coronado called these "Spanish skirts," as they look like the ruffles on a hoop skirt.

When you reach the floor of the canyon, the road crosses the languid **Prairie Dog Town Fork of the Red River,** which carved most of the gorge during the Pleistocene epoch. After climbing the other side of the canyon for about a mile, you have a view of the winding stream below. The ascent grows steeper until you attain the tableland again.

After crossing the grain fields of agricultural Armstrong County, the drive ends about 15 miles farther on in **Claude,** the county seat. From here, you can continue about 40 miles to **Palo Duro Canyon State Park** (806-488-2227. www.tpwd.state.tx.us/park/paloduro/paloduro.htm. Adm. fee) by taking Rte. 1151 west 29 miles to Rte. 1541. Then head south 8 miles to Rte. 217, which leads to the park. The park **Visitor Center** has exhibits on the area's human and nat-

Oklahoma's Quartz Mountains

Blair to Lone Wolf on Oklahoma 44

● 16 miles ● ½ hour ● All year

This short spin takes you through an outcrop of the Wichita Mountains in southwestern Oklahoma, detouring for wonderful bird's-eye views of Lake Altus-Lugert.

From **Blair,** a small farm town and bedroom community for Altus Air Force Base, drive north on Rte. 44. Cotton fields stretch away on both sides of the road, with the bumpy Quartz Mountains rising on the horizon ahead of you.

After 7 miles you cross the **North Fork Red River,** and the **Quartz Mountains,** peppered with enormous sienna boulders, suddenly loom up beside the road. Once sacred ground and a witer camp for Kiowa and Comanche Indians, the area now attracts vacationers, who come to **Quartz Mountain State Park** (580-563-2238. www.tour oklahoma.com/Pages/resort3.html) and its lakeside resort.

Turn left at the state park entrance for an enchanting 4-mile round-trip detour through the 4,300-acre park. Passing a small amusement park, the road ascends to a steep pass that falls away on the right, affording gorgeous views of 6,300-acre **Lake Altus-Lugert.**

Back on Rte. 44, head north along the lake. If the water is low, you can glimpse foundations of the former town of **Lugert,** flooded in the 1920s to create the lake. After 6 miles the drive ends in the small agricultural community of **Lone Wolf.**

ural history; a road plunges 600 feet to the canyon floor, where you'll find hiking and horse trails.

Oklahoma

Wichita Mountains

I-44 to Oklahoma 54 on Oklahoma 49

● 30 miles ● 1 hour ● All year

Just off I-44, this route traverses the Wichita Mountains Wildlife Refuge in southwestern Oklahoma, providing exquisite views of the rocky Wichitas, the refuge's many lakes, and such prairie grazers as buffalo, Texas longhorn, and elk.

From I-44 follow Rte. 49 west through a small residential area near the town of Medicine Park and out past cattle ranches and stands of cottonwood and oak. In just over 6 miles you enter the 59,020-acre **Wichita Mountains Wildlife Refuge** *(580-429-3222. http://southwest.fws.gov/refuges/oklahoma/Wichita)*. You can see close up the rugged, boulder-strewn peaks that arose about 250 million years ago when enormous pressure within the earth fractured blocks of granite and gabbro (cooled magma) and forced them up 1,000 feet and more above the level plain.

Continue about 2 miles through mixed-grass prairie interspersed with

187

Wichita Mountains

oak forests to the turnoff for **Mount Scott.** This 2.5-mile spur road winds up the mountain, with views of the Wichitas to the west and flat plains all around. From the lookout on top, you can see **Fort Sill Military Reservation** to the south. Dating from 1869, it holds the grave of Apache leader Geronimo.

Back on Rte. 49, go west through open rangeland with a backdrop of red-rock hills. A herd of 550 bison graze along here, as well as 300 Texas longhorn. Just beyond the turnoff for Rte. 115, the **Quanah Parker Visitor Center** has good exhibits on local geology, flora, and fauna.

The road now passes several small lakes and picnic sites. In about 7 miles you'll spot a prairie dog town, with **Elk Mountain** rearing up to the south. Rte. 49 ends 6 miles west of the refuge at the junction with Rte. 54.

Talimena Scenic Byway

Talihina, Oklahoma, to Mena, Arkansas, on Oklahoma 1 and Arkansas 88

● **54 miles** ● **2 hours** ● **Spring through fall. Spring bloom occurs in April and May; fall foliage peaks from mid-October to early November.**

Built in the late 1960s expressly for grand views, this two-lane highway ripples over the gentle Ouachita Mountains along the border of Oklahoma and Arkansas. Evergreen and deciduous trees shoulder the road, the latter making for gorgeous floral displays in spring and brilliant color in autumn.

Catering to Choctaw Indians and cattle ranchers, **Talihina** (Choctaw for "iron road") was founded by missionaries in the late 1880s, when the Frisco Railway came through the mountains. The byway's name derives from a combination of the towns that form its end points—Talihina and Mena. It lies within the 1.6-million-acre **Ouachita National Forest** *(501-321-5202. www.fs.fed.us/oonf/ouachita.htm),* the South's oldest (established in 1907) and largest national forest. Ouachita is an Indian word meaning either "good hunting grounds" or "hunting trip," and these woods still hold plentiful deer, squirrel, and other wildlife.

A Visitor Information Station about 7 miles northeast of **Talihina,** at the junction of U.S. 271 and Rte. 1, marks the start of the designated byway. Just 0.3 mile past the information station you come to **Choctaw Vista,** on the west end of **Winding Stair Mountain,** part of the **Ouchita Mountains.** From here you can look out on the beautiful dark blue hills and valleys through which the Choctaw traveled on their way west from Mississippi, in compliance with the 1830 Indian Removal Act.

For the next several miles the road cuts through a forest of shortleaf pine and scrub oak. Along here, too, grow prairie grasses such as little bluestem. The east-west lay of the Ouachita Mountains has caused separate plant communities to develop on either side: Post oak, blackjack, and serviceberry predominate on southern slopes, while the rich soil of the northern slopes supports white oak, hickory, dogwood, and papaw.

View from Rich Mountain, Talimena Scenic Byway

About 5 miles past the forest entrance, stop at **Panorama Vista** for wonderful, sweeping views of the mountains and the small farming villages tucked into the **Holson Valley.** Hang glider enthusiasts often launch from here on weekend days with easterly winds. Golden eagles, vultures, and hawks also soar on the updrafts.

Continue on to **Horse Thief Springs** *(Mile 16)*. In the late 1800s, horse thieves in transit between Texas and Missouri often rested from their labors here. The road now swoops back and forth down Winding Stair Mountain, giving you constantly shifting views. The Ouachita Mountains once extended to the Appalachians, before the Mississippi separated the ranges. The 300-million-year-old sandstones and shales of the Ouachitas were thrust up, folded, and faulted. Fault lines are visible in places along the drive, including the area around **Robert S. Kerr Arboretum and Nature Center** *(Mile 23. www.fs.fed.us/oonf/ oklahoma/nra/kerr.html)*. Three short trails here interpret the environment.

For several miles past the nature center the byway follows the crest of **Rich Mountain** through a forest of dwarf oak stunted by severe ice storms and southerly winds. At about mile 40, the **Old Pioneer Cemetery** holds the graves of 23 people who homesteaded here between the mid-19th and the mid-20th centuries.

Dutchmen's breeches

Two miles beyond, the **Queen Wilhelmina State Park** *(501-394-2863. www.arkansasstateparks.com)* features dramatic southerly views from the crest of Rich Mountain. The park centers around a rustic stone lodge. Originally constructed at the turn of the century and since rebuilt, the lodge was named for the queen of Holland, whose country held a substantial stake in the local railroad.

Three miles east of the park stands the highest point on the drive, **Rich Mountain Fire Tower** (2,681 feet). From this vantage, you have fine views of the forested mountains and of the ribbon of road snaking over the ridges.

The drive ends at the **Visitor Information Station** *(501-394-2382)* in **Mena.** A timber and cattle town, Mena sprang to life in 1896 when the first train of the Kansas City Southern Railroad came chugging through the mountains.

Arkansas

Arkansas 7

Hot Springs to Harrison on Arkansas 7

Country store in the Arkansas Ozarks

● **160 miles** ● **1 day** ● **Spring through fall. Peak fall foliage times vary; check locally.**

Over forested hills and through friendly mountain towns, Rte. 7 curves and rolls south to north in the rugged highlands of western Arkansas. Along the way, the road passes fine rural scenery, a national park, two national forests, several state parks, and a national river. In addition to these, expect to find plenty of down-home hospitality in the cafés and craft shops that line the road.

The drive begins in **Hot Springs,** the boyhood home of former President Bill Clinton. As it cuts through town, Rte. 7 becomes Central Avenue and passes a block of lush landscaping that graces a row of elegant bathhouses dating back to the 1840s. The Spanish Renaissance-style Fordyce Bathhouse (1915) now serves as the Visitor Center for **Hot Springs National Park** *(501-623-1433. www.nps.gov/hosp)*. Established in 1832 by President Andrew Jackson as a special national reservation, the park considers itself the oldest holding in the national park system. The city of Hot Springs itself, built into high limestone bluffs, encompasses part of the park.

For a grand view of the city and surroundings, turn right on Fountain Street and drive up twisting Hot Springs Mountain Drive to **Hot Springs Mountain Tower** *(501-623-6035. Adm. fee).*

Returning to Rte. 7, head north past a stretch of small motels and Victorian houses that soon becomes a 5-mile blur of flea markets, mobile homes, and billboards.

After leaving this behind, the highway travels up a tree-lined valley that heralds the natural beauty to come. At mile 7 turn left at the small town of Fountain Lake and continue on Rte. 7 another 6 miles to Mountain Valley, the town where the famous spring water is bottled. Just north of town, you can detour 7 miles west on Glazypeau Road, then north on Rte. 227 to

Lake Ouachita State Park *(501-767-9366. www.arkansasstateparks.com)*, nestled at the edge of Arkansas' largest man-made lake. The lake's 975 miles of shoreline encompass 48,000 acres.

North again on Rte. 7, you can make an 8.5-mile detour to crystal mines by turning left on Rte. 298. You can rummage around yourself in these mines for the sparkling stones. After the tiny town of Jessieville, Rte. 7 enters **Ouachita National Forest,** 1.6 million acres in the east-west-running Ouachita Mountains. The **Ranger Station** *(501-984-5313)* on the left has exhibits, information, and a short interpretive trail.

The road now begins winding up and down hills, presenting glorious views of low mountains and deep hollows. For the next 15 almost uninhabited miles you see gentle slopes of pines and hardwoods, steep rock walls, and the worn **Ouachita Mountains,** which look their finest in the dazzling hues of autumn.

At mile 42, cross the **Fourche La Fave River** and turn left into **Quarry Cove Park** to see impressive **Nimrod Dam and Lake.** Completed in 1942 for flood control, the 97-foot-high dam stretches 1,012 feet across the lake's east end. The resulting miles of shoreline offer excellent opportunities for fishing, swimming, and waterskiing.

Beyond here, Rte. 7 weaves uphill from the river and soon opens to views of Nimrod Lake and the surrounding hills. By the time you reach Ola, the woods alternate with soothing pastures and green farm fields. For the next few miles the air is redolent of pine woods and cured hams. In addition to hams, numerous wayside shops sell handmade quilts, pottery, honey, jams, and furniture.

191

In the small town of Centerville you can detour 16 miles east on Rte. 154 to lovely **Petit Jean State Park** *(501-727-5441. www.arkansasstateparks.com)*, which features dramatic overlooks, 95-foot-high Cedar Falls, and a lodge.

After returning to Centerville, follow the byway past wide fields of

Arkansas Ozarks

soybean and grain that extend to the distant mountains.

In 8 miles you reach the historic river port of **Dardanelle.** Take a left at the sign for **Dardanelle Powerhouse and Riverview Park,** a worthwhile 1.5-mile digression that leads to excellent views of the mighty **Arkansas River** and Lake Dardanelle Dam, with its towering spillways. **Lake Dardanelle State Park** *(501-967-5516. www.arkansasstateparks.com)* lies just to the northwest of town on Rte. 22. A 7-mile excursion west on Rte. 155 takes you up a zigzagging mountain road to **Mount Nebo State Park** *(501-229-3655. www.arkansasstateparks.com),* where you'll be rewarded with wonderful views of the **Arkansas River Valley.**

As you cross the Arkansas River at the north end of Dardanelle, you'll see on the north shore the prominent grain elevators at the **Port of Dardanelle,** where barges dock to load shipments of locally grown soybeans and grains.

Fordyce Bathhouse, Hot Springs National Park

North of here, the byway passes through fast-paced Russellville before returning to the uncluttered vistas of hill country. After a gradual climb up through fields and forested hills, you arrive in about 7 miles in the small town of **Dover,** where you can check out the abundance of local crafts and antiques, many sold from people's homes.

Five miles beyond, the drive enters **Ozark National Forest** *(501-968-2354. www.fs.fed.us/oonf/ozark),* whose steep-flanked mountains offer a more rugged aspect than the Ouachitas to the south. Oak and hickory predominate in the million acres of forest. Views grow more spectacular as you travel north, and a sign warns that the road is "crooked and steep next 36 miles."

Bending through a gently sloping forest, you pass signs announcing **Booger Hollow,** a tongue-in-cheek hillbilly trading post. Along with cheap souvenirs, it sells real crafts, sorghum, smoked ham, and other backwoods wares hawked by area shops.

The limpid, undammed waters of the Buffalo National River have long attracted canoeists and anglers.

About 10 miles farther on, you pass through the village of **Pelsor,** whose family-run general store has been around since 1922. Just north the forest opens to marvelous views in all directions. Stop at one of the pullouts or at the access to the 165-mile-long **Ozark Highlands Trail,** a mile beyond Pelsor.

After 9 miles you come to the quaint highland village of **Cowell,** with its little church and pond. Past this, the drive offers more fabulous views of the valley and rumpled ridge to the west.

Three miles north of Cowell, you can divert a mile west on Rte. 16, then northwest on County Rd. NE28 (gravel) 3 miles to **Alum Cove Natural Bridge,** a fascinating 130-foot-long rock span.

Back on Rte. 7, for the next several miles you twist along the side of **Judea Mountain,** through meadows, hollows, and coves. If you want to savor the spectacular scenery and some country cooking, stop at **Cliff House Inn** *(870-446-2292),* which hangs over the edge of the Ozarks' deepest canyon—the Arkansas "grand canyon."

Just north, the byway enters **Jasper,** a gateway to the Buffalo National River. The town has craft shops, cafés, motels, and river outfitters. As you cross the **Little Buffalo River** on the way out of town, notice the exposed limestone and sandstone walls. The road continues through the **Boston Mountains** (part of the Ozarks) before descending once again, this time down to the **Buffalo National River.**

Before crossing the bridge here, stop for information at **Pruitt Ranger Station** *(870-446-5373.*

Fishing on Buffalo Natl. River

Mid-March–Sept.). Designated as a national river in 1972, this wilderness protects such animals as bobcats, minks, and bears.

After passing **Mystic Caverns,** where you can tour two mountain caves, the road begins to smooth out somewhat, the hills flattening into green pastures where horses and cattle graze beside barns.

193

Soon you come to the drive's end in the resort town of **Harrison,** "crossroads of the Ozarks." Here, next to the local high school, a little-known piece of the past survives: **Baker Prairie,** a remnant of the vanishing

Canoeists along the Buffalo

tallgrass prairie that once blanketed much of the country's midsection. For information on it, visit the **Tourist Information Center** *(870-741-3343)* on U.S. 65 north.

The Levee

Loop from Lake Chicot State Park on Arkansas 257, 144, County Road 59, and the levee

● 30 miles ● 1 hour ● All year. Best in early morning and late afternoon. About half the drive is on a one-lane gravel-topped levee that limits speeds to no more than 25 mph.

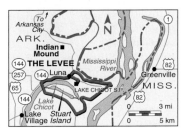

Following the Mississippi River, this adventurous loop travels the levees and back roads of southeastern Arkansas. Along the way, you have views of fertile farmlands, swamps, streams, abundant water birds, and other wildlife.

Start at **Lake Chicot State Park** *(870-265-5480. www.arkansasstate parks.com)*, situated on Arkansas' largest natural lake. The 20-mile-long oxbow lake is thought to have formed about 500 years ago when the Mississippi River changed course. From here head north on Rte. 257, then left on Rte. 144. Turn right after 1.3 miles by the grain bins at the intersection of unmarked Luna Road, which leads to the levee.

Drive up onto the gravel-topped levee and turn right. Running 640 miles along the Arkansas and Mississippi Rivers, this ranks among the world's longest continuous levees. After a flood in 1927 broke through the former levee, construction on the present one began. Although the levee follows the Mississippi, views of the river are limited.

At mile 3.6, you pass the site of Columbia, a bygone county seat that was flooded in 1855, then burned by Union troops in 1864. Along here too, on the left, the sloughs and borrow pits from which soil was taken to build the levee harbor a wonderful variety of birds, including cattle egrets, great blue herons, and sometimes ducks. Birds and beavers feed among the willows and cypress knees at the edges of these pits.

After about 6 miles the levee turns abruptly southwest; continue for another mile and a half to **Leland Chute,** a side channel of the river, where unusual paddlefish are sometimes caught. Farms stretching into the distance on the other side of the levee grow cotton, soybeans, milo, winter wheat, and rice.

Pink smartweed

Continuing on the levee 3 more miles, you can glimpse the northeastern end of Lake Chicot. In late summer the woods and shore here explode with the chatter of migrating ibis, herons, egrets, and endangered wood storks. After 2 more miles, you can cross the cattle guards and head west on pavement. Or you can continue exploring the levee to the south, and in 4.3 miles you'll arrive at the grand **Mississippi River.**

If you choose to take the paved road west, in a couple of miles you'll see the 1898 **Hyner Cemetery,** resting place for Italian immigrants who came to work the area plantations and frequently died of malaria. Two miles farther on, the road passes **Whiskey Chute** and **Stuart Island** (on the right), headquarters for a band of early 19th-century river pirates. Then you cross

On the levee

195

the dam over crescent-shaped Lake Chicot and intersect Rte. 144. From here you can take a 3-mile detour left and visit **Lake Village.** Settled in the mid-1800s, it is now an upscale resort town of nice houses and lakeside docks that are in striking contrast to some of the humbler dwellings in the rest of the county. Or continue the tour by turning right and then left (in 0.2 miles) onto unmarked County Road 59.

Just beyond this turn stands the lovely old Georgian manor house *(Private)* that was once the centerpiece of 10,400-acre **Yellow Bayou Plantation** (circa 1850). After 4.5 more miles past farmlands and banks colored by seasonal wildflowers, you reach the **Chicot Pumping Station.** The three-story facility, built by the Army Corps of Engineers, diverts muddy waters to the Mississippi. A **Visitor Center** details the project.

If you take the levee 14 miles north, you arrive in **Arkansas City,** historic seat of Desha County. The views along the way are excellent, but there are few turnoffs and no facilities.

To continue the loop, turn toward the pumping plant and head south on the levee. In 2 miles you see to the left the **Panther Forest Crevasse,** created by a 1912 break in the levee that flooded Lake Village. Anhingas and ducks favor the deep water here.

A half mile farther along, notice on your right the earth mound at the field's edge. It was constructed by Native Americans about 600 years ago. Continue 3.7 miles south on the levee past more views of fields and backwaters to the turnoff at Luna. In a half mile the loop ends back at Rte. 144.

Southwest

Utah, Arizona, New Mexico, Colorado

Utah

Logan Canyon

Logan to Bear Lake on U.S. 89

● **40 miles** ● **1 to 2 hours** ● **Spring through fall**

This scenic route in northern Utah through Wasatch-Cache National Forest's Logan Canyon is part of U.S. 89, which runs most of the way between the Mexican and Canadian borders. Along the way it passes many of the West's great sights, including the Grand Canyon, the Great Salt Lake, and Grand Teton, Yellowstone, and Glacier National Parks. Here the highway slips between towering limestone walls and shadows the Logan River. After a 3,000-foot climb, the road opens up to spectacular views of Bear Lake, shining jewel-like turquoise. Moose, elk, and deer are abundant in Logan's forests, and you can often spot them along the drive.

Outside of **Logan,** U.S. 89 shoots straight into Logan Canyon, passing a **Forest Service Information Center** *(Logan Ranger Dist. 435-755-3620)* on the right. Beyond the building to the right, the gently sloping terraces are embankments left over from ancient Lake Bonneville, which once covered 19,500 square miles of northwestern Utah. The first 4 miles pass three small dams, popular with fly fishermen. At the **Spring Hollow Campground Area,** the pleasant, 1-mile interpretive **Riverside Nature Trail** skirts the Logan River's rich riparian habitat; you can see beavers and their lodges. For spectacular views, skilled hikers can head up the precipitous, 4-mile **Crimson Trail** to the top of the limestone cliffs.

Continue along U.S. 89 about 15 miles to a good side trip. It begins on Tony Grove Road and winds up nearly 7 miles through aspen groves to **Tony Grove Lake** at 8,100 feet. The tranquil, pristine 25-acre lake nestles against steep rock cliffs—a glacial basin formed more than 10,000 years ago.

Back on U.S. 89, the route continues to climb, passing the **Beaver Mountain Ski Resort** *(435-753-0921),* until it reaches 7,800-foot **Bear Lake Summit** and then drops down to an overlook for **Bear Lake.** The 20-mile-long lake sparkles a blue-green reminiscent of the tropics. Some 8,000 years ago,

Oak Creek Canyon drive, near Sedona, Arizona

earthquakes isolated the lake from the Bear River, creating an unusual water chemistry and eventually nurturing four unique fish species.

Down by the lake, **Garden City** contains a marina and numerous shacks selling local raspberry jam and delicious raspberry shakes. Wide, sandy swimming beaches line the lake along the road southeast to Laketown.

Ashley Natl. Forest Scenic Byway

Vernal to Manila on U.S. 191, Utah 44, and Forest Road 218

● **67 miles** ● **3 hours** ● **All year**

Tucked into the northeastern corner of Utah, this route climbs across high desert country into lush evergreen-aspen forests as it traverses the eastern flank of the rugged Uinta Mountains, one of the few chains that run east-west in the hemisphere. Highlights include breathtaking rim views of Flaming Gorge and the twisted rock maze of Sheep Creek Canyon.

Before beginning the drive, stop in **Vernal** to see the **Utah Field House of Natural History State Park and Dinosaur Gardens** *(235 E. Main St. 435-789-3799. http://parks.state.ut.us/parks/www1/utaf .htm. Adm. fee)* for a good overview of area wildlife, geology, and Indian prehistory, including a room full of fluorescent rocks and a garden with full-size dinosaur reproductions. On U.S. 191 geologic signs plot the route as it progresses steadily back through time from the Cretaceous, about 80 million years ago, to the Precambrian, about a billion years ago. After nearly 6 miles the dry desertscape of juniper and sagebrush gives way to **Steinaker State Park** *(435-789-4432. http://parks.state.ut.us/parks/www1/stei.htm. Adm. fee),* a 780-acre lake that offers good trout and bass fishing. Three miles farther is **Red Fleet State Park** *(435-789-4432. http://parks.state.ut.us/parks/www1/redf.htm. Adm. fee).* Ask for directions to the Jurassic dinosaur footprints across the lake.

After Red Fleet the road switchbacks uphill, passing the gray gravel detritus of a large open-pit phosphate mine. Used for fertilizer, the phosphate-rich rock originated from the decomposition of billions of microscopic marine organisms some 225 million years ago. About 17 miles from Vernal, **Windy Point** offers good views of the **Ashley Valley** and reservoirs below. The road leaves the juniper-covered terrain, crosses high rolling grassland—a favorite wintering area for elk—and enters **Ashley National Forest**

Flaming Gorge National Recreation Area

(435-789-1181. www.fs.fed.us/r4/ashley). Four miles later the Red Cloud-Dry Fork drive (see sidebar) heads off to the left to camping and picnic grounds.

Fourteen miles from the Red Cloud turnoff, a side trip on U.S. 191 descends northeast for 6 miles to the **Flaming Gorge Dam and Visitor Center** *(435-885-3135. Visitor Center Mem. Day-Labor Day)*, site of the Green River dam that created the 91-mile-long Flaming Gorge Reservoir. A self-guided, 20-minute tour takes you to the power plant. In summer watch for ospreys on the small islands in the reservoir.

Return to Rte. 44; after nearly 4 miles, the turnoff for the **Red Canyon Overlook**

Toward Sheep Creek Canyon off Utah 44

appears on the right. The forested, 1.5-mile drive little prepares the visitor for one of Utah's most unforgettable vistas. The breathtaking vertical red-rock cliffs of Flaming Gorge plummet more than 1,300 feet to the reservoir below. A rim trail leads along the edge for incredible views of the **Green River.** Farther down the road, the **Visitor Center** *(435-889-3713. Mem. Day-Labor Day)* hangs precariously on the cliff's edge.

Back on Rte. 44, look for Milepost 14. **Sheep Creek Canyon,** a must-see 13-mile side trip *(Closed in winter)*, splits off to the west on FR 218. After nearly 7 miles the road passes Palisades Campground and enters **Sheep Creek Canyon Geological Area,** where upthrusts and erosion have created strange rock sculptures. Almost 8 miles later, the craggy rock walls narrow as the road passes **Big Spring.** Here, water pours out of the rock wall until there's barely room for road, creek, and cottonwood

Red Cloud-Dry Fork

Forest Road 018

● 45 miles ● 2 hours ● Summer. higher elevations snow-covered from late fall to mid-spring; the partly dirt route is usually closed in winter. Passage not recommended in wet weather. *See map p. 198.*

Seventeen miles north of Vernal on U.S. 191, this partly dirt road penetrates the Uinta (you-inta) Mountains' deep canyons and high-elevation forests laced with trout streams. (The road receives moderate to heavy use in the summer.)

From inside the **Ashley National Forest** *(435-789-1181)* boundary off U.S. 191, FR 018 cuts west across open grassland toward forests of lodgepole pine. (Near the FR 018 turnoff, there's a place to park for the 32.5-mile round-trip East Park Loop bike trail.) At 3 miles FR 018 (Red Cloud Loop Road) turns left, while the paved road leads north to the **East Park Reservoir.**

For the next 24 miles, FR 018 passes through groves of aspens, open meadows, and pine forests, offering some breathtaking views of Uinta peaks, including 12,240-foot **Marsh Peak,** one of the range's highest. Mule deer and elk are common; bobcat, coyote, mountain lion, and bear are also present, though they are rarely seen.

The road continues past **Dry Fork Overlook,** with a spectacular view of **Brownie Canyon** far below. From here, the road drops 2,000 feet in 10 miles, descending into **Dry Fork Canyon,** with picnic and camping sites. At about Mile 43 the road passes **Dry Fork,** site of a thriving community in early frontier days. A wall of prehistoric Indian petroglyphs is visible 1.5 miles south of Dry Fork on the **Sadie McConkie Ranch** *(Donation).*

199

trees. (Camping is prohibited from June to October because of the danger of flash floods.) Bighorn sheep were recently reintroduced into this area. The road widens to reveal the dirty white cliffs of Navajo sandstone from the Jurassic period, when dinosaurs roamed here, and then at the junction with Rte. 44 it passes picnic sites beneath cottonwoods. It's worthwhile to backtrack 4.5 miles east on Rte. 44 to the **Flaming Gorge Overlook,** whose sweeping vistas of red, yellow, and green rock cliffs caused explorer Maj. John Wesley Powell to dub it a "flaming, brilliant red gorge." The rest of the route passes over desertscape to the town of **Manila.**

Mount Nebo Scenic Byway

Utah 132 east of Nephi to Payson on Forest Road 015

● 38 miles ● 1½ hours ● Spring through fall; closed in winter

Though not far from the traffic of I-15, this central Utah route leaves civilization behind, climbing quickly into the quiet forests and far-reaching vistas of the Wasatch Range. Gently rising and falling over aspen-clad ridges and hills, the road passes under the nose of Mount Nebo and by a passel of peaceful mountain lakes. Mule deer and elk abound.

Begin the route 6 miles east of **Nephi** on FR 015. You'll head into the southernmost section of the **Uinta National Forest** *(435-623-2735. www.fs.fed.us/r4/uinta),* rising into the **Wasatch Range.** The road skirts gray, fingerlike rock outcroppings and passes Pole Canyon Road, which pushes northeast into groves of quaking aspen until it reaches **Bear Canyon.** Turn off at the **Ponderosa** and **Bear Canyon Campgrounds;** these peaceful sites, beneath a canopy of mixed conifers, rustle with animals. The **Nebo Bench Trail** leaves from here, climbing up into the 28,500-acre **Mount Nebo Wilderness** and eventually reaching the mountain's summit.

Back on the road, you'll switchback up the broad-backed mountains, through aspen and evergreen forests, to the **Devils Kitchen Geologic Interest Site.** A short walk takes you to an observation deck, passing informative signs about the vegetation. The natural rock amphitheater below features a strange landscape of knob-shaped pinnacles of red sandstone and conglomerate known as hoodoos.

Continue along the road for about 2 miles to the **Mount Nebo Overlook.** Like gnomes with pointy hats, white firs cling to the steep sides of the mountain, at 11,877 feet the tallest peak in the Wasatch Range. Long swathes on the mountain's flanks remain clear of vegetation, either because of thin soil, landslides, or avalanches. Early Mormon settlers named Mount Nebo after a mountain in Palestine; the name comes from a word meaning "sentinel of God."

The road continues past FR 014, which shoots down **Santaquin Canyon** along a trout stream to I-15. Just beyond the turnoff, **Utah Lake Overlook** offers stunning views of the turquoise waters of **Utah Lake** to the north and

Dawn along FR 015, Mount Nebo Wilderness

the flat desert beyond. The picturesque **Payson Lakes** at Mile 24 lure rainbow trout fishermen in droves. Heading off the mountain toward **Payson,** the road curves down into a narrow canyon, past maples that flash brilliant red in fall.

Colorado River Scenic Byway

Moab to I-70 on U.S. 191 and Utah 128

● 44 miles ● 2 hours ● All year

Hugging the southeast side of the Colorado River as it winds below sheer cliffs of Wingate sandstone, this route passes isolated side canyons and the spectacular pinnacles known as Fisher Towers. Rafters and kayakers ply the muddy rapids, and sand beaches line the water's edge. The lively town of **Moab** is a base for river runners, mountain bikers, four-wheel-drive enthusiasts, and rock climbers *(Moab Information Center 435-259-8825).* Five miles to the north lies **Arches National Park** *(435-259-8161. www.nps.gov/ arch. Adm. fee);* also nearby are the red-rock canyons of **Canyonlands National Park** *(435-259-7164. www.nps.gov/cany. Adm. fee).*

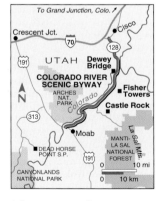

 Drive 2 miles north of Moab on U.S. 191, then turn right on Rte. 128 for the Colorado River Scenic Byway. A band of roadside vegetation provides a lovely counterpoint to the red and orange hues of the sandstone cliffs. Three miles in, the road passes **Negro Bill Canyon,** named after an early settler. A 2-mile hike up the canyon leads to views of **Morning Glory Natural Bridge.** High across the river from the trailhead lie 1,000-year-old Pueblo granaries.

The **Big Bend Recreation Area** offers a rest spot and sand beaches as the river makes a sweeping U-turn. Above Big Bend the Colorado picks up speed, and rapids begin to riffle the water. Several miles later, the canyon widens, and the road leaves the river. At about Mile 15, Castle Valley Road heads east, winding up through knolls to **Castle Valley** and views of the high, often snowcapped **La Sal Mountains.**

Colorado River with Fisher Towers and La Sal Mountains

Continuing north on Rte. 128 for several more miles, you'll see to the south the impossibly slender shape of **Castle Rock,** site of several recent car commercials. At about Mile 21, a 2.2-mile, graded dirt road turns right off Rte. 128 toward **Fisher Towers Recreation Site,** with views of soaring rock pinnacles. The 900-foot-high **Titan** and other pinnacles are remnants of an ancient floodplain. A 2-mile hike crosses to the foot of the spires, ducks through narrow canyons, crosses a steel ladder, and passes convoluted rock formations. The hike ends with spectacular views of adjacent **Onion Creek Canyon.** Five miles beyond Fisher Towers, the road crosses the river near the 1916 **Dewey Bridge** and heads through desert to I–70 near Cisco.

Bicentennial Highway

Hanksville to Blanding on Utah 95

● 133 miles ● ½ day ● Spring and fall

Miles of southeastern Utah's desert little prepare you for the panoramic views of sparkling Lake Powell against the sheer red-rock cliffs of the Glen Canyon National Recreation Area. From Lake Powell the route continues southeast through sheer red-rock canyons, passing world-famous natural bridges as well as numerous Anasazi ruins. Finished in the bicentennial year of 1976, this route samples an extraordinary range of scenery, history, and geologic wonders.

From **Hanksville,** Rte. 95 sweeps south through miles of open desert, with the imposing **Henry Mountains** to the west.

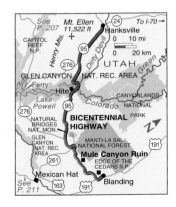

Rugged and remote, these mountains support mountain lions and a herd of nearly 400 bison. After about 10 miles an unimproved road heads west up to **Bull Creek Pass,** where a 4-mile trail near Lonesome Beaver Campground leads to the summit of 11,522-foot **Mount Ellen** and sweeping Utah views. Some 11 miles from the turnoff, the **Little Egypt Geologic Site** offers views of sphinxlike formations eroded from the Entrada sandstone.

About 9 miles farther along, the route descends into the red rock of **North Wash Canyon** and passes **Hog Springs Picnic Grounds,** where a trail over a bridge leads past walls of Wingate and Kayenta sandstone eroded over the past 100 million years. Six miles later the road enters the **Glen Canyon National Recreation Area** *(520-608-6404. www .nps.gov/glen),* then, after another 5 miles, arrives at the **Hite Overlook.** From atop the mesa the views of **Lake Powell** are extraordinary. Clear bands of brown and red sediments form cakelike layers in the eroding mesas. Look for **Hite Marina** in the far distance across the lake. This is the northernmost area of Lake Powell, a huge reservoir created by the Glen Canyon Dam on the Colorado River some 190 miles to the southwest. The road weaves down the cliff, crossing a bridge over the deep canyon of the **Dirty Devil River,** then another over the **Narrow Canyon of the Colorado River.**

> Arches are created by wind and rain and appear on the skyline, while natural bridges are carved by stream erosion and lie deep in canyons.

Shortly after crossing the Colorado, a road heads west to **Hite Marina-Campground** *(435-684-2278),* a primitive campground and one of Lake Powell's four full-service marinas. Nearby ruins suggest that prehistoric Indians used Hite as a point to ford the Colorado. Just past Hite, several access roads lead down to small side canyons flooded by Lake Powell. Rte. 95 continues southeast through **White Canyon,** past the rock formations of **Jacob's Chair** and **Cheesebox Butte.** Rising to 6,000-foot **Cedar Mesa,** the route enters a pinyon juniper forest and reaches the entrance to **Natural Bridges National Monument** *(435-692-1234. www.nps.gov/nabr. Adm. fee).* Continue 4 miles to the Visitor Center for a guide to the 9-mile loop-drive. Over eons, streams have cut deep into the white sandstone of **White** and **Armstrong Canyons** and left three spectacular natural bridges, each bearing a Hopi name: **Sipapu, Kachina,** and **Owachomo.** At each stop, trails lead down to the bridges on the floor of the canyon. The easy, 0.6-mile round-trip **Horsecollar Ruin Overlook Trail** winds around a sheer cliff face to a dramatic view of Anasazi ruins far below.

Back on Rte. 95, you can see an Anasazi habitation with below-ground structures at the **Mule Canyon Ruin and Rest Stop.** Archaeologists stabilized a 700-year-old tower and kiva, or

Owachomo Bridge, Natural Bridges Natl. Mon.

ceremonial chamber. One mile southeast of here lies **Cave Towers,** reachable by foot on a rough road just east of the entrance to Mule Canyon Ruin. At the head of precipitous **Mule Canyon** sit seven towers more than 900 years old. Other structures are visible halfway up in the cliff walls.

Rte. 95 continues east from the ruins, then jogs north across **Comb Wash** and up through a passage cut out of **Comb Ridge.** Extending 80 miles from the Abajo Mountains south to Kayenta, Arizona, this steeply eroded monocline—a bend in the Earth's crust—long hindered travel in Utah's southeastern corner. Just ahead, **Butler Wash Rest Stop,** another cliffside ruin, is well worth visiting. The 1-mile round-trip trail crosses washes and smooth, slippery rock, known as slickrock, to an overlook of cliff dwellings above a dead-end canyon.

Continue on to **Blanding** for a visit to the **Edge of the Cedars State Park** (435-678-2238. *Follow signs to*

Temples of the Sun and Moon, Cathedral Valley

NW edge of town. http://parks.state.ut.us/ parks/www1/edge.htm. Adm. fee), the site of a small ancestral Puebloan village and a museum with a large collection of native objects, some of them rare.

Cathedral Valley

Utah 24 near Caineville to I-70 at Fremont Junction

● 56 miles ● 1 day ● Spring through fall. High-clearance vehicles only. Not advisable in wet weather. Check conditions at Visitor Center (435-425-3791).

This maintained dirt road into the northern end of **Capitol Reef National Park** crosses a desertscape of twisting canyons and upthrust rock to Upper Cathedral Valley and its 500-foot monoliths.

Follow Rte. 24 east of the park Visitor Center for 11 miles. Turn off at the marked **Fremont River Ford.** (If the river is too high, go to Caineville farther along to access the valley.) The road follows the **Hartnet,** a region of low cliffs, canyons, and sandy valleys. At Mile 14, a 1.2–mile side road cuts west to a steep drop-off and the **Lower South Desert Overlook,** with views of the contorted terrain of the **Waterpocket Fold.** Some 17 miles beyond the ford, the road passes the **Lower Cathedral Valley Overlook.** Take the easy 1-mile walk to the rim to see the pinnacles known as the **Temple of the Sun** and the **Temple of the Moon.** The road continues to the Upper Cathedral Valley Overlook Spur Road. Turn right in just under a half mile for splendid views. After a series of steep switchbacks, you'll be treated to more views of the **Upper Cathedral Valley.** Soon the road goes north, paralleling a volcanic dike, into the **Last Chance Desert.** As you head toward I-70, to the west will be the **Thousand Lake Plateau,** and to the east the **San Rafael Swell** badlands.

Utah 12 Scenic Byway

*Panguitch through Bryce Canyon and Capitol Reef
National Parks on Utah 12, 63, and 24*

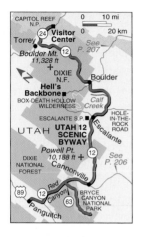

● **122 miles** ● At least ½ day ● Spring and
fall. Be sure to check road and weather
conditions before taking any unpaved side
routes. Admission fees to national parks

Some of Utah's most outstanding high desert
scenery unfolds along this route, which begins near
the pale orange spires of Bryce Canyon and ends
amid the immense sandstone domes of Capitol
Reef. Between these two national parks, this remote
highway snakes along narrow ridgetops, carves
through red-rock canyons past prehistoric Native
American ruins, and ascends 11,000-foot Boulder
Mountain for breathtaking views. Only paved in
its entirety since 1985, Rte. 12 serves as the road-
head for many small but scenic side roads offering
unparalleled opportunities to delve into one of
continental America's last explored frontiers.

The route begins at the county seat of **Panguitch,** an Old West town
dotted with redbrick houses full of Mormon history, and heads southeast
toward Bryce Canyon. About 2 miles past the intersection with U.S. 89, Rte.
12 enters **Dixie National Forest** *(435-
865-3700. www.fs.fed.us/dxnf)* and
rolls through **Red Canyon,** a fairy-
like world of curiously sculptured
limestone formations colored brilliant red by iron oxides and accent-
ed by large ponderosa pines. Outlaw
Butch Cassidy often hid out here.
At 9 miles, the national forest's
Red Canyon Campground *(435-676-
8815)* offers full camping facilities.
The orange-tinted cliffs and spires
of Bryce Canyon appear to the
southeast as the road ascends to the
flats of the **Paunsaugunt Plateau.**
Twelve miles from U.S. 89, Rte. 63
branches off to the south, passing
Ruby's Inn *(435-834-5341)*, a de-
scendant of the original "Tourist
Rest" located near Bryce Canyon's
rim. Some 2 miles beyond, this road
enters **Bryce Canyon National Park**
*(435-834-5322. www.nps.gov/brca.
Adm. fee).* The road along the rim
skirts 12 huge amphitheaters that
drop a thousand feet. With no

Red Canyon, east of Panguitch

Cottonwood Canyon Road

Cannonville to U.S. 89 E of Paria Ranger Station

● 46 miles ● 2 hours ● Spring through fall ● Southern part of route is graded dirt, which is impassable when wet and hard to navigate when too dry.

The paved portion of this southern Utah road—originally planned as a route between Bryce Canyon and Lake Powell—shoots 7 miles south of **Cannonville** to the entrance of the **Kodachrome Basin State Park** *(435-679-8562. http://parks.state.ut.us/parks/www1/koda.htm. Adm. fee)*, a name suggested by 1940s visitors from the National Geographic Society. Monolithic spires known as chimneys tower up from the valley floor. Once the area had springs and geysers, which gradually filled up with sediment and solidified. The soft Entrada sandstone eroded, leaving these odd desert spires. The road leads to **Chimney Rock;** from there a 1.5-mile round-trip trail takes you to a formation known as **Ballerina Slipper** and to a sandstone arch. Continue along the route for 10 miles to where a short side road leads to **Grosvenor Arch.** Named for Gilbert H. Grosvenor, the first full-time editor of the NATIONAL GEOGRAPHIC magazine, the magnificent sandstone buttress actually contains two arches. The road then passes into **Cottonwood Canyon,** through a slickrock desertscape of colorful red and white eroded rock. The road continues to Rte. 89, paralleling the **Paria River** and affording views of the **Cockscomb,** a jagged upthrust of the earth's crust.

shoulder in places, the single-lane road through the dense mixed-conifer forest can become crowded, especially on weekends.

Grosvenor Arch, Kodachrome Basin S.P.

Half a mile from the excellent Visitor Center, a short loop-road heads east to the rim at **Sunset Point,** a vantage point for the 6-square-mile **Bryce Amphitheater,** the scenic heart of the park. **Sunrise Point** offers superb views of the many-spired **Queen's Garden,** rock formations suggesting a queen facing her court, and of **Powell Plateau** in the distance. **Queen's Garden Trail** descends into the formations, known as hoodoos. Other hikes from Sunrise Point descend to the formations known as **Thor's Hammer** and **Wall Street.** The road continues to the rustic, remodeled 1920s **Bryce Canyon Lodge** *(435-834-5361. April-Oct.).* Well worth taking is a horse or mule ride *(call the lodge for information)* that begins at the lodge and descends to the canyon floor through a surreal landscape of tortured bristlecone pine and red rock.

From the Visitor Center continue 2 miles along the park road to a left turn for **Inspiration** and **Bryce Points,** where the 0.5-mile **Under-the-Rim Trail** begins. From here, **Silent City** looks like a congregation frozen in its seats. Bryce's many freeze-thaw cycles—about 200 a year—help nature sculpture these spires and spindles. The park road continues for 14 more miles, passing other lookouts, canyons, and an arch before ending at **Rainbow** and **Yovimpa Points** for views up to 200 miles to **Navajo Mountain** and the **Kaibab Plateau** in Arizona.

Retrace the park road to rejoin Rte. 12, which runs across the northern edge of the park. Follow it eastward into **Water Canyon. Mossy Cave** has a 1-mile round-trip trail that goes to a small cave and waterfall. From the park, the road drops south through the small towns of Tropic and Cannonville, the roadhead for the Cottonwood Canyon Road (see p. 206).

About 13 miles past Tropic, stop at a pullout for stunning views of the salmon-colored cliffs of 10,188-foot **Powell Point,** an early landmark in Maj. John Wesley Powell's survey of the Southwest. The road continues toward Escalante across the high pastures of the **Table Cliff Plateau.** Seventeen miles beyond the pullout, another one provides views of a Fremont granary built high in the cliff face. Primarily hunter-gatherers, the Fremont Indians occupied the area between A.D. 1050 and 1200.

A mile west of Escalante is **Escalante**

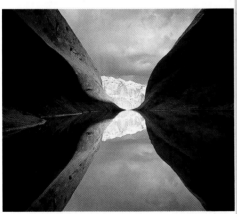

Waterpocket Fold, Capitol Reef National Park

State Park and Visitor Center (*435-826-4466. http://parks.state.ut.us/parks/www1/esca .htm. Adm. fee).* **Wide Hollow Reservoir** offers trout fishing, while a 1-mile nature trail leads to a petrified forest, with brightly

Burr Trail

Boulder to Utah 276

● **66 miles** ● **½ day** ● **Spring and fall. Check road conditions at Visitor Center (435-425-3791).**

This spectacular, partly dirt byway cuts across the rugged canyonland of southeastern Utah, descending precipitously to the giant Waterpocket Fold at the southern end of Capitol Reef National Park.

Heading southeast out of Boulder, the route weaves around white domes and rounded buttes of Navajo sandstone before crossing **Deer Creek** and coming to a primitive campground after 6 miles. The road descends into the narrow confines of **Long Canyon,** its fractured sandstone walls shooting hundreds of feet above the road. After 12 miles the **Long Canyon Overlook** affords sweeping views of **Circle Cliffs Basin.** Just before a series of switchbacks descend steeply into the **Waterpocket Fold,** a giant monocline, or fold in the earth's surface, a spur road (4-wheel drive needed) heads 3 miles north into **Upper Muley Twist Canyon,** past several arches. At the end, a short hike leads to the **Strike Valley Overlook,** with breath-taking views of the Waterpocket Fold. Crossing the fold, the Burr Trail drops 1,000 feet in

a mile. Take Notom-Bullfrog Road south 30 miles to Rte. 276. A left turn will lead you to the Bicentennial Highway (see p. 202) and a right turn to the Glen Canyon National Recreation Area.

Bryce Canyon National Park at sunrise

colored rock logs and a view of the early Mormon town of **Escalante.** Hell's Backbone, a spine-tingling, high-mountain, dirt-and-gravel road accessible in good weather, heads north from Escalante and overlooks **Box-Death Hollow Wilderness** area. The gravel-and-dirt Hole-in-the-Rock Road cuts south from Escalante 18 miles to the twisted slickrock desertscape of **Devil's Garden.** The side road ends at the **Hole-in-the-Rock,** a spot where in 1879-80 some 200 Mormon pioneers with 83 wagons and 1,200 head of livestock penetrated a notch in the canyon wall 2,000 feet above the Colorado River.

The 29 miles between Escalante and Boulder are so dramatic that you might not need to leave the road. It crosses **Calf Creek** near the **Calf Creek Campground** (435-826-5499), where a 5.5-mile trail leads to 126-foot **Calf Creek Falls.** In this area, known as the **Hogback,** the road twists along the crest of a narrow ridge with spectacular views of Calf Creek far below.

Continue on 6 miles to **Boulder,** where **Anasazi State Park** (435-335-7308. http://parks.state.ut.us/parks/www1/anas .htm. Adm. fee) offers a close-up view of the ancient Pueblo people, who, along with the Fremont Indians, occupied this region in prehistoric times. University of Utah archaeologists uncovered an 87-room village here in the late 1950s, one of the largest ancestral Puebloan communities west of the Colorado River. The state park has re-created a six-room dwelling and museum. From Boulder, the Burr Trail (see p. 207) leads southeast to Lake Powell and the Glen Canyon National Recreation Area.

Rte. 12 heads north from Boulder and enters a landscape of sagebrush and pinyon pine. It ascends the broad flanks of **Boulder Mountain,** which sits on the **Aquarius Plateau,** one of the continent's highest timbered plateaus. In fall, stands of fire yellow aspen play against the evergreens. Views from several overlooks, such as **Point Lookout,** are exceptional. The tangled canyons and colored sandstone cliffs of **Capitol Reef** lie in the foreground, while the imposing **Henry Mountains** and **Navajo Mountain** dominate the horizon. The road descends to the junction with Rte. 24 near Torrey.

Turn right onto Rte. 24 and enter **Capitol Reef National Park** (435-425-3791. www.nps.gov/care. Adm. fee), which preserves a portion of the **Waterpocket Fold,** a great wrinkle in the Earth's crust—known to geologists as a monocline—that reveals its raw colors and layers. For a hundred miles the fold's

208

Paiute Indians believed that Bryce Canyon's rock configurations were once animal-like creatures who changed into people. But they were bad, so Spirit Coyote turned them to stone.

Kimberly–Big John Road

Junction to I-70 near Fremont Indian S.P. on Utah 153 and FR 123 and 113

● **40 miles** ● **3 hours** ● **Summer and fall. Generally passable by high-clearance vehicles, but dangerous in wet weather. Closed winter and spring.**

At altitudes ranging from 6,000 to 11,500 feet, this southwestern Utah dirt road explores a corner of the **Fishlake National Forest** *(435-438-2436. www.fs.fed.us/recreation/forest_descr/ ut_r4_fishlake.html),* ascending the naked slopes of the **Tushar Mountains** and passing an old mining town.

From the town of **Junction** on U.S. 89, head west on Rte. 153 into the national forest, passing **Puffer Lake** and **Elk Meadows,** with its downhill ski area.

Near **Beaver Canyon,** take Forest Road 123 north to the **Big John Flat,** ascending the **Tushar Mountains.** Three peaks soar above 12,000 feet, and a half dozen others top 11,000 feet. On their flanks, high mountain meadows burst with wildflowers in late summer. Their open summits provide sweeping views of south and central Utah. At the northern and eastern flanks of the mountains, the road joins FR 113 and passes **Kimberly,** a turn-of-the-century gold-mining boomtown. The road continues on to I-70.

parallel ridges rise from the desert like the swells of giant waves. Exposed edges of the uplift have eroded into a dramatic slick-rock wilderness of massive domes, cliffs, and a maze of twisted canyons. Stop at the **Visitor Center** to plan your park visit. To take the Cathedral Valley drive (see p. 204) into the isolated northern end of the park, continue on Rte. 24 to the departure point 11 miles beyond the Visitor Center.

Zion National Park Scenic Byway

I-15 to Mount Carmel Junction on Utah 9

● **54 miles** ● **½ day** ● **April through October. Adm. fee to park**

This route penetrates some of Utah's most dramatic scenery: the confines of Zion Canyon, where massive sandstone cliffs shoot 2,000 to 3,000 feet overhead. From the canyon floor the road climbs through two narrow tunnels to high slickrock plateaus, an undulating moonscape of petrified sand dunes smoothed and then cracked over time. Each minute of the day presents a changing array of color.

From St. George take I-15 north for 8 miles and go east on Rte. 9 toward Zion. You'll pass the **Quail Creek State Park** *(435-879-2378. http://parks.state.ut.us/parks/www1/quai .htm. Adm. fee).* From the fast-growing town of Hurricane, the road climbs **Hurricane Cliff,** where views of the **Pine Valley Mountains** unfold. Paralleling the northern banks of the **Virgin River,** the road skirts the base of **Hurricane Mesa, Smithsonian Butte,** and the **Eagle Crags** before arriving

The West Temple after a spring snowstorm, Zion National Park, Utah

at the quaint Western town of **Springdale,** just before the entrance to **Zion National Park** *(435-772-3256. www.nps.gov/zion. Adm. fee).*

The new **Zion Canyon Visitor Center** lies just inside the park and offers a film and an excellent bookstore. After 2 miles Zion Canyon Scenic Drive goes north, while Rte. 9 heads east up Pine Creek. First take the must-see 7-mile scenic drive, which follows the bubbling waters of the **North Fork Virgin River.** The canyon has an average width of half a mile, with walls 2,000 to 3,000 feet high.

Desert varnish—oxidized iron and manganese—colors the towering walls of the **Beehives** and the **Sentinel** to the west. **Zion Lodge** *(435-586-7686)* operates cabins and motel rooms year-round. Horse and mule rides are available from March through November *(435-772-3810. Fee).* Across the road near the lodge is the parking lot for the **Emerald Pools.** A stroll on a well-maintained trail takes you to a series of pools, ledges, and waterfalls at the base of the cliffs.

Back on the road, a half mile ahead, is the **Grotto Picnic Area,** the trailhead for 5,990-foot **Angels Landing,** reached via 22 dizzying switchbacks. It's not for people who fear heights, but the views of the canyon are superb. The canyon road continues to **Weeping Rock,** where a pull-off offers excellent views of the sandstone behemoth called the **Great White Throne,** rising some 2,500 feet above the Virgin River.

The Zion Canyon Scenic Drive ends where the canyon narrows at the **Temple of Sinawava,** an immense natural amphitheater named for the Spirit Coyote of the Paiute Indians. The **Riverside Walk,** 2 miles round-trip, begins here and winds north

Zion–Mount Carmel Highway, Utah

along the river; hanging wildflowers adorn the canyon walls in season. Here and elsewhere in the park look out for the tiny denizens of this realm, including canyon tree frogs, pocket gophers, and more than 270 bird species.

Back at the beginning of the scenic drive, Rte. 9 splits off east along **Pine Creek,** switchbacking up to the **Zion–Mount Carmel Tunnel,** a monumental engineering feat when bored out of the rock mountain in 1930. As it climbs to the high eastern plateaus, the narrow roadway passes several open windows that look off into the canyon. (Large vehicles are escorted through the tunnel at a nominal charge.) After the tunnel Rte. 9 becomes the Zion–Mount Carmel Highway. A small parking area to the right is the trailhead for the **Canyon Overlook Trail.** Fences enclose much of the half-mile trail as it threads a narrow course along the lip of a canyon. The trail ends at a sheer dropoff and excellent views of Pine Creek and lower Zion Canyon.

Mormon pioneers saw the sculptured rocks here as "temples of God" and called the canyon Little Zion after the celestial city.

Back on Rte. 9, the upper eastern plateaus seem a world apart from Zion Canyon. Ancient sand dunes roll upward to sheer cliff faces. Frequent pull-offs offer opportunities to explore the slickrock. A mile before the park's East Entrance, stop at the pull-off for views of **Checkerboard Mesa,** whose weathered sandstone beds have been uniformly cracked by freezing and thawing cycles. From the park entrance, the highway continues past high pastures to **Mount Carmel Junction.**

211

Arizona

Monument Valley

Prickly pear

Kayenta to Mexican Hat on U.S. 163 and Rte. 42B

● 26 miles ● 2 hours ● All year

Few thrills compare with driving north on U.S. 163 across the endless sagebrush and red sand desertscape of northern Arizona and coming upon Monument Valley. Immense mesas, buttes, and pinnacles of raw sandstone rise like phantom ships on a silent sea. Swirled slickrock, precarious spires, and domed formations hardly seem of this world, a mélange of reds, oranges, and yellows against a brilliant blue sky.

The drive begins just south of **Kayenta,** a Navajo town established as a trading post in 1910 by archaeologist John Wetherill. U.S. 163 shoots past a 7,096-foot rock monolith named **Agathla,** or "piles of wool," by the Navajo. Just after 6 miles, an overlook on the right offers good views of Agathla and its neighbor across the highway, **Owl Rock**—a red sandstone formation with protruding "ears." At mile 15 the large formations of

Monument Valley buttes

Monument Valley come suddenly into view. A million and a half years of weathering have worn away huge amounts of soft rock, leaving these monoliths with their erosion-resistant caps of DeChelly sandstone.

After crossing the Utah border at mile 21, a side road (Rte. 42B) leads 4 miles east to the **Monument Valley Navajo Tribal Park** *(435-727-3353. Adm. fee)*. At this intersection Native Americans sell jewelry, pots, and samples of delicious Navajo fry bread. After a mile the side road dips back into Arizona, passing vendors offering horseback trips, and comes to the valley **Visitor Center,** site of a small museum, campground, gift shop, and the road-head for a 17-mile, dirt loop-trail into the formations. Jeep tour operators sell off-road excursions from the parking lot, but you can also guide yourself with a booklet from the Visitor Center. The ride is rough, and recommended for high-clearance vehicles only. **John Ford Point,** 3.5 miles along the drive, celebrates the director who filmed such Westerns as *Stagecoach* here. Three miles later you'll see the figures of **Totem Pole** and **Yei-Bi-Chei,** thin pinnacles that seem far too fragile to be rock.

Navajo woman

Heading back west and crossing U.S. 163, Rte. 42B continues to **Goulding's Lodge** *(435-727-3231)*. Established as a small trading post in 1920, Goulding's grew world famous as a haunt of Ford and John Wayne when filming here. A small museum contains local film memorabilia, as well as photographs and Anasazi artifacts. Return to U.S. 163 and go 5 miles north to the drive's end at **Mexican Hat,** a small town on the San Juan River named for a precariously balanced rock formation reminiscent of a large sombrero.

Oak Creek Canyon Drive

Flagstaff to Sedona on U.S. 89A

● 27 miles ● 2 hours ● Spring through fall. Can be very congested in summer. Best in fall when cottonwoods turn yellow and crowds thin out.

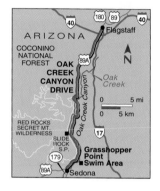

On the southern edge of the great Colorado Plateau that produced such marvels as Grand, Zion, and Bryce Canyons lies an equally stunning, but far more intimate spot—Oak Creek Canyon. For the past 3 million years, Oak Creek has carved a 12-mile-long, 2,000-foot-deep slice along the fault line into the ancient geologic past. From the ponderosa pines of Flagstaff to the red-rock desertscape of Sedona, the Oak Creek Canyon Drive reveals layers of dazzling red sandstone, tan limestone, purple siltstone, all eroded into curious shapes. Shady cottonwoods and a year-round water source attract a wide variety of animals, and the Forest Service has established numerous camping and picnic grounds along the short route.

213

Rte. 89A leaves the bustle of **Flagstaff,** a former lumber town in the shadows of the rugged **San Francisco Mountains,** and travels through the thick ponderosa pines of the **Coconino National Forest** *(520-527-3600. www.fs.fed .us/r3/coconino).* After 3 miles the road passes the small **Lindbergh Spring Roadside Park,** a good spot for a close-up look at ponderosas. Their clusters of three long needles distinguish them from other pine species.

After 8 miles atop the plateau, the road comes to the **Oak Creek Overlook** on the left, at the lip of a great escarpment known as the **Mogollon Rim.** Thirty million years ago, seismic forces thrust this section of earth's crust thousands of feet above the surrounding land.

A short loop-trail, where Native Americans sell crafts, brings you to the edge of a sheer drop. From this 6,400-foot vantage point, you'll see a diversity of plant life resulting from the dramatic elevation changes and relative abundance of water. Douglas-fir and white fir cling to the cliff walls. Water-loving trees, such as alder, willow, oak, and walnut, thrive along the creek. Dense brush dominates the dry hillsides. Where the canyon widens, desert plants appear.

From the overlook, the road— which began as a cattle trail and was

Oak Creek, Coconino National Forest

later adapted to wagons—switchbacks precipitously downward for 2 miles to the Pumphouse Wash Bridge. About 17 miles south of Flagstaff, a day-use area leads to the canyon's most popular hike, the **West Fork Trail,** a moderate 3-mile walk into **West Fork Canyon,** past fern forests and sandy beaches under sheer walls.

The rich red hues of red-rock country come from oxidized iron in sedimentary rock deposited 280 million years ago.

The road continues, passing camp sites and pic-nic grounds along the Oak

Touring Oak Creek Canyon area

Creek. Above, layers of sedimentary rock mark the rock walls. In age and composition they are like the rocks in the top third of the Grand Canyon.

Halfway through the canyon drive, **Slide Rock State Park** *(520-282-3034. www.pr.state.az.us/parkhtml/sliderock.html. Adm. fee)* appears on the right. Beyond the orchard and down some steps, a path leads to the site of the park's most popular activity. Here, the creek bubbles through a shoot of smooth Coconino sandstone, and the air fills with shouts as people ride the natural slide. (Be sure to bring water socks and jeans—the ride can be bumpy.) In summer you must arrive before 11 a.m. to park. Not far beyond Slide Rock is Oak Creek's other popular swim spot, **Grasshopper Swim Area,** with deep pools and soaring cliffs.

Just after this swim area, a pull-off on the north side of Midgely Bridge serves as the trailhead for the **Wilson Mountain Trail,** which pushes west into the **Red Rocks–Secret Mountain Wilderness.** Though strenuous—the trail rises 2,300 feet in 5.6 miles—the spectacular views extend several hundred miles and encompass **Verde Valley, Sedona,** and **Oak Creek Canyon.** An equally strenuous alternative is the **North Wilson Trail,** which starts north of the Encinoso Picnic Area and joins the Wilson Mountain Trail. Two miles from Midgely Bridge, the road passes out of the canyon and into **Sedona,** an arts community set among spectacular red-rock formations.

Apache Trail

Apache Junction to Tonto Natl. Mon. on Arizona 88

● **46 miles** ● **3 hours** ● **Fall through spring. The 25-mile Tortilla Flat–Roosevelt Dam section is dirt—avoid in wet weather, if bothered by heights, or if driving an RV; best driven south to north so as to stay on inside lane near cliff wall.**

Shadowing the ancient footpaths of Apache Indians, this partly unpaved route claims an abundance of switchbacks and dazzling views as it skirts the craggy Superstition Mountains just east of Phoenix, plunges into the sheer rock canyons of the Salt River, and encounters blue desert lakes. Along the spine-tingling section between Tortilla Flat and Theodore Roosevelt Dam, the road drops 1,500 feet in several miles.

From **Apache Junction** take the Rte. 88 for 5 miles to **Lost Dutchman State Park** *(480-982-4485. www.pr.state.az.us/parkhtml/dutchman.html. Adm. fee)*, which offers a good introduction to the native Sonoran Desert scrub-plant community on its easily accessible Native Plant Trail. Other more ambitious paths, such as the **Siphon Draw Trail,** lead up the sheer escarpment of **Superstition Mountain.** Of the legends that give the mountain its name, none is more famous than the story of Jacob "The Dutchman" Waltz, who allegedly discovered a mine and hid a cache of gold here in the 1870s. It remains undiscovered. Gold seekers continue to visit 4,553-foot **Weaver's Needle,** a volcanic plug visible north of the park at the **Needle Vista Viewpoint.**

Now inside the nearly 3-million-acre **Tonto National Forest** *(602-225-5200. www.fs.fed.us/r3/tonto)*, the road curves up through saguaro cactuses to a view of 10-mile-long **Canyon Lake,** azure blue against a desertscape of steep brown cliffs. Four lakes—**Saguaro** to the west, **Canyon, Apache,** and **Theodore Roosevelt**—were created in the early 20th century by damming the **Salt River** for irrigation and flood control. At Canyon Lake's edge, the **Acacia Picnic Area** offers swimming, **Palo Verde Recreation Site** contains a boating ramp, and **Boulder Recreation Area** has a fishing ramp and

215

Agave and yucca in the Superstition Mountains, Tonto National Forest

pavilion. **Canyon Lake Marina** *(602-944-6504)* features the **Lakeside Restaurant and Cantina** and offers lake cruises on *The Dolly (Arizona Steamboat Cruises 480–827–9144. Fare)*. The road winds around the lake for several miles, climbs again, and descends into **Tortilla Flat,** an old stagecoach stop and the only town along the Apache Trail. The ramshackle stores are right out of a Hollywood set, and the bar has saddles for seats and prickly pear ice cream.

Beyond Mesquite Flat, the dirt road begins, heading to **Fish Creek Hill,** the highlight of the drive. A short trail leads cliffside for panoramic views of sheer-walled **Fish Creek Canyon.** From here, the road descends precipitously 800 feet in the next mile, with sharp switchbacks narrowing in places to a car's width, before crossing a one-lane bridge over **Fish Creek.** A small pull-off after the bridge is the trailhead for a trail up the creek.

In 1911 President Theodore Roosevelt traveled the Apache Trail by car for the dedication of the Roosevelt Dam.

The road winds along Fish Creek and other small streams until it descends to views of 17-mile-long **Apache Lake,** flush against the eroded, multilayered desert rock face known as the **Painted Cliffs of the Mazatzal Mountains.** From one of the overlooks a road drops a mile down to **Apache Lake Marina and Resort** *(520-467-2511),* which has a marina, boat ramp, restaurant, and campground.

For the remaining 10 miles the road snakes along the narrow waters of Apache Lake, pushing between tall hills past the **Burnt Corral Recreation Site** to **Theodore Roosevelt Dam.** When built between 1903 and 1911, it was the world's largest masonry dam at 280 feet high and 723 feet long. Beyond the dam, 23-mile-long **Theodore Roosevelt Lake** spreads into the surrounding desert. Continue east to the **Roosevelt Lake Visitor Center** *(520-467-3200)* for displays and an observation deck.

Though the official Apache Trail ends here, it's worth continuing 5 miles east on Rte. 88 to **Tonto National Monument** *(520-467-2241. www.nps.gov/ tont. Adm. fee)* for a peek at the prehistoric Salado people. From the Visitor Center a lovely trail winds up 350 feet to cliff dwellings, one of the nation's best preserved Salado sites. In the 14th century, population pressures forced the Salado up into caves, where they built a 19-room community. Call in advance for a guided 3-hour (round-trip) hike to the even more spectacular 40-room Upper Ruin.

216

Globe to Show Low

U.S. 60

● 87 miles ● 2 to 3 hours ● All year. Temperatures can vary greatly from canyon to rim, especially in winter.

Well-traveled and well-built, U.S. 60 runs across the transition zone that connects Arizona's arid southern desertlands with the cool forested mountains of the Colorado Plateau. As it gains nearly 3,000 feet in elevation, the road passes the mesa and buttes of the San Carlos Apache Reservation, plunges more than 2,000 feet into the Salt River Canyon, and races up the Mogollon Rim to the edge of the White Mountains. It begins in semi-desert and ends in the nation's largest contiguous stand of ponderosa pine. When snowmelt engorges the Salt River, water rushes over the Mogollon Rim and through beautiful canyons—excellent for white water rafting and kayaking *(For outfitters, call the Globe Ranger District 520-425-7189).*

Before embarking on the drive, stop at the **Besh-Ba-Gowah Archaeological Park** *(Jesse Hayes Rd. 520-425-0320. Adm. fee),* a site 1 mile southeast of **Globe** that in the 13th and 14th centuries was a

Cibecue Falls

Salado pueblo with more than 200 rooms. Shell and turquoise jewelry and polychrome pottery were traded here.

Leaving Globe, a former silver- and copper-mining town, U.S. 60 climbs through the southeastern corner of the **Tonto National Forest** *(520-425-7189)*, a sea of desert shrub, semi-desert grasslands, and mesquite-choked washes. **Apache Peaks, Chrome Butte,** and **Rockinstraw Mountain** rise in the distance. After more than 16 miles, the road passes the **Jones Water Campground** on the right, a shady oasis of oak trees amid the hills. As the road climbs toward the crest of nearly 6,000-foot **Timber Camp Mountain,** the vegetation becomes pinyon pine and juniper and then ponderosa pine.

Continuing along U.S. 60, the route enters the **San Carlos Apache Reservation,** once home to the Apache leader Geronimo, and drops down to cattail-fringed **Seneca Lake** on the left. If you walk around the lake to the right, you'll see dramatic **Seneca Falls.**

217

From Seneca Lake the road continues to drop, opening up to breathtaking views of the **Salt River Canyon,** with its colorful sedimentary and basaltic rock faces and plunging cliffsides. The best pull-off, **Hieroglyphic Point,** provides an extraordinary view of geologic history from cliffs that descend 2,000 feet. Before gawking at the chasm, search out the thousand-year-old petroglyphs in the rocks near the foot of the stairs.

Great winding switchbacks weave down the cliff face to a bridge, rest area, and trails down to the bubbling **Salt River,** so named by the Pima Indians and early Europeans for its salty composition. The river drains 2,500 square miles and drops more than 10,000 feet, offering excellent white-water rafting. Some of the best begins here at the bridge and extends 52 miles to Theodore Roosevelt Lake. Across the bridge lies the **White Mountain Apache Reservation** and a small store where hiking and fishing permits are available *(White Mountain Apache Game and Fish Dept. 520-338-4385)*. A dirt road leads some 3 miles west along the Salt River to **Cibecue Creek.** A rugged, mile-long scramble northeast along the creek ends at a spectacular **Cibecue Falls.** Stop at the store before starting out to check on road conditions and pick up required permits.

U.S. 60 climbs out of the Salt River Canyon; at several pull-offs you can scan far below for the rusted hulks of old cars. From the main canyon the road passes over rounded mountains and offers views of the massive **White Mountains** to the northeast. It climbs the **Mogollon**

An 1873 boom-town, Globe is said to have gotten its name when someone found a hunk of silver with cracks resembling continents.

Roadrunner

Rim, the sharply defined southern edge of the upthrust Colorado Plateau. Atop the rim and higher, the road enters deep ponderosa pine forests. At 6,331 feet it reaches **Show Low,** a frontier town whose ownership was once decided in a poker game.

White Mountains Drive

Alpine to Hon Dah on Forest Road 249, Arizona 273, 261, and 260

● 68 miles ● 3 to 4 hours ● Spring through fall. Parts of the drive are closed in winter.

This route in central Arizona near the New Mexico border penetrates the high, remote forests of the White Mountains, passing pristine Big Lake and skirting Mount Baldy, a sacred Apache site and one of Arizona's highest peaks. The eastern portion of the route falls within the Apache-Sitgreaves National Forests; the west-

ern half is under the jurisdiction of the White Mountain Apache Reservation.

This route begins off the Colorado Trail Scenic Byway (see p. 219), 1.5 miles northwest of **Alpine,** and heads west on well-maintained gravel FR 249, arriving at the open meadows of **Williams Valley** after 4.5 miles. Especially popular in winter, the area has 5 miles of gentle trails and a toboggan run. Five miles from here, the road passes a small lake and picks up the meandering **Black River,** following it to **Three Forks,** the pretty

Wetlands along Arizona 273, Apache-Sitgreaves National Forests

Indian pink

confluence of three streams. The grasslands offer excellent opportunities to spot elk and mule deer. One mile later is the turnoff to **Big Lake** and the **Big Lake Visitors Center** (*Spring-summer*). A Forest Service pamphlet serves as an excellent guide to the short **Big Lake Nature Trail** that loops behind the center. The access road continues on to the dock, where you can rent a boat or buy fishing equipment.

Go north on Rte. 273. The route passes **Crescent Lake** and picks up Rte. 261, entering large tracts of treeless grassland interrupted only by volcanic rocks. Twelve miles from Big Lake, the road passes peaceful, 164-acre **Mexican Hay Lake,** packed with mallards, teals, buffleheads, and other ducks in fall. The route descends from the **White Mountains** to the plateau and joins Rte. 260 west of Springerville.

Head west past grasslands, where pronghorn often graze. And ancient

Mexican Hay is a small, weedy lake, thus the name— but fly fishermen have landed 15-inchers there.

volcanic cinder cones rise to the right. About 7.5 miles from the turnoff, the highway passes a 5-mile side road (Rte. 373) to the small resort town of **Greer,** which lies in a pretty canyon near the **East** and **West Forks of the Little Colorado River.** Along the side road are the short **Butler Canyon Nature Trail,** several campgrounds, and a cross-country ski area.

Rte. 260 continues west into the **White Mountain Apache Reservation** (*Hiking and fishing permits 520-338-4385*) after 7 miles and crosses the turnoff to Rte. 273, which leads south to Sunrise Lake and Sheep's Crossing, where trails head into the **Mount Baldy Wilderness** and to 11,590-foot **Mount Baldy.** The trail to Baldy stops short of the summit. Back on Rte. 260, continue on to the casino town of **Hon Dah,** past a handful of mountain lakes.

Coronado Trail Scenic Byway

Clifton to Springerville on U.S. 191

● **123 miles** ● **4 to 6 hours** ● **All year, but plowed weekdays only during snow season. Includes sharp curves and steep drop-offs.**

Some 450 years ago Francisco Vásquez de Coronado passed near this route on his expedition to find the fabled Seven Cities of Cíbola. Paralleling the border with New Mexico, the route skirts the eastern edge of the Apache-Sitgreaves National Forests, passes one of the nation's largest open-pit copper mines, then switchbacks up (427 curves between Clifton and Alpine) to cross the jagged edge of the Mogollon Rim. In its first 60 miles the winding highway climbs 5,000 feet, passing from the Upper Sonoran Desert to high alpine meadows and crossing as many life zones as you'd find from Mexico to Canada.

The route begins in **Clifton,** an early copper-mining town tucked into a canyon hewn by the **San Francisco River.** U.S. 191 twists and curves over mine tailings, passes a copper

Apache-Sitgreaves National Forests

concentrator at about 5 miles, and edges along the lip of an immense pit. At nearly 10 miles an observation point affords spectacular views of the Phelps Dodge Mine and the procession of trucks, tiny-looking from here, that haul 125,000 tons of copper ore out each day.

The route continues for another 5 miles along the mine, past piles of rubble with rocks containing copper ore. Suddenly the road follows a little creek bed up into rocky **Chase Canyon.** Slow down to 10 miles per hour for the next 5 miles. The road squeezes between colorful rock faces and dramatic drops, crossing from one side of the ridge to the other for about 15 miles, until the terrain flattens out to grassland and juniper-pinyon forest.

The route continues over ridgelines and mountainsides for another 18 miles, then passes a small parking area where you can take a half-mile hike up to a watchtower atop 8,786-foot **Rose Peak.** Some 17 miles farther, after passing the **Stray Horse Campground,** U.S. 191 ascends the **Mogollon Rim,** the southernmost edge of the Colorado Plateau, and comes to 9,346-foot **Blue Vista.** Outstanding views open to the southeast and west, a tangle of peaks and canyons enveloped in soft blue haze.

Aspen in fall

After Blue Vista the highway winds through thick, "aspect sensitive" forests: North-facing ridges bear spruce, fir, and aspen, while those facing south support oak and ponderosa pines. Seven miles later the road passes **Hannagan Meadow,** with a lodge and store; it's a good point of departure for cross-country skiing.

For the next 23 miles, the route curves along the eastern edge of the **White Mountains,** past thick aspen groves and alpine meadows alive with Indian paintbrush, columbines, and lupines in late July and August. In the small town of **Alpine** you can find good hiking information at the Alpine Ranger District *(520-339-4384)* of the **Apache-Sitgreaves National Forests** *(www.fs.fed .us/r3/asnf).* (The White Mountains Drive, p. 218, begins 1.5 miles north of Alpine on FR 249.) From Alpine U.S. 191 gently rises and falls over wide-flanked mountains past Arizona's third highest peak, 10,912-foot **Escudilla Mountain,** an old volcano inside the **Escudilla Wilderness Area.** The pleasant 3-mile hike on the **Escudilla National Recreational Trail** traverses an area burned by fire more than 40 years ago and ends at the Forest Service's fire tower for spectacular views. After crossing a wide, grassy valley, the road passes the **Nelson Reservoir,** a thin, mile-long lake with ducks, ospreys, and migratory birds in season. Seven miles from the reservoir, the route descends to flatlands and the town of **Springerville.**

Mount Lemmon Drive

Coronado National Forest to Mount Lemmon on Catalina Highway

● 60 miles round-trip ● 3 hours ● All year. Summer weekends can be crowded.

In 25 miles of hairpin and blind turns, this spectacular drive climbs more than 6,300 feet, winding up the southern flank of the Santa Catalina Mountains to 9,157-foot Mount Lemmon. Beginning in the saguaro cactus forests of the arid Sonoran Desert, it passes through five distinct life zones, ending in a cool mixed conifer forest more reminiscent of Canada than southern Arizona.

Seventeen miles northeast of Tucson, the Catalina Highway crosses into the **Coronado National Forest** *(520-670-4552. www.fs.fed.us/r3/coronado)* and heads across shallow canyons guarded by tall saguaro cactuses to the **Babat Duag Viewpoint** at 2.5 miles. You'll see the **Tucson Basin,** as well as the rugged **Rincon Mountains** to the southeast.

After 3 miles the road enters narrow **Molino Canyon.** You can get a good look at it from the **Molino Canyon Overlook.** Beyond the canyon lies 4,200-foot **Molino Basin,** site of a campground and trailhead and the

Mount Lemmon Drive through Coronado National Forest

transition zone from desert scrub to oak tree vegetation. Climbing higher, the trees change from oak to juniper in Bear Canyon to cypress, sycamore, pine, and walnut in upper **Bear Canyon.** After 14 miles, at 6,400-foot **Windy Point,** come the drive's most sweeping views: the **Tucson Basin, Santa Rita, Huachuca,** and **Patagonia Mountains,** and occasionally the **Sierra de San Antonio** of Mexico, far to the south. A half mile later, **Geology Vista** offers interpretive information.

The road continues up through ponderosa pine forests to 7,400-foot **San Pedro Vista,** with views looking north to the San Pedro River Valley. A couple of miles after the vista, the **Palisade Information Station** *(Santa Catalina Ranger District 520-749-8700)* has informative ecological exhibits and acts as the trailhead for the **Butterfly** and **Crystal Springs** hiking trails. Just before reaching Summerhaven, the end of the road, a 2-mile spur road leads to the **Mount Lemmon Ski Valley** *(520-576-1321),* one of the country's southernmost ski resorts. An unmarked, mile-long trail takes you from beyond the ski area through a quiet forest to near Mount Lemmon's summit.

222

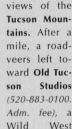

ARIZ. Tucson
Cortaro
10 0 5/mi
0 5 km
Picture Rocks
TUCSON MOUNTAINS DRIVE
TUCSON MOUNTAIN REGIONAL PARK
SAGUARO N.P.
GATES PASS ROAD
Old Tucson
Arizona-Sonora Desert Museum
86
SANDARIO RD.

Flowering saguaro

Tucson Mountains Drive

Tucson Mountain Park to Saguaro National Park on Gates Pass, Kinney, and Golden Gate Roads

● 22 miles ● 2 hours ● All year. Partly graded dirt and gravel; fine for passenger cars.

In minutes this road leaves the sprawl of Tucson and enters a magical forest of immense saguaro cactuses. On the way it passes an exceptional desert museum.

At the edge of the **Tucson Mountain Regional Park,** the road winds past saguaros to Gates Pass for great views of the **Tucson Mountains.** After a mile, a road veers left toward **Old Tucson Studios** *(520-883-0100. Adm. fee),* a Wild West theme park and movie set. About 1.5 miles north of the turnoff lies the **Arizona–Sonora Desert Museum** *(520-883-2702. www.desertmuseum.org. Adm. fee),* a feast of outdoor exhibits about the life-forms that inhabit the Sonoran Desert, including mountain lions, rattlesnakes, hummingbirds, and peccaries. Innovative exhibits tell about the saguaro cactus, which can grow 60 feet high and live 150 years. A mile past the museum, the road enters **Saguaro National Park** *(www.nps.gov/sagu)* and comes to the **Red Hills Information Center** *(520-733-5158),* with a paved **Cactus Garden Trail** and good information about the park. The gravel Bajada Loop Drive passes rocks adorned with Indian petroglyphs at the **Signal Hill Picnic Area,** while various trails lead into the saguaro forests and explore the rocky ridges of the Tucson Mountains.

New Mexico

Gila Scenic Byway

Loop from Silver City on New Mexico 15, 35, and 152 and U.S. 180

● 118 miles ● ½ day ● All year. Many curves make driving slow. Some sections are not recommended for RVs and trailers. Trail to cliff dwellings closes at 4 p.m.

Within the high desert forests of Gila National Forest, this southwestern New Mexico route penetrates some of the nation's largest and most remote tracts of wilderness. It passes a couple of Old West towns, winds to ancient cliff dwellings, and bypasses an immense open-pit copper mine. Make sure to leave time to visit the cliff dwellings.

The route begins at **Silver City,** a mining town that boomed in the 1870s when silver was discovered behind the present-day Grant County courthouse. The town's colorful history is told at the **Silver City Museum** *(312 W. Broadway. 505-538-5921. Closed Mon.).*

223

From town, the route climbs north on Rte. 15 for 6 miles into the **Pinos Altos Range** and reaches the town of **Pinos Altos,** or "tall pines," which hugs the Continental Divide at 7,840 feet. After a brief gold boom in the late 19th century, the town went bust. The famous bar at the **Buckhorn Saloon** *(505-538-9911),* along with its fine restaurant, keep the sleepy town alive.

After Pinos Altos the road loses its center line and narrows considerably as it winds through the Pinos Altos Range, heading up **Cherry Creek** past a couple of rustic picnic areas shaded by ponderosa

West Fork of the Gila River, Gila Cliff Dwellings N.M.

pines and cottonwoods. Eighteen miles after Pinos Altos, the route drops steeply to **Sapillo Creek** and **Grey Feathers Lodge** *(505-536-3206),* a wildlife sanctuary and popular destination for bird-watchers. At the creek, Rte. 15 intersects with Rte. 35, but continue north for 17 miles to the Gila Cliff

Gila Cliff Dwellings National Monument

Dwellings National Monument. On its way up to the cliff dwellings, the road climbs steeply through a series of switchbacks, passing the **Senator Clinton P. Anderson Scenic Overlook** after almost 7 miles. The **Gila River Canyon** lies 2,000 feet below, while spectacular vistas of the **Gila Wilderness** spread to the horizon. After the overlook, Rte. 15 crosses a level ridge with open views and then descends sharply to a bridge across the **Gila River** and a primitive camping site.

Four miles later, the road reaches **Gila Cliff Dwellings National Monument** *(505-536-9461. www.nps.gov/gicl).* Drive straight ahead to the **Visitor Center,** which offers good displays and information about the peoples who inhabited this remote area for a millennium or more. Be sure to pick up the informative guide. The road to the dwellings passes the **Lower Scorpion Campground,** which features a quarter-mile trail leading to a small cave dwelling. (The short paved path to the right ends at a series of ancient red pictographs painted with hematite.) The parking area for the major cliff dwellings lies just beyond the campground. A 1-mile loop climbs 175 feet to the dwellings on the southeast-facing cliff. Five caves contain a remarkable series of 42 rooms connected by passageways. Some 40 to 50 Pueblo Indians lived in these dwellings in the late 13th century.

> Ruins of circular pit houses show that people known as the Mogollon inhabited the Gila area at least 14 centuries ago.

Retrace the route to Sapillo Creek and take Rte. 35 southeast for 4 miles to **Lake Roberts,** a pretty lake surrounded by pines. As the road winds around the lake, it passes **Vista Village,** an archaeological site undergoing excavation. It's believed that prehistoric Indians occupied an 18- to 25-room pueblo here. The road continues up a wide valley and again crests the Continental Divide before reaching the **Mimbres River Valley** and coming on the **Mimbres Ranger District** *(505-536-2250)* outside the town of Mimbres.

At the town of San Lorenzo, the route intersects Rte. 152 (see Hillsboro-Kingston Ghost Towns, p. 225), which heads west 8.5 miles to the overlook of the **Phelps Dodge Santa Rita Copper Mine,** an immense hole in the earth. Continue on to Central, where U.S. 180 takes you back to Silver City.

Hillsboro-Kingston Ghost Towns

Hillsboro to San Lorenzo on New Mexico 152

● 34 miles ● 2 to 3 hours ● All year

Switchbacking into the thick forests of the Black Range, this route in southwest New Mexico winds past two old boomtowns before cresting at 8,194-foot Emory Pass. Rugged and remote, the route offers many chances to enjoy the vistas of the **Gila National Forest** *(505-388-8201. www.fs.fed.us/r3/gila).*

The route begins in **Hillsboro,** a pretty tree-lined community that was a gold boomtown in the late 1800s. The **Black Range Museum** *(505-895-5233. Closed Tues.-Wed. and Jan.-Feb.)* tells about town life and lore, including the story of Sadie Orchard, a colorful brothel-keeper. Nine miles beyond town, the route passes sleepy **Kingston,** once home to at least 22 saloons, three newspapers, and an opera house. Stop in at the **Black Range Lodge** *(505-895-5652)* to learn about this history-rich area.

From Kingston, the road switchbacks up about 10 miles to **Emory Pass,** where you get views of the former boomtowns and beyond to the **Rio Grande Valley** and **Caballo Reservoir.** Two trails begin here, both about 4 miles long: one to 10,011-foot **Hillsboro Peak,** the other to 9,668-foot **Sawyers Peak.** The road descends into cool forests, eventually reaching **San Lorenzo** in the Mimbres River Valley.

Black Range wildflowers

Heart of the Sands

White Sands Natl. Monument

● 16-miles round-trip ● 1 hour
● Fall through winter. Adm. fee

Waves of brilliant white sand dunes ringed by distant towering peaks make this southwestern New Mexico drive one of the most unusual in the Southwest. Ever shifting, the gypsum dunes can reach up to 60 feet high and move 12 to 16 feet per year. Enclosed by the White Sands Missile Range, White Sands National Monument closes occasionally for an hour or two for missile testing. Hikers should exercise caution: It's easy to lose one's bearing in this tractless desert, especially during sandstorms.

225

At the beginning of the route, the **Visitor Center** of **White Sands National Monument** *(505-479-6124. www.nps.gov/whsa. Adm. fee)* offers interpretive information on this unusual geologic feature. The sun evaporates water from nearby Lake Lucero and alkali flats, leaving a thin crust of tiny gypsum crystals, which the wind blows into dunes. In this harsh, dry environment, a species of mice, lizards, snakes, and scorpions have adapted light coloration to survive.

For about 3 miles the road skirts the edge of the dunes, where saltbush comes right up to the road. Fine, snowlike sand blows across the road and the parking lot for the **Big Dune Trail** on the left. This 1-hour nature hike climbs up a 60-foot dune past gnarled cottonwoods and provides many chances to follow animal tracks.

Rabbitbrush, White Sands National Monument

As the road pushes farther into the dunes, vegetation gradually disappears, though you see an occasional yucca plant whose roots stretch down as far as 30 to 40 feet. In the heart of the dunes, swirling sand prevents plants from taking root (and the absence of plants causes the sand to swirl). At the end of the 8-mile road, the **Alkali Flat Trail** leads 2.3 miles through the dunes. Wide parking lots offer ample opportunity to park and hike or sand-surf some of the steep dune faces.

226

El Malpais

I-40 east of Grants to Quemado on New Mexico 117 and 36

● 78 miles ● 2 to 3 hours ● All year

As recently as a couple of thousand years ago, massive volcanic eruptions poured rivers of molten lava into a remote valley in the high desert of west-central New Mexico. The route explores this bizarre world, winding between the flow's eastern edge and a series of high sandstone cliffs. In addition to the unforgettable fields of tortured black rock, views include a giant sandstone arch and distant cinder cones and craters.

As you begin your drive south from I-40, you see the lava flows immediately to the west. After 9 miles, Rte. 117 passes the ranger station for the **El Malpais National Conservation Area** *(505-287-7911. www.nps.gov/elma)*, which offers good displays on the region's culture. A mile later the route goes by a side road to the **Sandstone Bluffs Overlook,** a 1.5-mile drive to a picnic area atop yellow sandstone bluffs. Here you'll get the area's best views of El Malpais, the "bad country" in Spanish. Across the valley are the **Zuni Mountains,** and, to the north near Grants, sits 11,301-foot **Mount Taylor,** a volcano that blew 1.5 to 3 million years ago.

Five miles later the **Zuni-Acoma Trail** offers an opportunity to examine different forms of lava rock up-close. The 7.5-mile footpath follows an old Indian route connecting the pueblos of Acoma and Zuni. Be careful: The rock is rough on shoes, the hike is hot during the summer, and the cairns marking the trail are sometimes difficult to follow. An easier walk begins 3 miles farther at the **La Ventana Natural Arch,** one of New Mexico's largest arches, carved by wind and water out of Zuni sandstone. Just after the arch, the road comes to the **Narrows,** where lava flowed close to the 500-foot-high sandstone cliffs. A picnic area loops around to the cliff face. About 3 miles beyond, the road crosses a grassland where cinder cone volcanoes appear on the distant horizon.

View from Sandstone Bluffs Overlook

Not far past Rte. 41, the Chain of Craters Back Country Byway (Rte. 42) heads north on a gravel road that follows a line of volcanic cinder cones along the Continental Divide. The 36-mile route is generally passable in high-clearance vehicles, but may not be in rain or snow.

Rte. 117 continues across desolate stretches of the North Plains, where pronghorn often cavort, and climbs into pinyon pine forests. At Rte. 36 head south to the small town of **Quemado** on U.S. 60.

Turquoise Trail and Sandia Crest

Tijeras to I-25 south of Santa Fe on N.M. 14 and 536

● **48 miles (plus 28-mile round-trip to Sandia Crest)** ● **½ day**
● **In winter bundle up for Sandia Crest.**

A pleasant alternative to I-25, the Turquoise Trail connects Albuquerque and Santa Fe, passing through several small mining towns that retain the charm of the Old West. The route's highlight is the Sandia Crest National Scenic Byway, a side road that shoots up nearly 4,000 feet through Cibola National Forest to the top of 10,678-foot Sandia Crest for spectacular views of Albuquerque. In its 14-mile length, the side road curves through four life zones, the equivalent of driving from New Mexico to Canada's Hudson Bay.

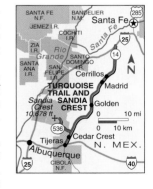

The route begins in **Tijeras,** a small town that's home to a ranger station of the **Cibola National Forest** *(11776 Hwy. 337. www.fs.fed.us/r3/cibola. 505-281-3304)* and an interpretive walk through the archaeological site of the **Tijeras Pueblo,** where several hundred people lived 600 years ago. Rte. 14 ascends from Tijeras across the eastern flank of the **Sandia Mountains** and through ponderosa pines to busy **Cedar Crest,** a suburb of Albuquerque.

After nearly 4 miles, Rte. 536 (the Sandia Crest National Scenic Byway) leads northwest to Sandia Crest. About a mile up, the byway passes the **Tinkertown Museum** *(505-281-5233. April-Oct.; adm. fee)*, a kitschy private museum with a Western town and miniature circus in a building made from 40,000 bottles. For the next 6.5 miles the road curves past several rest stops and the **Sandia Peak Ski Area** *(505-242-9052)*, developed by the Civilian Conservation Corps in 1938. At 8,651 feet, the **Balsam Glade Picnic Ground**

has tables beneath a thick stand of ponderosa pines. (Here, dirt-and-gravel Rte. 165 descends 5 miles into **Las Huertas Canyon** to the trailhead for **Sandia Cave.** A gentle, 1-mile trail leads to the cave, site of famous archaeological excavations that revealed human occupation some 12,000 years ago.)

Back on Rte. 536, the road continues to climb to **Sandia Crest,** where an observation deck affords spectacular views of **Albuquerque,** the **Rio Grande,** and distant **Mount Taylor.** In addition to a restaurant, the peak offers several good hikes, including the **Peak**

Adobe church, Golden

Nature Trail, an easy half-mile loop along the limestone ledge and through stands of spruce and fir. Retrace the route back to the Turquoise Trail.

The Turquoise Trail winds for another 44 miles through a rolling desert of stunted pinyon pine and juniper, passing the dusty former boomtowns of **Golden; Madrid,** with its craft shops and New Age artists; and **Cerrillos,** once boasting 21 saloons and four hotels catering to prospectors. The towns along the trail now draw Hollywood film crews. The Turquoise Trail ends at I-25, just south of the lively, historical state capital, **Santa Fe.**

228

High Road to Taos

Española to Ranchos de Taos on N.M. 76, 75, and 518

● 54 miles ● 3 to 4 hours ● All year

Pressing into the Sangre de Cristo Mountains past 13,000-foot peaks, this route is the most scenic between Santa Fe and Taos. The small, isolated mountain towns sprinkled along the way retain the flavor of the early Spanish settlers who came here four centuries ago.

From Española on U.S. 84, Rte. 76 cuts east about 9 miles to **Chimayó.** Its adobe **Plaza del Cerro** is probably the Spanish Southwest's only surviving fortified plaza. Just north of the plaza, **Ortega's Weaving Shop** *(505-351-4215)* carries the beautiful wool products of a family that has been

weaving for eight generations. Pilgrims travel from all over the Southwest to visit the **Santuario de Chimayó** *(505-351-4889)*, legendary as a center for curing the sick. The sanctuary has five colorful sacred paintings on wood,

Along the High Road to Taos

while a room off the sacristy features a hole from which cure seekers pull handfuls of earth to rub on their bodies. Don't miss the famous **Rancho de Chimayó** *(505-351-4444. Closed Mon. Nov.-April)*, a restaurant in a 19th-century hacienda-style building.

From Chimayó, Rte. 518 climbs into forest past **Cordova.** A road curves south to the tiny hillside town; signs invite you to visit artisans who carve figures from aspen and cedar. After climbing nearly 7 more miles, the route cuts through **Truchas,** once a Spanish outpost high on a mesa beneath 13,102-foot **Truchas Peak.** With views of the **Rio Grande Valley,** Truchas was the setting for Robert Redford's film *The Milagro Beanfield War.* As you enter town, the adobe building with the cross serves as the meeting place for the Brotherhood of the Penitentes, a secret religious society famous for their self-flagellation rites.

From Truchas the High Road to Taos enters the **Carson National Forest** and, for the last 35 miles, winds up and down through forests, past several small towns. The highlight of this leg is the tiny town of **Trampas,** about 8 miles northeast of Truchas. The **San José de Gracia Church,** built in

Santuario de Chimayó, Chimayó

the late 1700s, remains one of the most beautiful of colonial-era churches. At Peñasco follow Rte. 75 to Rte. 518. The end of the High Road is **Ranchos de Taos,** where you can visit **San Francisco de Asis** *(505-758-2754),* the 18th-century mission church that captivated painter Georgia O'Keeffe. You can complete the drive by taking Rte. 68 to **Taos,** an artist colony with a square surrounded by adobe buildings.

Enchanted Circle

Loop from Taos on U.S. 64 and N.M. 38 and 522

● 85 miles ● 4 to 5 hours ● All year. Ski areas draw crowds to the route over winter weekends.

In moments, this northern New Mexico route leaves the bustle of Taos and climbs into a remote, high-altitude world of cool forests, crystal lakes, windswept valleys, and tiny towns filled with Wild West history. It encircles 13,161-foot Wheeler Peak, the state's highest mountain, and passes some of the nation's most popular ski areas.

Head east out of **Taos** on U.S. 64. The route climbs through **Taos Canyon's** thick evergreen forests, passing several campgrounds and picnic spots. After 18 winding miles through the **Carson National Forest** *(505-758-6200. www.fs.fed.us/ r3/carson)*, the road curves over a 9,101-foot pass, then descends to grasslands and the ski town of **Angel Fire** *(Chamber of Commerce 505-377-6661 or 800-446-8117)*, 3 miles down Rte. 434. A mile beyond the Angel Fire turnoff, you'll see the sail-like chapel of the **Vietnam Veterans National Memorial** *(505-377-6900)* occupying a windblown hill on the left. In another 5 miles, **Eagle Nest Lake**

Indian woman at Taos Pueblo

emerges on the right. To the west, across the **Moreno Valley,** rises **Wheeler Peak,** contained within the **Wheeler Peak Wilderness** *(Questa Ranger District 505-586-0520)*, an area laced with hiking trails. At the town of Eagle Nest, U.S. 64, now a side road, heads around the north end of the lake to quiet **Cimarron Canyon State Park** *(505-377-6271. www.emnrd.state.nm.us/nmparks/ pages/parks/cimarron/cimarron.htm)*, with campsites and good fly-fishing on the **Cimarron River.**

From Eagle Nest take Rte. 38 for several miles to the ruins of **Elizabethtown,** a gold boom site in the mid-1860s. The route continues across the valley, climbing up to 9,820-foot **Bobcat Pass** and back into Carson National Forest before descending into the resort town of **Red River** *(Chamber of Commerce 505-754-2366)*, once a mining

camp and now a center for outdoor activities. Several miles after Red River the road passes a molybdenite mine, then slips through towering rock cliffs. At the village of Questa, detour north about 3 miles on Rte. 522, then turn left on Rte. 378 for a worthwhile 13-mile side trip to the **Wild Rivers Recreation Area** *(505-758-8851)*, which skirts the edge of the **Rio Grande Gorge.**

The drive continues south from Questa on Rte. 522, passing the turnoff for the **D.H. Lawrence Memorial** *(505-776-2245)* at San Cristobal, where the writer lived in the early 1920s. Soon you'll run into the intersection of U.S. 64 and Rte. 150 with Rte. 522. From here, detour west on U.S. 64

for 8 miles to the **Rio Grande Gorge Bridge,** with stunning vistas of the gorge. To reach the world-famous **Taos Ski Valley** *(505-776-2291),* head northeast on Rte. 150. Just past the intersection, look for tiny Museum Road on the right to reach the **Millicent Rogers Museum** *(505-758-2462. www.millicentrogers.org. Adm. fee),* an excellent gallery devoted to Native American and Hispanic art. Two miles down Rte. 522, you pass signs for **Taos Pueblo** *(505-758-1028. Call ahead for schedule; vehicle fee),* one of the country's largest multistoried pueblos. The drive ends back in Taos.

Colorado

Columbine

San Juan Skyway

Loop from Ridgway through Ouray, Silverton, Durango, Cortez, Dolores, Telluride, and Placerville

● **236 miles** ● **1 to 2 days** ● **All year. Mountain passes sometimes close in winter.**

231

As its fanciful name implies, the San Juan Skyway flirts with the heights, climbing to more than 10,000 feet three times as it charts a ragged loop through the mountains and high deserts of southwestern Colorado. Starting at Ridgway, this spectacular route heads south over the crest of the San Juan Mountains and passes through the historic mining towns of Ouray and Silverton. It drops into red-rock canyons near Durango and sails west across the desert to Mesa Verde National Park, where you can walk through 800-year-old ancient Pueblo cliff dwellings. Returning north, the road climbs back into the heart of the San Juans, pausing at Telluride before descending again to Ridgway.

Begin 4 miles north of town at **Ridgway State Park** *(970-626-5822. http://parks.state.co.us/ridgway. Vehicle fee);* U.S. 550 tops a dry hill and the southern skyline suddenly fills with the jagged crest of the **San Juan Mountains.** Carved by glaciers, these bony peaks are a mass of overlapping flows of lava and ash that spewed through layers of sedimentary rock beginning 40 million years ago.

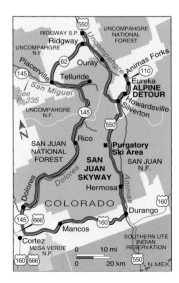

Cross the valley floor to **Ridgway,** an 1891 railroad and ranching town at the base of 14,150-foot **Mount Sneffels,** then continue south along the **Uncompahgre River** toward a deep cleft in the mountain front. The valley narrows under peaks rising at least 6,000 feet above the river, and the road caroms between red-rock cliffs and foothills covered with scrub oak, aspen, juniper, and pinyon pine.

An abundance of hot springs and large herds of elk and deer once made this valley a favorite winter camp for the Ute. The elk and deer still winter here, but the Ute were forced out of the San Juans during the 1870s after prospectors found rich lodes of gold and silver.

At **Ouray,** named for a Ute chief, multicolored cliffs squeeze the valley against the base of 14,000-foot peaks. **Ouray Hot Springs** *(970-325-4638. Adm. fee),* a municipal pool, steams at the north end of town. Drive through the historic district of ornate 1880s buildings, turn right, and follow the gravel road to **Box Canyon Falls** *(Adm. fee Mem. Day-Labor Day),* a thunderous plume plunging over smooth walls of dark limestone.

From Ouray, U.S. 550 switchbacks up into the mountains, offering splendid vistas back down to Ridgway. Waterfalls and creeks spill from the high cliffs and side canyons into **Uncompahgre Gorge,** the deep gash to your right. **Abrams Mountain,** 12,801 feet, looms over the head of the canyon.

Mesa Verde archaeologists have found more than 4,000 sites—from multistoried dwellings to cliff-side villages—that belonged to the Anasazi, ancestors of the Pueblo Indians.

There's no bracing yourself for what comes next. Just drive up the short series of hairpin turns, top the rim of the gorge, and let your pulse soar. Vivid red peaks burst into view, with broad smears of orange and red gravel streaming down their flanks into the dark surrounding evergreens. It's an astonishing, surrealistic sight, and yet the peaks carry the mundane labels of **Red Mountain No. 1, No. 2,** and **No. 3.** The road curves beneath these amazing peaks, running through a wide meadow and passing the debris of an active mining history: shacks, mills, heaps of gravel.

You climb nearly to tree line before arriving at 11,075-foot **Red Mountain Pass,** and then the road begins its 10-mile, 1,700-foot descent into Silverton.

Telluride beneath the San Juan Mountains

Look for deer and elk as you pass through the U-shaped valley framing **Bear Mountain,** 12,987 feet. Soon, the road drops, curves left, and runs across the wide floor of the **Animas River Valley** toward 13,338-foot **Kendall Mountain.** Go left at the junction with Rte. 110 and drive into **Silverton.**

Incorporated in 1876 and spared the fires that wiped out other old mining towns, Silverton retains its rickety historic look. Brush up on the region's past at the **San Juan County Historical Museum** *(970-387-5838. Mem. Day–mid-Oct.; adm. fee).* Then consider a side trip to the ghost town of **Animas Forks** (see Alpine Detour, p. 234). While you knock around town, the **Durango & Silverton Narrow Gauge Railroad** *(970-247-2733. Fare)* might come chuffing up the valley. This coal-fired

Cliff Palace, Mesa Verde National Park

steam train runs several times a day between Silverton and Durango.

From Silverton, head south on U.S. 550 and climb Sultan Mountain to **Molas Pass,** with its fine view of the **West Needle Mountains,** the **Grenadier Range,** and other peaks rising over tiny **Molas Lake.**

The road winds for 7 miles along the contours of the mountains to **Coal Bank Pass,** then tilts downward, leaving the mountains behind and heading for the plateau and canyon country around Durango. With the 4,000-foot drop in elevation, the forests change from spruce and fir to ponderosa pine and Gambel oak. As you descend, you'll see the condos and trails of **Purgatory Ski Area** *(970-247-9000)* on the right, and then pass under the **Hermosa Cliffs,** a long band of high sedimentary rocks.

The **Animas River** runs through the forested gorge to the left. Soon, the gorge widens into a broad, flat-floored canyon with red-rock walls rising over the trees. In **Hermosa** the lush canyon floor of grass and hayfields is fast yielding to vacation houses and golf courses.

The red-rock cliffs give out before you arrive in **Durango,** an 1880s railroad town that boomed with the San Juan mines. Elegant brick and stone Victorian buildings line its downtown streets. At the end of Main Street, you'll find the yellow 1882 train depot, a historic landmark and starting point for the narrow-gauge railroad to Silverton.

From Durango, follow U.S. 160 west through a rolling terrain of minor canyons and mesas. The **La Plata Mountains** rise to the north over a dark forest of low-growing trees. After about 23 miles the broad dome of **Sleeping Ute Mountain** appears on the western horizon. **Mesa Verde** stands to the left. You pass Mancos and drive about 8 miles across a flat, grassy plain to **Mesa Verde National Park** *(970-529-4465. www.nps.gov/meve. Adm. fee).* The park protects the ruins of ancient Pueblo villages and dwellings built here between A.D. 550 and 1270. Roads cross the top of the mesa, where the ancestral Puebloans grew crops, and wind along the rims of side canyons, where you see the dwellings under overhanging cliffs. Rangers lead tours of the major dwellings, including **Cliff Palace** and **Balcony House** *(Free tour tickets at Visitor Center).* Views from the mesa are extraordinary.

Continue along U.S. 160 toward Cortez, then follow Rte. 145 north 7.5 miles and turn left at the junction with Rte. 184 to visit the **Anasazi Heritage Center** *(970-882-4811),* an innovative museum depicting the evolution of the ancient culture. Self-guiding trails lead to two sets of ruins.

Once again on Rte. 145, you follow the **Dolores River** back into the San Juan Mountains. As the road gains elevation, it cuts through layers of

233

OLD TOWN SQUARE

Silverton stagecoach

sedimentary rock that bulged upward as magma rose through the Earth's crust and formed the mountains above Rico.

About 10 miles from Rico, you'll see 13,113-foot **Lizard Head Peak** off to the left—an isolated column of rock jutting from a broad, rounded mountaintop. A couple of miles farther, pull over at **Lizard Head Pass,** 10,222 feet, for another incredible view of the toothy San Juan crest, which soars 3,000 feet above the road. From right to left, these are **Sheep Mountain, Yellow Mountain,** and the **Ophir Needles.** You glide down over a meadow toward the Ophir Needles, pass **Trout Lake,** and then plunge down the mountainside. Huge, glaciated valleys open up to the right under broad amphitheaters of 13,000-foot peaks.

Then the road stops at a T-intersection. Turn right and drive toward the booming ski town of **Telluride.** Founded as a mining town during the late 1870s, Telluride boasts a magnificent downtown district of Victorian buildings, including a bank Butch Cassidy robbed in 1889. **Bridal Veil Falls** drops 365 feet from the cliffs behind town. Skiing resurrected Telluride, a near ghost town for decades.

From Telluride, Rte. 145 and the **San Miguel River** burrow down through sedimentary layers into a canyon lined by vermilion sandstone cliffs. At **Placerville** turn right on Rte. 62 and climb 11 miles to the **Dallas Divide.** As you top the pass, a spine of naked rock heaves into view, slicing upward from gentle foothills. Most peaks exceed 12,000 feet. From the divide, you glide back down to Ridgway.

234

Alpine Detour

Silverton to Animas Forks on Colorado 110

● 12 miles ● ½ day ● Early summer through fall. Gravel road. Closed in winter. *See map p. 231.*

This jolting, backcountry road connects Silverton with Animas Forks, a weather-beaten ghost town high in the San Juan Mountains. The route winds through spectacular forested canyons crowded with 13,000-foot peaks and passes the remains of several other abandoned mining camps and mills.

At the northern edge of **Silverton,** turn right on Rte. 110 and follow the **Animas River** over its flat gravel bed toward a narrow canyon cut into the mountains ahead. At the **Mayflower Mill,** idle since 1991, look for ore buckets dangling overhead from an aerial cableway that spans the canyon and rises to a glacially carved cirque. Below the cirque, **Arrastra Creek** tumbles down the canyon.

The canyon widens at **Howardsville,** a tiny cluster of shacks, cabins, and industrial buildings where miners have toiled sporadically since the 1870s. To gain some appreciation for their work, consider an underground tour of the **Old Hundred Gold Mine** *(970-387-5444. Mid-May–mid-Oct.; adm. fee).*

At **Eureka** the road passes a mill foundation, narrows to one lane with turnouts, and hugs the chasm walls. The reddish peak straight ahead is **Cinnamon Mountain.** Waterfalls spill from **Niagara Peak.**

At nearly tree line you bump to a halt in **Animas Forks.** Laid out in 1877, it once thrived as a busy mining town. Today, its collapsed houses rot amid wildflower meadows. An astounding crest of naked gray rock, **Niagara Peak,** looms down the valley.

Unaweep-Tabeguache Scenic Byway

Whitewater to Placerville on Colorado 141 and 145

● 133 miles ● 5 hours ● All year

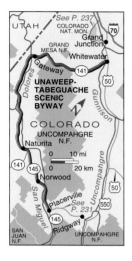

West of Colorado's mountain ranges lies a vast, arid region of plateaus and mesas and deep river canyons, that snake through smooth walls of vivid red stone. At the heart of this beautiful land stands the Uncompahgre Plateau, a huge, flat mass of rock extending for a hundred miles between Grand Junction and Telluride.

This drive crosses the plateau through Unaweep Canyon, a 1,000-foot gorge, then skirts the plateau's southwestern flank, following red-rock canyons carved by the Dolores and San Miguel Rivers. Toward the end of the drive, the road climbs over a mesa offering terrific views of the San Juan Mountains.

The route starts on Rte. 141 at **Whitewater,** south of Grand Junction. Across the arid **Gunnison River Valley** stands the **Uncompahgre Plateau,** known to the Ute as Tabeguache—"where the snow melts first." The plateau rose twice: first as a mountain range that eroded down to its roots of Precambrian granite and gneiss, then again carrying its present load of sedimentary rock.

Soon you enter **Unaweep Canyon,** its floor a jumble of boulders, gravel, and sandy soils dotted with juniper and pinyon pines. Geologists think the canyon was cut by the ancestral Gunnison River, which shifted to its present course as the plateau rose the second time.

Stop at **Grand Valley Overlook** for a long, backward view, then continue 6 miles to Divide Road and turn left. By now, the canyon resembles a broad trough. Its wide, grassy floor runs between palisades of gray granite capped by forested red-rock cliffs.

Divide Road climbs 2 miles to a cattle guard. Park there and walk to the edge of the bluff for an excellent view of the canyon and of the **Great Unconformity**—the distinct line between gray Precambrian granite and vivid red Triassic sandstone that represents a gap in the geologic record of roughly 2.2 billion years.

Return to Rte. 141 and go 4.5 miles to **Unaweep Divide.** Here, **East Creek** and **West Creek** flow in opposite directions. This topographic oddity named the canyon: In Ute, Unaweep means "canyon with two mouths." You pass the ruins of **Driggs Mansion** (a sign explains its history) and, after about 12 miles, the canyon suddenly narrows. In this tight chasm, stop at **West Creek Picnic Area,** a lovely shaded swimming hole.

Just 1.4 miles beyond, the road punches out of the chasm into a broad red-rock gorge. You just crossed the **Uncompahgre Fault** and are now on the west side of the Uncompahgre Plateau.

Hawks, eagles— even peregrine falcons—nest among Unaweep Canyon's cliffs, while mountain lions and bobcats prowl the side canyons for deer and rabbits.

Dolores River, San Juan National Forest

After a few miles you arrive in Gateway and enter the **Dolores River Canyon.** Broad walls of vermilion rock soar 1,500 feet above rustling cottonwoods along the river. Emerald flecks of juniper and pinyon pine speckle the smooth layers of red, pink, peach, and beige rock. From Gateway the road climbs along the Dolores and San Miguel Rivers through all those sedimentary layers.

Continue driving for about 30 miles along the sandy banks of the lovely Dolores, then climb 300 feet above the river to an overlook for **Hanging Flume.** Miners bolted this 7-mile-long wooden trough to the canyon wall in 1889 to carry water to a placer gold mine. Soon you pick up the **San Miguel River** and pass some uranium tailings ponds. Across the river a defunct mill marks the site of a uranium company town.

You go through Naturita, then climb out of the canyon on Rte. 145 and cross the broad back of **Wright's Mesa.** Ahead rise the jagged peaks of the **San Juan Mountains;** to the north, the flat Uncompahgre Plateau.

Beyond Norwood the road dives again to the San Miguel River, where you'll find a mix of trees reflecting the shift between desert and mountain: juniper, Gambel oak, willow, Douglas-fir, ponderosa pine, blue spruce, aspen—all grown in compelling contrast to the brilliant red cliffs. At **Placerville** you can pick up the San Juan Skyway (see page 231).

Colorado National Monument

Rim Rock Drive

● **23 miles** ● **1 hour** ● **All year. Admission fee**

Colorado National Monument, near the Utah border in west-central Colorado, lies along the northeastern edge of the Uncompahgre Plateau. This huge chunk of the earth's surface rises more than 2,000 feet above the Grand Valley of the Colorado River. Rim Rock Drive hugs the plateau's edge and offers a tour of soul-aching beauty among juniper and pinyon pine highlands, red-rock cliffs, and deep side canyons.

Take Rte. 340 from Grand Junction to Monument Road and the **East Entrance** *(970-858-3617. www.nps.gov/colm. Adm. fee)*, where you start the long, switchbacking drive to the top of the plateau. As you climb, you pass through 200 million years of accumulated sedimentary rock—tilted in great slabs, standing as isolated columns, crumbled over steep boulder fields, and curving sensuously overhead in continuous, smooth cliffs.

At the top, pull into **Cold Shivers Point,** which overlooks the deep, narrow trough of **Columbus Canyon** and offers a stunning view across the **Grand Valley.** The plateau's core has risen twice, first as the base of a mountain range that eroded away. Then, after layers of rock reburied the core, it rose again while the valley floor sank.

At **Red Canyon Overlook,** about 2.5 miles up the road, parallel walls of red stone rise 500 feet over a broad, relatively flat canyon floor. White-throated swifts flit through the void, and along the rim, pinyon jays hop among the pine branches. You might see a coyote or a yellowheaded collared lizard, but most of the monument's wildlife is hard to spot. Bighorn sheep and bobcats do live here, though.

Interpretive signs at the next three overlooks (**Ute Canyon, Fallen Rock,** and **Upper Ute Canyon**) offer a quick geology lesson on how erosion forms the many side canyons spilling from the edge of the plateau. Farther along the rim, stop at **Highland View,** where you get an excellent vista across the Grand Valley to the distant badlands of the **Book Cliffs,** which rise about 1,200 feet above the **Colorado River.**

237

Monument Canyon

Drive another mile to **Artists Point,** where an eroded ridge of rock juts into the canyon and ends in a descending series of stone pinnacles the color of sunset. Around the corner you'll find the **Coke Ovens Trail,** a half-mile path to a spectacular overlook at the tip of the **Coke Ovens.** These are massive columns of red stone roughly 400 feet high and rounded at their tops like kilns or coke ovens. Other interesting formations crowd **Monument Canyon** and help enrich Kodak shareholders.

The overlook at **Grand View** is one of the best spots in the park to see how the core of the plateau rose beneath its overlying layers of sedimentary stone. From the railing, look north across the canyon and trace the red cliffs as they curve downward to the right. The dark gray knobs of coarse rock beneath the cliffs are gneiss and schist, the 1.5-billion-year-old core of the plateau. The overlying layers tilted, warped, and sometimes broke as the core was heaved upward and the valley floor fell.

Continue on Rim Rock Drive to the **Visitor Center** for an overview of the park's geology, plants, and animals. Nearby, you'll find picnic tables and a campground. If you have time, stroll one of the nature trails: **Alcove** (through the pinyon pines) and **Window Rock** (to the rim).

You get your last high-altitude view from the plateau at **Distant View,** then the road switchbacks to the valley floor through **Fruita Canyon.** Stop at **Balanced Rock View** to admire the 600-ton boulder perched on a pedestal of red sandstone, and at **Redlands View** to trace the meandering fault line between the fallen valley floor and the risen block of the plateau.

Peak to Peak Scenic Byway

Central City to Estes Park on Colo. 119, 72, and 7

● 55 miles ● 2 hours ● All year

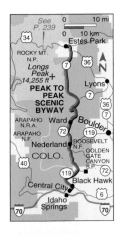

This high mountain drive traverses the eastern flank of Colorado's Front Range, seesawing over forested ridges and running crosswise to almost every major valley between Central City and Estes Park. Sights include historic towns, 13,000-foot peaks, and portions of Rocky Mountain National Park.

Begin the drive on Rte. 119 at the mining, now casino, towns of **Central City** and **Black Hawk.** A gold strike here in 1859 kicked off Colorado's first gold rush and helped pay for the towns' elaborate Victorian buildings. Nine miles beyond Central City, turn into **Golden Gate Canyon State Park** *(303-582-3707. http://parks.state.co.us/golden_gate. Adm. fee)* for the 100-mile vista of the **Front Range** from **Panorama Point.** Back on 119, you descend toward Nederland

Hiking to Long Lake, Indian Peaks Wilderness

through hilly lodgepole forests. Turn left on Rte. 72 and after a few miles look for the **Indian Peaks** to the northwest. Summits exceed 13,000 feet and lie within the popular **Indian Peaks Wilderness.** At the junction with Rte. 7, turn left and go 2.5 miles to an overlook for your first good view of peaks in **Rocky Mountain National Park** (see next drive). The great domed summit to the north is **Mount Meeker,** 13,911 feet. As you continue north, the forest opens up, and you begin to move through meadows peppered with stands of ponderosa pine typical of the park's east side. Look for elk, deer, and coyotes.

About 3 miles beyond Meeker Park, pull over at the **Enos Mills Memorial.** Mills was an innkeeper and naturalist who lobbied for the creation of the national park and spoke at its 1915 dedication. His homestead cabin *(Tours Mem. Day-Labor Day)* stands at the eastern edge of a meadow. Here you also get the best view of **Longs Peak.** Soaring 14,255 feet, it towers a mile above the valley floor. Every year some 10,000 people attempt its summit.

Head north about 2 miles to Rocky Mountain National Park's **Lily Lake Visitor Center** *(970-586-5128. Mid-June–mid-Aug.),* with exhibits on geology, plants, and animals, and have a look over the rim of **Fish Creek Canyon.** Then continue on Rte. 7 as it drops 1,300 feet down the north wall of the canyon to the town of **Estes Park,** which sprawls among rolling meadows.

Trail Ridge Road

Estes Park to Granby on U.S. 34 through Rocky Mountain National Park

● 55 miles ● ½ to 1 day ● Open from about Memorial Day to mid-October. Be prepared for crowds between mid-June and mid-August. Admission fee to park

Trail Ridge Road crosses the broad back of Colorado's Front Range through Rocky Mountain National Park. It rises to 12,183 feet, well above tree line, and rolls along over a gentle landscape akin to the world's Arctic regions. Tremendous views open up of peaks, deep valleys, and, often, the churning violence of approaching thunderstorms. Expect to be pelted by hail one moment, baked by sunshine the next. But you get more than stunning top-of-the-world vistas on this drive. You skirt wide meadows where bighorn sheep, elk, and deer browse. You follow streams and rivers—including the meek headwaters of the Colorado—and plunge through subalpine forests.

Start in **Estes Park,** a growing resort town in a wide basin first homesteaded in 1860 by Joel Estes. At nearly every turn, the flat summit of **Longs Peak** (14,255 feet) and its companion peaks loom over the rooftops. Follow U.S. 34 past the 1909 **Stanley Hotel** *(970-586-3371. Tours, rooms, meals),* built by the inventor of the Stanley Steamer automobile.

The road winds along **Fall River,** squeezing between high forested ridges studded with immense domes of exposed granite. Pick up a map for **Rocky Mountain National Park** *(970-586-1206. www.nps.gov/romo. Adm. fee)*

at the **Fall River Entrance Station** and drive 1.7 miles to **Sheep Lakes** in **Horse-shoe Park,** a meadow at the foot of the **Mummy Range.** Salty soils here draw bighorn sheep, but also look for mule deer and, especially in fall, elk.

Fall aspen leaf on lichen

Follow Trail Ridge Road through Horseshoe Park and up the slope to **Deer Ridge Junction,** where you'll turn right. Park first, though, and stroll to the edge of the hill overlooking **Moraine Park** and Longs Peak. This parkland, or mountain meadow dotted with stands of ponderosa pine, is typical of much of the national park's east side.

You leave the parkland behind as the road begins to rise into the forest of Engelmann spruce, subalpine fir, and limber pine. About 2 miles from Deer Ridge Junction, stop at the **Beaver Ponds,** where a self-guided nature trail leads through an active beaver colony.

At **Many Parks Curve,** 9,640 feet, a boardwalk offers an expansive view of Moraine Park, Horseshoe Park, and other long, glaciated basins carved out during the Ice Age. **Estes Valley,** just visible beyond **Deer Mountain,** looks glaciated but wasn't. Four miles and 1,200 vertical feet up the road, stop at **Rainbow Curve,** the last turnout before tree line. Here, the stresses of an increasingly harsh climate show in the trees. Some wind-blasted trunks grow branches only to leeward, and 100-year-old, sapling-size dwarfs grow horizontally, protected by boulders. The trees give out completely as the road traverses a knife-edged ridgeline, and soon you've arrived in the wide, rolling meadows of the alpine tundra. A deep canyon drops off to the left toward an incredible panorama of the park's major peaks.

Stop at **Forest Canyon Overlook,** 11,716 feet, and take the footpath down to the platform. A peaks-finder chart identifies the summits, which run across your field of vision for 20 miles. Glaciers carved the bowls and basins, spires and ridges that make this ragged mass of gneiss and granite a pleasure to look at. A valley glacier also gouged out **Forest Canyon,** 2,500 feet below.

The road parallels the summits for 2 miles to **Rock Cut** at 12,110 feet, where a steep, self-guided, 1-mile round-trip nature trail climbs a hill. Worth every gasping breath, it offers more than views of mountains rising over colorful wildflower meadows. You'll also learn about the adaptations plants and animals make to survive a very short growing season, wind speeds of 150 mph, and intense sunlight.

The road roughly follows a 10,000-year-old trail where prehistoric people hunted.

U.S. 34 reaches its highest point between the **Lava Cliffs** and **Gore Range** turnoffs. Stop at the **Alpine Visitor Center** *(June-Sept.)* for more about the alpine tundra. If you've brought binoculars, you can usually see a dozen or more elk in a glacial amphitheater beneath the center's viewing platform. The road descends quickly to **Medicine Bow Curve,** a hairpin with a view of the **Medicine Bow Mountains,** 20 miles north. It also overlooks the headwaters of the **Cache la Poudre River,** a silver thread meandering over the treeless floor of a long valley.

You slant down through a subalpine forest and soon approach a small lake, **Poudre Lake.** At its far end lies **Milner Pass,** where you can plant a foot on either side of the **Continental Divide.**

Continue your descent through the forest 2 miles to **Farview Curve,** with its impressive view of the **Never Summer Mountains** across the wide **Kawuneeche Valley.** That timid little stream winding across the valley is the **Colorado River. Grand Ditch,** the faint diagonal line cutting across the Never Summers, intercepts meltwater for farmers near Fort Collins.

Follow the switchbacks down to the valley floor and drive about 14 miles along enormous meadows. Stop at the parking area for **Never Summer Ranch,** a preserved, 1920s-era dude ranch nestled in the forest. A half-mile walk leads to the cluster of ranch buildings erected by John Holzwarth after Prohibition shut down his Denver saloon.

Displays at the **Kawuneeche Visitor Center,** about 8 miles from the ranch, focus on animals and plants that live on the colder, wetter west side of the park. Historic **Grand Lake Lodge** *(970-627-3967. June–mid-Sept.)* perches on a mountain slope overlooking Grand and Shadow Mountain Lakes. You'll enjoy sitting on its veranda for a drink or a meal. **Grand Lake**—a jewel surrounded by mountains and enormous glacial troughs—is Colorado's largest natural lake.

The road continues south along **Shadow Mountain Lake,** which, like **Lake Granby** a little farther along, is a huge reservoir impounding the Colorado River. Water is carried by tunnel through the mountains for use on the east slopes. You'll find many picnic areas, campgrounds, and boat ramps along the lake's perimeter, most of which is in the **Arapaho National Recreation Area** *(970-887-4100).* The high mountains to the southeast are part of the **Indian Peaks Wilderness,** a popular backpacking area accessible from the Arapaho Bay campground on Lake Granby.

The road continues for about 5 miles over rolling hills to **Granby.**

The "parks" here are mountain meadows created when Ice Age glaciers melted, leaving lakes that eventually silted up and drained.

241

Fog-bound Trail Ridge Road near the Continental Divide

Rocky Mountains

Montana, Wyoming, Idaho

Montana

Going-to-the-Sun Road

St. Mary to Apgar through Glacier National Park

● 50 miles ● 2 hours ● Late spring through fall; closed October to early June. Best driven in the morning. Good chance of wildlife sightings. Adm. fee to park

High in the mountains of northwest Montana, Glacier National Park sprawls over a magnificent landscape of jagged peaks, deep mountain lakes, and steep-sided valleys. Crossing the park's backbone from east to west, Going-to-the-Sun Road climbs from the fringe of the Great Plains to the Continental Divide, then drops into the lush rain forests of the McDonald Valley. The route passes ribbon-like waterfalls, vibrant wildflower meadows, and turquoise streams.

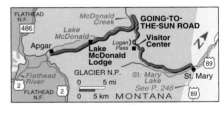

From the town of **St. Mary** head a mile west to the entrance to **Glacier National Park** *(406-888-7800. www.nps.gov/glac. Adm. fee)*. The drive begins at the east end of **St. Mary Lake.** Ten miles long, the lake occupies a trough gouged by a huge glacier thousands of years ago. Along its upper end, peaks of sedimentary rock sweep up 4,500 feet.

From here, the road curves through meadows colored by wildflowers and bordered by aspen and lodgepole pine. The haunts of elk and deer, these meadowlands also provide homes for mice, voles, gophers, and squirrels. Look for hawks circling above, on the prowl for lunch.

Continue past the Rising Sun Campground to **Wild Goose Island Turnout,** with its famous view of an islet dwarfed by mammoth peaks. Three miles up the road at **Sun Point,** a short path climbs to a fine lake overlook, where a peaks-finder chart identifies the major summits. All of them suffered the glorious vandalism of the Ice Age. Cirques, knife-edged crests, horns, and broad U-shaped valleys track the flow of glaciers inching down from high summits to fill valleys like this one.

Within a mile of Sun Point, the road begins to climb through a massive layer of vermilion mudstone. On the left, a 1.5-mile trail leads to **St. Mary Falls,** one of the loveliest cascades in the park. Across the lake, look for

Avalanche Creek, Going-to-the-Sun Road, Glacier National Park, Montana

Virginia Falls dropping through the forest.

At the **Jackson Glacier Turnout** a sign explains how the glacier, barely visible over the treetops, has shrunk to just a quarter of the size it was in the mid-19th century. Black bears thrive in these deep subalpine forests of Engelmann spruce and fir, as do weasels, red squirrels, porcupines, and great horned owls.

Going-to-the-Sun Road opened in 1933 after years of arduous construction. Every spring it takes about two months to clear the road of snow.

After another mile the road breaks out of the forest and into a broad, open slope rimmed by mountains. Stop at the hairpin turn and crane your neck to see 10,014-foot Mount Siyeh standing over the apex of the curve, with 9,642-foot Going-to-the-Sun Mountain to the right and Cataract and Piegan Mountains on the left. Grizzly bears roam the scrubby amphitheater enclosed by the peaks, and bighorn sheep and mountain goats browse along the upper slopes.

As you drive toward Logan Pass, the road edges along the nearly vertical cliffs of **Piegan Mountain,** and a waterfall thunders right onto the pavement. At 6,646 feet, **Logan Pass** is one of the best areas in the park to spot mountain goats. You might see them crossing the road, but if you don't, stop at the **Visitor Center** and hike to the **Hidden Lake Overlook.** The 1.5-mile boardwalk trail rises through a wide basin of rock terraces overgrown with wildflowers, ending at the brink of a spectacular hanging valley. Even if you don't see goats, you won't be disappointed.

From Logan Pass, you descend along the broad face of the **Garden Wall,** a knife-edged crest stretching along the Continental Divide. In Glacier, the

St. Mary Lake and Wild Goose Island

Monkey flower, arnica, and Indian paintbrush

divide not only separates Pacific and Atlantic watersheds, but it also forms a climatic divide. Tree species typical of the northern Rockies grow on the cooler, drier east side, while the west side fosters cedars, hemlocks, and other trees found in Northwest rain forests.

After about 5 miles you come to **Bird Woman Falls Overlook,** with views of a white ribbon of water cascading off a hanging valley enclosed by (left to right) Mounts Oberlin, Clements, and Cannon. The turnout also overlooks deep, glaciated **McDonald Valley.**

For the next 4.5 miles the road slants down through an area still recovering from a 1967 lightning fire. Silver trunks of dead trees stand like ships' masts over a lush carpet of fireweed, black cottonwood, mountain maple, young lodgepole pine, and a variety of berry bushes.

Soon the road makes a sharp turn to the left and glides down through the forest to the floor of the valley. Here, you pick up **McDonald Creek,** a rippling sheet of glacier blue water that races over a bed of red and green pebbles. Its waters draw white-tailed deer and moose.

Pull over at the **Avalanche Exhibit** for a neck-crimping view of Mount Cannon and its avalanche chutes, then drive 3 miles to an unmarked turnout on the right side. Short paths through cedars and hemlocks lead to **Red Rock Point,** where McDonald Creek zigzags between tilted blocks of red mudstone and rests in murmuring turquoise pools.

Just a mile down the road, the **Trail of the Cedars** makes a short loop through a forest of cedar and hemlock. The trail also passes the mouth of **Avalanche Creek,** where sapphire waters swirl over bloodred rock.

It's hard to get enough of McDonald Creek, and a footbridge and trail at **Sacred Dancing Cascade** follows the creek past a series of rapids and falls. There's also a turnout at **McDonald Falls.**

Soon, though, the road pulls away from the creek and bores through a dense forest of cedar, hemlock, larch, white pine, and birch, emerging at **Lake McDonald Lodge** *(406-756-2444),* a fine rustic structure with an immense lobby of stone and timber and a public dining room. **Lake McDonald** itself occupies a deep trench 10 miles long, 1.25 miles wide, and 472 feet deep. Views of it from the road are limited because of an intervening strip of thick forest, but you'll find dozens of turnouts with paths leading through the trees to wide pebble beaches. The beaches seem made for picnics, the red and green pebbles for skipping across the water.

Going-to-the-Sun Road near Logan Pass

At the southwest end of the lake, follow signs to the village of **Apgar,** where the drive ends with a sweeping view up Lake McDonald to the mountains above Logan Pass.

Yellowstone National Park to Glacier National Park

● 377 miles ● 2 days ● All year

This lightly traveled route between Yellowstone and Glacier National Parks crosses Montana through an epic western landscape that sprawls along the base of the northern Rockies. It traces the sinuous course of the Yellowstone River to Livingston, then cruises through wide intermontane basins full of sagebrush and pronghorn. North of White Sulphur Springs, the road climbs over a gentle, forested range of mountains, scrambles around in gullies and canyons, then breaks out onto the Great Plains, crossing the Missouri River at Great Falls. Rollicking through the foothills of the awesome Rocky Mountain Front, it finally drops into the St. Mary Valley at the eastern edge of Glacier National Park.

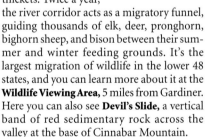

From **Gardiner,** follow the **Yellowstone River** northwest through a semiarid valley of steep, gravelly hills thinly covered by grass and sagebrush. Across the river you can see two prominent summits: 9,652-foot **Sepulcher Mountain** on the left and 10,992-foot **Electric Peak** to the right.

Broad, deep, and swift, the Yellowstone rushes between stony banks and coasts past narrow sand beaches shaded by gnarled juniper trees and rustling willow thickets. Twice a year, the river corridor acts as a migratory funnel, guiding thousands of elk, deer, pronghorn, bighorn sheep, and bison between their summer and winter feeding grounds. It's the largest migration of wildlife in the lower 48 states, and you can learn more about it at the **Wildlife Viewing Area,** 5 miles from Gardiner. Here you can also see **Devil's Slide,** a vertical band of red sedimentary rock across the valley at the base of Cinnabar Mountain.

Mule deer

U.S. 89 continues 8 more miles through this broad canyon before the hills crimp down into **Yankee Jim Canyon,** a narrow gorge the Yellowstone has cut through Precambrian metamorphic rock.

Soon the road exits the gorge and heads across the expansive, undulating floor of **Paradise Valley,** spreading between the **Gallatin** and the **Absaroka** (Ab-SORE-kuh) **Ranges.** Above the river rise black basalt cliffs, which give out as you pass a rest area. Suddenly, the entire Absaroka massif stands before you—a grand alignment of peaks bulking up more than 4,500 feet above the valley and forming a backdrop to Livingston.

Seven miles beyond the rest area, you'll pass the turnoff for **Chico Hot**

Absaroka Range near Livingston

Springs *(406-333-4933. Adm. fee)*, one of Montana's finest commercial soaking grounds, with a saloon and two restaurants to match.

In the midst of the sun, sweat, and dust of summer, the shaded banks and cool waters of the Yellowstone River are always inviting. One of the best sites on the river lies 10 miles past Chico: **Mallard's Rest Fishing Access** occupies a flat bench of sand and gravel under huge cottonwoods. Here, you can let the broad, dimpled sheet of the Yellowstone run across your toes while you gaze into the glacially carved high country of the **Absaroka-Beartooth Wilderness.**

Twelve miles north the road enters **Livingston,** an 1880s railroad town with a colorful historic district. Its **Depot Center** *(200 W. Park St. 406-222-2300. May-Sept.; adm. fee)*, a 1902 Northern Pacific train depot designed by the architectural firm that did New York City's Grand Central Station, now houses a railroad museum. Across the street stands another town landmark—**Dan Bailey's Fly Shop** *(406-222-1673)*, legendary among fly fishing enthusiasts.

Landing a trout

From Livingston U.S. 89 joins I-90 briefly, rounds the northern spur of the Absaroka Range, and heads north. Crossing the Yellowstone for the last time, it enters **Crazy Mountain Basin,** a broad, rumpled floor of grass and sagebrush that extends from Livingston nearly to White Sulphur Springs. The **Bridger Range** rises to the west, and the jagged crest of the **Crazy Mountains** cuts into the eastern sky. Below them, the **Shields River** meanders across dry ranch fields, sometimes pooling into backwater sloughs and ponds rimmed with cattails, reeds, and cottonwoods. Deer, owls, kingfishers, woodpeckers, beavers, minks, and muskrats live in the wetland areas. Out on the flats pronghorn are everywhere, while hawks, coyotes, and badgers are on the

Aspen grove, Two Medicine Valley

prowl for gophers and other rodents.

As the Crazy Mountains sink from view, the **Castle Mountains** rise straight ahead like a forested granite dome. On the western horizon, the **Big Belt Mountains** replace the Bridger Range. As you enter **White Sulphur Springs,** look for the impressive Victorian mansion standing atop the highest hill in town: **The Castle** (406-547-2324. Mid-May–mid-Sept.; adm. fee). It was built of hand-hewn granite in 1892 by a local rancher and mine owner; today, it's a house museum.

From White Sulphur Springs, the road crosses the **Little Belt Mountains,** which look like big swells on a prairie-grass sea. As you climb higher, a forest thickens around you, but the trees open often into meadows where you're likely to see elk and deer in the evening. The road tops out at 7,393-foot **Kings Hill Pass,** then drifts down through the forest along **Belt Creek.** As you descend to drier elevations, the trees shift from lodgepole pine and Engelmann spruce to drought-resistant ponderosa pine.

At Monarch the road breaks away from Belt Creek to avoid a major chasm of 1,000-foot cliffs, then climbs over the open backs of the surrounding hills to a scenic turnout. From here you can see the cliffs plunging down to Belt Creek. **Sluice Boxes State Park** (406-444-3750. www.fwp.state.mt.us/cgi-bin/parks.pl?16) occupies part of the chasm (follow the signs at the bottom of the hill).

Cattle drive along U.S. 89

U.S. 89 continues to follow Belt Creek and its ribbon of trees and shrubs through a wide, dry canyon to the junction with U.S. 87/Mont. 200. Turn left to continue on U.S. 89 and cross 15 miles of rolling prairie to the outskirts of **Great Falls,** which straddles a gorge cut by the Missouri River. When the Lewis and Clark expedition encountered this gorge in 1805, they were forced to spend nearly two weeks portaging around it. A series of five dams has extinguished some of the grand cascades that once thundered here, but the road along the river is worth driving for its views of the Missouri.

To reach the river, turn right on the U.S. 87 bypass. Stop first at the **Lewis and Clark National Historic Trail Interpretive Center** (4201 Giant Springs Rd. 406-727-8733. Mem. Day-Oct. daily, Tues.-Sun. rest of year; adm. fee), which details the expedition from beginning to end. **Giant Springs Heritage State**

Park on the river *(406-454-5840. www.fwp.state.mt.us/cgi-bin/parks .pl?14. Adm. fee)* is just up the road; catch up on the area's plants and animals at the park **Visitor Center.** Continue to Giant Springs, a small pond of crystalline water welling up through a bed of lush aquatic plants. Huge trout glide around in a display tank at a fish hatchery beside the springs.

Return to the U.S. 87 bypass and follow the river into town. Turn left on 14th Street to reach the **C.M. Russell Museum** *(400 13th St. N. 406-727-8787. www.cmrussell.org. Closed Mon. Oct.-April; adm. fee)*, home of the world's most extensive collection of paintings, sculptures, and drawings by the cowboy artist Charles M. Russell.

From Great Falls, follow I-15 to the Vaughn exit and continue on U.S. 89 across a corner of the **Great Plains** toward the **Rocky Mountain Front.** This seemingly endless barricade of high serrated peaks slid out onto the prairie about 70 million years ago—the leading edge of an overthrust belt of mountains that now extends from Helena north into Canada and west to Kalispell. It's a vast tract of wild land that gathers Glacier National Park, three contiguous wilderness areas, and several national forests into an ecosystem that is larger than the states of Delaware and Rhode Island combined.

Abundant on the prairie along U.S. 89, pronghorn can cruise about as fast as cars, clocking in at speeds above 55 mph.

Just north of Fairfield, **Freezeout Lake** spreads across the prairie with the mountains as a distant backdrop. Freezeout is a major stopover for migrating waterfowl, and its skies explode each spring and autumn with flocks of gabbling snow geese and tundra swans.

About 10 miles farther along, the drive passes the small town of **Choteau.** At the north end of town, you can stop at the **Old Trail Museum Complex** *(406-466-5332. Closed Sun.-Mon. Sept.-May).* More than simply an interesting pioneer museum, the complex also sponsors excursions to local dinosaur fossil sites between May and September.

From Choteau to Browning the highway bobs along over prairie swells as it heads toward the Rocky Mountain Front. During the 19th century, the Blackfeet Indians controlled the buffalo country east of the mountains here, though they were occasionally challenged by the Kootenai and Flathead tribes who lived to the west. In Browning, the heart of the Blackfeet Indian Reservation, stop at the **Museum of the Plains Indian** *(406-338-2230. Closed weekends Oct.-May; adm. fee June-Sept.)*, which celebrates the traditional life of the northern Plains tribes with exhibits of clothing, weapons, tools, and ceremonial gear.

Beyond Browning, the highway swings toward the mountains, bounding over lateral moraines left by glaciers that mauled the peaks and plowed their way down to the plains about 10,000 years ago. Before long, you climb into the

Wooden church, Ringling, Montana

foothills and then descend the northeastern flank of **Divide Mountain** into the **St. Mary Valley.** The drive ends at the eastern entrance to **Glacier National Park** (see Going-to-the-Sun Road, p. 243), where you have a stunning view of the massive mountains that characterize the park's terrain.

Beartooth Highway

Red Lodge to Yellowstone National Park on U.S. 212

● 68 miles ● 3 hours ● Late spring to fall. Generally closed mid-October to Memorial Day. Major switchbacks

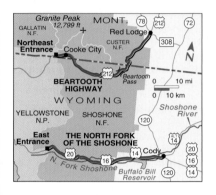

From the rarefied heights of Montana's alpine tundra to the thirsty soils of Wyoming's High Plains desert, this spectacular drive winds through some of the most beautiful and varied landscapes in the Yellowstone region.

As you come into Red Lodge from the north on U.S. 212, the **Beartooth Plateau** looms over the surrounding prairie foothills as a hulking mass of black, rounded mountains. The plateau, an immense block of metamorphic rock, was heaved up through the Earth's crust about 50 million years ago. Much later, an enormous ice cap smoothed its surface and flowed down into the plateau's side canyons, hollowing them into spacious U-shaped valleys.

250

Red Lodge is an 1880s coal-mining and ranching town lined with turn-of-the-century redbrick storefronts and hotels catering mainly to skiers and visitors to Yellowstone. Here you can visit the **Beartooth Nature Center** *(N end of Red Lodge. 406-446-1133. Adm. fee),* which exhibits native wildlife.

The road follows **Rock Creek** into the mountains, winding through grassy hills that soon give way to heavily forested mountains. Rocky outcrops interrupt evergreen forests, and an occasional spire juts over the trees. About 13 miles from Red Lodge, the road climbs away from the creek, and suddenly the vista opens up toward the 1,800-foot cliffs that bend around the head of the valley in a tight semicircle.

After 5 miles of dramatic switchbacks, stop at the **Vista Point** scenic overlook. Here, at 9,200 feet, a short path leads to the tip of a promontory with phenomenal views across **Rock Creek Canyon** to the high, rolling country of the Beartooth Plateau. Signs brief you on the geology, plants, and animals of the area.

As you continue on U.S. 212, the trees give out entirely and you begin crossing a landscape of low, rounded hills covered with grasses, sedges,

Angler on Beartooth Lake

and lavish summer wildflowers. Soon the road cuts back to the rim of the canyon, and from the narrow turnouts you can see a chain of glacial lakes, including **Twin Lakes,** 1,000 feet below. Even in July, enough snow accumulates against the headwall here to draw skiers.

View of Twin Lakes from Beartooth Pass

As you pass by the ski lift, the **Absaroka Range** breaks over the southwest horizon in a row of jagged volcanic peaks. Wildflower meadows lead to the west summit of **Beartooth Pass,** at an exalted 10,947 feet.

The brutal climate at this elevation—frigid, wind hammered, dry—deters the growth of trees and shrubs, and the plants that do grow here have adapted in remarkable ways. Some convert sunlight to heat, and many conserve water the way desert plants do.

Only marmots, squirrels, pikas, and mountain goats live here year-round. The goats frequent the cliffs called **Quintuple Peaks,** to your immediate right. Grizzlies passing through dig up the meadows for roots and for squirrels, and bighorn sheep summer among the boulder fields. If you scan the sky, you may see hawks, eagles, or falcons sweeping the high country in search of rodents.

Alpine wildflowers

From the pass, you descend to a landscape where scattered islands of pine and spruce eke out a living amid knobs of granite and fields of wildflowers. Hundreds of tiny ponds and several small lakes shimmer in glaciated depressions.

As you approach the turnoff for **Island Lake Campground,** two prominent spires of the Absaroka Range swing into view: 11,708-foot **Pilot Peak** and 11,313-foot **Index Peak.** Beyond here, you descend through a forest of lodgepole and whitebark pines toward 10,514-foot **Beartooth Butte.** Soon you pass **Beartooth Lake,** a great picnic spot nestled against the butte's 1,500-foot cliffs.

When the road breaks out of the trees, look to the left across a deep canyon to see **Beartooth Falls** cascading through the forest. In another mile follow the gravel road to **Clay Butte Lookout,** a fire tower with a smashing view of some of Montana's highest mountains.

Watch for deer, moose, and elk in the meadows as the road moves down the flank of the plateau to the **Pilot and Index Overlook.** You're looking at the northeastern edge of the Absaroka Range, an eroded mass of lava, ash, and mudflows that began forming 50 million years ago.

Continue 5.5 miles to an unmarked bridge over **Lake Creek** and take the short path back to a powerful waterfall thundering through a narrow chasm. A completely different sort of cascade fans out over a broad ramp of granite in the trees above **Crazy Creek Campground,** 2.5 miles farther.

From here the road picks up the **Clarks Fork River** and follows it through what is left of a centuries-old forest, much of which fell victim to the great Yellowstone fires of 1988. Soon the road passes through the tiny tourist crossroads of **Cooke City,** begun as a 19th-century mining camp. In 1877 the Nez Perce retreated through this area on their way to Canada. Four miles beyond, the drive ends at the northeast entrance to **Yellowstone National Park** (307-344-7381. www.nps.gov/yell. Adm. fee).

Lake Creek, Shoshone National Forest

Wyoming
North Fork of the Shoshone

East entrance of Yellowstone National Park to Cody on U.S. 14/16/20

● 52 miles ● 2 hours ● Spring through fall. Yellowstone's east entrance closed in winter. *See map p. 250.*

From Yellowstone's east entrance, the drive descends through dense evergreen forests into the high, semiarid country surrounding Cody and its famous Western museum.

Beginning at the east edge of Yellowstone, U.S. 14/16/20 follows the shallow waters of **Middle Creek** to **Pahaska Tepee** (307-527-7701. www .pahaska.com. Mid-May–mid-Oct.), a modern dude ranch built around one of Buffalo Bill Cody's hunting lodges. Behind a roadside curio shop, the rustic lodge holds mounted elk heads, a big fireplace, and burl furniture.

After the lodge, you pick up the **North Fork Shoshone River.** As you descend through the forest, cliffs and narrow columns of bulbous rock carved by water begin to rise through the trees. These formations, including **Chimney Rock,** are the remains of ancient volcanic mudflows. Soon, the forest thins to a peppering of juniper scattered along the canyon cliffs. The **Wapiti Ranger Station** *(307-527-6921)* here in the canyon was built in 1903 as headquarters for **Shoshone National Forest** *(www.fs.fed.us/r2/shoshone).*

Following the curves of the river beneath red rock, you coast out of the canyon into a wide valley, hugging the shore of **Buffalo Bill Reservoir** and **Buffalo Bill State Park** *(307-587-9227. http://spacr.state.wy.us/sphs/buffalo.htm).*

If you stop at the **Buffalo Bill Dam Visitor Center** *(307-527-6076),* you can gaze down into **Shoshone Canyon,** an impressively deep gorge between Cedar and Rattlesnake Mountains. A roadside exhibit partway down the gorge explains the geology of Rattlesnake Mountain.

As the road emerges from the gorge onto the desert floor of the **Big Horn Basin,** you'll see isolated **Heart Mountain** off to the northeast. It slid off the Beartooth Plateau and came to rest north of Cody.

Entering **Cody** from the west, look for **Trail Town** *(307-587-5302. Mid-May–mid-Sept.; adm. fee).* A mix of replicated and authentic frontier buildings, it offers shops, eateries, and period exhibits. Drive downtown to see Cody's **Buffalo Bill Historical Center** *(720 Sheridan St. 307-587-4771. www.truewest.com/BBHC. May-Nov.; adm. fee).* Perhaps the best Western museum in the northern Rockies, it has one of the finest collections of Western painting and sculpture, a Plains Indian museum, a world-renowned collection of firearms, and a treasure trove of Buffalo Bill memorabilia.

Colter's Hell hot springs, Shoshone River

Big Horn Mountains Scenic Byway

Dayton to Shell on U.S. 14

● 60 miles ● 2 hours ● Late spring through fall; pass occasionally closed in winter

This splendid drive over the broad back of the Big Horn Mountains rises from the Tongue River Valley, booms across meadows, then dives into a dazzling gorge on the range's west side.

From **Dayton,** U.S. 14 leaves the shaded banks of the **Tongue River** and winds through rolling prairie foothills toward the dark eastern front of the **Big Horn Mountains.** The range formed 60 million years ago, when a section of

Precambrian "basement" rocks—some of them 2.9 billion years old—was forced through the surface. The Precambrian rock carried with it a cap of

Big Horn Mountains

mostly eroded sedimentary rock.

About 10 miles from Dayton, stop at the **Sand Turn Pullout** on the flank of the mountains. Here, a sign identifies Buffalo Tongue Rock, one of the sedimentary rock layers that tilted as the Big Horns rose. Within a mile, the road begins traversing the north wall of **Little Tongue River Canyon.** Pull over at the turnout for **Fallen City,** a steep field of huge limestone chunks that tumbled from the ridgeline across the canyon.

After this the road switchbacks up through a deep lodgepole pine forest that slowly gives way to expansive subalpine meadows, typical of the Big Horn crest.

At Burgess Junction, an hour detour on U.S. 14A will bring you to **Medicine Wheel,** an ancient stone circle sacred to Indians. Back on U.S. 14, you'll soon reach **Granite Pass,** elevation 9,033 feet, whose vast, grassy meadows attract elk and deer. As you descend to **Shell Canyon,** stop at **Shell Falls Interpretive Site,** where a self-guided nature trail hugs the rim of a granite-lined chasm overlooking the falls. Exhibits cover canyon geology, plants, and animals.

254

Pebbling a barren plateau high in the Big Horn Mountains, the Medicine Wheel is an enigmatic message from a people long gone.

Below the falls, the drive gets even better. You pass two roadside exhibits showing where bighorn sheep tend to congregate during winter. Then the canyon narrows and you plunge into a slender gap that curves between high walls of smooth, colorful rock. Cliffs of pink, orange, beige, and reddish brown rise hundreds of feet from the swift waters of **Shell Creek.** Savor the view because it lasts only about a mile before the road punches out of the western flank of the Big Horns and heads across the desert floor to the town of **Shell** and the drive's end.

Snowy Range Road

Laramie to Saratoga on Wyo. 130 and 230

● 85 miles ● 3 hours ● Late spring through fall; closed in winter

Easily one of the most spectacular drives in Wyoming, the Snowy Range Road crosses the Medicine Bow Mountains in southern Wyoming, passing expansive wildflower meadows, tiny alpine lakes, and high glaciated cliffs before descending to the plains. It's the sort of drive that makes you want to stop the car, get out, amble around, and smell the lousewort.

From **Laramie** take Rte. 130 west across a broad, grassy flat toward the **Medicine Bow Mountains.** A dark band across the western horizon, they were raised along a fault roughly 65 million years ago. Look for coyotes, pronghorns, and hawks as you drive the 27 miles to **Centennial,** a small town founded in 1876 in hopes of gold that never panned out.

From Centennial, you climb into a forest of lodgepole pine, aspen, subalpine fir, and Engelmann spruce. As you gain elevation, wide meadows covered with thick mats of grass and summer wildflowers dot the forest, frequented by deer, elk, and moose. About 10 miles from Centennial, the high peaks of the **Snowy Range,** part of the Medicine Bow Mountains, burst into view. This impressive crest of 1,000-foot cliffs is composed of glaciated quartzite two billion years old. From the plains, the grayish-white quartzite looks like snow during the dry hot months, when the ground cover is gone.

Weaving through high mountain country and past alpine lakes, this drive is a welcome relief from the dry Wyoming flatlands.

For a closer look, drive 3 miles to the **Sugarloaf Recreation Area** and rumble a mile down a rough road of glacial gravel to the picnic area. Here, you'll find two tiny alpine lakes nestled among wildflower meadows at the foot of **Sugarloaf Mountain.**

Return to the main road and drive a mile to the **Libby Flats Observation Point,** at the summit of a 10,847-foot pass. A stone turret here overlooks a landscape dotted with boulders and dwarf subalpine fir. On clear days, you can see as far south as Rocky Mountain National Park in Colorado. A peaks-finder chart points out **Medicine Bow Peak,** at 12,013 feet the Snowy Range's highest.

Making a 26-mile descent through arid foothills, across a sagebrush

255

Summit of the Snowy Range Road

plain, and over the **North Platte River,** the drive reaches the junction with Rte. 230. Turn right and go 7.5 miles to **Saratoga,** which offers a public hot springs and the **Wolf Hotel** *(101 E. Bridge St. 307-326-5525),* built in the 1890s as a stage stop.

Centennial Scenic Byway

Dubois to Pinedale on U.S. 26 and U.S. 189/191

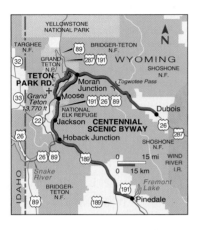

● **162 miles** ● **1 day** ● **All year. Pass occasionally closed in winter**

One of the finest drives in the Rockies, the Centennial Scenic Byway charts a long, doglegging course through the mountains and river valleys of northwest Wyoming. Along the way, it passes nearly every major sight in the region—the Wind River Range, the Tetons, the Snake River, and the Green River Valley. Get an early start so you can catch the morning light on the Tetons and still make Pinedale in time to watch the sun set on the Winds.

The byway begins at **Dubois** (DOO-boyce), in a portion of the **Wind River Valley** where the surrounding terrain shifts from colorful arid badlands to densely forested mountain slopes. Before leaving town, stop at the innovative **National Bighorn Sheep Interpretive Center** *(907 W. Ramshorn. 307-455-3429. Closed Jan.-April; adm. fee).* Next door you'll find the **Wind River Historical Center/Dubois Museum** *(307-455-2284. June-Sept.; donation),* a good pioneer, archaeology, and natural history museum.

U.S. 26 climbs from town between layer-cake badlands and the gentle eastern flank of the **Wind River Range.** To the northeast rears 11,920-foot Ramshorn Peak, part of the volcanic Absaroka Range. Beside the road, the **Wind River** curves over beds of cobblestone, sliding past evergreens and aspens, washing through thickets of willows, and sometimes wetting the feet of moose, elk, and fishermen.

About 17 miles from town, pull over at the **Tie Hack Memorial,** which venerates the tough, mostly Scandinavian lumberjacks who hacked railroad ties from these forests until the 1930s. Within a few miles, the crenellated battlements of the **Breccia Cliffs** and then **Pinnacle Buttes** burst over the tree-tops. Be sure to stop at **Falls Campground** to stroll the rim of the waterfall. Nearby, Forest Road 515 leads to historic **Brooks Lake Lodge** *(307-455-2121)* at the foot of soaring Pinnacle Buttes.

U.S. 26 rises steadily through a forest of rough-barked Engelmann spruce, smooth silvery-barked subalpine fir, and towering lodgepole pine. In meadows rife with wildflowers, be on the lookout for moose, elk, deer, even bear. Soon, you cross **Togwotee** (TOE-guh-dee) **Pass,** elevation 9,544 feet, and descend to **Teton Range Overlook,** with its incomparable view of Wyoming's best known mountains. A peaks-finder chart identifies individual summits, including the 13,770-foot Grand Teton.

Drive out of the mountains onto the floodplain of the Buffalo Fork River, and you're soon in **Grand Teton National Park** *(307-739-3600).* From **Moran Junction,** Yellowstone National Park lies 27 miles north. At Moran you can also also pick up the Teton Park Drive (see page 258).

Rte. 26 turns south, however, and passes through a wetland area. Look for moose, elk, and bison along here. Continue south over gently rolling terrain to the **Snake River Overlook,** perched above a wide bend of the river with one of the classic views of "The Grand" and its attendant peaks. Bald eagles and ospreys sometimes glide over the river. From here, the drive heads south through **Jackson Hole** to **Moose Junction,** where you'll find the main park **Visitor Center** and the chuck wagon tepee of legendary **Dornan's** *(307-733-2522)* with fine views of the Tetons. About 6 miles south of Moose, a fence encloses the **National Elk Refuge** *(307-733-9212. http://nationalelkrefuge.fws.gov. Adm. fee),* where more than 10,000 elk gather every winter. Sleigh rides among the elk start from refuge headquarters. Nearby, take a sharp left turn into the **Jackson National Fish Hatchery** *(307-733-2510)* to see cutthroat trout bred for Wyoming and other states. Back on Rte. 26, the **National Museum of Wildlife Art** *(307-733-5771. Adm. fee),* a mile beyond, displays works by some of the nation's finest wildlife artists.

> A bull moose in rut is a belligerent animal, known to charge anything that annoys it—other bulls, people with cameras, cars, and even locomotives.

Soon you arrive in **Jackson,** a former ranch town turned tourist mecca. If you want to avoid the traffic cruising past its boutiques, art galleries, restaurants, bars, and outfitters, take the truck route and follow U.S. 189/191 south. Seven miles from Jackson you hit the **Snake River** and follow it to **Hoback Junction.** Here, the **Hoback River** joins the Snake, and their combined waters rush into the **Grand Canyon of the Snake River.** In summer, you can watch rafts full of paddlers race through the white water by taking a short detour down U.S. 26/89.

The byway, though, follows U.S. 189/191 up **Hoback Canyon,** through winter range for deer, elk, moose, and bighorn sheep. The Hoback River, a good trout stream, sweeps by forested campgrounds and by lovely picnic areas. If soaking in a mountain hot spring sounds inviting to you, turn left on the Granite Creek Road 11 miles south of Hoback

Junction and drive up the side canyon there to a rustic commercial pool.

Southeast of Bondurant, the road drops out of the mountains onto the sagebrush flats of the **Green River Valley.** Bursting over the eastern foothills, the crest of the **Wind River Range** rises more than 13,000 feet and includes Wyoming's highest summit, 13,804-foot Gannet Peak. A heavily glaciated mass of Precambrian rock, the Winds were formed 55 to 60 million years ago.

The wide Green River Valley lay at the heart of the 19th-century fur trade. Trappers roaming the West rendezvoused here summers to trade their "plews" for

Nez Perce Peak in the Tetons

Teton Park Drive

Moran Junction to Moose Junction on Teton Park and Jenny Lake Loop Roads

● 25 miles ● 2 hours ● Closed late Oct. to early May. Adm. fee. *See map p. 256.*

This drive swings through the scenic heart of **Grand Teton National Park** (307-739-3600. www.nps.gov/grte), a preserve built around one of Earth's most dramatic geologic statements.

From U.S. 26/287, turn right at **Moran Junction**, pick up a park map at the entrance station, and drive about 3 miles to the **Oxbow Bend Turnout.** Here you get a classic view of **Mount Moran** towering above a bend in the **Snake River.** This unforgettable fang of Precambrian rock, along with its companion peaks, soars some 6,000 feet above the flat floor of Jackson Hole. Below the turnout, ponds formed by river meanders attract moose, otters, swans, bald eagles, and herons.

The **Tetons,** young mountains that are still growing, began rising from the earth just 5 to 10 million years ago, but they are composed of rocks 2.5 billion years old. As the mountains rose, the valley floor sank, creating the spectacular landscape of today. At **Jackson Lake Junction,** turn left and drive along Jackson Lake to **Signal Mountain Road,** which climbs to the summit of Signal Mountain and offers a grandstand vista of Jackson Lake, the Tetons, and the other ranges that ring Jackson Hole.

Return to the main park road, then turn right at **North Jenny Lake Junction** and follow the one-way loop road into the scenic center of the Tetons. Load your camera for the **Cathedral Group Turnout,** with its tremendous close-up views of **Mount Owen, Teewinot Mountain,** and the nearly vertical north face of the **Grand Teton.** From the picnic area at **String Lake,** take the short trail to **Leigh Lake,** with its unrivaled views of **Mount Moran.** The **Jenny Lake Turnout** offers a stunning vista of the Tetons.

Continue on the main park road to the **South Jenny Lake** area. Take the 3-mile trail around the lake or pay for the boat ride. On the other side, a trail of less than a mile leads to **Hidden Falls** and **Inspiration Point—** the most popular short hike in the park.

Back on the park road, the **Menor–Noble Historic District** features a restored 1890s homestead and cable ferry across the Snake. The park's nearby **Moose Visitor Center** has exhibits on the natural history of the area. The drive ends just beyond, at the junction with U.S. 26.

> Officially, a local man named W.O. Owen is recognized as the first to climb the Grand Teton in 1898, but a U.S. Geological Survey team claims to have gotten there before him in 1872.

Bull elk in velvet

Tetons towering above the Snake River, Jackson Hole, Wyoming

goods caravanned from Missouri. Their brief tenure, 1824-1840, is celebrated at the **Museum of the Mountain Man** *(U.S. 189/191. 307-367-4101. May-Oct.).* End your tour by following Fremont Lake Road to **Fremont Lake,** which stretches beneath the Winds.

Idaho

Big Hole Mountains Drive

Swan Valley to Victor on U.S. 26 and Idaho 31

● **21 miles** ● **½ hour** ● **Spring through fall.** *See map p. 260.*

This short drive over eastern Idaho's Big Hole Mountains rises from the banks of the Snake River, winds along the rim of a narrow gorge, and tops a lovely mountain pass overlooking Wyoming's Teton Range.

Start 3.5 miles west of the town of **Swan Valley,** where U.S. 26 crosses the **Snake River,** southern Idaho's principal waterway and a major tributary of the Columbia. Here the river sweeps north around a high, arid hill, then enters a deep canyon cut into basaltic lava and hardened volcanic ash. For a quick side trip follow the signs 1.5 miles to **Fall Creek Falls,** a 60-foot cascade over travertine outcroppings.

Return to U.S. 26 and continue to the town of Swan Valley, where you turn left onto Rte. 31. Gliding over rolling fields of wheat and barley, the road runs toward the forested slopes of the **Big Hole Mountains,** then climbs

Blue columbine

to the rim of **Pine Creek Canyon.** A couple of turnouts offer good views of this narrow cleft in black basalt that flowed as lava onto the floor of Swan Valley almost two million years ago.

Within a mile or so the gorge ends, and the road runs along the floor of a small valley. **Pine Creek,** a good fishing spot for cutthroat and rainbow trout, meanders through thickets of willow and dogwood. Moose, elk, and deer browse the bottomlands.

After several miles, you begin climbing through another, longer canyon to the top of 6,764-foot **Pine Creek Pass.** From here, a 4-mile round-trip on Rainy Creek Road rambles through wildflower meadows with great views of the Teton Valley and the sea of broad-backed mountains to the southwest.

Coming off the pass, Rte. 31 winds down out of the forests and onto the wide, flat floor of the **Teton Basin,** where you get a sweeping view of the gentle western slopes of the **Tetons,** including the **Grand Teton**—that distinctive prong of gray rock jutting over the foothills.

The drive ends in **Victor,** fast becoming a bedroom community for Jackson, Wyoming, which is just over the Teton Range to the east.

Mesa Falls Scenic Byway

Ashton to U.S. 20 on Idaho 47

● 28 miles ● 1 hour ● Spring through fall

In all of Idaho, there remain just two undisturbed waterfalls of any real consequence. Both thunder through a narrow chasm carved by the Henrys Fork River in eastern Idaho, near Yellowstone National Park. The Mesa Falls Scenic Byway visits both of them, offers good views of the Teton Range, and passes through forests and meadows frequented by deer, elk, and moose.

From **Ashton,** drive east on Rte. 47 toward the toothy skyline of the **Teton Range,** which thrusts up 7,000 feet. Keep an eye out to the north for **Big Bend Ridge,** the western flank of a volcano that erupted 1.3 million years ago.

The road soon curves to the north and drops to the floor of a forested gorge. Stop near the **Warm River Bridge** to look for trout and for the ospreys, bald eagles, and river otters that feed on them. Driving out of the gorge, you come to a narrow ridge separating **Warm River Canyon** (right) from the **Henrys Fork Canyon** (left). Dense forests hide canyon

260

vistas, but an overlook offers a glimpse of the Tetons and a bend of the Warm River. A turn-off 3 miles beyond leads to **Lower Mesa Falls.** Along the paved trail to its rim, the sound of hissing thunder rises from the canyon, as far below the river squeezes between columns of basalt, then plunges 65 feet.

Return to the byway, drive a mile to the turnoff for **Upper Mesa Falls,** and follow the road down the canyon wall to a large parking area. A footpath here skirts the ruins of a turn-of-the-century log lodge, then leads to viewing platforms of the 114-foot falls. One platform stands at the very edge of the cataract. (In 1981 the hydroelectric industry proposed to dam both upper and lower falls. Fortunately, the plans were thwarted.)

The road continues past a dozen heavily logged miles of **Targhee National Forest** *(208-652-7442. www.fs.fed.us/tnf)*, then joins U.S. 20.

Upper Mesa Falls

Sawtooth Drive

Boise to Shoshone on Idaho 21 and 75

● **246 miles** ● **2 days** ● **All year; occasionally closed in winter**

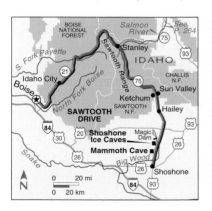

Starting from the desert floor at Boise, this drive climbs into central Idaho's spectacular Sawtooth Range then winds down through Sun Valley to the volcanic desert floor.

Built in a rare spot of shade along the edge of Idaho's southern desert, **Boise** took root as a mining center and military post during the Idaho gold rush of the 1860s. As befits a state capital, Boise offers several museums. For state history, visit the **Idaho Historical Museum** *(Julia Davis Park. 208-334-2120. www.state.id.us/ishs. Donation);* for a look at a living stream, stop at the **Morrison Knudson Nature Center** *(600 S. Walnut Ave. 208-368-6060. Tues.-Fri.);* for rare birds, go to the **World Center for Birds of Prey** *(6 miles south on S. Cole Rd. 208-362-8687. Adm. fee).*

From downtown Boise take Warm Springs Avenue as it curves through the city's outskirts and connects to Rte. 21. This follows the Boise River into a shallow canyon. In 7 miles, you pass the turnoff for **Sandy Point** *(208-344-0240. May-Oct. Adm. fee),* a lovely bathing area beneath the high wall of Lucky Peak Dam.

As you climb into the swollen brown hills above Boise, expansive views open up behind you of the **Snake River Plain**—a vast sheet of basaltic lava flows capping thousands of feet of volcanic ash. Scrambling upward, the road follows a twisting side canyon into ever cooler and moister surroundings. Grass thickens, ponderosa pines begin to sift in among the gullies and ravines, and soon you find yourself driving through a proper forest.

Approaching **Idaho City,** the terrain flattens, and heaps of cobblestones appear on the forest floor among the trees—the leavings of placer miners who swarmed here after gold was discovered in 1862. Soon, Idaho City grew into a tough mining town of 20,000 souls, more than a few prone to violence. Many original buildings survive, including the 1864 territorial penitentiary, where period graffiti includes "Judge Bears is a sun of a bich [sic] and everybody knows it." To learn more, stop by the **Boise Basin Museum** *(Montgomery and Wall Sts. 208-392-4550. Mem. Day-Labor Day; adm. fee).*

Short-eared owl

Continuing north along forest-edged Rte. 21 takes you over **Mores Creek Summit,** 6,117 feet, and, 10 miles beyond, into the **Lowman Burn.** This area was scorched by forest fires in 1989; for the next 24 miles roadside exhibits explain the fires and their aftermath. Four miles past Lowman, one of the signs overlooks **Kirkham Hot Springs,** where the **South Fork Payette River** flows through a chasm of white granite.

Along the South Fork, the road runs through a forest of towering ponderosa pines. After the turnoff for **Grandjean** (hot springs and lodge), it winds up through lodgepole pines and Douglas-firs to 7,056-foot **Banner Summit.** Here, you start driving through broad meadows ringed by forest—likely areas to see elk, deer, coyotes, and hawks. This is the northern fringe of the **Sawtooth National Recreation Area** *(208-727-5013. www.northrim.net/ sawtoothnf/snra)*—756,000 acres that encompass four mountain ranges, several large lakes, lush evergreen forests, the source of the Salmon River, and such uncommon wildlife as mountain goats and bighorn sheep.

Born Lakes in the White Cloud Mountains, Sawtooth National Recreation Area

Suddenly, the shattered crest of the **Sawtooth Range** bursts over the treetops. Stop at the **Park Creek Overlook,** 18 miles from Banner Summit, for a terrific view of the peaks rising over a wetland meadow frequented by elk and deer. Continue 6.5 miles through evergreen forests interrupted by wide grassland meadows to **Stanley,** a mining town turned ranching town now catering to fishermen, hunters, backpackers, and white-water boaters. At Rte. 75, you can begin the Salmon River Scenic Route (see p. 264) by turning left. This drive turns right, following the **Salmon River** south through **Sawtooth Valley.**

The core of the Sawtooths is made of pink granite that rose from the earth's crust 50 million years ago. Glaciers draped the peaks several times, gouging out cirques and ridges and piling up the large moraines that still dam the lakes. The high peaks, many over 10,000 feet, lie within the **Sawtooth Wilderness,** an enticing landscape for day hikes and backpacking trips. Pick up information at the **Stanley Ranger Station** *(208-774-3000. Mon.-Fri., and Sat. in summer),* 3 miles south of town.

> **A chaotic mass of splintering crags, knife-edged ridges, and jagged rock towers, the Sawtooth Range punctuates the horizon for miles.**

Follow the signs to **Redfish Lake Visitor Center** *(208-774-3376. Mid-June–Labor Day),* overlooking the biggest lake in the recreation area. The stunning sheet of turquoise water, ringed with beaches and lodgepole pine forests, is nearly overwhelmed by a mass of peaks so close they seem to overhang the lake. From **Redfish Lake Lodge** *(208-774-3536. Mem. Day-Sept.; fee for boat)* an excursion boat crosses to a wilderness hiking trail.

263

The lake was named for the thousands of sockeye salmon that once spawned here in autumn. Today, Idaho sockeye and chinook live on the brink of extinction, due largely to dams on the Columbia and Snake Rivers that catch oceanbound smolts in their turbines.

Return to Rte. 75 and stop at the **Sawtooth Hatchery** *(208-774-3684. Tours Mem. Day-Labor Day),* 1.5 miles south, where spawning runs of chinook salmon and steelhead trout are raised. From the hatchery, the road continues across the valley floor, past the sites of **Sawtooth City** and **Vienna** (1870s mining towns), then up a broad hillside to the **Galena Overlook.** Here, 2,000 feet above the valley floor, you gaze down the full length of the Sawtooth Range. That squiggle of willows traces the headwaters of the **Salmon River,** which eventually gathers most of the water in central Idaho and funnels it through a canyon that ranks as one of the deepest on the continent.

Rafters on the Salmon River

Soon you top 8,701-foot **Galena Summit** and drop into the forested **Big Wood River Valley.** The colorful **Boulder Mountains** rise to your left. As you drive south, the valley opens up into rolling hills and benchlands. The Big Wood River winds amid the increasingly arid foothills toward **Ketchum,** a popular ski town. Turn left on Sun Valley Road and follow the signs to **Sun Valley** *(800-634-3347 or 208-726-3423),* with its historic 1936 lodge and upscale vacation houses. Along the bike path east of town, the **Hemingway Memorial,** a bust of the writer, is tucked into the cottonwoods alongside Trail Creek.

Return to Ketchum and head south on Rte. 75 to **Hailey,** where you can drive past poet Ezra Pound's boyhood home *(Private)* at 314 Second Avenue S. Beyond Hailey, trees give way to hills, then the hills dissolve into hayfields. Pull over at the sign for **Magic Dam,** where you can get an idea of the vastness of the **Snake River Plain,** a flatland of black lava that paves southern Idaho. Geologists believe it to be the track of a hot spot that melted the earth's mantle 17 million years ago. Some attribute the melting to a huge meteorite crashing into the area.

A mile beyond at **Shoshone Ice Caves** *(208-886-2058. May-Sept.; adm. fee),* guided tours lead through a lava tube partially filled with ice. Eight miles south, you tour **Mammoth Cave** *(May-Sept.; adm. fee)* at your own pace, using a propane lantern. Stocked as a fallout shelter during the Cold War, Mammoth is worth a stop just to see the entrance office, stuffed with scruffy taxidermied animals. Pigs, chickens, and peacocks run in the yard.

Idaho 75 between Stanley and Ketchum

The byway ends 12 miles south in **Shoshone,** whose older buildings are made of lava blocks.

Salmon River Scenic Route

Stanley, Idaho, to Darby, Mont., on Idaho 75 and U.S. 93

● **184 miles** ● **½ day** ● **Spring through fall**

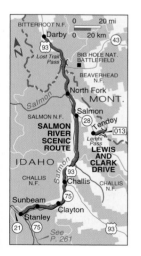

This scenic route follows central Idaho's largest river north from its headwaters in the Sawtooth Range through desert canyons to the tiny town of North Fork, where the waters swerve suddenly to the west and leave all roads far behind. The drive then heads back into the mountains, following the path of Lewis and Clark over Lost Trail Pass and down into the Bitterroot Valley. It's a gorgeous drive and one that also touches on major historical themes—exploration, fur trapping, mining, settlement, and Indian conflicts.

The route begins in Stanley, on the flat floor of Stanley Basin and in full view of Idaho's most spectacular peaks, the **Sawtooth Range.** Follow Rte. 75 east to the **Stanley Museum** *(208-774-3517. Mem. Day-Labor Day),* which summarizes the area's mining and ranching past in a small, historic ranger station.

Paralleling the **Salmon River,** the road soon slants down into a forested gorge lined with granite outcroppings.

See P. 261

The river—clean, cold, and swift—drops 15 feet a mile, charging through turbulent rapids and sweeping past several hot spring pools. **Sunbeam Hot Springs,** the best known and most obvious of the springs, trickles down a rocky slope about 11 miles from Stanley. Less than a mile beyond the springs, the river stalls out in deep pools of emerald green and turquoise at the crossroads town of **Sunbeam.** The dynamited remains of the only dam ever built on the Salmon River stand below an overlook.

As it rushes across central Idaho, the Salmon River cuts one of the deepest gorges on the continent.

If you detour about 10 miles up Yankee Fork Road, you'll find the ghost towns of **Bonanza** and **Custer,** built during the area's 1870s gold rush. The **Yankee Fork Gold Dredge,** still standing here, operated from 1940 to 1952.

Follow the river 2.5 miles east of Sunbeam to **Indian Riffles,** which overlooks spawning beds for chinook salmon. Years ago, chinook and sockeye salmon migrated through here in such numbers that locals said you could almost walk across the river on the backs of spawning fish. No longer. Hydroelectric dams on the Columbia and Snake Rivers have endangered both species. In 1994 only 96 chinook and just one sockeye returned to spawn.

The road continues along the Salmon River through small canyons that get wider and drier as you descend. Beyond Clayton, the river bends to the northeast and runs through a valley surrounded by high desert hills. This eroded volcanic landscape was carved from ash and lava that spread across the region 50 million years ago from calderas lying northwest of Challis.

265

Approaching the junction with U.S. 93, you pass under a towering cliff of rust-colored rock. Bighorn sheep frequent the area, and so did bison in earlier times. At the **Bison Jump Archaeological Site,** a sign describes how Indians drove small herds of the animals over the cliff.

At the junction of Rte. 75 and U.S. 93 stop at the **Land of the Yankee Fork Visitor Center** *(208-879-5244. Closed weekends Nov.-May)* to see exhibits on the region's geology, history, and mining methods—from pick-and-shovel to shaft mines.

As you head north from **Challis,** founded in 1878 to supply the mining camps, look for pronghorn dotting the desert floor and hawks wheeling overhead. To the southeast rise the gravelly, colorful ramparts of the **Lost River Range.**

Salmon River and the Sawtooth Range

Soon you cross the **Pahsimeroi River** and round the northern flank of the **Lemhi Range.** About 18 miles past Challis, both road and river punch through a narrow gorge that widens into a spectacular canyon. The walls soar hundreds of feet above the river to cliffs that cut a gap-toothed silhouette across the sky. Just south of Salmon, you begin to cross the **Lemhi Valley.** On the far side are the Beaverhead Mountains, a massive block of Precambrian sedimentary rock that slid east during the general uplift of the Rockies some 70 million years ago.

Follow U.S. 93 to **Salmon,** an 1860s mining town and now a center for ranchers, loggers, and river runners. Here, you can pick up the Lewis and Clark Drive (see sidebar), tracing the explorers' route over Lemhi Pass.

Heading north, the road runs through yet another canyon carved by the Salmon. Look for great blue herons, cliff swallows, deer, pronghorn, and maybe even river otters. At North Fork the river plunges west into the **Salmon River Canyon,** one of the continent's deepest gorges. Rushing across the vast wilderness of central Idaho, the river is no less forbidding today than it was when early explorers named it the River of No Return.

U.S. 93 tunnels through dense forests to **Lost Trail Pass,** 7,014 feet, named in 1805 by the bewildered northbound party of Lewis and Clark. In 1877, during their epic flight for freedom, the Nez Perce also crossed east through these mountains into the Big Hole Valley. At the **Big Hole National Battlefield** (*15 miles E on Rte. 43. 406-689-3155. www.nps.gov/ biho. May-Sept.; adm. fee*), you can walk over the ground where the Nez Perce beat back the army.

From the pass, you descend into the **Bitterroot Valley,** a region heavily dependent on logging. Stop at the **Indian Trees Campground** to admire stands of mature ponderosa pines, whose reddish, plate-like bark can smell like vanilla.

South of **Darby,** the high peaks you'll see to the left are the Bitterroots; the low-lying mountains to the right are the Sapphires, which once overlay the Bitterroots. As the Bitteroots rose, the Sapphires slid 50 miles to their present location.

Lewis and Clark Drive

Tendoy to Lemhi Pass on Idaho 28 and FR 013

- 11 miles ● 1 hour
- Late spring through fall.
See map p. 264.

This steep gravel road climbs through the arid foothills of the Bitterroot Range to Lemhi Pass on the Continental Divide. Here you'll find, as Lewis and Clark did, one of the headwaters of the Missouri River.

From Rte. 28, turn east at Tendoy and south at the T-junction immediately beyond, picking up Forest Road 013, as it follows along beside Agency Creek.

The road climbs a wooded crease between the hills, lush with willows, alders, and cottonwoods. After almost 10 miles, you reach **Lemhi Pass,** elevation 7,373. From the buck rail fence that marks the Continental Divide and the border between Montana and Idaho, you can look west over hump-backed hills to the **Lemhi Range** and east to the **Horse Prairie Valley.** Signs here commemorate Lewis's and Clark's crossing of the pass but say little about the Lemhi Shoshone, Nez Perce, and Blackfeet who had beaten this path so thoroughly that the white explorers called it a "highway."

Turn right beyond the signs and follow the short road to the **Sacajawea Historical Area,** honoring the Lemhi Shoshone woman who helped Lewis and Clark. Here you'll find a shady campground, and, just north of it, one of the sources of the **Missouri River** welling from a hillside. When Meriwether Lewis arrived here in 1805, he wrote, "I had accomplished one of those great objects on which my mind had been unalterably fixed for many years; judge then the pleasure I felt in allaying my thirst with this pure and ice-cold water."

Lake Coeur d'Alene

Coeur d'Alene to Potlatch on Idaho 97, 3, and 6

● 92 miles ● 2 hours ● Spring through fall

This trip through the forested mountains of Idaho's panhandle skirts the shoreline of Lake Coeur d'Alene, then bounds over hilly terrain all the way to Potlatch. Along the way, forests of ponderosa pine, cedar, hemlock, and larch alternate with open farmland and marshy river bottoms.

East of the town of Coeur d'Alene, take the Rte. 97 exit from I-90 and head south. The road runs along **Wolf Lodge Bay,** an arm of **Lake Coeur d'Alene** stretching beneath high cliffs. Fall salmon runs draw about 60 bald eagles to the bay every year.

Follow Rte. 97 for 4.5 miles as it hugs the shoreline of the bay, then switchbacks up a cliff to a rest area. Here, a short gravel trail leads to a platform overlooking Wolf Lodge Bay and **Beauty Bay.** This is about as panoramic a view of the lake as you'll find along this road, because the forests are too thick and the lake too serpentine to afford more than quick glimpses.

Twenty-three miles down the road, you come to **Harrison,** a timber town that boomed from 1890 to 1917, when a huge fire wiped out the dominant lumber company. A mile south of town, a geology exhibit describes how Lake Coeur d'Alene formed in the **St. Joe River Valley.** Geologists now think the glaciers that dammed the river date back 70,000 to 130,000 years.

Turn right at the junction of Rtes. 97 and 3, and drive over fertile farmland beside the St. Joe River to **St. Maries,** where the **Hughs Historical House** *(538 Main Ave. 208-245-3563)* has exhibits on the town's timbering heritage. Then head south 15 miles on Rte. 3 and make a right on Rte. 6.

Beyond **Emida,** Rte. 6 runs for about 10 miles through a very dense forest of hemlock, cedar, larch, and white pine before arriving at the **Giant White Pine Campground.** The namesake pine stands near the parking lot: a soaring column of gray scaly bark 6 feet in diameter. Its total height approaches 200 feet and its age exceeds 400 years. At the turn of the century, loggers felled thousands of these giants, mainly to make matches.

From here, the road continues west, dropping out of the forest to the farmland around **Potlatch,** a company town established in 1905 by Potlatch Lumber.

Sunset on Lake Coeur d'Alene

Northwest

Alaska, Washington, Oregon

Alaska

George Parks Highway

Wasilla to Fairbanks on Alaska 3

● 323 miles ● 1½ days ● June to mid-September. Summer days offer as much as 21 hours of daylight, but by early September heavy snow can fall in Fairbanks. Mileages are designated by mileposts.

Linking the state's two largest cities—Anchorage and Fairbanks—with Denali National Park and Preserve, this highway travels through the kind of scenery that defines the Alaskan interior: tundra and muskeg, the continent's highest peaks, glaciers, forests, wild rivers, and lonely expanses inhabited only by moose, grizzlies, foxes, wolves, and a wealth of birds.

The Parks begins at its junction with the Glenn Highway (see page 272) in the **Matanuska-Susitna Valley,** 35 miles northeast of Anchorage. Alaska's breadbasket, the Mat-Su stretches in a long fertile swath between the Chugach and Talkeetna Ranges.

Vintage buildings at the **Old Wasilla Town Site and Visitor Center** *(Mile 42.2. 907-373-9071)* testify to the isolation and self-sufficiency of the area's old-time bush communities in the days before the Parks was built. (The highway dates back only to 1971.) Wasilla's original log community hall houses the **Dorothy G. Page Museum** *(323 Main St. 907-373-9071; adm. fee),* an evocative collection of personal artifacts. The nearby **Iditarod Museum** *(Knik Rd. 907-376-5155. Summer daily, fall-spring weekdays)* displays pictures and videos of Alaska's world-famous Iditarod Trail Sled Dog Race, which covers the 1,150 miles from Anchorage to Nome. At Wasilla's sprawling outdoor **Museum of Alaska Transportation and Industry** *(Mile 46.7 exit at Rocky Ridge Rd., follow signs. 907-376-1211. www.alaska.net/~rmorris/mati1.htm. May-Sept. daily, Oct.-April Tues.-Sat.; adm. fee),* hybrid planes, trains, and other conveyances celebrate sourdough ingenuity in coping with Alaska's weather, terrain, and size.

Leaving Wasilla, the highway soon picks up the **Little Susitna River** *(Mile 57.1),* thronged by migrating

Bandon Beach, southern Oregon coast

Mount McKinley, Denali National Park and Preserve

salmon in late spring and midsummer. At mile 67.2, the **Nancy Lake State Recreation Area** *(907-495-6273. www.dnr.state.ak.us/parks/units/nancylk.htm)* also features similar wetlands, as well as several lakes and a canoe trail.

A couple of miles farther on, you will see the turbid **Susitna River** conveying its gritty cargo of silt rasped by glaciers sliding past Alaska Range peaks. The Willow Creek Parkway at mile 70.8 offers access to riverside wetlands flanking the Susitna's **Delta Islands.** The Hatcher Pass Junction Road at mile 71.2 leads to the **Willow Creek State Recreation Area** *(907-269-8400)*, noted for its profusion of wildflowers.

Weather permitting, northbound views of 20,320-foot **Mount McKinley,** highest peak in North America, begin about mile 76. Also called Denali—meaning the "high one" in an Athapaskan dialect—the peak rises 15,000 feet above the surrounding terrain.

For a taste of bush-community life, exit at mile 98.7 and follow the 14.5-mile road to **Talkeetna** (population 450), at the meeting of the Susitna, **Chulitna,** and **Talkeetna Rivers.** Established as a riverboat station in 1910, Talkeetna is now a popular staging area for climbing expeditions to Mount McKinley.

Northbound from the Talkeetna turnoff, the Parks crosses the Susitna *(Mile 104.3)* and traverses a boggy region favored by harvesters of edible fiddlehead ferns. Some of the finest stands of white birch in Alaska can be seen for several miles on both sides of the river. About 28 miles beyond, you enter **Denali State Park** *(907-745-3975. www.dnr.state.ak.us/parks/units/denali1.htm. Facilities closed mid-Oct.–mid-May)*. This primitive 324,240-acre state preserve shares the natural wonders but not the crowds of the adjoining national park.

A wide-open, sparsely timbered tundra basin humped with moraines and flanked by soaring ridges, Broad Pass exudes a profound solitude that affects many travelers.

Few McKinley views match the one from the turnout at mile 135.2, where signs identify various **Alaska Range** landmarks. In another 20 miles you will be able to see the rugged **Eldridge Glacier,** just 6 miles west of the road.

Turnouts along here lead to creeks, beaver ponds, and good fishing spots. Near **Little Coal Creek** *(Mile 163.8),* you see the imposing **Kesugi Ridge** rising steeply to the east.

At mile 174, the road crosses the bridge above 260-foot-deep **Hurricane Gulch,** then continues north to **Broad Pass** *(Mile 201.3),* whose summit marks a watershed divide: From here, north-flowing streams drain into the Yukon River and south-flowing into Cook Inlet. Descending toward the **Jack River,** the highway rides the crest of a long hill running parallel with similar ridges, with **Summit Lake** in between. These are drumlins, carved by glaciers moving parallel to their lengths.

The Denali Highway *(Closed Oct.–mid-May)* intersects at sleepy **Cantwell,** an Alaska Railroad flag stop. North of town, the road skirts the **Reindeer Hills** and joins the **Nenana River,** popular with canoeists and kayakers. River and road cross at mile 215.7 beside 5,778-foot **Panorama Mountain.** Toward evening, sunlight and shadows on 4,476-foot **Mount Fellows** *(Mile 234)* can be gorgeous.

Traffic builds near the entrance to **Denali National Park and Preserve** *(Mile 237.3. 907-683-1266 or 907-683-1267 in summer; 907-683-2294 rest of year. www.nps.gov/dena. Park open year-round; services May-Sept., depending on weather; adm. fee).* Only the first 15 miles of the interior park road are open to private vehicles; shuttles provide further access. Reservations on the shuttle are a must. The park's renowned beauty and wildlife attract heavy summer crowds. The **Visitor Center,** 0.7 mile from the highway, has information.

North of the park entrance, the highway negotiates the steep **Nenana River Canyon.** Its luminous slopes are rich in phyllite, a lustrous rock containing small particles of mica. Scan the heights above **Moody Bridge** *(Mile 242.9)* for Dall's sheep.

This region is rich in coal, and between miles 247 and 251 dark seams stripe the eastern bluffs. The Usibelli Coal Mine, east of Healy, is Alaska's top producer. Between Healy and the **Rex Bridge** *(Mile 279.8),* the highway follows the Nenana over boggy terrain, then veers east away from the river.

In the town of **Nenana** *(Mile 304.5)* the highway rejoins the Nenana River at its confluence with the 440-mile-long **Tanana River,** one of Alaska's few commercially navigable inland waterways.

Denali shuttle bus yielding to a grizzly

271

Between Nenana and Fairbanks, far horizons suggest the scale of Alaskan terrain. The plain extending west from mile 318 includes **Minto Flats State Game Refuge** *(907-459-7213),* a primordially pristine wildlife sanctuary. Look south for a wide perspective on the circuitous Tanana.

The Parks ends near downtown **Fairbanks,** at the junction with Rte. 2. Don't miss the **University of Alaska Museum** *(907-474-7505. www.uaf.alaska.edu/museum. Adm. fee),* the state's premier cultural, historical, and scientific showcase. The nature walk through fields and woods at 1,800-acre **Creamer's Field Migratory Waterfowl Refuge** *(1300 College Rd. 907-459-7307)* offers glimpses of moose, fox, and snowshoe hare.

Glenn Highway

Anchorage to Glennallen on Alaska 1

● 189 miles ● 1 day ● June to mid-September. Be aware of heavy traffic, winter frost heaves and bumps, and many narrow stretches. Mileages are designated by mileposts.

Angling across south-central Alaska, this drive begins at Cook Inlet and follows glacially carved river valleys between the towering peaks of the Chugach and Talkeetna Mountains to the foot of the wild Wrangell Mountains.

Leaving Anchorage, the highway skirts **Knik Arm,** a fjord off Cook Inlet, and the western reach of the **Chugach Mountains.** Great views and the possibility of seeing moose, bear, and Dall's sheep justify a 13-mile side trip to **Chugach State Park Visitor Center** (*Eagle River Exit at Mile 13.4. 907-345-5014 www.dnr.state.ak.us/parks/units/chugach. May-Labor Day*).

Alaska's Athapaskan and Russian heritage live on at the **Eklutna Historical Park** (*Mile 26 exit. 907-696-2828. www.eklutna.com. Adm. fee*), where Orthodox churches and colorful cemetery "spirit houses" combine Russian-Slavic and Tanaina Athapaskan design.

Take the Old Glenn Highway from mile 29.6 and loop 18.6 miles through the **Matanuska Valley Colony,** a Depression-era agricultural project that relocated some 200 impoverished Great Lakes farm families. The old and new routes rejoin in **Palmer,** a pleasant town of 3,000 in the **Matanuska Valley,** named for the river that irrigates its rich farmlands.

About 17 miles from Palmer the **Independence Mine State Historical Park** (*Mile 49.5 exit onto Hatcher Pass Rd. 907-745-2827. www.dnr.state.ak.us/parks/units/indmine.htm. Daily June-Labor Day, weekends rest of year. Fee for tours*) is a relic from the region's gold mining past. About a mile farther on, the **Musk Ox Farm** (*907-745-4151. May-Sept.; adm. fee*) breeds the hoofed, shaggy Ice Age survivors that were hunted nearly to extinction in the 19th century. Their ultralight underwool, called qiviut, is worked by an Eskimo knitting cooperative.

Heading east, the Glenn High-

Bald eagle

way follows the **Matanuska River** between the northerly **Talkeetna Mountains** and the southerly Chugach. Aspen and cottonwood color autumn along here, and there's an impressive view of 4,541-foot **Pinnacle Mountain** at mile 66.5, where the transparent **Kings River** joins the muddy Matanuska. Turnouts at miles 70.6 and 71 offer river access.

272

Moose crossing Glenn Highway

At mile 93 you can see **Monument Glacier,** a rock glacier formed from the stony debris carried by an ice glacier. Trails from **Matanuska Glacier State Recreation Site** *(Mile 101)* lead to unobstructed views of 1,000-foot-thick **Matanuska Glacier.** *(Access to its base is by private road from Mile 102. 907-745-2534. Adm. fee.)* Striated by broken rock, the glacier flows 27 miles from 13,000-foot-high Chugach ice fields. It once reached Knik Arm, flowing through what is now the Matanuska Valley. Turnouts at mile 102.8 and 107.8 offer photogenic perspectives.

Between mile 107 and 118, look for Dall's sheep on 6,300-foot **Sheep Mountain** to the north. Wildflowers bloom profusely along this stretch, including pink fireweed (named for its quick reappearance after fires) and yellow-eyed, blue-petaled alpine forget-me-not, the state flower.

Around 3,000-foot **Tahneta Pass** *(Mile 122)*, sparse stands of stunted black spruce struggle to survive in sodden muskeg. The views are splendid from 3,322-foot **Eureka Summit** *(Mile 129.3)*, the Glenn's loftiest pass and the divide of the Matanuska, Susitna, and Copper River systems. Looking east from mile 131 you'll see the **Wrangell Range,** which reaches

Road crews take full advantage of the short Alaskan summer. That can mean gravel, dust, and sometimes mud.

elevations exceeding 16,000 feet. This is caribou country, and in autumn you may spot migrating herds.

Tazlina Glacier and 20-mile-long **Tazlina Lake** appear near mile 156. Abundant meltwater keeps hundreds of lakes and ponds brimming. A 20-mile side road at mile 159.8 leads to **Lake Louise,** a good spot for fishing and boating.

The falling-down "drunken forests" seen in this area are the result of trees growing in soil too soggy to hold them upright. At mile 176.6, a turnout affords a fine view east across **Copper River Valley** to the Wrangells. An interpretive sign identifies 14,163-foot **Mount Wrangell,** a steaming, semi-dormant volcano. The Wrangell peaks, among the highest in mammoth

Wrangell–St. Elias National Park and Preserve, dominate easterly vistas as you approach Glennallen and the junction with Rte. 4, the Richardson Highway (see below).

Richardson Highway

Glennallen to Valdez on Alaska 4

● 115 miles ● ½ day ● June to mid-September. Mileposts record mileages in reverse, from Valdez to Glennallen.

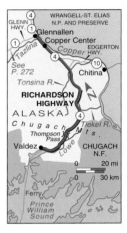

The Richardson Highway got its start as a treacherous gold rush trail heading to the Klondike. This portion of the historic route travels through south-central Alaska, skirting volcano country, passing through tundra and forest, and arcing over barren ridges where glaciers slide from ice fields.

Begin east of **Glennallen** by heading south on the Richardson Highway from its junction with the Glenn Highway (see p. 272). Stop at the viewpoint near mile 112 for a long vista across the **Copper River** to a quartet of snowcapped peaks, highest of the **Wrangell Mountains.** The tallest two, **Mount Sanford** and **Mount Blackburn,** exceed 16,000 feet. Near mile 111 you'll cross the **Tazlina River,** where there is an ideal picnic spot. The Tazlina—"Swift River" in Athapaskan—flows from Tazlina Glacier, north of Valdez, into the Copper River at Glennallen.

274

At mile 106 a 6.5-mile loop road leads to **Copper Center,** a gold rush-era refuge for snowbound tenderfeet. The vintage log **Copper Center Lodge** *(907-822-3245)* offers rustic rooms and sourdough-style fare. Two adjoining old log bunkhouses contain the **George Ashby Memorial Museum** *(June-Aug. Mon.-Sat.),* an eclectic multicultural display of artifacts that include items from early Russian settlements.

Fishing from a floatplane, Willow Lake

At the **Wrangell–St. Elias National Park and Preserve Visitor Center** *(Mile 105 between the Copper Center loop-road turnoffs. 907-822-5234. www.nps.gov/wrst. Daily Mem. Day-Labor Day, Mon.-Fri. rest of year),* you can obtain information on this 13.2-million-acre area, America's largest national park.

Heading south from here, you'll cross rolling hills of paper birch, black spruce, and willow trees, a region favored by homesteaders earlier in this century. The **Willow Lake Turnoff** *(Mile 87.7)* offers an excellent view of the ice fields of the Wrangell Mountains, and a mile farther on you come to the roaring Trans-Alaska Pipeline System's **Pump Station 11.** Signs explain how two or three pumps move about 1.8 million barrels of oil a day 800 miles from Prudhoe Bay to Port Valdez.

The Edgerton Highway *(Mile 82.6)* permits an easy 33-mile side trip to **Chitina** (pop. 49), a former railroad stop and supply center on the Copper River. In the summer, hordes of dip-netters gather here for the annual salmon runs.

Fisherman on the Little Tonsina River

Back on the Richardson, opposite Tonsina Lodge *(Mile 79)* you'll see layers of silt, sediments, and cobbles dropped by melting icebergs, evidence that a deep glacial lake once covered the area. As you travel the **Tiekel River Valley,** watch for grazing moose along the 20-mile stretch beginning at the **Little Tonsina River State Recreation Area** *(Mile 65.1. 907-269-8400).* Nearby **Pump Station 12** also has an interpretive viewpoint.

275

Silence reigns again along the **Tiekel River,** where, beginning around mile 60, you'll see beaver dams and lodges. In summer, deep red dwarf fireweed and blue arctic lupine decorate the roadside. The riverside rest area at mile 47.9 looks up at 7,217-foot **Mount Billy Mitchell,** and a couple of miles beyond, grassy **Stuart Creek** attracts nesting trumpeter swans in spring and summer.

From Valdez, a day-long ferry voyage across Prince William Sound to Seward sets up a lovely drive north on the Seward Highway back to Anchorage.

As the highway angles through the **Tsina River Valley,** the sheer cliffs rising from the moraines were worn smooth by passing glaciers. When the valley narrows, stop to savor the soothing murmur of rushing streams and take in the nearly 360-degree panorama of soaring peaks. From here the highway climbs to **Worthington Glacier** *(Mile 28.7).*

Continue on to barren 2,678-foot **Thompson Pass** *(Mile 26),* which holds Alaska's seasonal snowfall record (81 feet!). Snow patches on the pass often last through summer. Push your hand into one: Its density suggests how the weight of accumulating snow layers compacts the underlayers into ice so dense its crystals absorb all but the blue spectrum of light, thus giving glaciers their distinctive blue color.

The stone ramparts of the **Chugach Mountains** loom as you descend to **Heiden Canyon** and the **Blueberry Lake State Recreation Site** *(907-269-8400),* considered one of Alaska's most idyllic alpine settings. Around mile 16, you'll enter precipitous **Keystone Canyon.** White-water enthusiasts relish the challenges of the **Lowe River,** which tumbles through the gorge. Look above the highway for terraced remnants of the original **Valdez-Eagle Trail,** built for horse-drawn sleds and wagons. Violent feuds among competing

Mount Drum, Wrangell Mountains

early railroaders left the roadside tunnel *(Mile 14.9)* unfinished. Along this stretch, waterfalls cascade into the canyon.

You'll emerge from Keystone Canyon beside the gravel plain of the **Lowe River Delta** and cross the moraine of **Valdez Glacier** *(Mile 0.9).* **Valdez Arm,** an 11-mile-long fjord, is America's northernmost ice-free harbor. The old Valdez townsite was abandoned after its waterfront was submerged during the devastating 1964 earthquake.

Prickly rose

As you approach Valdez, watch for **Duck Flat,** a migratory waterfowl sanctuary, and nearby **Crooked Creek,** where spawning salmon converge in midsummer and fall. An observation platform permits a close look at the fish. This and other local phenomena are superbly explained at the downtown **Valdez Museum** *(907-835-2764. www.alaska.net/~vldzmuse. Summer daily, fall-spring Mon.-Sat.; adm. fee),* which celebrates the region's dramatic human and geologic history. Once in Valdez, stop by the **Alyeska Pipeline Visitor Center** *(Tatitlek St. 907-835-2686)* for details and information about the pipeline's history and construction.

Seward Highway

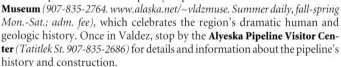

Anchorage to Seward on Alaska 1 and 9

● 127 miles ● ½ day ● June to mid-September. Mileposts record mileages in reverse, from Seward to Anchorage.

A remarkably compact sampler of Alaska's trademark natural phenomena, this National Forest Scenic Byway in south-central Alaska includes fjords, glaciers, mountain ranges, alpine lakes and meadows, evergreen forests, and wildlife-rich wetlands.

From Anchorage take either the New or Old Seward Highway south. They merge as Rte. 1 near **Turnagain Arm,** an easterly extension of **Cook Inlet** gouged by Ice Age glaciers.

At the **Anchorage Coastal Wildlife Refuge** *(907-267-2344. www.state.ak.us/adfg/wildlife/region2/refuge2/acwr.htm)* you'll gain a sense of Alaska's dramatic geology: Looking 75 miles west, you can see 11,070-foot **Mount Spurr,** an active volcano looming above the forbidding **Alaska Range,** one of North America's highest mountain systems. Easterly views are dominated by the jagged ridges of the **Chugach Mountains,** lifted by colliding continental plates to over 13,000 feet, then crushed by ancient glaciers. Across Turnagain Arm the spires of the **Kenai Mountains** crown the spruce and hemlock wilderness of the Chugach National Forest.

Backcountry skier, Turnagain Pass

Around mile 117 you'll see **Potter Marsh,** a watery expanse of sedges and willows. Stroll across the wetland on the elevated boardwalk; if you're here in spring and summer, look for pairs of trumpeter swans, Canada geese, mallards, and pintails. From mid-July to mid-August the wetland teems with fish, including chinook salmon that average 3 feet and 40 pounds.

Two miles farther on, Rte. 1 passes the **Potter Section House,** a camp for crews who maintained the railroad in this area during the age of steam. The site now serves as **Chugach State Park Headquarters** *(907-345-5021. www.dnr.state.ak.us/parks/units/chugach. Closed weekends).*

For the next 36 miles the highway follows Turnagain's north shore. The phenomenal bore tides here, with ranges of 40 feet, occur about $2\frac{1}{4}$ hours after low tide in Anchorage and are seen best from turnouts between miles 95 and 90. Don't venture onto these flats, whose deep quicksands have proved fatal! Stop at **Beluga Point** near mile 110 for a sweeping panorama of Turnagain Arm and the possibility of seeing the white whales for which the point is named.

As you continue south on Rte. 1, near mile 80 you'll see what remains of

277

Seward Highway along Turnagain Arm

Portage, a village abandoned after the 1964 earthquake dropped the site onto a tidal plain. At the motor vehicle loading area for the **Alaska Railroad** *(907-265-2494 for reservations, 907-265-2607 for recorded schedules. www .alaskarailroad.com),* you can drive onto flat-cars for a half-hour run over wetlands and through pitch black tunnels to **Whittier.** Here, the ferries of the **Alaska Marine Highway** *(800-642-0066 in the continental U.S. and Canada, 907-272-4482 in Alaska. http://akmhs .com. Fare)* head across **Prince William Sound,** passing mammoth Columbia Glacier on their way to Valdez and Cordova.

Aurora borealis lighting the Alaskan wilderness

Back on Rte. 1, you soon see **Portage Glacier,** which offers a superb opportunity to gauge the colossal power of Alaska's fabled mountain-crushing rivers of ice. Drive 5.2 miles, past **Explorer** and **Middle Glaciers,** to the **Begich Boggs Visitor Center** *(907-783-2326. Summer daily, weekends rest of year).* Stroll the gravel beach of milky **Portage Lake,** where icebergs calved by the glaciers melt into graceful shapes. During August and September nearby **Williwaw Creek** churns with spawning salmon.

Near mile 78 you'll hook around the end of Turnagain Arm and cross the broad **Placer River Delta.** The river's silty gray waters flow from nearby ice masses. The ascent to 988-foot **Turnagain Pass** follows the steep **Ingram Creek Canyon** to alpine meadows that in summer are as green as billiard tables and decorated with wildflowers. Stands of hemlock, spruce, and cottonwood quiver in summer breezes, and the cottonwood flash tawny yellow in autumn. Above tree line are slopes of glinting stone polished by long gone glaciers. At the pass near mile 68 you'll see low mounds on the flats south of the rest stop. These are moraines—gravel terraces deposited by retreating glaciers. The scars on the mountainside east of the road mark avalanche paths.

The mudflats of Turnagain Arm are flooded daily by a fast-moving bore tide whose 40 foot range ranks it as one of the greatest in the world.

Near mile 56 you'll come to the Hope Highway, a 17.7-mile route north and west to the historic gold-mining community of **Hope** on Turnagain's south shore. Bear left to stay on the byway and follow **Canyon Creek** to **Summit Lake Lodge** *(Mile 44. 907-244-2031. Closed in winter).* The handsome, peeled-log lakeside inn is an excellent place to stop and sample hearty Alaskan cuisine.

At mile 37 bear left onto Rte. 9 for Seward. Nearby **Tern Lake** is a noted birdwatching site deep in the **Kenai Mountains.** You might also want to check out the local sourdough color in **Moose Pass,** a spunky hamlet in the crook of Y-shaped **Upper Trail Lake.**

Alaska, Washington

Starting around mile 24 you'll skirt the southern reach of **Kenai Lake,** whose 24-mile-long bed was gouged by glaciers. Farther on, placid **Snow River** backwaters flank the highway. Patrolled by beavers and grazed by moose, these pools are thick in summer with yellow pond lilies that resemble golden teacups on floating saucers of jade.

Stop at **Grayling Lake Trailhead** *(Mile 13)* for a long view east up the pristine **Snow River Valley**. Near mile 4, a good 9-mile road leads to **Exit Glacier** in **Kenai Fjords National Park** *(907-224-2132 or 224-3175. www.nps.gov/kefj)*. An easy half-mile trail ends at the glacier's 150-foot-high seracs, spires of broken blue ice at its base. An arduous 3.5-mile trail

Incoming tide on Alaska's Cook Inlet

leads to the glacier's source, **Harding Ice Field,** third largest on the continent.

When you arrive in **Seward,** take a leisurely walking tour of the town. This ruggedly hospitable sportfishing center on **Resurrection Bay** has been the Kenai Peninsula's principal port since 1903. From Seward you can take the ferries of the Alaska Marine Highway to points west and east.

279

Washington

Mount Baker Scenic Byway

Glacier to Artist Point on Wash. 542

● 24 miles ● 1 hour ● Summer to early fall. Final portion to Artist Point is closed in winter. Not for acrophobics.

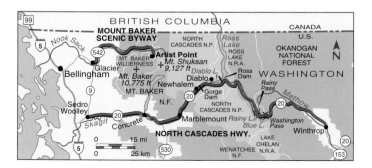

Mount Baker Scenic Byway

Embraced by the Mount Baker Wilderness, this spur road takes you deep into the kind of rugged high country usually seen only by backpackers. For the last 10 miles the switchbacking drive gains 3,200 feet in elevation, affording you panoramic views of the Cascade Range.

Start by picking up information at the Forest Service's **Glacier Public Service Center** *(360-599-2714 summer only)*. From here the scenic byway follows the **North Fork Nooksack River** through a forest of old-growth and second-growth evergreens. After about 7 miles, Wells Creek Road leads south less than a mile to **Nooksack Falls,** a stunning 175-foot-high waterfall. Back on the byway, you soon pass several turn-outs with views of a thrashing, white-water stretch of the river hundreds of feet below.

After 13 miles, you pass the **Silver Fir Campground.** Here, through a forest of big trees, you begin to glimpse the burly, glacier-clad mountains ahead. Within a couple of miles the high country comes into full view as the road leaves the dense forests and snakes steeply up the exposed sides of the mountains. Plentiful turnouts allow you to stop and savor the view.

In another 7 miles you enter **Heather Meadows,** where the ground is dominated by eponymous heather and the sky is dominated by 9,127-foot **Mount Shuksan,** a massive patriarch ornamented with rock outcroppings, jagged ridges, and hanging glaciers. A half mile farther, aptly named **Picture Lake** reflects Mount Shuksan in its placid waters. On the other side of the lake, you'll come to the **Mount Baker Ski Area** *(360-734-6771. To accommodate skiers, the road to this point is open year-round).* On summer weekends, guided nature walks leave from the **Heather Meadows Visitor Center,** a mile farther up the road.

From the Visitor Center the road climbs past sobering rock slides and stunted conifers until it reaches the sublime alpine, where earth and sky blur into one. For the last couple of miles, the byway seems suspended in air as it twists skyward, passing a number of trails along the way. The drive makes a stunning finish at 5,140-foot **Artist Point,** where the easy, mile-long **Artist Ridge Trail** puts 10,775-foot **Mount Baker** in your lap.

North Cascades Highway

Sedro Woolley to Winthrop on Wash. 20

● 128 miles ● 4 hours ● Late spring to early fall. Road closed from Ross Dam east through Washington Pass November to April. No major services for the 86 miles from Marblemount to Winthrop. *See map page 279.*

This highway travels from the verdant pastureland of Washington's rainy west to the sagebrush ranching country of the eastern hills and valleys. In between, it weaves past the high peaks and dense forests of North Cascades National Park and surrounding national forest lands.

On its way from Canada to Mexico, the 2,600-mile-long Pacific Crest Trail wanders through the spectacular North Cascades high country, even crossing the road in places.

Begin in Sedro Woolley with a stop at the **National Park/National Forest Information Office** *(On Rte. 20. 360-856-5700).* From here Rte. 20 rolls east through the lower **Skagit River Valley**—a mosaic of farms, orchards, and small ranches edged by low mountains covered in evergreens. The peaks here are grain silos, and the animal life consists of cattle, horses, and sheep.

After some 24 miles, you'll enter the town of **Concrete,** named for the material it produced from the 1930s to the 1950s, when it functioned as a company town. Most of its public buildings are still made of concrete.

East of Concrete, the valley narrows as the mountains grow higher, closing in on the **Skagit River,** a federally designated wild and scenic river. During the winter, keep an eye out along the river for bald eagles. The Skagit chum salmon run then attracts hundreds of the birds, making this one of the largest gatherings of eagles outside Alaska.

About 18 miles farther on, the road enters **Marblemount,** entrance to the "American Alps," as the northern Cascades are called.

Ross Lake National Recreation Area

Six miles east of Marblemount, you cross **Bacon Creek** and enter the **Ross Lake National Recreation Area,** which is part of **North Cascades National Park** *(360-856-5700)*. Husky mountains lean in and force the road to cling tightly to the thin ribbon of flatland along the Skagit. In places the river, its course ever steeper, roars through rocky gorges.

Black bear cub

A turnoff 9 miles beyond leads to the **North Cascades Visitor Center** *(206-386-4495. Daily spring-fall, weekends in winter)*, where fine exhibits explain the natural history of the region. A half mile farther, Rte. 20 passes through **Newhalem,** a little company town built by Seattle City Light to house the workers who operate the three dams on the Skagit.

The first of these, **Gorge Dam,** plugs the river about 3 miles east of Newhalem. Just past it, a high bridge arches above slender, 242-foot **Gorge Creek Falls.** About 3 miles beyond the falls, a turnoff leads to **Diablo.** Here, **Seattle City Light's Tour Center** *(206-684-3030)* offers rides on an incline railway *(Fare)* up the side of Sourdough Mountain, as well as half-day package tours *(Fare)* of the area.

After the Diablo turnoff, the highway skirts dammed reservoirs; turnouts provide sweeping views of these bodies of water and the surrounding mountains. At the **Diablo Lake Overlook,** interpretive signs explain that the green-blue color of the water is the result of rock flour. These suspended particles of fine glacial sediments are washed down from the high country.

Curving along **Diablo Lake** for another 2.5 miles, Rte. 20 passes a turnout for the **Happy Creek Forest Walk,** a 0.3-mile boardwalk that leads through a forest of venerable Douglas-firs towering above their younger offspring. The older firs survived a fire long ago and provided the seeds for the regeneration of the grove.

About 4 miles beyond, the road enters **Okanogan National Forest** *(509-996-4000. www.fs.fed.us/r6/oka)*. Climbing southeast along **Granite Creek,** you drive through splendid raw mountains, past turnouts that provide good views and trails that lead into the backcountry.

After 20 miles, you crest 4,860-foot **Rainy Pass,** where a mile-long, paved path leads to mountain-ringed **Rainy Lake.**

About 4 miles east, the **Blue Lake Trail** ascends 2 miles through forests and meadows, with superb views to the east of

Downtown Winthrop

7,720-foot **Liberty Bell Mountain** and the 7,807-foot **Early Winters Spires. Blue Lake** lies in a gorgeous alpine bowl, whose steep slopes are popular with mountain goats.

Two miles farther on, the road tops 5,477-foot **Washington Pass,** the highest point on the highway. From here, a panorama of peaks lies before you. For the next 15 miles the road descends sharply between big mountains and big trees until it levels out in the **Methow Valley.** Here, dense forests give way to open ponderosa pine woodlands and ranchlands on the drier east side of the northern Cascades. The highway signs warning drivers to watch for horseback riders and cattle define the character of the valley.

The drive ends in **Winthrop,** a re-created frontier town with Old West facades, wooden sidewalks, and the **Shafer Museum** *(285 Castle Ave. 509-996-2712. Daily June-Sept., weekends in May),* with exhibits on turn-of-the-20th-century mining, logging, and farming in the area.

Sherman Pass Scenic Byway

Republic to U.S. 395 on Wash. 20

● **37 miles** ● **1½ hours** ● **Late spring to early fall**

Traveling through the sprawling ranch country east of the Cascades, this drive offers a taste of classic sagebrush-covered western hill country.

The scenic byway begins about 3 miles east of **Republic** on Rte. 20. After angling 5 miles through rolling ranchland edged by stands of ponderosa pine, western larch, and Douglas-fir, you cross into the **Colville National Forest** *(509-738-7700. www.fs.fed.us/cvnf).*

Climbing 4 miles, the road traverses a burned landscape created by the 1988 White Mountain fire, which blazed through some 20,000 acres. Big trees survived the fire while the underbrush burned, opening up space for new growth. Amid the lush grass and wild-flowers now growing, you might spy deer or the flash of a bluebird.

A 3-mile climb through both burned and unburned forests brings you to 5,575-foot **Sherman Pass.** The **Kettle Crest National Recreation Trail** here leads north to wildflower meadows, and a quarter-mile spur ascends to a fine vantage point atop **Columbia Mountain,** with panoramic hundred-mile views that include **Sherman Peak** to the south and **Wapaloosie Mountain** to the north. At **Sherman Overlook,** about a mile down the byway, a short interpretive trail with generous vistas provides information on plant life and the area's fire history.

As the highway travels through the dense forests along **Sherman Creek,** look for the occasional beaver dam and the

Western larch in autumn

prominent summit of 5,838-foot **Paradise Peak** on the southern horizon.

At about mile 30, an interpretive trail explains early logging in the area. From here, the byway descends to enormous **Franklin Roosevelt Lake,** a portion of the **Columbia River** now harnessed as a reservoir by Grand Coulee Dam, some 90 miles downstream. After edging the reservoir for several miles, the byway ends at the junction with U.S. 395, 3 miles west of Kettle Falls.

Olympic Peninsula

Aberdeen to Hoodsport on U.S. 101, Wash. 109, the Moclips Highway, and the Dungeness Scenic Loop

● **278 miles** ● **2 days** ● **Spring through fall**

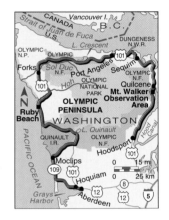

Following the perimeter of the Olympic Peninsula, this drive rambles through fern-clad rain forests and alpine meadows, past wild remote beaches, and into classic logging towns. Above it all rise the glacier-streaked Olympic Mountains.

284

Start in downtown **Aberdeen,** with a visit to the **Grays Harbor Historical Seaport** *(360-532-8611. Tour fee).* The seaport's centerpiece, the **Lady Washington,** is a full-size replica of the tall ship that sailed into these Northwest waters in 1788—the first American vessel to land in the region.

Heading west on U.S. 101, you pass the **Polson Museum** *(360-533-5862. June-Sept. Wed.-Sun., Oct.-May weekends; adm. fee),* about 3 miles outside town. Once the home of lumber baron Arnold Polson, the 26-room mansion now houses exhibits on logging and shipping.

Fishing boat, Hoquiam

Less than a quarter mile farther on, you cross the **Hoquiam River** and enter downtown **Hoquiam.** U.S. 101 turns north here, but you take Rte. 109 west. As you pass through town, keep an eye out for **Hoquiam's Castle** *(515 Chenault Ave. 360-533-2005. Tours by appointment, summer only.),* the meticulously restored Victorian fantasy of yet another lumber baron.

Outside Hoquiam, the road skirts **Bowerman Basin,** part of which is protected as the **Grays Harbor National Wildlife Refuge** *(360-753-9467).* Renowned among birders, the basin and its mudflats play host to half a

Ruby Beach, Olympic National Park

million migrating shorebirds every spring.

The highway skirts **Grays Harbor** for 2 miles, then veers into a forest of young trees that were planted to repair the wounds of clear-cutting. In a dozen miles, the road meets the ocean and turns north, following the shoreline for about the next 15 miles. Along this stretch, you'll pass small towns, oceanfront homes, tourist facilities, Sitka spruce forests, and broad sandy beaches.

Just past Moclips, you'll enter the **Quinault Indian Reservation.** Turn east onto the Moclips Highway, part of which is unpaved but usually well graded. After winding 20 miles through forests of young and middle-aged Douglas-fir and western hemlock, you rejoin U.S. 101.

As you head north, you'll notice that the clear-cuts and young trees give way to some respectably tall timber: you're now in the **Olympic National Forest** *(360-956-2400. www.fs.fed.us/r6/olympic).* About 5 miles into the forest, you begin passing stands of old-growth Douglas-fir and Sitka spruce. If you detour about a mile down South Shore Road, you'll find the quarter-mile **Rain Forest Nature Trail** leading through a forest, dripping with hanging moss, made unbelievably lush by some 140 inches of rain a year. Another minute down the road brings you to deep, clear **Lake Quinault** and the lovely old **Lake Quinault Lodge** *(360-288-2900).* If you continue 10 miles farther east, South Shore Road enters the interior portion of spectacular 922,626-acre **Olympic National Park** *(360-452-0330. www.nps.gov/olym).*

Colorful tide pool creatures

Back on U.S. 101, you curve for the next 28 miles through a forested landscape that runs the gamut from inspiring old-growth to one of the largest clear-cuts you'll ever see. A couple of spur roads along

Olympic National Park

this stretch allow you to detour into the interior of the peninsula and the national park.

U.S. 101 reaches the **Pacific Ocean** at the southern end of a 57-mile sweep of seashore that represents a coastal segment of Olympic National Park. For 10 miles you follow this virtually undeveloped shoreline, with short trails providing access to a variety of beaches. About 1.5 miles after entering the park you'll come to the pullout for **Beach #1.** (In an abject failure of imagination, most of these beaches are numbered instead of named.) The trail here tunnels through Sitka spruce, ending abruptly at the rim of a 100-foot-high cliff, with views of wild sandy beaches ribbed by the driftwood bones of fallen forest giants.

At rocky **Ruby Beach,** 9 miles farther on, waves pound sea stacks and shorebirds skitter around the edges of tide pools that teem with sea stars, sea urchins, mussels, and hermit crabs.

After this the highway turns inland, leaves the park, and parallels the **Hoh River** for about 10 miles before crossing it and heading north through another forested landscape. Along the way, you pass **Den's Wood Den** *(360-374-5079),* featuring chain saw sculpture that ranges from toadstools to panthers.

Ten miles north, U.S. 101 enters **Forks,** a quintessential Pacific Northwest logging town, where locals favor "hickory" shirts and pickup trucks. At its south end, look for the Visitor Center *(800-44-FORKS)* and the **Forks Timber Museum** *(360-374-9663. Mid-May–mid-Oct.),* displaying antique logging equipment and a collection of photographs of pioneering loggers.

Olympic National Park sprawls across the Olympic Peninsula in a wild tumult of rain forest, seashore, rock-ribbed pinnacles, icy rivers, alpine meadows, and glaciers.

For about the next 30 miles, you head north along the **Sol Duc River,** then east up the **Sol Duc Valley,** through heavily logged national forest lands and a few tiny towns. When the highway again reenters Olympic National Park, the trees and mountains return, and you soon see the western tip of **Lake Crescent,** a beautiful dark blue glacial lake framed by thick fir forests.

Clinging tightly to the southern shore of the lake for the next 10 miles, the road passes numerous viewpoints, interpretive signs, and turnouts. About 7 miles from the western tip of the lake, a short road leads to the historic 1916 **Lake Crescent Lodge** *(360-928-3211. May-Oct.)*, with its wonderful view of the lake. A mile-long trail here winds through a forest of Douglas-fir to 90-foot-high **Marymere Falls.**

After Lake Crescent, the highway leaves the park and picks up the shoreline of **Lake Sutherland,** then **Indian Creek,** and finally **Lake Aldwell.** At this point you can look out across the **Strait of Juan de Fuca** to Vancouver Island in Canada.

Tiger lilies

About 5 miles farther on, **Port Angeles,** a town of about 19,000 people, faces toward the ocean. Teeming with activity, its waterfront docks berth ferries going to and from nearby Victoria, British Columbia, and ships loaded with timber, bound for ports around the world. At the **City Pier** an observation tower offers fine views of the waterfront and the strait.

The 20-some miles of U.S. 101 east of Port Angeles constitute the route's most developed stretch. To avoid some of this, turn left about 12 miles from Port Angeles onto the Dungeness Scenic Loop. Signs lead the way as the route twists and turns through pastoral **Dungeness Valley,** noted for its berry farms and unexpectedly sunny climate; in the rain shadow of the **Olympic Mountains,** it gets an average 17 inches of rain a year.

About 3 miles from U.S. 101 you'll come to the **Dungeness National Wildlife Refuge** *(360-457-8451. www.dungeness.com/refuge. Adm. fee).* Its principal feature is the **Dungeness Spit,** a 5.5-mile-long finger of sand that hooks far out into the strait. If you hike to the lighthouse at the end of the spit, along the way you may spot harbor seals, loons, great blue herons, and, in spring and fall, huge flocks of migrating shorebirds.

From the refuge, the loop curves along the edge of the strait, then heads inland to **Sequim** (pronounced Skwim). Here, you rejoin U.S. 101 as it hugs the shorelines of **Sequim Bay** and **Discovery Bay** before turning south through a restful blend of wooded hills, scattered farms and ranches, and small towns. About 30 miles beyond Sequim, the famous oyster-producing town of **Quilcene** sits beside **Quilcene Bay,** an arm of the Hood Canal.

For a grand view of the bay and canal—a natural and quite beautiful cul-de-sac off Puget Sound—continue 5.5 miles south to FR 2730 and take it 4 miles to the 2,804-foot **Mount Walker Observation Area.** In addition to the canal, on a clear day you can see the high **Olympics, Mount Baker, Mount Rainier,** and even the **Seattle Space Needle.**

Just south of the road to Mount Walker, U.S. 101 comes face-to-face with the **Hood Canal** and hangs tightly to its western shore for the remainder of the drive. You'll pass marshes speckled with birds, oyster farms, waterfront homes, and small towns sporting seafood cafés.

The drive finishes near the south end of the Hood Canal in **Hoodsport.**

Mount Adams Drive

Randle to Packwood on Wash. 131, Cispus Road, and Forest Roads 23, 2329, 56, 2160, and 21

Glacier Creek, Gifford
Pinchot National Forest

● 67 miles ● 4 hours ● Summer to early fall.
Gravel roads require slow speeds but can be
negotiated by ordinary passenger cars.

This drive in southern Washington feels almost like a hike, as it follows a series of paved and unpaved roads deep into the Gifford Pinchot National Forest. Along the way, it passes lakes, rivers and creeks, old-growth forests, and memorable mountain views.

From **Randle,** turn south on Rte. 131. After going 2 miles, make a left turn onto Cispus Road. You'll pass a bucolic blend of small ranches, farms, and orchards for several miles until you cross into the **Gifford Pinchot National Forest** *(Cowlitz Valley Ranger District, 360-497-1100; Packwood Information Center, 360-494-0600. www.fs.fed.us/gpnf).* At this point the road designation changes to FR 23.

Once in the national forest, the drive tunnels through a classic western Cascades old-growth forest that is anchored by massive Douglas-firs. To truly appreciate their size, walk up to one of these evergreen skyscrapers. You'll probably find that its trunk is bigger around than you are tall, and its tip towers some 250 to 300 feet above your head.

Cruising 3 miles through the big trees, you come to a narrow, steep gravel logging road on the left that climbs almost 2 miles to **Layser Cave.** You can walk through the quarter-mile-long cave, which was inhabited seasonally by prehistoric peoples for 3,500 years.

Back on FR 23, keep an eye out for wildlife. The undergrowth limits visibility, but birds and small mammals are common and you may even spot deer and elk. You may also encounter logging trucks roaring down this paved section of the loop, so be on the lookout.

A number of trails branch off FR 23 along this stretch, and even a short hike, like the quarter-mile **Camp Creek Falls Trail** 7 or 8 miles from the Layser Cave turnoff, yields many discoveries. **Camp Creek Falls** itself plunges 30 feet over a rocky ledge, and if you move slowly along the trail, you might see a 6-inch banana slug chomping on leaves or a newt stepping in slow motion across the forest floor.

From here, the road enters a shaded corridor overarched by the forest and soon picks up the **Cispus River.** For the next 15 miles, you stay with the river as it meanders down the valley.

Deer and elk roam the broad river valley and adjacent coniferous forest, most of it still vaunting old growth. Ridge after ridge of mountains, striped with avalanche chutes, rim the horizon. If you're here in the fall, the road-side trees burn bronze and gold in the autumn sun.

After about 10 miles, you'll see a snow-draped peak in the east; that's **Mount Adams,** the 12,276-foot volcano for which this route is named. At about the same point, the old-growth forest becomes inter-spersed with clear-cuts and younger stands. Many of the trees seem to have sprouted whiskers: A pale green lichen, called old man's beard, hangs in profusion from both the trunks and the branches.

A couple of miles farther on, you leave FR 23 and turn left onto FR 2329, which soon brings you to **Takhlakh Lake.** The large, tree-lined lake is exquisitely backdropped by

Mount Adams and Takhlakh Lake

Mount Adams. Picnic tables and campsites take full advantage of the view, and a mile-long trail leads around the lake. An interpretive sign explains that Mount Adams lacks the single point of a classic volcano, because it comprises several cones. In the 1930s people mined sulfur from the mountain.

289

FR 2329 follows along the northern edge of the **Mount Adams Wilderness,** passing through young and old forests, pocket meadows that in spring and summer are radiant with wildflowers, and ancient lava flows spewed out from the mountain. Along the way, Mount Adams frequently punctuates the southern sky, while 14,410-foot **Mount Rainier** rises far to the north. Shimmering ribbons of icy, clear water flow from the nearby mountainsides, giving rise to lovely little gardens of wildflowers and bright green mosses.

Some 10 miles past Takhlakh Lake, turn right onto FR 56 and follow it along the Cispus River for about a mile, then turn left on FR 2160. After 2 miles, turn right on FR 21. Passing several more groves of enormous Douglas-fir, the road tightropes along a mountainside high above **Johnson Creek** for several miles before it ends at the junction with U.S. 12, just south of **Packwood.**

Mount St. Helens

Randle to Lower Smith Creek Trailhead on Wash. 131 and Forest Roads 99, 25, 90, and 83

● 103 miles ● 6 hours ● Late spring to early fall. This route provides a less traveled alternative to the more accessible western side of the Mount St. Helens National Volcanic Monument. *See map page 288.*

This drive winds through a landscape that is testament to both the destructive forces of nature and its regenerative ability.

From U.S. 12 in **Randle,** take Rte. 131 south past grassy fields, ranches,

View of Mount Adams sunrise from Mount St. Helens National Volcanic Monument

and the **Cowlitz River.** After 2 miles Rte. 131 forks right, and in another mile the bucolic scenery gives way to forests as you enter the **Gifford Pinchot National Forest** *(Cowlitz Valley Ranger District, 360-497-1100),* and the road becomes FR 25.

For the next 17 miles the drive angles through a mix of old-growth and second-growth coniferous forests with hiking trails and picnic areas. Turn right on FR 99, a 17-mile spur road that penetrates deep into the heart of **Mount St. Helens National Volcanic Monument** *(360-247-3900. www.fs.fed.us/gpnf/ mshnvm).* Established in 1982, the monument protects the awesome terrain created by the eruption of Mount St. Helens. One in a string of Cascades volcanoes, it exploded at 8:32 a.m. on May 18, 1980, spewing out rock, ash, and gas at a speed of 200 miles an hour. The heat of the blast melted glaciers that in turn caused mudflows and floods, wreaking further destruction on the region. Today, the area is slowly recovering its former beauty.

The landscape of this national monument was formed in a moment, when the top 1,300 feet of Mount St. Helens blew off, devastating 200 square miles.

Climbing through a handsome forest of Douglas-fir, FR 99 gives you a good look at a before-the-cataclysm picture. After about 8 miles on this road, a turnout will provide you with your first good look at an after-the-cataclysm picture. Here, the nearest trees still standing have been reduced to bare gray sticks, and more distant trees, those closer to the volcano, have been slammed flat to the ground by the blast. Hunching into the sky 10 miles away is the beheaded volcano itself. Behind you, however, a surprisingly sharp division exists between the unaffected forest and the ravaged one.

A mile farther, the 0.4-mile-long **Meta Lake Trail** offers a glimpse of the resiliency of life: Saplings poke through pumice; birds flit through shrubs; fish and frogs inhabit lakes; and you might glimpse elk and deer.

For its final 8 miles the winding, sometimes precipitous road runs through the carnage. Along the way turnouts have interpretive signs explaining this volcanic terrain, and several trails enable you to walk out into the blast area—otherwise off-limits to hikers. Now and then, you might also catch glimpses of the glaciated crown of **Mount Adams** on the eastern horizon.

The road ends at the **Windy Ridge Viewpoint.** Here, less than 5 miles from Mount St. Helens, you can look across into the gaping crater created when the northeast flank of the mountain blew out, leaving a chasm 1.2 miles wide and 2.4 miles long. Forest Service interpreters and interpretive signs provide details.

Retrace your route along FR 99, then turn south on FR 25. The mosaic of forests here survived the blast, though they were coated by gritty ash that covered the land, even as far away as western Montana. Occasionally you'll catch fine views of Mount St. Helens and the monument area, notably from the **Clearwater Viewpoint,** about 8 miles from the FR 25/99 junction.

Through Mount St. Helens N.V.M.

Sixteen miles beyond, drive west on FR 90 along the north side of **Swift Reservoir.** Making one last sally into the monument, the drive turns north 11.5 miles farther on at FR 83 and heads through a beautiful forest of spruce and fir. Two miles on FR 83 brings you to a short side road up to **Ape Cave,** actually two lava tubes—an upper one 1.5 miles long and a lower one half as long. You can hike through both, but you'll need a flashlight.

291

The next 5 to 6 miles along FR 83 offer closeup views of the looming, unexploded south side of Mount St. Helens. After crossing a lahar, a broad floodplain formed by a river of hot mud and ash, the drive ends a few miles farther on at the **Lower Smith Creek Trailhead,** where you can hike along a mudflow-scoured canyon.

Lupine and balsamroot

Oregon
Columbia River Gorge

Troutdale, Oregon, to Maryhill Museum of Art, Washington, on the Historic Columbia River Highway, I-84, and Wash. 14

● 90 miles ● 3 hours ● Early spring to late fall. *See map p. 294.*

The drive travels the length of the dramatic Columbia River Gorge National Scenic Area, whose natural beauty is complemented by ample civilized pleasures. You can dine at an elegant restaurant, raft down a wild river, or hike in an old-growth forest.

Start in downtown **Troutdale,** just off I-84, where 257th Avenue intersects the Historic Columbia River Highway. In about a mile you'll cross the **Sandy River** and pass by **Lewis and Clark State Park** *(Day-use only)* before reaching the 292,000-acre **Columbia River Gorge National Scenic Area** *(541-386-2333. www.fs.fed.us/r6/columbia)*. For the next 8 miles the drive passes scattered houses, parks, farms, produce stands, and small towns.

Historic Columbia River Highway

A pullout at the **Portland Women's Forum State Park** will give you your first look at the gorge itself. Extending far upriver, the view includes the broad **Columbia River** and some of the brown-black columnar basaltic cliffs, covered with dense green vegetation, for which the gorge is famous. This cleft in the earth was carved by water over millions of years. Floods at the end of the last ice age swept down the ancestral Columbia River, scouring the gorge.

Construction on the highway began in 1913. Now, only two stretches of the older original road are still drivable. The 35-mile section beginning in Troutdale is the longest original portion remaining.

Leaving the pullout, you soon reach the drive's high point: the **Vista House** *(503-695-2230. Mid-April–mid-Oct.)*, a lovely stone building perched atop a 733-foot promontory overlooking the river. Inside, you'll find displays on the natural history of the gorge and the crafting of the highway.

After Vista House, the narrow, winding highway slips down through deep forests to the river's edge. About 2 miles past Vista House, **Latourell Falls** signals the beginning of the many waterfalls you'll encounter. Tallest of them all is 620-foot **Multnomah Falls,** viewable from a short, steep paved trail about 8 miles farther on.

Of special interest is **Oneonta Gorge.** This deep, narrow slash in basaltic cliffs rises hundreds of feet above your head, while the **Oneonta Creek** squeezes down to just a few yards as it courses through. The perpetually cool, moist, shaded conditions here nurture a profusion of ferns, mosses, lichens, and other plants, some found nowhere else.

Begun in 1913, the old historic highway has been called a "poem in stone," its intricate stonework and graceful bridges blending with the natural surroundings.

When the historic highway ends, you have to tolerate about 9 miles of traveling east on I-84. Five miles down this stretch, you may want to stop for a tour of the **Bonneville Dam** *(541-374-8820. Self-guided tours daily)*. Four miles past the dam, exit at Cascade Locks to visit **Cascade Locks Marine Park.** Here you can tour the **Cascade Locks Historical Museum** *(541-374-8535. Summer; donation)* or cruise the Columbia River aboard the stern-wheeler **Columbia Gorge** *(541-374-8619. Summer; fare)*.

From Cascade Locks, the soaring **Bridge of the Gods** *(Toll)* crosses the river into Washington, where you pick up Rte. 14. Head east on Rte. 14 and in about a mile take a left on Rock Creek Drive to visit the **Columbia Gorge Interpretive Center** *(509-427-8211. Adm. fee)*, which features displays on the gorge's human and natural history.

Continuing along the river in the shadow of forested mountains, the road passes bird-rich wetlands and a couple of small towns. Leaving the wet west slopes of the **Cascade Range,** you move into the drier eastern side. For the

292

Vista House, Columbia River Gorge

next 40 miles, the annual rainfall decreases about an inch a mile.

Out on the Columbia River, you'll probably see fishing boats and enormous grain barges loaded down with wheat. You might also see windsurfers, because the gorge attracts these sports enthusiasts from throughout the world. They come here because of the vigorous wind that constantly funnels through what is the only sea level corridor in the Cascade Range.

After some 20 miles the road enters serious ranching, farming, and orchard country. Towns become fewer and smaller, broad-shouldered plateaus are silhouetted against the sky, and red-tailed hawks ride the thermals that rise from basaltic cliffs. In some places, notably around **Murdock**, you'll get great views of **Mount Hood**, across the river in Oregon.

About 3 miles past Murdock, **Horsethief Lake State Park** *(509-767-1159. April-Oct. Mile-long rock art trail accessible only by guided tour Fri.-Sat.)* boasts wonderful Native American petroglyphs and pictographs.

For the last 18 miles of the drive, you cruise atop grassy open tableland, often far above the river. A mile after the road leaves the Columbia River Gorge National Scenic Area, you'll find the **Maryhill Museum of Art** *(509-773-3733. www.maryhillmuseum.org. Mid-March–mid-Nov.; adm. fee)*. Built in the 1920s as the private residence of famed railroad man and social visionary, Sam Hill, this edifice on the bluffs above the Columbia is now a respected art museum.

Mount Hood

Sandy to Hood River on U.S. 26 and Oregon 35

● **72 miles** ● **2 hours** ● **Late spring to early fall. April is blooming season for Hood River Valley orchards.**

Making a half circle around Oregon's highest peak—volcanic, snow-mantled Mount Hood—the drive then cruises through the rich orchard country of the Hood River Valley.

Begin in the town of **Sandy**, "gateway to Mount Hood," where the classic cone of the 11,235-foot volcano dominates the eastern sky. As you head

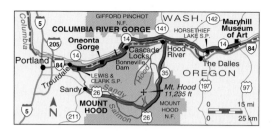

east on U.S. 26, you move into a forested landscape. After about 15 miles, you come to the **Mount Hood Information Center** *(503-622-4822)*, which offers regional information. Half a mile past the center, the aptly named **Wildwood Recreation Site** *(503-622-3696. Mid-May–Sept.)* contains forests of Douglas-fir, red alder, and bigleaf maple, threaded by hiking trails beside the **Salmon River.**

In 2 miles you reach the **Zig Zag Ranger Station** *(503-622-3191)* for the **Mount Hood National Forest** *(www.fs.fed.us/r6/mthood)*. The ranger station features the **Wy'East Rhododendron Gardens,** showcasing the plants that create a lush understory in these Oregon forests.

Heading into the national forest, the highway curves past some sizable trees and along the sides of some strapping mountains. The stark, rocky southwest flank of **Mount Hood** can be seen from time to time through the trees. Many trails lead into the forest from the highway; the **Mirror Lake Trail,** about 10 miles from the Zig Zag Ranger Station, is a justifiably popular 1.4-mile hike to a lovely lake. The trail continues up **Tom, Dick, and Harry Mountain.**

As you sail through the Hood River Valley on Route 35, the fruit orchards are a feast for the eye, especially during the spring blooming season.

A mile or two past the Mirror Lake trailhead, you may want to turn north onto Timberline Road and proceed 6 miles up to **Timberline Lodge** *(503-272-3311)*. A 1930s WPA project, the finely crafted timber-and-stone lodge sits above tree line, high on the side of Mount Hood. Besides its breathtaking views, it has a perpetual snowfield that attracts skiers year-round.

Back on U.S. 26, go 2 miles to the junction with Rte. 35 and head north toward the town of Hood River. Almost immediately you come to the intersection with FR 3531, which leads to a pioneer woman's grave site. If that makes you curious about what crossing these mountains in a covered

294

Mount Hood reflected in Trillium Lake

wagon was like, take the 1-mile trail from here to **Barlow Pass** along a remnant of the **Barlow Road.** Built in the 1840s, this dirt track was the first road across the Cascades.

For the next 20 miles you descend through a forest of Douglas-fir, hemlock, and pine, catching glimpses of Mount Hood as you play tag with the **East Fork Hood River.** The road finally emerges into the **Hood River Valley,** Oregon's premier fruit-growing district, with pears and apples leading the way. The profusion of fruit stands along the roadside here also sell cherries, nectarines, marionberries, peaches, and apricots—and often ladle out free homemade cider as well.

The drive ends in the town of **Hood River,** where the **Hood River** itself and its 15-mile-long valley run into the **Columbia River.** You can get a different perspective on the valley by taking the tourist train operated by the **Mount Hood Railroad** *(541-386-3556 or 800-872-4661. Fare).*

Mount Hood National Forest

Northern Oregon Coast

Tillamook to Pacific City on local roads

● 39 miles ● 1 hour ● All year

A microcosm of the entire Oregon coast, this drive offers beaches stitched with driftwood, misty capes blanketed by thick rain forests, and tiny towns where almost every café has an ocean view.

Start in **Tillamook,** a town famous for its cheddar cheese. The largest manufacturer, **Tillamook County Creamery Association** *(2 mi. N of town at 4175 Hwy. 101 N. 503-842-4481),* allows self-guided tours of its impressive factory. The county's **Pioneer Museum** *(2106 Second St. 503-842-4553. Adm. fee)* houses a natural history collection and historical artifacts.

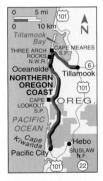

Near the museum, at the junction of U.S. 101 and Third Street, signs saying "Three Capes" mark the beginning of the drive. At Bayocean Road, veer to the right. For the first few miles the route curves past green pastures speckled with dairy cows until it reaches **Tillamook Bay.**

Near **Bayocean Spit,** a side road provides views of pelicans, gulls, and herons working the tidal flats. From the spit, the drive cuts southwest through thick coniferous forests.

Bob Straub State Park, Pacific City

Cape Kiwanda

After 2 miles you come to **Cape Meares State Park** *(503-842-4981)* on the open ocean. Stop to see the lighthouse and the Octopus Tree, a Sitka spruce with a 50-foot circumference.

Continue south on Cape Meares Loop Road. More views are waiting 2.5 miles beyond in the tiny town of **Oceanside.** From the bluff at the north end of town, you can see **Three Arch Rocks National Wildlife Refuge** *(541-867-4550)*, offshore rocks teeming with birds and sea lions.

After winding along the beach for a couple of miles, take **Netarts Bay** Drive along the shoreline of Netarts Bay. Look for sea lions resting on sandbars.

Now the drive picks up Whiskey Creek Road and enters deep forests on its way to **Cape Lookout State Park** *(503-842-4981. www.prd.state.or.us. Vehicle fee mid-May–mid-Sept.)*. Park trails lead through a lush rain forest to the tip of the cape, with 40-mile views up and down the coast.

From here, take the Cape Lookout Road to Sand Lake Road and turn right. Heading inland, you pass more forests, pasturelands, and sand dunes, before rejoining the coast. Soon, you see the radiant red-and-yellow sandstone cliffs of **Cape Kiwanda** standing against the fury of the Pacific. During summer, fishing dories launch into the rushing surf here.

The drive ends in **Pacific City,** where the dunes and beaches of **Bob Straub State Park** *(503-842-3182)* offer solitude.

Central Oregon Coast

Yachats to North Bend on U.S. 101

● **70 miles** ● **2 hours** ● **All year**

The northern part of this route is a vintage Oregon coast blend of seashore and forest, while the southern section skirts the incomparable Oregon dunes.

In **Yachats** (pronounced yah-HOTS), a small but charming coastal town, the U.S. 101 bridge over the **Yachats River** marks the beginning of this drive. A mile south, you enter the **Cape Perpetua Scenic Area** *(541-547-3289. Mem. Day-Labor Day, weekends in winter)*. At the **Devils Churn** here, waves rumble up a narrow channel and explode against massive rocks. Just beyond, a side road climbs 2 miles to the **Cape Perpetua Overlook.** Highest point on the Oregon coast, it offers views of the **Pacific,** the coast, and the towering **Coast Range.**

The **Cape Perpetua Visitor Center,** on U.S. 101, is the access point for numerous trails that fan out to tide pools, old-growth forests, and Native American shell middens.

For the next 23 miles, a string of state parks and waysides hold rocky shores and sandy beaches, where sandpipers scamper at the edge of the surf and harbor seals loll. In the area's deep forests, you might see elk browsing. At **Heceta Head Lighthouse State Scenic Viewpoint** *(Near Mile 172. 541-997-3851. Lighthouse tours. Parking fee),* you can visit the lighthouse and a mile farther on the **Sea Lion Caves** *(541-547-3111. Adm. fee).* The vast cavern houses a raucous colony of Steller sea lions. Five miles beyond at the little **Darlingtonia State Wayside,** a boardwalk leads through bogs thick with carnivorous cobra lilies.

Just south of here U.S. 101 quits the coast, leveling out as it enters the fast-growing town of **Florence.** The **Old Town** waterfront has a pleasant mix of galleries, cafés, and shops.

Across the **Siuslaw River,** you enter the **Oregon Dunes National Recreation Area** *(541-271-3611.*

Pacific rhododendron, Oregon Dunes National Recreation Area

297

www.fs.fed.us/r6/siuslaw/oregondunes), its 31,500 acres stretching along 40-some miles of coastline. Right away you see dunes, but they're mostly covered by forest. In fact, the Oregon dunes are not a sea of pure sand but a blend of open dunes, tree islands, wetlands, forests, and lakes.

About 6 miles inside the recreation area you'll come to a side road for the **Siltcoos Recreation Corridor.** The recreation area has a broad sandy beach fronting the ocean and a trail that follows a wildlife-rich estuary of the **Siltcoos River.** Farther along U.S. 101, turn right at the Carter Lake Campground and walk the half-mile **Taylor Dune Trail.**

About a mile down U.S. 101, you can look across waves of sand that reach heights of several hundred feet at the **Oregon Dunes Overlook.** From

Sunset over Heceta Head Lighthouse State Scenic Viewpoint

here, the road continues south past forests and lakes until it hits civilization at **Gardiner,** on the **Umpqua River.** This tiny town was named after the owner of the brigantine Bostonian, which went down off the coast in 1850. Salvage from the ship was used to build the town.

Across the Umpqua, in the larger town of **Reedsport,** the **Oregon Dunes Headquarters** *(541-271-3611)* has brochures, displays, and a film on the dunes. Four miles farther, the drive passes the town of **Winchester Bay.** A brief detour into town will bring you to a marina, the **Umpqua Lighthouse,** a nice park, and some savory clam chowder.

After Winchester Bay, U.S. 101 once again passes by forested dunes and lakes as it returns to the east side of the Oregon dunes. After about 9 miles you can hike into the **Umpqua Dunes,** an outstanding dune system, via a quarter-mile trail out of the **North Eel Campground.** Reaching heights of 400 feet, the Umpqua Dunes are among the highest dunes in the recreation area.

From North Eel, you pass through a familiar landscape of forests and lakes for another 11 miles. The drive ends in the coastal town of **North Bend.**

Southern Oregon Coast

Bandon to Brookings on U.S. 101

● **81 miles** ● **3 hours** ● **All year**

This route showcases the Oregon coast's rough side, where stalwart cliffs and sea stacks stand against the Pacific's relentless assault. But away from the coast, the drive takes on a tamer tone as it passes through pleasant little towns and farmlands.

Start in **Bandon,** a small seaside town with a surprising variety of activities. You can visit the town's famous cheese factory, birdwatch at **Bandon Marsh National Wildlife Refuge** *(541-867-4550),* relish the huge winter

waves that pound the coast, or shop in **Old Town.** At **Cranberry Sweets** *(First and Chicago. 541-347-9475)* courageous visitors may want to try a local favorite—cheddar cheese fudge.

As you leave Bandon on U.S. 101 south, you quickly enter farmland. After 3 miles you'll see the first of many cranberry bogs, as cranberries are the major crop around here. During the fall you may also spot farmers in their hip waders out harvesting these tart berries.

In 3 more miles you encounter another of this area's distinctive products:

U.S. 101 near Cape Sebastian

carved myrtlewood. At several roadside factories along the route, you can tour the facilities and buy items carved of this beautiful hardwood.

For the next 25 miles or so U.S. 101 stays inland, passing sheep ranches, forests, little towns, jam-and-honey stands, and more cranberry bogs. When you rejoin the Pacific at **Port Orford,** a detour of a couple of blocks in the middle of town will give you a generous ocean view. At the town's **Battle Rock Park,** a beach and picnic area are placid memorials to the fierce 1851 battle fought here between Indians and the first pioneers, who came by sea to build a settlement.

From Port Orford the road rapidly climbs into the **Coast Range,** edging along high above the sea and providing views limited only by the curve of the earth. Hundreds of feet below, waves hammer the shore. This landscape continues as you cross the boundary into **Humbug Mountain State Park** *(541-332-6774. www.prd.state.or.us).* Even more spectacular vistas await at the top of **Humbug Mountain;** a 3-mile trail leads to its 1,756-foot summit.

> Oceanside bluffs serve as box seats where you can sit and watch hulking Pacific waves break against the rocks.

After veering inland for a few miles to get around Humbug Mountain, the road once again slithers along the mountainsides right above the ocean. As it comes down to sea level, you have access to miles of virtually deserted sand beaches ornamented by twisted pieces of driftwood.

When the road enters the **Rogue River Valley,** it travels through the more settled lower reaches of the **Rogue River,** one of the nation's premier wild and scenic rivers. To see the wilder side of the river, take one of the jetboat trips offered by local outfitters. These excursions go as far as 52 miles upriver. Across the river in **Gold Beach,** you can also take a look around the

Rogue River Museum *(At Jerry's Rogue Jets. 800-451-3645).* The museum details the history of boating and settlement along the Rogue River.

After Gold Beach, the drive climbs out of the Rogue River Valley and back into the Coast Range. About 8 miles south of the Rogue River, a short side road leads to the top of **Cape Sebastian** and a panoramic view of the mountains and ocean. From Cape Sebastian the highway drops to the shore, passing by 3 or 4 miles of beaches backed by low dunes.

A few miles beyond, U.S. 101 ascends to new heights, literally and figuratively; this final 14-mile stretch of coast is stunning, especially at **Samuel H. Boardman State Park** *(541-469-2021.*

Samuel H. Boardman State Park

www.prd.state.or.us). Extending along the coast for nearly 10 miles, the park consists of a narrow strip of forests and clifftops poised dramatically between U.S. 101 and the ocean. For the most part, you can't see the ocean from the highway, but a number of overlooks, side roads, waysides, and trails provide plenty of vistas.

You might want to stop and admire the scenery from the **Oregon Coast Trail,** which winds through the park. This 3-foot-wide trail traverses a steep slope with views of immense sea cliffs, pocket coves, wind-twisted trees, sea stacks, and a vast sweep of the Pacific. Descending through a spruce forest to some dunes, you cross the open sand above the crashing surf and climb up to a path that cuts through a dense blanket of waist-high coastal scrub. In spring and winter you're likely to spot migrating gray whales. Similar scenes of this monumental meeting between land and sea can be savored from dozens of other vantage points.

Beyond the park, the drive continues a couple of miles to its terminus in the fishing town of **Brookings.**

Rogue Umpqua Scenic Byway

Roseburg to Prospect on Oregon 138, 230, and 62

● **120 miles** ● **½ day** ● **Late spring through fall**

This byway in southwest Oregon offers the rare opportunity to drive alongside two of the country's stellar wild and scenic waterways— the North Umpqua and Rogue Rivers—both a feast of rapids, waterfalls, gorges, storied fishing holes, and serene stretches of cold, clear mountain water.

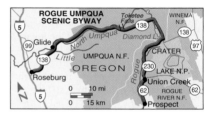

From the quiet town of Roseburg, head east on Rte. 138. For the next 16 miles the road passes through farmland on its way to the **North Umpqua River,** which stages a dramatic entrance in the town of Glide. Below the town's **Colliding Rivers Viewpoint,** the North Umpqua and **Little River** meet.

Leaving Glide, the road follows the North Umpqua up into the forests of the **Cascade Range.** The river narrows into impressive rapids at several points, particularly at the pullout at mile 21.5. Stop a half mile later at **Swiftwater Park,** where a viewing platform has interpretive signs explaining the North Umpqua's renowned salmon and steelhead runs. The 77-mile **North Umpqua Trail** begins across the river here.

Among fly-fishing enthusiasts the next 30 miles of the North Umpqua are world famous for summer steelhead runs. Much of this stretch is framed by the towering basaltic cliffs of the **North Umpqua River Canyon.**

About 9 miles past Swiftwater Park you enter the **Umpqua National Forest** *(541-672-6601. www.fs.fed.us/r6/umpqua).* Trails are plentiful here, often leading to waterfalls. Near the Toketee (say TOE-ke-tee) Ranger Station, the gorgeous half-mile trail to 120-foot-high **Toketee Falls** winds above a narrow, rocky gorge resounding with the North Umpqua's turbulence. The trail ends at a viewing platform high above the feathery falls. Another half-mile trail to one of southern Oregon's highest waterfalls, 272-foot **Watson Falls,** starts a mile up Rte. 138.

About 18 miles farther on, a detour on FR 4795 takes you to capacious **Diamond Lake,** backdropped by thick coniferous forests and

Bridge over the Rogue River

the snow-covered peaks of the Cascades, including 8,363-foot **Mount Bailey.** A detour of about 5 miles on Rte. 138 leads to **Crater Lake National Park** *(541-594-2211. www .nps.gov/crla. This entrance is closed in winter; adm. fee).* The ink blue waters of Crater Lake fill the caldera of dormant Mount Mazama.

To continue on the drive, head right on Rte. 230. Three miles farther on, you'll enter the **Rogue River National Forest** *(541-858-2200. www.fs .fed.us/r6/rogue),* where the Rogue River emerges from underground lava tubes. For a view down on the peaks and ridges around Crater Lake, stop at the **Crater Rim Viewpoint,** a couple of miles into the national forest.

For about the next 20 miles, Rte. 230 descends past trees and occasional lava flows almost two million years old. As you get lower, lodgepole pines give way to mostly old-growth incense cedars, Douglas-firs, mountain hemlocks, and white firs. Dropping into the Rogue's canyon, the road meanders alongside the river.

Rte. 230 soon ends, and you join Rte. 62 south. In 1.5 miles you'll come to **Union Creek,** an historic Civilian Conservation Corps center that is now a tiny hamlet. On the north end of Union Creek, you can hike the **Rogue Gorge Trail.** The short, paved path leads to an observation platform overlooking the 25-foot-wide, 40-foot-deep chasm—actually a collapsed basalt lava tube now occupied by the river.

At **Natural Bridge,** a mile south of Union Creek, a short interpretive trail offers more great views of the Rogue. At one point here, the river actually disappears as it travels underground for some 200 feet through another ancient lava tube, forming a natural land bridge.

Continuing 4 more miles through stands of looming sugar pines, ponderosa pines, and Douglas-firs, the drive passes **Mammoth Pines Nature Trail.** This quarter-mile interpretive loop leads through an old-growth coniferous forest.

The drive ends about 6 miles farther on, when it emerges from Rogue River National Forest and enters the small logging town of **Prospect.**

Toketee Falls

Cascade Lakes Highway

Bend to Sunriver on Oregon 372, County Rtes. 46 and 42

● 83 miles ● 3 hours ● Summer through fall. Portions of the route are closed in winter.

Weaving through a classic Cascades landscape, the highway passes massive volcanoes, murmuring streams, forests of awesome evergreens, lava flows, glittering lakes, and meadows full of wildflowers.

Head southwest out of **Bend** on Rte. 372, following the signs to Cascade Lakes and Mount Bachelor. After about 3 miles you start climbing into ponderosa pine forests characteristic of the drier east side of the Cascades. Soon you cross into the **Deschutes National Forest** *(541-383-5300. www.fs.fed.us/r6/deschutes/welcome.html).* A viewpoint 5 miles into the forest lets you contemplate an immense swath of the eastern Cascades, including some extensive lava flows.

As you continue climbing, the forest becomes a dense mix of pine, fir, hemlock, and spruce. About 7 miles past the viewpoint, you round a bend and **Bachelor Butte** suddenly fills the horizon. After about 5 miles a turnoff leads up to the **Mount Bachelor Ski and Summer Resort** *(541-382-2607. Lift open to travelers Mem. Day-Labor Day; fare);* a chairlift ascends to the 9,065-foot summit of this volcano. On clear days, the wraparound view here takes in the surrounding peaks.

Back on the drive, now called Rte. 46, you have more dramatic views of other volcanoes and mountains, with **Broken Top** hulking in the foreground. A side road a mile or so past the ski-area turnoff leads a half mile to a short trail with great views of **Todd Lake** and the snow-crowned mountains that rear above it. Fringed by spruce and fir forests, Todd Lake is favored by American dippers, which dive into it with abandon. This is the first of many beautiful mountain lakes along the drive; most were formed when ancient lava flows dammed or redirected rivers.

Running the Upper Deschutes

Forging on between Bachelor Butte and Broken Top, the road skirts the marshy north end of **Sparks Lake.** Then it curves around **Devils Hill,** a jumble of dark lava boulders, some of which are adorned with pictographs painted long ago by Native Americans.

You can get a closeup look at this fascinating area by parking at **Devils Lake** and walking back along the highway to **Devils Hill.** At its base lie a lovely little pond and a meadow that is sprinkled with wildflowers during the summer.

As Rte. 46 swings south, it edges the 286,708-acre **Three Sisters**

Cascade Lakes Highway below South Sister Mountain

Wilderness *(Hiking permits available at most trailheads)*. Here, you pass more lakes and lava formations and more views of Bachelor Butte and other towering Cascades giants. Opportunities for hiking, fishing, boating, and picnicking abound, particularly if you make a stop at **Elk Lake,** where there's even a sandy beach.

Six or seven miles past this lake, the highway pulls alongside the **Deschutes River.** From its source in nearby **Little Lava Lake,** it begins its journey to Washington. For the next few miles you follow the river, only 25 feet wide at this stage.

Skiing Mount Bachelor

After river and road part company, you continue for several miles along a wild natural boulevard lined with pines, firs, and hemlocks; watch the forest edge for deer. For more wildlife, turn off at the **Osprey Point** and **Crane Prairie Reservoir.** Here, a short trail through the forest opens onto the reservoir, where dead trees cradle the nests of a variety of birds, including ospreys. From Osprey Point itself, you may also spot geese, ducks, river otters, great blue herons, and sandhill cranes.

About 3 miles past Osprey Point, turn east onto Rte. 42 as it passes groves of monumental ponderosa pines. About 3 miles from the junction, the Deschutes River reappears, and, if you stop at the observation platform overlooking the river, you may spot kokanee—a landlocked species of salmon.

For the next 15 miles or so the drive leads through a mix of pristine and cut-over pine forests. Soon houses begin to reappear, heralding a return to civilization and the end of the drive in the town of **Sunriver,** a resort community catering to summer vacationers and winter skiers. To visit Sunriver, turn left on South Century Drive.

McKenzie-Santiam Pass Loop

Loop from Sisters on Oregon 242 and 126

● 85 miles ● 3 hours ● Late summer to early fall. Oregon 242 closed in winter. Not recommended for RVs or trailers

Nature began working on the scenery in this region some three million years ago, when volcanic activity first gave rise to the High Cascades. In the shadow of 10,000-foot volcanoes, this National Forest Scenic Byway passes lava flows, unspoiled lakes, old-growth forests, a wild river, and an abundance of waterfalls.

Start in **Sisters** at the junction of Rte. 126 and Rte. 242. Head southwest on Rte. 242, a narrow highway that within minutes leads into the ponderosa pines of the **Deschutes National Forest** *(541-383-5300)*. Stop at **Windy Point,** at mile 11.5, for your first clear look at the Cascades' volcanic nature. From this 4,909-foot viewpoint, you look out over a sprawling lava flow, with snow-topped **Mount Washington** in the background.

Several pullouts provide opportunities to stop and explore, and 3 miles past Windy Point the road travels right through a flow. The Forest Service has made this 75-square-mile sea of rock quite inviting. Right next to the highway is the **Dee Wright Observatory,** which perches atop the 5,324-foot crest of **McKenzie Pass.**

Willamette National Forest

Olallie Creek, Willamette Natl. Forest

Built from lava blocks in the 1930s by the Civilian Conservation Corps, the observatory provides a 360-degree view of the lava field, the craters from which the molten rock poured, and several high volcanic cones. The half-mile **Lava River Trail** leads onto a flow, with interpretive signs on the natural history of the area.

From the observatory, the drive passes into the **Willamette National Forest** (*541-465-6521. www.fs.fed.us/r6/ willamette*) and continues through the lava jumble for another 2 or 3 miles. Then you reenter lush, wet forests typical of the west side of the Cascades.

During the next 11 miles you'll encounter a few small lava flows topped with trees that are windswept and stunted. As you descend, brawny Douglas-firs stretch heavenward and vine maples, brilliant gold during autumn, ensnare the understory. The road is tortuous and slow, which is just as well as it gives you time to spot the poorly marked trailhead for **Proxy Falls.** This short trail weaves through old-growth forest, taking in two beautiful waterfalls along the way.

Back on the highway, you'll drive another 9 miles through forests so thick that they sometimes make a virtual tunnel of the road. When Rte. 242 ends at Rte. 126, you head north on this straighter, more heavily trafficked but still scenic road.

305

For the next 20 miles you'll be traveling against the flow of the **McKenzie River** as it rushes downstream past fine old-growth forests, pleasant lakes, and lava flows. The **McKenzie River National Recreation Trail** runs mostly along the west side of the river, and there are several points at which you can pick up the 26-mile-long footpath. After about 13 miles on Rte. 126, you pass **Koosah Falls,** and a half mile beyond, **Sahalie Falls.**

Seventy and a hundred feet high respectively, both falls gush from the mouth of the forest and thunder into misty pools surrounded by radiantly green moss and grass.

A mile beyond the turnoff for Sahalie Falls is **Clear Lake,** the headwaters of the McKenzie River. About 4 miles farther on, you leave McKenzie River country and continue east on Rte. 126, a major trans-Cascades route.

After climbing to 4,817-foot **Santiam Pass,** the road

Fall color along Oregon 126

slowly descends through forests, with some exhilarating views of **Mount Washington.** Passing lakes, lava flows, and old-growth forests, you're soon back in Sisters.

Aufderheide Natl. Scenic Byway

Blue River to Oregon 58 on Forest Road 19

● 60 miles ● 2½ hours ● Spring through fall. Generally closed November-early April due to heavy snowfall. *See map page 304.*

On the west side of the Cascade Range, this National Forest Scenic Byway follows three rivers through the lush, largely undeveloped lands of the **Willamette National Forest** *(541-465-6521).*

Start the drive 3.5 miles northeast of the town of Blue River, where Rte. 126 intersects FR 19 south—the Aufderheide Byway. Almost immediately, take a detour down a side road that leads 1 mile to the **Delta Campground** and **Nature Trail,** a half-mile interpretive path that introduces you to the verdant old-growth forests of the western Cascades.

Back on FR 19, you soon come to the **South Fork McKenzie River,** tamed at this stage by 452-foot-high **Cougar Dam,** which you can see from the viewing area about 3 miles ahead. **Cougar Reservoir** swallows the river for the next 6 miles before it emerges as a cold, clear stream. To the east you can see the high peaks of the **Three Sisters Wilderness.**

About 13 miles farther, the road swings along the **Roaring River,** a main tributary of the South Fork McKenzie. A pulloff a mile later overlooks the river, full of trout.

Picking up the **North Fork of the Middle Fork of the Willamette River**—a designated wild and scenic river—the byway follows its cascading, sparkling waters among giant trees. Flattening out, the river and road roll on to meet the **Middle Fork Willamette** and Rte. 58, where the drive ends.

Elkhorn Drive

Loop from Baker on Oregon 7 and 410, County Rte. 24 and 1146, FR 73, and U.S. 30

● 106 miles ● 4 hours ● Summer to early fall. Road between Sumpter and Anthony Lakes frequently closes due to snow.

This National Forest Scenic Byway circles through a pretty parcel of the Elkhorn Mountains, laden with ghost towns, hulking gold dredges, abandoned mines, and other remnants of the 1860s gold boom.

Begin in historic **Baker** by picking up information at the **Wallowa-Whitman National Forest Reception Office** *(1550 Dewey Ave. 541-523-6391. www.fs.fed.us/r6/w-w. Mon.-Fri.).*

The drive heads south out of town on Rte. 7, following the **Powder River** through

Roaring River, Willamette National Forest

Countryside near Baker

ranch country. After 13 miles you enter the **Wallowa-Whitman National Forest** and grasslands cede to ponderosa pine forests. Watch for elk, deer, ducks, and geese for the next 10 miles, especially at the **Mowich Loop** picnic site. Three miles past the loop, the depot for the **Sumpter Valley Railroad** *(541-894-2268. www.svry.com. Weekends Mem. Day-Sept.; fare)* offers a vintage, steam-train tour of the valley, which still shelters a fair amount of wildlife.

About 2 miles past the depot, turn north onto Rte. 410 and follow the Powder River another couple of miles to **Sumpter.** Once a 15-saloon boomtown of 3,500, Sumpter is now home to only about 175 people. A historic gold dredge still stands in the **Sumpter Valley Dredge State Heritage Area** *(South end of town. 541-894-2486. www.prd.state.or.us).*

From Sumpter you'll climb into the **Elkhorns** on Rte. 24, with some fine views of the mountains. About 16 miles out of town, the road enters **Granite,** an old mining center that's now a virtual ghost town. As you continue, the road becomes FR 73.

Local stop, Sumpter

About 6 miles past Granite, you'll drive alongside **Crane Flats,** an extensive series of meadows favored by elk and deer. After crossing the **North Fork of the John Day,** a designated wild and scenic river famed for its salmon and trout, turn right and follow the river. After 5 miles, you leave the river and climb about 9 miles to 7,392-foot **Elkhorn Summit,** with its vistas of the **Blue Mountains** and beyond. Just past the summit lie several pocket lakes, where you can hike, swim, canoe, picnic, or camp.

For the next 10 miles the road descends through evergreen forests to the **Baker Valley.** Cutting south through this beautiful pastoral setting, follow Rte. 1146 to Haines, then pick up U.S. 30 to return to Baker.

Hells Canyon Byway

Elgin to Hells Canyon on Oregon 82, 86, and 350, and Forest Road 39

● 135 miles ● 4 hours ● Summer to early fall. No services beyond Joseph.

From the Wallowa Valley, a broad corridor of grass framed by big mountains and dotted with ranches, the drive climbs into the Wallowa Mountains. Passing old-growth forests and clear-running rivers, it reaches that fabled split in the earth known as Hells Canyon.

Start in **Elgin,** where the police department, city hall, and a movie theater are housed in a 1912 brick opera house. As you head east out of town on Rte. 82, shimmering grass ripples across hillsides and cattle graze. In a dozen miles the road enters the canyon of the **Wallowa River,** through which you drive for the next 10 miles.

Around mile 22, you emerge in the heart of the **Wallowa Valley.** Bales of hay pebble the fields here, barns glow a vivid red in the strong sunlight, and horses snort steam as they gallop across early morning pastures. Leaning over the valley from the south are the snowy peaks of the **Wallowa Mountains.**

The town of **Wallowa,** a few miles ahead, is a place whose residents wear cowboy hats and boots and a sign in someone's front yard reads: "Will buy or trade deer or elk skins." **Enterprise,** about 18 miles beyond, is the

308

Gunsight Mountain and Anthony Lake, Wallowa-Whitman National Forest

metropolis of the region, with a population of some 2,000. On its western outskirts, the **Wallowa Mountains Visitor Center** *(541-426-4978. Closed winter weekends)* has information and grand views from the center's hilltop location.

As you continue southeast on Rte. 82, the Wallowas loom larger and larger. By the time you reach **Joseph,** the peaks of the **Eagle Cap Wilderness** are just a few miles away. For a small town, Joseph has a surprisingly cosmopolitan side, stemming in part from the presence of one of the nation's finest bronze foundries—**Valley Bronze** *(541-432-7445. Mem. Day–mid-Dec., closed Sun.-Mon. rest of year; adm. fee for tours)*, which forms the core of a thriving artistic community. The works of one of Oregon's most respected artists, David Manuel, as well as Native American artifacts, are featured at the **Manuel Museum** *(541-432-7235. Call ahead for hours, closed mid-Nov.–late Feb.; adm. fee).*

Just past the museum take a left on Rte. 350 to continue east. Proceed through farm country for 8 miles and turn right onto Wallowa Mountain Road (FR 39) toward Hells Canyon Overlook and Halfway.

Climbing quickly into forested mountains, the road crosses into the **Wallowa-Whitman National Forest** *(541-523-6391)* after 5 miles. Here charred trees recall the 1989 Canal Fire, which affected 23,000 acres. For several miles the road is flanked by a ghostly assemblage of skeletal tree trunks and branches, but you can also see many seedlings thrusting up through the scorched forest remains.

Past the burn area, older evergreen forests take over for the next 40 miles or so. Some of the ponderosa pines are colossal old-growth specimens, their bark the patchwork of yellow-red that has earned the trees their nickname—"yellow bellies."

Twenty-some miles beyond the forest boundary, a turnoff onto FR 3965 leads 3 miles to the **Hells Canyon Overlook.** From here, you can see down into the deepest canyon in

Chief Joseph of the Nez Perce cherished the Wallowa Valley, calling it the "beautiful valley of winding waters."

North America. Measuring 10 miles from rim to rim and 8,043 feet at its deepest point, this wild gorge is the handiwork of the Snake River.

Return to the Wallowa Mountain Road and continue through yellow-belly forests to

Hells Canyon Overlook

North Pine Creek. You can feel the high country begin to slip away as deciduous trees replace ponderosa pines and the mountains melt into hills. When the drive intersects Rte. 86, turn left and follow the road down into **Hells Canyon** and along the **Snake River** in Idaho. Near road's end at the **Hells Creek Recreation Site** *(541-785-3395. Summer)*, jetboats and rafts are available from outfitters for river trips on the designated wild and scenic portion of the river.

Far West
Nevada, California, Hawaii

Nevada

Lamoille Canyon Scenic Byway

Into the Ruby Mountains on Forest Road 660

● 24 miles round-trip ● 2 hours ● Spring through fall. Closed in winter.

Called the Yosemite of Nevada, Lamoille Canyon in northeastern Nevada is a deep, glaciated trough that descends in one long, gentle curve from the subalpine forests of the Ruby Mountains to the high desert plains southeast of Elko. Dozens of waterfalls spill from the cliffs. Bighorn sheep and mountain goats amble the high country. Hawks and eagles soar overhead.

To get there, follow Rte. 227 east of Elko for 26 miles to the well-marked start of the byway. The **Ruby Mountains**—a magnificent crest of broad, serrated peaks—seem to burst from the flat valley floor. About 10 miles wide and 100 miles long, the range is composed of a mass of metamorphic and igneous rocks faulted upward about ten million years ago.

FR 660 leads through **Humboldt National Forest** *(775-752-3357. www.fs.fed.us/htnf/humboldt.htm)* and dead-ends in **Lamoille Canyon,** a deep cleft in the mountains straight ahead. To the right of the canyon bulks 11,387-foot **Ruby Dome,** mauled by glaciers. Almost immediately you cross **Lamoille Creek,** a lush corridor of cottonwoods, willows, and aspens that zigzags up the canyon from the **Powerhouse Picnic Area** beneath the road. For a quick orientation on the historical and recreational features of the canyon, stop at the interpretive exhibit above the picnic area. A number of the peaks you see ahead top 10,000 feet.

Six miles up the road at **Glacier Overlook,** another exhibit explains the glaciers that moved through here during the Ice Age and identifies the spot where the tongues of ice converged. The U-shaped walls of Lamoille Canyon trace the glaciers' paths. Here, too, you may see bighorn sheep on cliffs across the canyon. Continue 2 miles to **Thomas Canyon Campground,** at the mouth of another glacial side canyon. A difficult trail wanders a couple of miles up the broad floor of **Thomas Canyon** to wildflower meadows and limber and whitebark pine forests.

Take the time to stroll the **Changing Canyon Nature Trail,** which starts 1.5 miles up the road at the pull-off for **Hanging Valley.** The short loop-trail and its accompanying brochure describe the canyon's formation and offer a primer of common plants and animals.

California 1 along the Big Sur coast

The **Terraces Picnic Area** is a quiet, off-road spot where you can admire a 1,500-foot cliff of metamorphic rock swirled with light-colored granite that curves for miles along the canyon's east wall. From here, the road coasts over nearly flat meadows, rich with grasses, sedges, and wildflowers.

Willow thickets cloak Lamoille Creek's meandering course. Within 2 miles you arrive at **Road's End,** a trailhead beneath an astounding ring of peaks that rise from a forest—and the end of the byway. The elevation here is 8,800 feet, some 2,700 feet above the byway's start.

The **Ruby Crest National Recreation Trail** begins here. It leads into the **Ruby Mountains Wilderness,** a 90,000-acre tract of lakes, forests, meadows, and glacial peaks where bighorn, mountain goats, and eagles live. But you don't have to hike far to see the backcountry. **Island Lake** lies just 2 miles away in a glacial cirque. And you can fish for brookies at **Lamoille Lake,** 2 miles up Ruby Crest. To return, retrace the route.

Ruby Mountains

Moapa Valley Drive

Overton through the Valley of Fire on Nevada 169

● 32 miles ● 2 to 3 hours ● Spring and fall. Summer temperatures frequently exceed 100°F.

The first glimpse of Lake Mead as the highway heads south from Overton is startling—it's as though a piece of sky had fallen to earth amid the seared desertscape of southeastern Nevada's Mojave Desert. Along Lake Mead's western shores, the route passes a museum on area prehistory, gives access to marinas and sandy beaches, and takes you through a land of tortured red rock known as the Valley of Fire.

Completed in 1936, the Hoover Dam near Boulder City tamed the Colorado River and provided a stable, year-round source of water for southern California. The dam's reservoir is **Lake Mead,** the nation's largest, stretching 110 miles north to **Overton.** Before leaving Overton, stop at the **Lost City Museum** (*721 S. Moapa Valley Blvd. 702-397-2193. Adm. fee*) on the right. With its artifacts and restored structures, the museum presents a fascinating glimpse into a community of Pueblo people who inhabited scores of villages along the nearby Muddy River before A.D. 1150.

Head south from Overton on Rte. 169. You'll pass a silica sand mine, and soon, across the stark desertscape, you'll see Lake Mead to the east. About 9 miles farther, Rte. 169 turns off to the west toward the Valley of Fire. First turn east and take a side road almost 3 miles down to **Overton Beach** for a close-up of Lake Mead.

Valley of Fire

Return to Rte. 169 and head west into the **Valley of Fire State Park** *(702-397-2088. www.state.nv.us/stparks/vf .htm. Adm. fee)*. The park road takes you through the 7-mile valley—a land of tortured sandstone turned red from oxidized iron and eroded into curious shapes. In 5 miles the road passes **Elephant Rock,** the **Seven Sisters** formations, and a short trail leading to petrified logs before arriving at the informative **Visitor Center.** From here, a road leads north to the **Petroglyph Canyon Trail,** a half-mile path through canyon walls decorated with petroglyphs. Continue on this road for 2 miles to **Rainbow Vista,** offering a spectacular view of canyons, domes, towers, ridges, and valleys in an amazing range of color. The road ends after 5.5 miles at the **White Domes,** immense blocks of white sandstone. Return to the Visitor Center and head west. You'll find a campground, more formations, and **Atlatl Rock,** where 84 steel steps lead up to a well-preserved wall of petroglyphs. As you exit the park, head east then south on Northshore Scenic Drive through the **Lake Mead National Recreation Area** *(702-293-8990. www.nps.gov/lame)* or go west toward I-15.

Red Rock Canyon Loop Drive

From the Red Rock Canyon National Conservation Area to Nevada 159

● 13 miles on a one-way road ● 1 to 2 hours ● All year. Open only during daylight hours. Summer temperatures soar into the 100s, so exercise caution.

Less than 20 miles from the glitter of Las Vegas, this route enters a world of arresting geology: sheer sandstone cliffs, deep canyons, and rugged vistas. With temperatures cooler than the surrounding desert and blessed with natural springs, this desert basin and deep canyon desertscape provide havens for wild burros, bighorn sheep, foxes, and coyotes.

Stop first at the Bureau of Land Management's **Visitor Center** at **Red Rock Canyon National Conservation Area** *(702-363-1921. www.blm.redrock.gov)* for displays about the area's geology and animal and plant life. From here, the drive climbs toward the **Calico Hills,** an outcropping of sandstone domes cut by deep canyons. At the end of the hills, a moderate 1.25-mile hike from the **Sandstone Quarry** leads to the **Calico Tanks,** holes in the rock that collect rainwater and attract wildlife.

Back on the road, views open to the west of the **Wilson Cliffs,** high

313

sandstone walls that reveal the **Keystone Thrust Fault**. About 65 million years ago, two of Earth's crustal plates collided so powerfully that 600-million-year-old gray limestone was thrust over the much younger red sandstone.

A mile-long side road to **Willow Spring Picnic Area** appears after 6.5 miles and penetrates **Red Rock Canyon,** where you can see Indian rock art on the sheer sandstone walls. The main route continues past **Ice Box Canyon** to the **Pine Creek Canyon Overlook** for an unexpected view of ponderosa pines, probably relics from the last ice age. The loop ends at **Rte. 159** after crossing a wide plain scattered with Joshua trees.

California

Rim of the World Scenic Byway

Mormon Rocks Fire Station to Mill Creek Ranger Station on California 138, 18, and 38

● 107 miles ● 4 hours ● All year. Traffic is thick on summer weekends, and winter brings throngs of skiers.

This delightful ride through the San Bernardino Mountains provides a lofty, forested reprieve from the dry, brushy flatlands east of Los Angeles, a gateway to recreational lakes and ski resorts, and a chance to trace some of the historic routes traveled by Indians, Mormon pioneers, and miners.

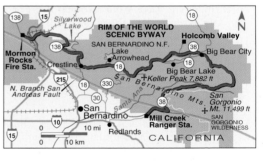

Your drive begins on Rte. 138 at the **Mormon Rocks Fire Station,** where you can walk a half-mile trail through coastal sage scrub and desert. It leads to views of the formations called **Mormon Rocks,** which are uptilted beds of pinkish sandstone. In 1851 Mormon pioneers passed here on their way to settle what became San Bernardino. Look for hawks and falcons.

Drive 5 miles east to the **Cajon Pass Overlook.** This historic pass was the conduit for the Old Spanish Trail (1830), the Santa Fe–Salt Lake Trail (1849), John Brown's Toll Road (1861), and the Santa Fe Railroad (1885), whose tracks are just ahead of you, with the Southern Pacific tracks beyond. Continue into **Horsethief Canyon,** through which Ute Indians moved stolen horses out of southern California during the 1830s and '40s. You are looking into the past in terms of vegetation, too: Before Spanish missionaries came to California, the bunchgrass scattered here was the most prevalent grass in the state.

Rte. 138 climbs past stands of California junipers toward the **Silverwood**

Big Bear Lake, California

Lake Overlook (6 miles from the Cajon Pass Overlook). The lake doubles as a recreational site and reservoir for southern California farms and communities. Below you lies the basin of the **West Fork Mojave River,** filled with chaparral. After driving another 6 miles or so you enter a forest of pine, Douglas-fir, incense cedar, and black oak, whose leaves turn bronze in autumn.

315

Go 11 miles to **Crestline,** a hub of subdivision development that began in the 1920s, and turn onto Rte. 18 heading east. If the day is clear (there are no guarantees in smog country), pull into a turnout and enjoy the far-ranging view from this steep mountain flank over the vast **San Bernardino Valley.** The **Santa Ana Mountains** rise to the southwest, the **San Jacintos** to the southeast.

About 10 miles farther, a side trip on Rte. 173 leads 2 miles to the resort community of **Lake Arrowhead** *(Chamber of Commerce 909-337-3715).* The picturesque, private lake is edged with white firs, sugar pines, and dogwoods. Return to Rte. 18 and continue east. To get on a first-name basis with the trees of the **San Bernardino National Forest** *(909-383-5588),* continue 2.5 miles to the **Heaps Peak Arboretum** and walk its 0.7-mile, self-guided trail.

Another side trip, on Keller Peak Road 5.5 miles ahead, takes you to the **Keller Peak Fire Lookout** *(May-Nov.),* a tower with a view of the 53,000 acres burned during the 1970 Bear Fire, and to the **National Children's Forest,** where replanting was partly financed by schoolchildren.

To tell the difference between a Jeffrey pine and a ponderosa pine, pick up the cones. Spines from Gentle Jeff turn inward; those from Prickly Pon turn out and will stick you.

Two miles beyond the Snow Valley ski area on Rte. 18, you crest a divide separating the mountains' drainage toward the Pacific Ocean and that flowing to the Great Basin. From here, you can see **San Bernardino Peak, San Gorgonio Mountain,** and **Big Bear Lake.**

Continue about 20 miles to Big Bear Dam. Rte. 18 leads you on a side trip to the communities along pretty **Big Bear Lake** *(Big Bear Resort Assoc.*

909-866-7000), which offers boating, waterskiing, and resort facilities. The scenic byway itself turns left at the dam onto Rte. 38, following the north shore. Past Fawnskin, look for the white-domed **Big Bear Solar Observatory** *(909-866-5791. www.bbso.njit.edu. July-Labor Day. Tours Sat.)*, operated by the New Jersey Institute of Technology. A bit farther, FR 2N09 leads to the left on an 5.5-mile side trip into the **Holcomb Valley,** where, starting in 1860, southern California's biggest gold rush took place. The **Big Bear Ranger Station,** ahead on Rte. 38, has a brochure for a self-guided drive.

Stay on Rte. 38 as it turns south through Big Bear City and heads out of town. Continue to **Onyx Summit,** at 8,443 feet the byway's highest point. Next you descend to **Barton Flats,** an expanse of forested landslide debris. The **Visitor Center** *(May-Oct. weekends)* here offers information on the 59,749-acre **San Gorgonio Wilderness** stretching southward around San Gorgonio Mountain (11,499 feet), southern California's highest peak. Drive on 4 miles to the **Landslide Overlook,** from which you'll see the scar on **Slide Mountain** where the slope gave way. Across the Santa Ana River Canyon you'll also spy a scratch that's the former route of the Rim of the World Drive. The canyon is technically a graben, or depression between faults.

Follow **Mill Creek Canyon** 7.5 miles as it descends into chaparral country. **Vista Point** turnout, 4 miles later, lies on the North Branch of the San Andreas Fault. Go past the Edison Mill Creek Powerhouse to the **Mill Creek Ranger Station** *(909-794-1123).*

Roadrunner, Death Valley

Death Valley

Olancha to Death Valley Junction on California 190

● 130 miles ● 3 hours, plus side trips ● All year, but summer is extremely hot. Be sure to carry drinking water, and set out with a full tank of gas. Adm. fee to national park

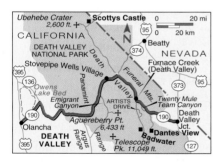

This southeastern California drive takes you into one of the world's great desert realms, Death Valley. This kingdom of extremes has the hemisphere's lowest elevation and highest temperatures (record high: 134°F). Facing its heat, mountains, and vast emptiness, a motorist sympathizes with the pioneers who crossed the 130-mile-long valley en route to California in 1849. "[It was] always the same," one wrote. "Hunger and thirst and an awful silence."

The drive starts west of Death Valley in nondescript **Olancha.** After skirting the dry **Owens Lake Bed** for about 15 miles, Rte. 190 jogs southeast, then climbs through the **Argus Range** past 5,000 feet and enters **Death Valley National Park** *(760-786-2331. www.nps.gov/deva. Adm. fee).* Then it descends into the **Panamint Valley,** where you may see low-flying military jets scream past on training runs. Geologically, this is basin-and-range country, from the **Sierra Nevada** range, towering behind you, eastward into Nevada.

Soon you climb into the **Panamint Range**. At Emigrant Campground turn right for a trip up **Emigrant Canyon;** after a dozen miles an unpaved 6.5-mile road leads past the site of Harrisburg, a vanished boom-town, and the Eureka Mine shaft to **Aguereberry Point** (6,433 feet), with a dizzying view into **Death Valley.**

When a pioneer party crested the Panamint Range and gazed back at the place that had nearly been their cemetery, one woman exclaimed, "Goodbye, Death Valley." The name stuck.

Back on the highway, drive into Death Valley and the tiny resort of **Stovepipe Wells Village.** There a 2.3-mile side trip leads to the mouth of **Mosaic Canyon** and a walk through winding halls of breccia and white marble, carved by water. Return to the drive and continue about 2 miles to sand dunes, mostly grains of quartz, that cover 14 square miles; hikers may see the tracks of creatures from stinkbugs to coyotes. Kangaroo rats eat the seeds of mesquite trees, one of the most common of 900 plant species in this "barren" valley.

Drive on to the junction where Rte. 190 turns south. A side trip to the north leads 36 miles to **Scottys Castle** *(760-786-2392. Adm. fee)*, a Mediterranean-style mansion with a 270-foot swimming pool, built in the 1920s on the dreams of prospector-hustler Walter Scott and the funds of Chicago millionaire Albert Johnson. Then drive about 9 miles west to **Ubehebe Crater,** a volcanic steam explosion pit with dark cinders atop lighter colored alluvial deposits.

317

Return south to the junction with Rte. 190 and take that road some 4 miles to the turnoff for **Salt Creek.** Along a short nature trail you'll see

Rocky hills of Death Valley

tiny desert pupfish whose ancestors swam in vanished Lake Manly 12,000 years ago. Drive on to the **Furnace Creek** area, where natural springs gush with more than 600 gallons a minute, supporting trees (tamarisk, date palms) and visitor accommodations (even a golf course!). The park

Visitor Center has geology and wildlife exhibits. At the foot of the **Funeral Mountains,** the mission-style **Furnace Creek Inn** *(760-786-2345)* made Death Valley a stylish winter resort in 1927. Built of adobe bricks and local travertine stone, the elegant oasis has a swimming pool fed by warm springs and a dramatic view of the valley.

From Furnace Creek take a side trip south on Badwater Road. After about 2 miles, pause for a walk up **Golden Canyon,** whose walls and mud hills seem to glow like gold at sunset. About 9 miles farther, turn right to the **Devils Golf Course,** a sharp jumble of rock-hard salt pinnacles created by evaporated brine risen from a deeper layer of mud. Then drive on to **Badwater** (279 feet below sea level), whose pools are saltier than the ocean. The hemisphere's lowest spot is several miles west, at minus 282 feet. On the return drive north, take a side jaunt on one-way **Artists Drive,** which winds some 10 miles through terrain streaked with iron oxides (yellow, red, pink) and volcanic minerals (green, purple), then through canyons cut into alluvial fans, common in the valley.

On rejoining Badwater Road, drive to Rte. 190 and turn right 4.5 miles to **Zabriskie Point,** where a stroll takes you to an overlook of badlands created from ancient lake beds, tilted and eroded. Drive on about a mile to a side trip on a one-way gravel road through **Twenty Mule Team Canyon,** part of the badlands seen from Zabriskie Point. After this road rejoins the highway, drive on to the turnoff for a 13-mile side trip to **Dantes View,** which shows you the essential Death Valley—alluvial fans, salt flats (with Badwater right below you), and the Panamint Range, topped by 11,049-foot **Telescope Peak,** across the three-million-year-old valley. Return to Rte. 190 and turn right; the drive ends in 18 miles at **Death Valley Junction.**

Kings Canyon Scenic Byway

Sequoia National Forest boundary to Copper Creek and return on California 180

● 100 miles round-trip ● 4 hours ● Late spring through fall. Route closes east of Hume Lake Road from around early November to mid-April.

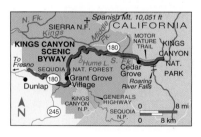

Along this drive you'll gaze up at giant sequoias and down into Kings Canyon, which is deeper than the Grand Canyon. The road has its ups and downs, too: It climbs 4,000 feet up the western slope of the Sierra Nevada, then drops 3,700 feet into the geological wonderland of the canyon depths.

Once you've entered the oak-studded hills of **Sequoia National Forest** *(Hume Lake Ranger District, 559-338-2251. www.r5.fs.fed.us/sequoia),* watch for colorful hang gliders taking off from the ridge about 2,000 feet above the highway and gliding to earth 1,000 feet below in **Dunlap Valley.**

Continue to the Big Stump Entrance Station to **Kings Canyon National Park** *(559-565-3134. www.nps.gov/seki. Adm. fee).* Here you'll see giant sequoias, a species that can grow more than 270 feet high and survive more than 3,000 years; they occur naturally only on the western slope of the Sierra Nevada. Loggers rampaged here between 1860 and 1890, and the **Big Stump Trail** loops for a mile among stumps, logs, and downed trees—reminders of the sequoia logging days. The living trees are young, second-growth sequoias.

Grant Grove Village has tourist facilities and a park **Visitor Center.** Just ahead, turn west on the side road to **General Grant Grove,** where a 0.3-mile trail leads to the world's third largest sequoia, the **General Grant Tree.** Standing 267 feet high, with a diameter of more than 40 feet, this 2,000-year-old giant is honored as the nation's Christmas tree.

Return to Rte. 180 and perhaps cross to take the narrow 2.6-mile side road to **Panoramic Point** (7,700 feet), where the view reaches from the Sierra Nevada's peaks to the canyons of the **Middle** and **South Forks Kings River.** Back on the highway, you'll leave the national park and reenter the national forest, and soon reach **Cherry Gap** (6,804 feet) and the **McGee Burn Overlook;** damage from a 1955 forest fire still shows. Two great granite ridges, **McKenzie** and **Verplank,** stretch toward the west.

Now the road descends into **Indian Basin.** About 1.5 miles from Cherry Gap a side road leads into **Converse Basin,** where some 8,000 sequoias were logged at the turn of the century. A mile-long trail takes you to the **Boole Tree,** at 269 feet tall the largest tree in a U.S. national forest.

319

General Grant Tree

Return to the highway. Just over a mile ahead is the side road to **Hume Lake,** offering sandy beaches and trout fishing. Or continue on the main route, which descends through cedars and pines until suddenly the view explodes to take in the impressive canyons of the Middle and South Forks

South Fork of the Kings River

Kings River. Ahead, **Junction Overlook** shows you the two forks flowing together against a backdrop of towering peaks. Look northward, lovers of superlatives: The 7,800-foot drop from **Spanish Mountain** (10,051 feet) to the river creates one of North America's deepest gorges.

Follow the South Fork's canyon to **Yucca Point,** where a 2.5-mile trail descends more than a thousand feet to the confluence of the roaring river forks. Just ahead at **Horseshoe Bend,** where the canyon narrows to a cleft less than 200 feet across, the river has cut a curve through weak layers in the folded metamorphic rock.

In another 2 miles you reach the riverbank. You can tour **Boyden Cave** *(Adm. fee),* hollowed from a marble formation by the slow forces of water. Drive on about 5.5 miles to **Grizzly Falls,** which tumbles down granite cliffs; the base is a good spot to picnic. Next the road ascends and reenters Kings Canyon National Park. All at once the V-shaped canyon changes to a U-shaped valley—evidence that this section was carved in the granite not by a river but by a broad mass of glacial ice. Naturalist John Muir termed the result "a rival to the Yosemite."

After crossing the South Fork Kings River, you reach **Cedar Grove,** a beautiful, mile-deep valley named for its incense cedars; there are abundant hiking trails and a ranger station. Drive a mile to **Canyon View,** a turnout with an unobstructed picture of the gorge. On the sandy flats below, red-barked manzanita defy drought. Ahead 2 miles, look for the quarter-mile trail to **Roaring River Falls,** which leaps through a granite slot to a pool 80 feet below.

In autumn the highway is edged with chokecherries (bitter and inedible), actually members of the rose family.

In another third of a mile, note the turnoff for the **Motor Nature Trail,** a rough dirt road leading 3.5 miles back to Cedar Grove; it's a one-way route, so drive it on the return trip. (At the trailhead, pick up a pamphlet on area geology.) For now, continue eastward as the road slices through ridges of rocky rubble—actually terminal moraines created when glaciers retreated, leaving their debris behind.

Soon you reach peaceful **Zumwalt Meadow,** formed when a glacial lake slowly filled with silt. In the shelter of granite walls, a mile-long nature trail takes in the river, mixed conifers, and meadow and bog vegetation, including Venus's-flytrap.

To the north, glacial abrasion scarred granite **North Dome** (8,717 feet). Drive half a mile to the viewpoint looking southeast toward **Grand Sentinel,** a mass of stone towers whose similarly angled summits indicate parallel fracture zones in the granite. The road ends just ahead at **Copper Creek;** trails link with the Pacific Crest Trail and lead into the high country of Kings Canyon.

The return trip offers fresh perspectives on all you have seen.

320

Tioga Pass

Yosemite National Park's Big Oak Flat Entrance Station to U.S. 395 at Mono Lake on California 120

● 66 miles ● 4 hours ● Late spring through fall; closed late October to Memorial Day. Admission fee to national park

Here is a chance to see Yosemite's backcountry—the granite peaks of the Sierra Nevada, shimmering lakes, glacial valleys, and wildflower meadows. You'll drive over the highest automobile pass in California before descending rocky, dramatic Lee Vining Canyon to Mono Lake. The route is decidedly less crowded than the road through Yosemite Valley.

Drive into **Yosemite National Park** *(209-372-0264. www.nps.gov/yose. Adm. fee)* at the **Big Oak Flat Entrance Station** and go east 8 miles on Rte. 120 (Big Oak Flat Road). Then turn left, following Rte. 120 as it becomes Tioga Road, whose points of interest will be handily marked with numbered "T signs." You begin a climb through mixed evergreen forests, but after about 14 miles the trees

Silver Lake, along the June Lake Loop

begin clearing and views broaden to the high country as you reach the vista point (T11) for **Mount Clark** (11,522 feet) and **Mount Hoffman** (10,850 feet).

At **Yosemite Creek** (T15) a granite canyon resembling a trough conducts snowmelt 7 miles downstream to Yosemite Falls. To learn to recognize trees along

June Lake Loop

California 158

● 15 miles ● 1 hour ● Late spring through fall. Road closes with the first big snowfall (usually in Nov.) and reopens about late April.
See map page 322.

On this drive you'll see five lakes and fascinating evidence of the passage of glaciers. This part of the eastern Sierra, having been raked by glacial ice, appears raw and rocky, but its aspect is softened when spring brings wild irises, and in late September the aspens turn gold. *(Info: Inyo National Forest 760-647-3044)*

Turn west from U.S. 395 onto Rte. 158 at the southern access point for the June Lake Loop. You climb a glacial moraine to its summit, called **Oh! Ridge** for its exclamation-inducing view of **June Lake** and **Carson Peak** (10,909 feet). Take the campground road to the right for a side trip to the sandy swimming beach at June Lake.

Now continue to June Lake village, where on your right rest two glacial erratics. These 30-ton boulders, amazingly balanced one atop the other, were left by retreating glaciers. Soon you glimpse **Gull Lake,** offering good trout fishing. Next the highway flanks the geologically unusual **Reversed Creek**; glacial debris blocked its course and made it reverse direction. On your right, aspens hide **Silver Lake** until it edges the road. The vegetation starts thinning as you reach **Grant Lake**, where you may see great blue herons.

Leaving the lake, you drive over another glacial moraine and descend toward **Mono Lake.** On your right rise the **Mono Craters**, plug-dome volcanoes formed of pumice and obsidian and explained on a sign nearby. Rejoin U.S. 395 at the northern entrance to the June Lake Loop.

321

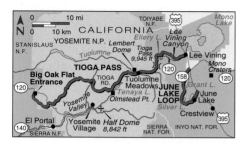

Tioga Road, stop ahead at a nature trail (T18) that identifies pines (Jeffrey, western white, lodgepole) and firs (red and white). Also stop at **Olmsted Point** (T24) and stroll a quarter mile for a look down **Tenaya Canyon** at **Half Dome**, the world-famous granite monolith rising nearly a mile above Yosemite Valley's floor.

You can picnic on the sandy beach at mile-long **Tenaya Lake.** The rock formations girding the lake exhibit glacier polish that prompted the Yosemite Indians to name it Py-wi-ack—Lake of the Shining Rocks. Then drive on, past the polished granite knob of **Fairview Dome** (T28).

Much-loved **Tuolumne Meadows** (8,600 feet) is the largest subalpine meadow in the Sierra Nevada. During the Ice Age this region lay buried under 2,000 feet of ice, and all the features you see—ponds, domes, horned peaks—were carved by glaciers. Today, meandering creeks and the **Tuolumne River** help flood the meadows in June. By July there are blossoms of wildflowers, such as Indian paintbrush and cinquefoil. Stop in at the

Tenaya Lake, Yosemite National Park

Tuolumne Meadows Visitor Center (*209-372-0263. Mem. Day-late Oct.*), a hub from which hiking trails radiate into the high country.

As you leave, look northward to **Lembert Dome** (T32), another piece of glacial sculpture. After 2 miles the road parallels the boulder-strewn **Dana Fork Tuolumne River** (T34). At T36 you have a clear view of **Mount Dana** (13,053 feet) and **Mount Gibbs** (12,764 feet), whose metamorphic rocks are often tinged with alpenglow in the evenings.

At **Tioga Pass** (9,945 feet) the road crests the state's highest auto pass, and you leave Yosemite National Park. Continue on Rte. 120 past glacially carved **Ellery Lake.** Now the road begins a plunge down **Lee Vining Canyon.** Six miles along, the road runs between moraines—ridges of rocky debris left by passing glaciers—that stand as high as 700 feet. Stop for information at the **Inyo National Forest Ranger Station** *(760-647-3044).* The route ends in just over a mile at U.S. 395 and **Mono Lake,** a haunting body of water that is 700,000 years old and studded with spires of white tufa.

Lake Tahoe

Loop from South Lake Tahoe on Calif. 89, Calif. 28/ Nevada 28, and U.S. 50

● 72 miles ● 3 hours ● All year. Tahoe can be jammed during summer weekends and August. Winter weekends are also crowded.

This route traces the perimeter of a majestic alpine lake 6,225 feet above sea level, ringed by the peaks of the Sierra Nevada and its Carson Range. The sparkling water, whose color varies from pale aquamarine near shore to deep sapphire, is so clear that you can see an object more than 75 feet down. The area's scenery is stunning: The lake was created by faulting, then during the last ice age glaciers created bays, U-shaped valleys, and jagged peaks, all offering outdoor recreation. For indoor recreation, gaming (casinos no longer call it gambling) is legal on the Nevada side of the state line. This line runs north-south through the 22-mile-long lake.

323

Set off from the city of **South Lake Tahoe** *(Visitors Bureau 530-544-5050 or 800-AT-TAHOE),* taking Rte. 89 northwest from U.S. 50. Stop in at the **U.S. Forest Service Visitor Center** *(530-573-2674. June-Oct.)* after about a mile. It maintains natural history trails through a conifer forest and a chamber on **Taylor Creek** for observing the fall salmon run. Adjacent **Tallac Historic Site** *(530-541-5227. www.tahoeheritage.org. Estates open spring-fall; fee for tours. Grounds open all year)* showcases

Heavenly Ski Resort, Lake Tahoe, California

luxury estates of the 1890s and early 1900s, when Lake Tahoe became a retreat for San Francisco's wealthy elite.

As you drive farther on Rte. 89, look southwest toward **Mount Tallac** (9,735 feet), where a cross of snow appears on the east face most of the year.

Continue on until the road threads a dramatic ridge, with **Cascade Lake** to your left and fabled **Emerald Bay** to your right. Pull off just ahead at **Inspiration Point** for a fine view of this bay and of Lake Tahoe's only island, **Fannette.** The island is topped with a stone teahouse, built in 1929 by heiress Lora Knight along with her 38-room **Vikingsholm** *(530-525-7277. www.vikingsholm.org. Mem. Day-Labor Day; adm. fee),* a mansion in the style of a Scandinavian castle. At the head of the bay, the house can be reached only by boat or steep footpath, which local wags say goes "1 mile down and 2 miles back up."

Cave Rock State Park at sunset

As you drive along the north side of Emerald Bay, look across the lake to the rounded granite peaks of the **Carson Range.** Continue to **D.L. Bliss State Park** *(530-525-7277. http://parks.ca.gov/north/sierra/dlbsp303.htm. Adm. fee),* named for a lumber baron who once owned 75 percent of Tahoe's lakefront property. The 957-acre preserve has beaches, an early 19th-century wooden lighthouse, and odd rock formations such as **Turk in Turban** and the 130-ton **Balancing Rock.** On the park's northern edge, off **Rubicon Point,** the lake floor drops to 1,411 feet, the deepest point along the shore.

Past **Meeks Bay,** whose mile-long beach was once a Native American fishing camp, you enter **Sugar Pine Point State Park** *(530-525-7982. http://parks.ca.gov/north/sierra/sppsp339.htm. Adm. fee)* and its 2,000 acres of shore and forest, including sugar and Jeffrey pines, incense cedars, and black cottonwoods. Take a look at **Phipps Cabin,** built by Indian fighter William Phipps in 1872, and the lavish 1902 **Ehrman Mansion** *(530-525-7232. July-Labor Day);* on its lakeside lawn you can enjoy a picnic and a million-dollar view.

> Lake Tahoe contains more than 37 trillion gallons of water—enough to cover a flat area the size of California to a depth of 14 inches.

Continue 9 miles to **Tahoe City** *(Visitors Bureau 530-583-3494 or 800-TAHOE 4-U),* a winter skiing hub for nearby Squaw Valley and Alpine Meadows. Summer attractions include the Indian and pioneer artifacts at the **Gatekeeper's Museum** *(530-583-1762. May-Oct.)* and the 1909 **Watson Cabin** *(530-583-8717. June-Labor Day)* Leaving town on Rte. 28, follow the developed shoreline 9 miles to **Kings Beach,** a long and often crowded strand. After you cross the Nevada line into Crystal Bay, casinos appear.

Soon comes touristy **Ponderosa Ranch** *(775-831-0691. May-Oct.;*

adm. fee), where television's *Bonanza* was filmed, and then you enter **Lake Tahoe–Nevada State Park;** stop at **Sand Harbor** *(775-831-0494)* for a picnic. About 5 miles after Rte. 28 merges into U.S. 50, a sign at **Logan Vista Point** explains that the virgin pine forests around Lake Tahoe were felled in the mid-1800s to build Nevada boomtowns; fir thickets replaced them.

Continue to **Cave Rock,** part of a volcanic rock in which caves were carved by waves. Then come **Zephyr Cove's** beach and facilities and the gambling hub of **Stateline.** Cross into California, and soon you're back in South Lake Tahoe, tying your drive into a neat circle. For the big picture, drive south on Ski Run Boulevard to the **Heavenly Ski Resort** *(775-586-7000),* where a new gondola *(fare)* ascends 2,800 feet up the slopes for a superb view of Lake Tahoe and surroundings.

Lassen Park Road

Manzanita Lake Entrance to Southwest Entrance of Lassen Volcanic National Park

● 30 miles ● 1½ hours ● Open June through October. Admission fee to park

On this scenic drive through 106,000-acre **Lassen Volcanic National Park** *(www.nps.gov/lavo),* you'll see nature's beauty—and power. The chain of volcanic activity has been unbroken for over two million years, with the most recent activity in 1914-15, when Lassen Peak staged a series of spectacular eruptions. Nearly every rock in the park was born of a volcano, and every hydrothermal feature on earth (except geysers) appears here. As foils to these violent features, there are evergreen forests and glacial lakes.

Enter the park at the **Manzanita Lake Entrance** and stop at the **Loomis Museum** *(530-595-4444. Adm. fee),* whose exhibits explain the area's volcanic history. Adjacent **Manzanita Lake** is a fall stopover for wood ducks and Canada geese. Continue to **Chaos Jumbles**, a 2-square-mile boulder field left 300 years ago during a rockfall from nearby plug-dome volcanoes, the **Chaos Crags.**

At Noble Pass the 1850s **Old Emigrant Trail** wends through. Ahead lies the **Hot Rock**—not a heisted diamond, but a 300-ton chunk of lava. It rode a mudflow

Sunset over Manzanita Lake and Lassen Peak

from Lassen Peak, 5 miles away, during the May 19, 1915, eruption. Drive on 2 miles to the **Devastated Area,** where the May 19 mudflow swept through. As an encore, on May 22 Lassen Peak spewed gas and volcanic debris 25,000 feet into the sky.

On the ascent to **Summit Lake** the road is edged by stands of quaking aspen and red fir. Past the lake, continue to the serene meadow at **Kings Creek.** Then go on to **Lassen Peak** (10,457 feet), where a 2.5-mile trail climbs the rocky slopes to the summit. Keep going about a mile to **Bumpass Hell,** a major hydrothermal area with hot springs, mud pots, and steam vents that you reach on a 3-mile round-trip hike. You can view the same features about 5 miles ahead on a short loop-trail at the **Sulphur Works,** the surviving vent system of ancient Mount Tehama, an 11,500-foot-high volcano that was 11 miles across at its base. Nearby **Brokeoff Mountain** (9,235 feet) is a remnant. You'll see sputtering mud pots and sniff clouds of reeking steam whose smell derives from hydrogen sulfide. This chemical dissolves in water to form sulfuric acid, which is decomposing the lava.

Go a mile to the **Southwest Entrance Station** and the drive's end.

Lost Coast

Ferndale to South Fork on Mattole Road

● **65 miles** ● **2 hours** ● **All year. For the best views as you descend toward the Pacific Ocean, drive north to south.**

Cape Mendocino

This little-traveled road climbs and dips through forests and windy ranchlands to one of the westernmost points in the contiguous 48 states, Cape Mendocino, with stops at two friendly settlements. Begin in the Eel River Valley at **Ferndale** *(Chamber of Commerce 707-786-4477),* an 1852 town that grew rich from creameries and enjoyed a boom in Victorian houses and commercial false-front architecture.

Follow Mattole Road out of town, zigzagging up slopes wooded with maples and evergreens. After 4 miles a wide view opens across forested valleys; then grassy hills appear. This stretch is called **Wildcat Ridge,** but the animals you're likely to see are hawks and windblown cows. The road descends to the **Bear River** and a ranch at **Capetown,** a former stage stop. A precipitous stretch continues on to **Cape Mendocino,** site of many shipwrecks. Here three large tectonic plates grind together just off the coast, creating one of the continent's most active earthquake zones. For some 5 miles you drive beside a tidal zone that rose about 4 feet during the April 1992 earthquake, giving the appearance of perpetual low tide. Most of the land is private, with limited beach access.

At **Petrolia** the state's first commercial oil wells were drilled in 1865. Ahead, a 5-mile detour on Lighthouse Road leads to the shore; a 3.5-mile trail then leads to an old lighthouse. This is the northern margin of the **King Range National Conservation Area** *(707-986-7731. www.ca.blm.gov/arcata),*

whose steep terrain, which includes 4,088-foot **King Peak,** defies highway engineers.

Return to Mattole Road and drive on to **Honeydew,** no more than a store yawning in the shade. This is the local hangout, so sit on the porch and gab. The road climbs, crossing the Mattole River and then **Panther Gap** (2,744 feet) as you enter **Humboldt Redwoods State Park** *(707-946-2409)* and **Rockefeller Forest,** which holds many of the world's remaining old-growth redwoods. Stop at **Giant Tree** and marvel at the champion coast redwood, soaring 363 feet. Ahead in **South Fork,** the road joins the Avenue of the Giants and U.S. 101.

Avenue of the Giants

Phillipsville to Pepperwood on California 254

● 31 miles ● 1½ hours ● All year. Autumn colors are vibrant. *See map above.*

For visitors to 51,000-acre **Humboldt Redwoods State Park** *(707-946-2409. http://parks.ca.gov/north/ncrd/hrsp.html)* in northern California, this route offers a quiet alternative to U.S. 101, which it more or less parallels. You'll see ancient redwoods soaring from the alluvial flats of the Eel River and enjoy miles of hiking trails. Interspersed are woodsy hamlets, as well as tourist bait.

Humboldt Redwoods State Park

(If you wish to buy a bear carved from a tree stump with a chain saw, this is the place.) Heading north on U.S. 101, take the **Phillipsville** exit and pick up a free "Auto Tour" pamphlet from the roadside box. On your left are views of the **South Fork Eel River.** Ahead, get a good look at redwoods from the short loop-trail through **F.K. Lane Grove.** About 6 miles farther you enter a typical stretch of bigleaf maples, black cottonwoods, and other deciduous trees that share space with the redwoods and sword ferns. Ahead, **Williams Grove** offers river access for fishing *(Mid-Oct.–Feb.)* and the park **Visitor Center** *(707-946-2263)* has exhibits on wildlife and local history.

Proceed 1.5 miles beyond Burlington Campground to **Weott,** a town that vanished under 33 feet of water during the 1964 Eel River flood; a pole on the right side of the road shows the high-water mark. Continue to the **California Federation of Women's Clubs Grove,** with its four-sided fireplace by architect Julia Morgan. Ahead, take the South Fork turnoff for **Founders Grove** and its trail to the 362-foot **Dyerville Giant,** the champion coast redwood until it fell in 1991; it was thought to weigh more than a million pounds.

Return to the Avenue of the Giants. About a mile north, the Mattole Road to Honeydew cuts off to the left (see Lost Coast drive, p. 326). Continue 7.5 miles to the **Drury-Chaney Groves** and walk one of the park's prettiest trails. The drive ends 2 or 3 miles farther at Pepperwood on U.S. 101.

California 1 North

Jenner to Mendocino

● 87 miles ● 3 hours ● All year. Try to drive northbound (in the lane farthest from the sheer drops), and avoid darkness and heavy fog.

On this wild northern California coast, the blue Pacific pounds itself white on mighty headlands. The skies shift from haunting fog to glorious sunshine, changing your mood in synchrony. Small towns alternate with state parks. Begin in **Jenner,** a charming, don't-blink-or-you-missed-it settlement near the mouth of the **Russian River.** Where the river slips into the sea at **Goat Rock Beach,** look down on the colony of harbor seals (pupping season: March-May). In the estuary you'll see ospreys, and **Penny Island** is home to several hundred species of birds.

The portion of Rte. 1 (known locally as Highway 1) that switchbacks along the cliffs north of Jenner was originally built in the 19th century. After about 4 miles stop at the **Vista Trail,** a 1-mile loop with amazing coastal views. Heading north, look for broken shale and sandstone in the road cuts near the mouth of Timber Gulch; here the earth-shaking **San Andreas Fault** crosses the coastline and vanishes northward on its circuitous coastal journey. As you proceed, the woods part to reveal the palisades of **Fort Ross State Historic Park** *(707-847-3286. http://parks.ca.gov/north/russian/frshp207.htm. Vehicle fee).* The 1812 fort, built by Russians to hunt sea otters and grow food for their Alaska outposts, has a reconstructed chapel and residences.

Fort Ross State Hist. Park

Continuing north, you enter 6,000-acre **Salt Point State Park** *(707-847-3221 or 865-2391. http://parks.ca.gov/north/russian/spsp248.htm),* where Indians once searched for salt to preserve seafood and tan hides. If you scuba dive or snorkel here at **Gerstle Cove,** a wet suit is a must; water temperatures average 52°F.

In another few miles you reach **Kruse Rhododendron State Reserve** *(707-847-3221. http://parks.ca.gov/north/russian/krsr206.htm),* whose 317 forested acres are splashed with blossoms in spring. Then Rte. 1 edges one of the coast's numerous marine terraces, formed by tectonic uplift and fluctuating sea levels that carved platforms and bluffs into the land. Next comes **Sea Ranch,** a 5,000-acre development among meadows, trees, and cliffs. You can decide whether the geometric boxes and angled roofs blend into the landscape as planned. Five marked trails allow public beach access.

Driftwood hunters should stop at **Gualala** (wa-LA-la) **Point County Park** to comb the strand. Farther north, near **Anchor Bay,** geologists found pebbles eroded from rocks that were originally deposited near Santa Barbara—350 miles south. They were carried along as the land west of the San Andreas Fault moved northward over some 20 million years.

After the town of Point Arena, turn left on Lighthouse Road and drive about 2 miles to **Point Arena Light Station and Museum** *(707-882-2777. Closed weekends Thanksgiving-Christmas; adm. fee).* A replacement of the 1870 lighthouse, it has the original Fresnel lens. The 115-foot tower is a good perch for spying gray whales from December through April. If you want to experience the loneliness of a lighthouse keeper, rent a bungalow overnight *(707-882-2777).*

Return to Rte. 1, which soon crosses the wide **Garcia River plain,** where white whistling swans arrive for the winter from Siberia and the Arctic. Continue to the beaches and dunes of **Manchester State Park** *(707-937-5804. http://parks.ca.gov/north/russian/mendo/msp147 .htm. Adm. fee).* Two miles offshore, **Arena Rock** is a submerged, 10-acre pinnacle where snorkelers and divers observe sea creatures such as the tiger rockfish. At the park's north end, near Alder Creek, the San Andreas Fault slashes out to sea.

After passing the town of Elk and the **Navarro** and **Albion Rivers,** you reach **Van Damme State Park** *(707-937-5804. http://parks.ca.gov/north/russian/mendo/vdsp 142.htm. Adm. fee),* a spot for snorkelers to gather abalone *(April-Nov., except July).* Brown "heads" bobbing in the ocean are often mistaken for sea otters, which no longer live here; they are air-filled bulbs of kelp. Tide pools hold sea stars and anemones. The park runs inland, too, along the fern-draped canyon of the

Mendocino coastline

Cow parsnip along California 1

Little River. Take Airport Road off Rte. 1 to the **Pygmy Forest Discovery Trail,** where nature practices bonsai on pine and cypress trees.

About 2 miles north of Little River is the Victorian village of **Mendocino.** An art colony since the 1950s, the town's highlights include the **Mendoci-no Art Center** *(707-937-5818),* gabled **MacCallum House** *(Inn and restaurant 707-937-0289),* and **Kelley House Museum** *(45007 Albion. 707-937-5791. Daily June-Aug., Fri.-Mon. Sept.-May; adm. fee).* The **Ford House Visitor Center and Museum** *(735 Main St. 707-937-5397. Donation)* displays a model of the town from the 1890s, when it had a 12-seat outhouse. Trails wind across **Mendocino Headlands State Park** *(707-937-5804. http://parks.ca.gov/north/ russian/mendo/mhsp158.htm),* which surrounds the village on three sides. The park epitomizes the north coast—bluffs, grasslands, tide pools, wave-carved tunnels, blue waters, gray whales, and views to expand the spirit.

Marin County

Golden Gate Bridge to Point Reyes National Seashore (with 8-mile round-trip up Mount Tamalpais) on U.S. 101, Calif. 1, and Panoramic Highway

● 34 miles ● 2 hours ● All year

This drive has all the classic sights of northern California, from a panorama of San Francisco Bay to redwood trees, from the San Andreas earthquake fault to migrating gray whales.

After crossing the **Golden Gate Bridge** north-bound on U.S. 101/Rte. 1, pass Sausalito and exit onto Rte. 1 just north of Marin City. Drive 3 miles and turn right on the Panoramic Highway, then, less than a mile ahead, turn left on Muir Woods Road to

Muir Woods National Monument *(415-388-2596. www.nps.gov/muwo).* These 560 acres embrace the Bay Area's only virgin redwood forest, with trees as high as 252 feet and at least 1,000 years old. Trails loop around Redwood Creek, beyond the Visitor Center.

Return to the Panoramic Highway, turn left, and continue to the Pan Toll Road. Turn right to ascend the east peak of **Mount Tamalpais** (2,571 feet), the mountain biking center of Marin County. A startling panorama takes in San Francisco, the bay, and the Pacific Ocean.

Drive back to the Panoramic Highway, turn right, and zigzag 4 miles downhill among grassy hills and forests of redwood and California bay to reach Rte. 1. Here **Stinson Beach** lies on a sandspit in front of **Bolinas Lagoon,** where great blue herons and snowy egrets fish. The road follows the shoreline and, 3.5 miles north of Stinson Beach, birds nest in the reserve at **Audubon Canyon Ranch** *(415-868-9244. Weekends mid-March–mid-July; donation).*

As Rte. 1 unwinds northward through the **Olema Valley,** its center line virtually traces the dreaded **San Andreas Fault.** On your left lies the **Point Reyes Peninsula,** which during the 1906 San Francisco earthquake jolted as much as 18 feet northwest, pulling roads and trees asunder. To walk an interpretive trail along the fault line, continue just north of Olema and turn left on Bear Valley Road to the Visitor Center for **Point Reyes National Seashore** *(415-663-1092. www.nps.gov/pore).* This preserve embraces forests, grasslands, coastal wetlands, and seashore. Migrating gray whales are easy to spy in winter from **Point Reyes Lighthouse.** The 71,000-acre preserve also shelters tule elk, marine mammals, and more than 430 species of birds. Nearly half the continent's bird species have been spotted here.

On the return drive, stay on Rte. 1, stopping at the **Muir Beach Overlook** for a view of the coastline and the Golden Gate Bridge. Continue to U.S. 101, which you can take back to the bridge.

Point Reyes National Seashore

Silverado Trail

Napa to Calistoga

● **29 miles** ● **1 hour** ● **Spring through fall. In spring mustard flowers carpet the Napa Valley. Summer is hot and crowded. Fall is grape harvest time. Winter brings 70 percent of the year's rainfall.**

The Silverado Trail runs parallel to Rte. 29, the main (and often clogged) traffic artery through the Napa Valley. This quieter back road offers glimpses of the nation's foremost wine region, about an hour northeast of San Francisco, as it was perhaps 30 years ago. Because the roadway dips and curves along the foothills, it offers gorgeous views of vineyards and mountains. Along the way you can stop in at small wineries for tours and tastings; most of the larger ones are along Rte. 29. The Silverado Trail was established in 1852, when floods swamped the valley's main road. By the late 1800s it was the wagon route from the cinnabar mines on Mount St. Helena, which marks the valley's north end, to the docks of San Pablo Bay to the south.

To begin the drive, go north on Rte. 29 through the city of **Napa** to Trancas Street; turn right, drive less than 2 miles, then turn left on the Silverado Trail. As you proceed, most of the grapevines surrounding you are Chardonnay, but when you reach the Yountville Cross Road after 8 miles, Cabernet Sauvignon begins its reign. Turn left at this cross-roads—one of many east-west links between the trail and Rte. 29—and go about a mile to the **Napa River Ecological Reserve.** This is a rare public access point to the river. The 73-acre riparian habitat reveals what the area looked like 150 years ago. A path winds among oaks, California bays, and willows; 150 bird species have been catalogued here.

Drive another mile on the crossroad for a side trip to **Yountville,** a cozy tourist town named for George Yount, who planted the valley's first grapes in 1838. Back on the Silverado Trail north, the valley opens up and allows you to grasp the picture of local geography. The mountains rising 1,500 to 2,000 feet on both sides of the valley are part of the Coast Range. Those that form the valley's western wall are covered in chaparral and Douglas-fir, while the less lofty, drier mountains to the east are generally cloaked in oaks and manzanitas. The mountains were created when sedimentary rocks buckled

332

Vineyard along the Silverado Trail

upward under great pressure, then were covered with volcanic lava and ash. Alluvial deposits made the rich soil that's perfect for wine grapes.

Continue to Rutherford Hill Road, passing countless vines and serene wineries; a right turn leads 0.5 mile to the **Auberge du Soleil** *(707-963-1211).*

Cabernet Sauvignon grapes

The renowned restaurant's outdoor deck seems to hang over the valley like a hot-air balloon.

A mile north on the trail brings you to Zinfandel Lane. For a side trip to **St. Helena,** a principal town of the Napa Valley, turn left and go about a mile to Rte. 29, then turn right. Highlights include the old-fashioned main street, and the **Robert Louis Stevenson Museum** *(1490 Library La. 707-963-3757. Closed Mon.),* devoted to the noted Scot.

Continuing north on the Silverado Trail to Taplin Road, notice one of the valley's original 60 or 70 stone bridges; another picturesque example stands a bit farther at Pope Street. About 10 miles farther, your drive ends upon turning left on Lincoln Avenue into **Calistoga,** settled in 1859. The mineral spas and hot mud baths of this resort town represent the last gasps of the volcanic activity that helped shape the Napa Valley. Another geothermal remnant, the **Old Faithful Geyser** *(707-942-6463. Adm. fee)* gushes 60 feet into the air every 40 minutes. There's a large model of the early resort at the **Sharpsteen Museum** *(1311 Wash. St. 707-942-5911).*

Above town looms 4,343-foot **Mount St. Helena,** formed when manifold ridges were covered with hundreds of feet of volcanic materials. A brief silver boom erupted here in the early 1870s; Silverado City boasted 1,500 people, several saloons, and a hotel. The boom went bust by the time Robert Louis Stevenson spent his honeymoon in a cabin there in 1880. Today Mount St. Helena is preserved as 4,747-acre **Robert Louis Stevenson State Park** *(8 miles north of Calistoga on Rte. 29. 707-942-4575. http://parks.ca.gov/north/silverado/ rlssp215.htm).* A rough trail ascends past the old Silverado Mine and Stevenson's cabin site to dramatic views over the Napa Valley.

333

California 1 South

Monterey to Morro Bay

● 123 miles ● 6 hours ● All year

Along this coastline, central California preserves its natural beauty and remembers its roots. The drive starts in historic Monterey, visits the art colony of Carmel, and threads through Big Sur, where mountain ridges plunge into the Pacific in a dramatic encounter between land and sea. Farther south, the landscape mellows to oak-studded hills as the road passes Hearst Castle on its way to Morro Bay.

Join Rte. 1 in **Monterey** *(Monterey Co. Convention & Visitors Bureau 831-649-1770. Closed weekends).* The town served as California's capital under Spanish, Mexican, and American flags, and by the early 1900s boasted an important sardine industry. Surviving sites include the **Royal Presidio Chapel, Monterey State Historic Park, Custom House, Casa Soberanes, Larkin House,** and other adobe buildings, as well as touristy **Fisherman's Wharf** and **Cannery Row,** home of the celebrated **Monterey Bay Aquarium**.

Drive 3 miles south on Rte. 1 to **Carmel-by-the-Sea** *(Monterey Co. Convention & Visitors Bureau 831-649-1770. Closed weekends)*, an upscale village of quaint cottages, restaurants, inns, shops, and art galleries fronted by a broad beach fringed with Monterey pines. Among the highlights are **Mission San Carlos Borromeo del Rio Carmelo,** second of the California missions, founded by Padre Junipero Serra in 1770; **Tor House,** the 1919 home of poet Robinson Jeffers; and mile-long **Carmel River State Beach,** with its pelicans and kingfishers.

From Carmel drive 3.5 miles south to **Point Lobos State Reserve** *(831-624-4909. http://pointlobos.org. Adm. fee)*, a 550-acre park encompassing coves,

Big Sur coastline

headlands, meadows, tide pools, and the nation's first undersea ecological reserve, covering 770 acres, with kelp forests 80 feet high. Trails lead past Monterey cypresses, which grow naturally only here and on the 17-Mile Drive (see p. 336). The park's 250 species of birds and mammals include black-tailed deer, gray foxes, sea otters, and sea lions. Migrating gray whales pass by from December through April.

One-time resident writer Henry Miller called Big Sur "the face of the earth as the creator intended it to look."

After driving through **Carmel Highlands,** where impressive houses perch on granite cliffs above the sea, you reach the start of **Big Sur,** which extends 90 miles south to San Simeon. On this fabled coastline, redwood groves reach skyward, the **Santa Lucia Range** plunges into the sea, and waves are beaten to froth on ragged rocks. It's a place of elemental power that can make human affairs seem inconsequential.

Rte. 1, opened in 1937, climbs as high as a thousand feet above the sea. One of the few easy-to-reach beaches is at **Garrapata State Park** *(831-667-2315. http://parks.ca.gov)*, about 2 miles south of Carmel Highlands. From **Soberanes Point** watch for sea otters, which are protected along the entire coast.

Sea otter

En route to Bixby Creek Bridge, 7 miles farther, you can choose to leave Rte. 1 and drive the 12-mile old Coast Road, which climbs through remote forests and canyons and offers silent ocean views before ending at Andrew Molera State Park (see below). The unpaved road is tortuous and impassable when it rains.

Much-photographed **Bixby Creek Bridge** is a single-span concrete arch more than 260 feet high and 700 feet long. Park at turnouts near either end to gawk or take pictures. Ahead, the highway passes **Hurricane Point,** a place of big winds and big views, and the mouth of the **Little Sur River.** Looking inland, you'll see 3,710-foot-high **Pico Blanco,** distinguishable by its lime deposits. Toward the sea, sand dunes soon appear, rolling toward the 1889 **Point Sur Light Station** *(831-625-4419. Tours Sat.-Sun.; adm. fee),* a state historic park. In 3 miles you reach 4,800-acre **Andrew Molera State Park** *(831-667-2315. http://parks.ca.gov. Adm. fee),* whose broad beach, oak and redwood forests, and stretch of the Big Sur River are accessible only by foot.

Pass through the settlement of **Big Sur,** which offers food and lodging, and head for **Pfeiffer Big Sur State Park** *(831-667-2315. http://parks.ca.gov. Adm. fee),* where the **Big Sur River** runs through 800 acres of redwoods, maples, sycamores, bay laurel, and ferns. Then go 1.5 miles south and turn right on the 2-mile road down **Sycamore Canyon** to the white sands of **Pfeiffer Beach,** where the surf roars through arched rocks.

Nearly 2 miles farther on the highway you come to **Nepenthe** *(831-667-2345),* an indoor-outdoor restaurant perched 800 feet above the sea and famous for its jaw-dropping view of mountains and coast. About half a mile south, on the left, look for the **Henry Miller Memorial Library** *(831-667-2574. Closed Mon.-Wed.),* perched among towering redwoods. It displays books

335

and memorabilia of the novelist who spent 18 years in Big Sur. Also stop 8 miles farther at **Julia Pfeiffer Burns State Park** *(831-667-2315. http://parks.ca.gov. Adm. fee),* whose terrain ranges from 3,000-foot-high ridges to an underwater preserve. Do walk the short trail along the seaside bluff to see **McWay Falls** pour 80 feet into a picturesque cove.

Ahead of you lies the southern stretch of Big Sur, wild and lonely. The road clings to a precipitous coastline, and the only settlements in the next 35 miles are Lucia, Pacific Valley, Gorda, and Ragged Point. From here onward, the landscape settles down to hills and pastureland. You'll spy the **Piedras Blancas Light Station** on a point supposedly named in 1542 by Spanish explorer Juan Rodríguez Cabrillo for its white rocks (so tinted by bird droppings).

After a spell away from the Pacific, the road reaches the town of **San Simeon,** a staging area for the 5-mile bus ride to **Hearst Castle** *(Tours only; reservations 800-444-4445. www.hearst castle.org. Adm. fee),* begun in 1919 by news-

California 1 near Big Sur

paperman William Randolph Hearst. Perched in the Santa Lucia Range, the 127-acre estate looks as if a piece of Europe had wafted to the Wild West. The 115-room main house and guesthouses mix classical and Mediterranean Revival styles, using European architectural elements, antiques, and artwork collected by Hearst.

Continue 7 miles to **Cambria,** an arty town nestled against hills where Monterey pines thrive in porous soil of decomposed sandstone. On the ocean side of the highway, at Moonstone Beach, look for moonstones and California jade. Drive on 6 miles to the microscopic colony of **Harmony,** where you can watch artists at work. Ahead on **Estero Bay,** small **Cayucos** dates from the coastal schooner era of the 1860s; the pier has good fishing for rockfish and perch, plus views of pelicans and cormorants.

The end of your route is **Morro Bay** *(Morro Bay Chamber of Commerce 805-772-4467),* easily identified by its landmark **Morro Rock.** A turban-shaped, extinct volcanic cone perhaps 50 million years old, it is 576 feet high and linked to the mainland by a 2,000-foot-long sandbar. Peregrine falcons live here. To learn about local wildlife, visit the **Morro Bay State Park Museum of Natural History** *(805-772-2694. www.mbspmuseum.org. Adm. fee).* Around Morro Bay you'll also see great blue herons and, from October to March, monarch butterflies in eucalyptus trees.

Mission San Carlos, Carmel

17-Mile Drive

Loop from California 1 Gate, midway between Monterey and Carmel-by-the-Sea

● 17 miles ● 1 hour ● All year. Admission fee

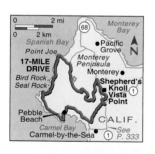

On this drive around the Monterey Peninsula, about 2.5 hours south of San Francisco, you'll see a series of marvels. Some are natural (a ragged, romantic shoreline, offshore rocks swarming with seals and seabirds, the 5,300-acre Del Monte Forest and its windswept cypresses); some are man-made (elegant houses, world-famous golf courses). To enter the drive, you can use four additional gates: Carmel *(Off N. San Antonio),* Morse *(Off Rte. 68),* Pacific Grove *(Off Sunset Dr.),* and Country Club *(Off Congress Ave. in Pacific Grove).* Your entrance fee includes a guide map with numbered stops, and there are plenty of directional signs.

You'll start on the inland portion of the route. Drive about a mile from the **Rte. 1 Gate** to the **Shepherd's Knoll Vista Point** to see the long, white arc of **Monterey Bay.** Now the road climbs to **Huckleberry Hill,** where you look over the **Monterey Peninsula,** a vast projection of the Santa Lucia Range. After threading your way downhill among luxury houses in a forest of Monterey and bishop pines, you pass a golf resort and reach the coast at **Spanish Bay.** At this spot Spanish explorer Gaspar de Portolá camped in 1769 while trying to find Monterey Bay; today you can picnic on the white-sand beach.

Continue to **Point Joe,** where the sea surges perpetually due to submerged rocks (although one theory says that ocean currents collide here). The area is a graveyard of ships that mistook Point Joe for the entrance to Monterey Bay.

To see tide pools, drive on to the 3-mile **Coastal Bluff Walking Trail.** Farther ahead, your nose will know when you're near **Seal** and **Bird Rocks,** the home of countless squealing gulls and cormorants. The barks of hundreds of harbor seals and California sea lions also fill the air. Continue to **Fanshell Beach,** a white crescent where harbor seals bear their pups each spring.

The drive's best view of the Pacific coastline is from the **Cypress Point Lookout;** the view sometimes stretches 20 miles down the coast to the **Point Sur Lighthouse.** Drive another mile to 13-acre **Crocker Grove,** a wildlife preserve with the oldest and largest Monterey cypress. The next stop is the wind-ravaged **Lone Cypress,** venerable symbol of the Monterey coast, on its

Lone Cypress, California

rocky knob. The road then loops out to **Pescadero Point,** the northern tip of Carmel Bay, then passes the famous Pebble Beach golf resort opened in 1919.

Conclude your drive either at the Carmel Gate or back at the Rte. 1 Gate.

337

Hawaii

Kalanianaole Highway, Oahu

Lunalilo Freeway (H1) to Hawaii 61 on Hawaii 72

● **20 miles** ● **1 hour** ● **All year**

Plumeria blossoms

Here's a handy escape route from Honolulu's Waikiki Beach. Replacing the madness and crowds is a quieter side of Oahu—the tropical fish of Hanauma Bay, sandy beaches and expert bodysurfing waters, and the forested back side of the **Koolau Range** *(Hawaii Visitors Bureau 808-923-1811).*

The route begins where H1 becomes Rte. 72, northeast of Diamond Head. (From Waikiki you can reach H1 via a scenic shoreline route: Drive east on Kalakaua Avenue to Diamond Head Road, which soon becomes Kahala Avenue and passes through a neighborhood of elegant oceanfront estates. Turn left on Hunakai Street, then right on Kilauea Avenue, and follow the signs to H1 east.)

You'll drive the length of 6-mile-long **Maunalua Bay.** Then, ahead of you, rise 1,208-foot **Koko Crater** (on the left) and 646-foot **Koko Head** (right).

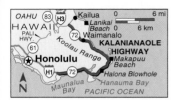

Continue to **Hanauma Bay State Underwater Park,** the island's most popular snorkeling spot. (Visit early to beat the crowds.) Hanauma began taking shape 35,000 years ago, when a volcanic explosion under the sea pushed up a cone of ash, silicate, basalt boulders, and limestone. Some 7,000 years ago the ocean eroded through the cone's wall, creating the bay. On the palm-fringed sand grows *pohuehue,* or beach morning glory. Caution: The wave-washed rock ledges and turbulent outer zones are dangerous.

Within the next 2 miles you reach the **Molokai Island Viewpoint** (the island of **Lanai** is also visible) and then the **Halona Blowhole,** where water rushes into an undersea tunnel and up through a crevice, spewing into the air; the effect is best during rough surf. Almost immediately past that is the brown-sugar-colored strand of **Sandy Beach Park,** where bodysurfing championships are held in the often treacherous surf.

Rte. 72 climbs away from the sea, then passes **Makapuu Point,** the easternmost spot on Oahu. (Look for the lighthouse.) You reach the coast again at **Makapuu Beach Park,** where bodysurfers ride waves as high as 12 feet and hang gliders soar from cliffs. Not far offshore lie **Rabbit Island,** an old volcanic crater occupied by wild rabbits and wedge-tailed shearwaters, and smaller Turtle Island. Across the road is **Sea Life Park** *(808-259-7933. Adm. fee),* offering performances by whales and dolphins, as well as a 300,000-gallon reef tank full of sharks and tropical fish.

Proceed 2.5 miles to **Waimanalo Beach Park,** with white sand and good swimming. Then comes the gate to **Bellows Air Force Station,** where

Hanauma Bay's turquoise waters and coral reefs are home to sea turtles and schools of angelfish, parrot fish, and other finned creatures so tame they'll eat from your hand.

Pali Highway through the Koolau Range with Honolulu in the distance

a good "local secret" beach opens to the public on weekends and holidays only. To your left rises the rugged green **Koolau Range,** the island's dominant mountain chain. About 4 miles past the ethnically Hawaiian town of **Waimanalo,** the route ends at Rte. 61. You can turn right to visit the bedroom community of **Kailua** (windsurfing at Kailua Beach Park, swimming at Lanikai Beach). Or turn left to take the scenic Pali Highway (Rte. 61) over the Koolau Range, stopping at windy **Nuuanu Pali Lookout** for a view of windward **Oahu,** then descending into Honolulu. Or simply return to Honolulu the way you came.

Hana Highway, Maui

Kahului to Hana on Hawaii 36 and 360

● 100 miles round-trip ● 6 hours ● All year. Since there are 54 bridges and more than 600 curves, don't drive this if you are in a hurry or suffer from motion sickness.

Known as one of Hawaii's most scenic routes, the Hana Highway winds along the coast past waterfalls and rocky streams, through rain forests, and among tropical blossoms and fruit trees. The twisting "highway," built in 1927 by convict labor, is well paved but narrow, with many stops while oncoming traffic crosses one-lane bridges. Set out early in the day, pull over for restless drivers behind you, and take it easy. It's the trip that counts here, not the destination.

Rte. 36 begins in **Kahului.** A surf-laced coastline and sugarcane fields appear alongside you on the 7 miles to **Paia,** the last place before Hana to fill your gas tank and picnic basket. Once a busy sugar plantation town, Paia has become a laid-back colony of hippies, craftspeople, and windsurfers, who show their stuff at **Hookipa Beach Park,** near the 9-mile marker past town.

The road climbs away from the coast through an area of increased rainfall that supports pineapple fields. Just past the 16-mile marker, the road is renumbered as Rte. 360, and mile markers go back to zero. This is the start of the "real" Hana Highway. Gardens and mailboxes sprout up when you reach tiny **Kailua,** where many residents work on the ditches that carry

Keanae Peninsula

rainwater from the wet uplands to the dry cane fields of central Maui. Along this stretch, guava trees and mountain apples are common. On the way out of town notice Norfolk pine, rainbow eucalyptus, and bamboo.

Past the 9-mile marker, stop at the short **Waikamoi Ridge Trail** to stroll among tall eucalyptus trees, their trunks twined with South American taro vines. On the road just ahead are **Waikamoi Falls** and **Puohokamoa Falls,** the latter a fine picnic spot surrounded by kukui nut trees, heliconias, and impatiens, with pools to swim in. Then continue just over a mile to **Kaumahina State Wayside Park** and its expansive view over the coastline.

The road runs along several hundred feet above the sea, then skirts U-shaped **Honomanu Bay** (entrance just past the 14-mile marker). The bay encloses a rocky, black-sand beach and rough water, while the verdant gulch behind it is home to African tulip trees with fiery red blossoms. After you climb the bay's far side, there is a small pull-off with a stunning view back over the bay.

In about 2 miles you reach the **Keanae Arboretum,** where trails lead to native and introduced plants (taro, breadfruit, banana, bamboo, ti, ginger). Just ahead is the road down to the **Keanae Peninsula,** an extension of land created by rough aa lava that spilled down from **Haleakala,** the dormant volcano that dominates eastern Maui. Down in quiet **Keanae** village, whose residents are mainly native Hawaiians, there is a restored 1860 stone church and cultivated patches of taro, the source of poi.

The 54 bridges along the Hana road have Hawaiian names with such poetic translations as Whirling Waters, Open Laughter, First Ruffled Waters, Prayer Blossoms, and Heavenly Mist.

You can get a good view of the peninsula from the small, unmarked **Keanae Overlook,** just past the 17-mile marker.

Now comes a stretch where the road climbs high above the ocean. Above this region, Haleakala's slopes receive an average 390 inches (and sometimes as much as 500 inches) of rain yearly, which accounts for the many waterfalls through here. One of the prettiest is beyond the 22-mile marker at the wayside park of **Puaa Kaa,** which has picnic tables beside a stream among tree ferns, guavas, and gingers.

Just after the Hana Gardenland nursery, you can take a side trip to the left on the rutted, muddy Ulaino road leading to **Piilanihale Heiau,** a large temple of fitted lava rocks built by a 14th-century chief.

Back on Rte. 360, stop at **Waianapanapa State Park,** which offers a black-sand beach and caves formed of collapsed lava tubes.

Wailua Falls, near Kipahulu

(The water inside sometimes turns red—some say because of clouds of small shrimp, while others cite the legend of a slain Hawaiian princess whose blood tinges the water.) Sweet-smelling plumeria blooms in the park, and you may see black noddy terns flying near the sea.

Within a few miles you reach the pastoral town of **Hana,** which is quiet

Vanda orchids

and unspectacular, though its setting between **Hana Bay** and the green hills is lovely and its mood timeless. The main businesses are ranching and the upscale **Hotel Hana-Maui** *(808-248-8211)*, started in 1946. Do see the Hawaiian artifacts and crafts on display at the **Hana Cultural Center** *(808-248-8622. Adm. fee)* and visit the 1838 **Wananalua Church,** built of lava rock.

Although the drive ends in Hana, the road continues as Rte. 31 to **Oheo Gulch,** part of **Haleakala National Park** *(808-572-9306. www.nps.gov/hale),* where numerous pools form in **Palikea Stream** as it descends from Haleakala.

In the nearby village of **Kipahulu,** you'll find the grave of aviator Charles Lindbergh at the **Palapala Hoomau Church cemetery.** Return to Kahului over the same route you came.

Hamakua Coast, Hawaii

Hilo to the Waipio Valley on Hawaii 19 and 240

● 51 miles ● 2 hours ● All year

This rugged coast—edged with cliffs, crossed by streams, lush with foliage and waterfalls—represents a real departure from the island's highly developed Kona and Kohala coasts. Begin your drive in **Hilo** *(Visitors Bureau, 250 Keawe St. 808-961-5797)* a tropical town whose warm weather and annual 137 inches of rain make it a garden and orchid-growing center. (The greatest profusion of orchid blooms is between February and April.) The **Lyman House Memorial Museum** *(276 Haili St. 808-935-5021. Adm. fee)* focuses on Hawaiian life and artifacts.

In the weathered, turn-of-the-century downtown district, Rte. 19 fronts **Hilo Bay;** take this route north. Between mile markers 3 and 4 there is a scenic point from which you can look back at the crescent of Hilo Bay. Bananas and wild sugarcane grow in this lush area. Between mile markers 7 and 8, turn right on the Onomea Bay Scenic Route, which parallels Rte. 19 for 4 miles, passing through an area that matches most people's idea of the "real Hawaii." The road is lined with Alexandra palms,

Sea cliffs and waterfall, Waipio Valley Overlook

mango trees, and red-blooming African tulip trees. Narrow stone bridges cross streams. Below a bluff you'll see the black rocks and crashing waves of **Onomea Bay,** where sea turtles swim. Along this route you can visit the **Hawaii Tropical Botanical Garden** *(808-964-5233. http://htbg.com. Adm. fee),* which preserves a seaside rain forest and displays more than 2,000 species of flowers and plants from around the world. Shore birds and sea turtles inhabit this beautiful jungle garden.

Rejoining Rte. 19, continue past mile marker 13 and turn left on Rte. 220 for a 3-mile side trip to **Akaka Falls State Park** *(Hawaii parks information 808-587-0300. www.hawaii.gov/ dlnr/dsp/hawaii.html).* There, a 0.5-mile loop leads you among bamboo groves, red ginger, impatiens, hanging orchids, and other rain forest plants to reach the falls, which plunge more than 440 feet down a volcanic cliff. After returning to the main road, drive north about half a mile to **Kolekole Beach Park.** Here **Kolekole Stream** (from Akaka Falls) meets the sea at a black-sand beach. The surf is dangerous, but the stream has pools for swimming, and this is a nice picnic spot.

Some people believe the ghosts of ancient Hawaiian nobility walk the Waipio Valley and you can hear their chants and see their torches.

You can also stop ahead at **Laupahoehoe Beach Park,** a grassy patch on a lava peninsula pounded by surf. Then continue 12 miles and take a 3-mile side trip to little-used **Kalopa State Park,** a rain forest on the lower slopes of

Along the Hamakua coast drive

Mauna Kea, with a 0.7-mile nature trail. Back on the main road, continue to the former sugar mill town of **Honokaa,** a quiet, multicultural hamlet, and turn onto Rte. 240, traveling about 9 miles to road's end at the **Waipio Valley Overlook.** From here you gaze over a fertile, mile-wide valley enclosed by pali (cliffs) as high as 2,000 feet. Far below you'll see taro patches and fish ponds, fruit trees (coconut, mango, guava, banana), waterfalls, and a black-sand beach split by **Waipio Stream.** The valley, inhabited for a thousand years, was in ancient times a hub of Hawaii's political and religious life, a home of chiefs. Although 2,500 people once lived here, that number dwindled drastically in the 1800s, and after a disastrous 1946 tsunami, most people moved topside. If you want to visit, the hourly **Waipio Valley Shuttle** *(808-775-7121)* plies the steep, treacherous road (suitable only for four-wheel-drive vehicles), or you can walk a mile down. (And up!)

Return to Hilo the way you came.

Chain of Craters Road, Hawaii

Hawaii Volcanoes National Park

- 46 miles round-trip ● 6 hours
- All year. Admission fee

Lava flow tour

From southeast Crater Rim Drive, Chain of Craters Road descends 3,700 feet until it ends sharply at a lava flow. From there it's usually a short walk to see flowing, red-hot lava. On the way you drive among the vast flows that spilled from the shield vent called **Maunu Ulu;** the lava expelled here from 1969 to 1974 would pave a highway around the Equator. (The smooth lava is pahoehoe, the jagged is aa.)

After 17 miles, a 2-mile trail leads to the **Puu Loa Petroglyphs,** some 15,000 figures and symbols carved in lava by early Hawaiians. Drive 2.5 miles to where the road meets the ocean at the **Holei Sea Arch,** eroded by waves in the sea cliffs. Swimming is unsafe. The current route ends near here, where lava has swamped the road. Since 1983, lava flows have buried more than 13 miles of highway, destroyed 10,000 acres of trees and plants, and added more than 500 acres of new land to the island.

Despite all the road changes, you still might see sizzling hot (2100°F) lava flows entering the water off the coast. Be sure to follow the guidance of park rangers as to where you can safely go.

Crater Rim Drive, Hawaii

Hawaii Volcanoes National Park

- 11 miles ● 2 hours
- All year. Admission fee to national park.

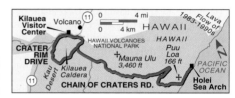

At **Hawaii Volcanoes National Park** *(808-985-6000. www.nps.gov/havo. Adm. fee)* you can actually witness the force that continues to build the Big Island of Hawaii—volcano power. Kilauea is one of the world's most active volcanoes. Steam rises from its caldera, and the terrain is a surreal moonscape of craters, cinder cones, and congealed lava flows. You'll circle Kilauea's rim, see a rain forest and a desert, and enter the realm of Pele, Hawaii's volcano goddess.

Begin with the natural history displays at the **Kilauea Visitor Center,** then cross the

343

Hapuu tree ferns and ohia forest on Kilauea

road to see the **Volcano House** *(808-967-7321)*, a historic hotel perched on the rim of the caldera. From its parking lot, walk the 0.3-mile **Earthquake Trail** for a view of **Kilauea Caldera** (2 miles across, 500 feet at its deepest) and Mauna Loa, the world's most massive mountain, rising 32,000 feet from seafloor to peak. **Mauna Loa** erupted in 1984, spewing forth a million cubic yards of lava per hour and ultimately covering almost 12,000 acres of land.

Now you'll drive clockwise around Kilauea's rim, soon entering a rain forest of ferns and red-blossomed ohia trees. Stop at the **Kilauea Iki** ("little Kilauea") **Crater,** which in 1959 was a lake of boiling lava with fountains 1,900 feet high; now you see a steaming black crust. Continue to the **Thurston Lava Tube** (0.3-mile loop-trail) to walk through a former conduit for molten rock. Among the nearby ohia trees and tree ferns you may see the apapane, a bright red honeycreeper that feeds on nectar and insects.

> The east rift zone of Kilauea has been flowing since 1983, so you may be able to see rivers of red molten rock, which reaches 2100°F.

Ahead stop at **Puu Puai Overlook**, where a 0.4-mile paved walkway leads along the **Devastation Trail.** (A member of your party can drive 0.7 mile ahead to the Devastation parking area to pick you up at trail's end.) This former rain forest area was obliterated by pumice and cinders from Kilauea Iki's 1959 eruption, but is being recolonized by both native and non-native plants. Ahead, impressively steaming **Halemaumau Crater** is said to be the home of Pele Honua Mea (Sacred Earth Person). Hawaiians still come to pay homage with dances on the crater's edge. Above the crater look for white-tailed tropic birds.

After this, you cross old lava flows, see the **Kau Desert** (created by natural acid rain), and view the **Southwest Rift Zone** (fractures in the weakened side of the volcano). Stop at the **Jaggar Museum** *(808-985-6000)* to look at diverse types of lava and bits of volcanic glass called Pele's tears. Then you pass the vents of **Steaming Bluff** and the volcanic gases and colorful rocks of the **Sulfur Banks.** Your circle concludes back at the Visitor Center.

Amaumau ferns on the edge of Kilauea Caldera

Lava from Kilauea sizzling into the Pacific Ocean

Sam Abell, NGP: 34.
Dean Abramson: 16t.
Ian Adams: 127.
Tom Algire: 23t, 242, 254.
AMERICAN LANDSCAPES: 241 (Rick Schafer), 292 (Rick Schafer), 297b (Rick Schafer), 298 (Rick Schafer), 299 (Ray Atkeson), 303t (Rick Schafer).
James L. Amos: 58b.
Scott Barrow Photography: 343t.
Tom Bean: 150, 212b, 214.
Annie Griffiths Belt: 14.
Craig Blacklock: 142t.
Paul O. Boisvert: 35, 37 (both).
Matt Bradley: 190, 191, 193 (both).
Robert Brodbeck: 123, 124.
Robert C. Clark: 106c, 108.
Kathy Clay: 58t.
Willard Clay: 26, 62, 211, 215.
Bob Clemenz: 325.
Carr Clifton: 12b, 63, 87b, 156b, 322.
Bruce Dale: 88.
Kent & Donna Dannen: 178, 238, 253.
Bob Devine: 301b, 309.
Michael DeYoung: 277b.
Jay Dickman: 4, 255.
Dick Dietrich: 192, 337t.
John Dominis: 341t.
Susan G. Drinker: 286-7
Dan Dry: 98.
Doug Dye: 248b.
Jack Dykinga: 220t, 222.
Tom Evans: 277t.
Russ Finley: 81.
Jeff Foott: 334b.
Stephen Frink/WATERHOUSE: 118b.
f/STOP PICTURES: 29 (Richard W. Brown).
John P. George: 204.
Georgia Department of Industry, Trade & Tourism: 111, 112.
Jeff Gnass: 13, 61, 83b, 125, 142b, 177, 232, 281, 282b, 313, 339, 343b.
Jon Gnass: 293.
Scott Goldsmith: 53, 55.
Philip Gould: 172, 174t, 175.
KEN GRAHAM AGENCY: 271 (Kim Heacox), 273 (Ken Graham), 276c (Dicon Joseph).
Charles Gurche: 74b, 296.
Acey Harper: 119.
Fred Hirschmann: 151, 217t, 220b, 224, 340.
Ralph Lee Hopkins: 218, 219, 229t, 287.
Paul Horsted/DAKOTA STOCK IMAGES: 152, 157.
Michio Hoshino: 278.
Leland Howard: 267.

William Hubbell: 49, 50.
George H.H. Huey: 185t, 203, 227
Randall Hyman: 166, 167.
Todd Jagger: 184.
Michael Javorka: 180t, 291b.
Frank Jensen: 210b.
Chris Johns: 338.
Dewitt Jones: 331.
Karen Kasmauski: 90.
Steve Kaufman: 274.
James Kay: 205.
Layne Kennedy: 145, 159.
Bern Ketchum: 163.
Stephen J. Krasemann: 16b.
Emory Kristof: 82.
Diane Kulpinski: 303b.
Susan Lapides: 44, 47.
Bill Lea: 86, 87t, 94, 95.
J.C. Leacock: 160, 240, 324.
Tom & Pat Leeson: 282t.
Danny Lehman: 199, 270.
Mark W. Lisk: 262b.
Robert Llewellyn: 317.
David Loeb: 136.
Chlaus Lötscher: 276t.
Bill Luster: 129.
Ivor Markman: 326.
John Marshall: 283, 284, 285t, 288, 294.
Ian C. Martin: 106t, 110b, 165, 194, 195.
Larry Mayer: 138, 149b.
Jack Parnell/MCCONNELL MCNAMARA & CO.: 51c, 54.
Steve McCutcheon: 275.
David P. McMasters: 84.
Michael Melford: 196, 262t, 263.
Neal Mishler: 246.
George F. Mobley: 96l.
David Muench: 45, 51t, 80, 101, 130, 162, 182, 198, 201, 225, 265, 312, 320, 329b, 334t, 342.
Marc Muench: 207, 319.
Vincent J. Musi: 41t, 56, 59, 64t, 67t, 68, 69, 71.
Cathy Nelson: 230.
G. Alan Nelson: 120, 140.
John Netherton: 96-7.
North Dakota Tourism Department: 148, 149t.
Jonathan Nutt: 176.
Frank A. Oberle: 164.
Pat O'Hara: 285b.
Carl Oksanen/ALPEN GLOW IMAGES: 259. back cover.
Richard Olsenius: 128, 187.
Jack Olson: 153.
Rob Outlaw: 210t.
Londie G. Padelsky: 321.
Laurence Parent: 158, 179, 186, 189t, 223, 228.
PICTURESQUE: 85 (Carl V. Galie), 92 (Edward Morgan).

Bob Pool: 295b, 302.
Ed Preston: 341b.
Jake Rajs: 10, 65, 66, 99, 103, 118t, 291t.
James Randklev: 12t, 23b, 25, 77, 109, 110t, 114t, 115, 117, 221, 231, 245b, 327, 336, 337b, 344.
John Reddy: 244, 247t, 248t.
Roger Ressmeyer/STARLIGHT: 345.
Paul Rezendes: 40, 46.
Cliff Riedinger: 272.
Joel Riner: 264.
J. Carlos Rojas: 279.
Ron Sanford: 156t.
Jim Schafer: 70b.
Phil Schermeister: 304, 305 (both), 307 (both).
Thomas A. Schneider: 122.
Stephen J. Shaluta, Jr.: 75, 78 (both).
Clyde H. Smith: 32.
Richard Hamilton Smith: 133, 137, 143.
Scott T. Smith: 2-3, 83t, 189b, 206, 257, 260.
Joseph Sohm/CHROMOSOHM MEDIA: 1, 27, 31, 33, 38-9, 79, 208.
Harley Soltes: 280, 289, 290.
Pam Spaulding: 100, 132, 251 (both), 252.
Tom Stewart: 20.
STONE :cover (James Randklev), 10 (Tom Bean).
James A. Sugar/BLACK STAR: 332, 333.
Medford Taylor: 24 (both), 28, 36, 41b, 42, 72, 73, 74t, 91, 116b.
Steve Terrill: 295t, 297t, 301t, 306, 308.
Tom Till: 64b, 107, 146, 169, 171, 174b, 202, 229b, 232-3.
Larry Ulrich: 116t, 212t, 213, 217b, 226, 234, 236, 237, 245t, 315, 329t, 330.
Randy Ury: 21.
Ben Van Hook: 105, 113, 114b.
Will van Overbeek: 180b, 183, 185c.
Jeff Vanuga: 258.
Salvatore Vasapolli: 19, 154, 261, 316.
Brian A. Vikander: 247b, 249.
Steve Wall: 30, 102.
Stuart Wasserman: 268.
H. Mark Weidman: 67b, 70t.
WEST LIGHT: 323 (Nik Wheeler), 335 (Charles O'Rear).
Mike Whye: 161, 168.
Chuck Wickham/TEMPERED LIGHT: 96r.
Cary Wolinsky: 135.
Garry Wunderwald: 250.

346

349